D1563755

FOUNTAIN OF DISCONTENT

The U.S.S. San Jacinto *Stopping the British Mail Steamer* Trent

U.S. Signal Corps Photo No. 111-BA-1911 (Brady Collection) in the National Archives

FOUNTAIN OF DISCONTENT

The *Trent* Affair and
Freedom of the Seas

GORDON H. WARREN

NORTHEASTERN UNIVERSITY PRESS

Boston 1981

Editors, Robilee Smith & Katherine Talmadge
Designer, Sandra Rigney of the Book Dept., Inc.

Library of Congress Cataloging in Publication Data

Warren, Gordon H   1944–
    Fountain of discontent.

    Bibliography: p.
Includes index.
    1. Trent Affair, Nov. 8, 1861.   2. United States—
Foreign relations—1861–1865.   I. Title.
E469.W3   973.7′2   80-24499
ISBN 0-930350-12-X

ISBN 0-930350-12-X

86 85 84 83 82 81   6 5 4 3 2 1

Printed in the United States of America

For my parents,
Harris G. Warren and Katherine F. Warren

Preface

IN THE HUNDRED AND TWENTY YEARS since it occurred, the *Trent* affair has attracted the attention of numerous historians and popular writers fascinated by this dramatic, even melodramatic, event. They have examined the *Trent* affair within the context of Anglo–American relations during the Civil War, observed it from the viewpoint of its chief participants, and explored its monographic features. Together, a score of books and articles form an interesting, though fragmented, record of the incident.

The *Trent* affair found its first historian in 1896, when Thomas L. Harris of Indiana University published an account that held the field for about three decades and is still sometimes cited. Although Harris's volume contained some unexplainable factual errors, as well as the obvious lack of great historical perspective, it was a conscientious attempt to survey the incident from several angles, including international opinion and law. However, the scholarly aspect of Harris's study is disfigured by a strong bias against England, whose press, people, and government he considered to be in league "heart and soul with the South." British military and diplomatic moves in relation to the seizure of Mason and Slidell were designed, Harris contended, to "browbeat and menace the United States."[1] Articles by Charles Francis Adams, Jr., and Richard Henry Dana, Jr., followed in 1911–12.[2] In another twenty years, the grandfather of modern Civil War diplomatic historians, Ephraim D. Adams, published a two-volume work on *Great Britain and the American Civil War* (New York: Longmans, Green, 1925). Adams's careful, if pedestrian, treatment

1. Thomas L. Harris, *The Trent Affair, including a Review of English and American Relations at the Beginning of the Civil War* (Indianapolis and Kansas City: Bowen-Merrill, 1896).

2. Charles Francis Adams, Jr., "The *Trent* Affair," Massachusetts Historical Society *Proceedings*, XLV (1911–12), 35–148; Richard Henry Dana, Jr., "The *Trent* Affair: An Aftermath," ibid., 508–30.

set the pattern for other histories, because his discussion of the *Trent* affair was based solely on Anglo–American relations and concentrated on diplomatic exchanges and popular excitement; the Adams study ignored military and naval preparations, world opinion, and international law. Adams viewed the emotional binge surrounding the *Trent* affair in both countries as a safety valve for public opinion, and stressed that the peaceful settlement of the crisis weakened London's conviction about Secretary of State William H. Seward's alleged hostility toward England and its people.

After Adam's work, historical interest in the affair apparently lagged; articles were infrequent, until a veritable outpouring of books occurred in the 1960s and 1970s. Because many of these works were biographical accounts, they tended, like most biographies, to emphasize the role of their subjects in key events, and served mainly to fill out the work of E. D. Adams.[3]

In other accounts of the Civil War period, the *Trent* affair appeared against the panorama of international relations. Robin W. Winks, in *Canada and the United States: The Civil War Years* (Baltimore: Johns Hopkins Press, 1960), examined its effect on Canadian security and public opinion, dismissing it as "a popular, but not necessarily a diplomatic, crisis." The security theme was emphasized in Kenneth Bourne's *Britain and the Balance of Power in North America, 1815–1908* (Berkeley and Los Angeles: University of California Press, 1967). Carefully relating British preparations for war, the weakness of Canadian defenses, and cabinet disagreement over military and naval policy, Bourne did not doubt the British government's willingness to accept a war, which he believed was avoided only because of the effect of its preparations on Washington. Lynn M. Case and Warren F. Spencer, in *The United States and France: Civil War Diplomacy* (Philadelphia: University of Pennsylvania Press, 1970), presented a superb history of the French side of the crisis; their study was marred only by its curious acceptance of the old conspiracy theory that Captain Charles Wilkes connived with Mason and Slidell in the capture. The first volume of Brian Jenkins's *Britain and the War for the Union* (Montreal: McGill-Queens, 1974) was superior in some ways to the Adams study. It contained a

3. Martin B. Duberman, *Charles Francis Adams, 1807–1886* (Boston: Houghton Mifflin, 1961); Glyndon G. Van Deusen, *William Henry Seward* (New York: Oxford University Press, 1967); David Donald, *Charles Sumner and the Rights of Man* (New York: Alfred A. Knopf, 1970); Daniel B. Carroll, *Henri Mercier and the American Civil War* (Princeton: Princeton University Press, 1971); John Niven, *Gideon Welles: Lincoln's Secretary of the Navy* (New York: Oxford University Press, 1973).

multidimensional treatment of the affair from the British–Canadian–American perspectives, emphasized diplomatic and military developments, but lacked analysis. A synthesis of recent scholarship is D. P. Crook, *The North, the South, and the Powers, 1861–1865* (New York: 1974). Based on secondary materials and published documents, it accepts the conclusions of recent scholars.

Articles dealing with the *Trent* affair have appeared in recent years, expanding knowledge and demonstrating the complicated background of a deceptively simple incident.[4] However, historians who expect to document elaborate responses by the Confederate government to the crisis will discover virtually nothing. Richmond, like the rest of the world, found itself a spectator to the drama.

Eighty-odd years passed after Harris's work before publication of another book-length account of the affair. In a preface to *The Trent Affair: A Diplomatic Crisis* (Knoxville: University of Tennessee Press, 1977), Norman Ferris wrote that "historians have heretofore failed to explain *why* a relatively trivial maritime incident threatened to touch off a trans-Atlantic war at the end of the year 1861." However, Ferris's book, while an improvement on previously published works, did not succeed in adequately explaining the why of the incident.[5]

The inadequacies of the literature—its partial quality, its confusions, its mistaken emphases—thus have obscured an interesting chapter in American history. In this volume, I have done my best to relate the realities of that time, now more than a century into the past, when peace hung in the balance, when war would have been the sheerest disaster, when the governments in Washington and London gradually came to their senses and chose a less dangerous path.

Many persons and institutions have assisted me in the preparation of this work. In particular I must thank the staffs of the Public Record Office, the British Museum, and the Historical Manuscripts Commission in London; the library of the University of Nottingham; the Bodleian Library; the National Maritime Museum in Greenwich; and the National Library of Wales. I also appreciate the cooperation of the staff of the Archives du Ministère des Affaires étrangères in Paris, especially for their patience with my halting French. On this side of the Atlantic, I could not have asked for better service than I received

4. Among them Harold B. Hancock and Norman B. Wilkinson, " 'The Devil to Pay!': Saltpeter and the *Trent* Affair," *Civil War History,* X (1964), 20–32; and F. C. Drake, "The Cuban Background of the *Trent* Affair," ibid., XIX (1973), 29–49.

5. Eight years prior to the Ferris study, in "The *Trent* Affair, 1861–1862," Ph.D. dissertation, Indiana University (1969), I had explained the reasons behind Britain's violent reaction.

from the officers and staff of the Public Archives of Canada, who made their facility a most pleasant place for research. Among numerous institutions in the United States that have aided in this endeavor are the Massachusetts Historical Society, the Library of Congress, the Rush Rhees Library of the University of Rochester, the General Sanford Memorial Library, Houghton Library of Harvard University, and the Office of Naval Records and Library of the National Archives.

In nearly a decade of research and writing on the *Trent* affair, I have been fortunate in having the generous support of several individuals. J. Garry Clifford of the University of Connecticut and Frank J. Merli of Queens College of the City University of New York carefully read the entire manuscript at various stages of development, pointing out errors and faulty prose, and suggesting other territory to explore. My father, Harris Gaylord Warren, professor emeritus of Miami University, performed the same tedious chores and also cleared up confusion caused by inventive punctuation. David M. Pletcher of Indiana University read the manuscript at an early stage and offered many helpful suggestions. Professor Zoltan Kramar of Central Washington University enlightened me with his explanation of the intellectual pedigree of some contemporary British military theorists. Although my wife, Suzanne, asked me not to clutter up the preface with the usual encomium to the spouse, I must ignore the request because her critical and iconoclastic view of the manuscript persuaded me that several scholarly, but otherwise boring, sections had to be eliminated. My mother-in-law, Sue Capehart, no model for all those bad jokes about such relatives, saved me a trip back east by researching some diplomatic and naval records in the National Archives that I missed on previous excursions.

Finally, I must add my gratitude and praise to those of other students who have had the great good fortune to come under the guiding hand of Robert H. Ferrell of Indiana University. His encouragement and reassurance were invaluable during the times experienced by all scholars who wonder whether their years of work on a subject will ever contribute to the advancement of historical knowledge. His incisive criticism of prose, organization, and arguments—known to a generation of students as "the Ferrell treatment"—helped me more than I know how to acknowledge.

Ellensburg, Washington   GORDON H. WARREN
August 1980

Contents

List
of
Illustrations

"The fountains of discontent in any society are many, and some lie much deeper than others."

—WILLIAM H. SEWARD

1.

The Capture of
Mason and Slidell

WHEN THE CIVIL WAR BEGAN in the spring of 1861 the Lincoln administration faced many problems, notably the possibility of European intervention. A host of Union war measures affecting foreign governments and their citizens involved the United States almost immediately in several unpleasant confrontations, which were exacerbated by the overbearing attitude of the State Department, alarmist reports from the Washington diplomatic corps, and reluctance of the powers to tolerate interference with neutral rights. Confederate dependence on imported war materials prompted an early Union blockade of the Southern coast and a spirited effort by Union naval officers to intercept all vessels suspected of an enemy destination or an errand for the Richmond government. Inevitably, incidents occurred, the tone of diplomatic correspondence worsened, and popular discontent mounted on both sides of the Atlantic. Within a few months, strained relations between the United States and Europe, especially Britain, provided the perfect medium for an international crisis. It needed only a catalyst.

Dark clouds scudded across the moonless, autumn sky as the C.S.S. *Theodora*, nudged by a breeze from the northwest, cast off her lines about midnight on October 12, 1861, and steamed slowly out of Charleston harbor.[1] Midnight departures had become commonplace at this Southern port, a mecca for blockade-runners, so the *Theodora* attracted scant attention. Union curiosity would have been unwelcome, because the *Theodora* carried more than a crew of profiteers; two Confederate commissioners, James Murray Mason and John Slidell, newly appointed to the courts of Queen Victoria and Napoleon III, were on board. Their primary mission was to seek recognition of Confederate independence, but their first task was to run the Union blockade; therefore, the gloomy weather and lack of fanfare suited them.

Mason and Slidell were not the first Confederate agents to try their skill at European intrigue. The previous March, William L. Yancey and A. Dudley Mann had traveled to Britain while T. Butler King and Pierre A. Rost had gone to France to establish formal diplomatic relations and to negotiate commercial treaties. Their subsequent failure to obtain official recognition for themselves or the Confederacy was not surprising. Only Mann possessed any diplomatic experience, a rather meager background consisting of negotiation with German courts and a tragicomic search for the Kossuth regime in revolutionary Hungary. Yancey's reputation as a defender of slavery had hardly endeared him to the British government, King was an undistinguished Georgia politician, and Rost's sole recommendation had been his ability to speak French. When it became apparent that the foursome had beguiled no one with their Southern charm and that it took more than a few battlefield victories and brave pronunciamentos to win international support, the Richmond cabinet decided to recall its discouraged diplomats and send more experienced men on a mission of indeterminate length.

Shortly after their appointment in late August, Mason and Slidell received instructions almost as difficult to execute as those given to American envoys many years before, in 1776. They were directed to prove to the French and British governments that the Union blockade was ineffective; to negotiate treaties of amity and commerce; and to urge recognition of Southern independence by stressing that European textile plants would need the Southern cotton, that the United States would soon cease to be a maritime competitor, and that Confederate success would establish a balance of power on the North American continent.[2] Discrediting the porous blockade required little effort; they needed only to present periodically the statistics of blockade violations compiled by the Confederate State Department, which would be generally verified in the dispatches of foreign consuls. But to negotiate commercial treaties and procure recognition of an insurgent body of slaveholders, Mason and Slidell would have to persuade European powers to abandon caution, moral principle, and international legal precedent. Undaunted by the challenge, the two men confidently expected the Confederate cause abroad to triumph with the aid of the world's most powerful monarch, King Cotton.

There was an Alice-in-Wonderland quality about Southern faith in the power of a cotton embargo to compel European recognition of Confederate independence and to intervene in the Civil War, and the record of overseas reliance on Southern cotton encouraged the fantasy. A fifth of the British population depended directly or indirectly on the cotton-manufacturing industry, which received 80 percent of its fiber from the South. Other European nations, especially France, also relied heavily on the American supply because of the low quality and high cost of cotton elsewhere. Southern readers of the British *Parliamentary Debates* were entertained annually by mournful accounts of the failure to develop alternative sources in India. Convinced that Europe's industrial fate was inextricably linked to their region, Southerners gradually (and, perhaps, inevitably) came to exaggerate cotton's importance. Although the South lacked all the attributes of a flourishing, modern economy—industry, a merchant marine, and capital reserves—Confederate spokesmen pointed with delight to "that little attenuated cotton thread, which a child can break, but which nevertheless *can hang the world*."[3]

The obsession with cotton's influence so deeply permeated every facet of Southern society that historian Clement Eaton has compared it with "the belief of the French people prior to World War II in the impregnability of the Maginot Line." The popularizer of the catch phrase "King Cotton," Senator James H. Hammond of South Carolina, typified the prevailing bravado when he asserted that no sane nation would make war on cotton because "without firing a gun, without drawing a sword . . . we could bring the whole world to our feet." Touring Hammond's state after the attack on Fort Sumter, the correspondent for the London *Times*, William H. Russell, found that Carolinians smugly expected John Bull to "make a great fuss about noninterference, but when he begins to want cotton he'll come off his perch." The general opinion was that England would have to recognize Confederate independence to avoid an end to the cotton supply, and a consequent revolt of the working class. "Look out there," a Charleston merchant said, pointing to a wharf piled high with bales, "there's the key will open all our ports, and put us into John Bull's strong box as well."[4] Cotton, as the instrument of Confederate international power, seemed invincible.

Ranking Confederate officials, who might have known better, subscribed to the King Cotton theory and made it the basis of diplomatic policy. In instructions to commissioners going abroad, the Confederate State Department in Richmond harped on the theme that Britain and France were so dependent on Southern cotton that terrible social and economic consequences would befall them if the Union blockade endured, and great benefits would result if it collapsed under foreign pressure. Unsure of how to convey these prospects without antagonizing the recipients, the Richmond statesmen merely suggested to their government's first diplomatic envoys that they make "a delicate allusion to the probability of such an occurrence." But the European governments ignored such hints, and, bolstered by mounting Union defeats, Confederate officials abandoned innuendo; by September 1861, they were calling on every nation "to throw the moral weight of its recognition into the scale of peace as soon as possible." Toward the end of September, instructions written for Mason and Slidell urged them to emphasize that a war that prevented the export of Southern cotton was "directed as much against those who transport and manufacture cotton as against those who produce the raw material," and that only by the establishment of Confederate independence would the question of cotton supply for Britain and France be satisfactorily settled.[5] Thus, through a combination of bribery, blackmail, and bluster—all prompted by the availability or scarcity of cotton—Mason and Slidell were to persuade European nations to recognize the Confederacy, agree to favorable commercial terms, and intervene against the Union. It was a measure of their innocence or arrogance that they never questioned the strategy or the certainty of its success.

Of the two envoys, James Mason, the ebullient master of Selma Plantation in Virginia, had the more attractive (if less luminous) personality. Having served in the House of Representatives and the Senate, where he fell under the influence of John C. Calhoun, Mason grandly considered the sectional dispute an uncompromisable quarrel between two different social and economic systems. Insouciance was Mason's most obvious quality. He had preached secession when most Southerners viewed it with horror, and happily led Virginia out of the

James M. Mason, Confederate Minister to Great Britain
U.S. Signal Corps Photo No. 111-B-5163 (Brady Collection) in the National Archives

Union in April 1861. His ten years as chairman of the Senate Foreign Relations Committee, his high social position, and his long friendship with President Davis might explain his appointment as commissioner to Britain; unfortunately, he was not a good choice. Like Yancey, his influence was impaired by a proslavery notoriety, which was highlighted by his authorship of the Fugitive Slave Act of 1850. Paunchy and perpetually frowning, with long bushy hair scratching the nape of his coat, Mason peered out from under heavy eyebrows at all adversaries of Southern independence. Many Northerners shared the opinion of Charles Francis Adams, Jr., the son of the American envoy to the Court of St. James's, that Mason was a dull-witted, typical Virginian, "very provincial and intensely arrogant." A New York paper, in the abusive editorial style of the day, once described Mason as a "cold, calculating, stolid, sour traitor" whose heart was "gangrened with envy and pride, his mien imperious and repulsive." Mason could be charming and gracious, and William H. Russell of the London *Times* regarded him as "a fine old English gentleman but for tobacco." Still, Mason lacked diplomatic talents. When the Confederate diarist Mary Boykin Chesnut heard of his appointment to London she thought it "the maddest thing yet." She could not picture him a diplomat. "He will say chaw for chew, and he will wear a dress coat to breakfast." Mrs. Chesnut's apprehensions were to be fully justified. Mason's incompetence eventually won him a British historian's criticism for proving "so unfitted for his task, that Lincoln would have done well to have paid his passage."[6]

Although the Confederate commissioner to France, John Slidell, had a less savory background than Mason, he was widely regarded as the more capable man. A native of New York, son of a tallow chandler (prompting snobbish wags to say that he had been "*dipped* not *moulded* into society"), he had fled the city in 1819, after seriously wounding a theater manager in a duel over the affections of an actress. One jump ahead of the sheriff for this affair and for debts incurred in a mercantile business failure, he sought refuge in Louisiana as a gambler and then a lawyer, eventually marrying a beautiful young Creole named Mathilde Deslonde. Like many attorneys, Slidell drifted into politics and soon antagonized Andrew Jackson by sympathizing with nullification. He championed his adopted state from 1843 to 1845 in the House of Representatives, where he worked for the sugar interests, and, in the interest of James K. Polk, he instigated the Plaquemines Parish scandals—a pitifully obtuse voting fraud—in the 1844 presidential election. In appreciation, President Polk appointed Slidell commissioner to Mexico to negotiate for the beneficial adjustment of the Texas boundary and to purchase New Mexico and California as part of the bargain, but the Mexican government refused to receive him. This helped set the stage for provocative American moves that led to the Mexican War. Slidell's star continued to rise. A United States Senator from 1853 to 1861, he managed James Buchanan's successful campaign for the presidency in 1856, opposed Stephen A. Douglas at every opportunity, and supported the Breckinridge-Lane ticket in 1860. By this time, to be sure, his star was at its zenith. One could see both success and failure in his statesmanlike visage—piercing gray eyes, iron-gray moustache, thin firm lips, dissipated face, and a roll of fat under the chin. He already had gained a reputation of being tricky, of being a wirepuller and "subtle, full of device, and fond of intrigue." It was said that if he were thrown into a dungeon he "would conspire with the mice against the cat sooner than not conspire at all."[7]

This adroit Louisianan's unorthodox powers of persuasion had earned him the North's abnormal fear as "the most dangerous person

John Slidell, Confederate Minister to France
U.S. Signal Corps Photo No. 111-B-4134 (Brady Collection) in the National Archives

to the Union the Confederacy could select for diplomatic work in Europe." Slidell had been offered a position in the first Confederate mission in March 1861; however, preferring to work alone and disliking Mann, he had declined. Now, seven months later, believing more strongly than ever in the imminent recognition of the Confederacy by European powers, he agreed to employ his special talents.[8] With luck he might imitate the example of Benjamin Franklin, who had journeyed to Paris on a similar mission less than a century earlier.

The Confederate agents faced a small problem concerning their escape from Charleston; since April, the Union had maintained a quasi-blockade of the Southern coast, concentrating a few dozen warships outside major ports, off the West Indies and Mexico, and in the Gulf Stream. The arrangement left hundreds of miles of coastline and scores of rivers, bays, inlets, and harbors unguarded, but a steam frigate and a sloop of war watched over the port of Charleston. Mason and Slidell initially planned to run the blockade on a privateer, the *Nashville*, and spent weeks on board the ship, frustrated by the tide, winds, and a heavy surf that made crossing the bar hazardous. When two more steamers joined the blockading squadron, the commissioners considered departing from Matamoros in Mexico, but discarded that route as time-consuming; finally, they changed to the *Gordon*, a privateer of lighter draft, especially suited for the escape plan, which called for a prolonged course close to shore.[9]

Mason and Slidell could not have chosen a more appropriate vessel. Built before the war for service as a coasting packet with occasional trips to Havana, the *Carolina*, as it was first named, had been refitted and commissioned the C.S.S. *Gordon* a week before Bull Run. Equipped with three guns and sidearms for a crew of fifty, she had gained a fearsome reputation for preying on Yankee merchantmen. Blockaders called her the "Black Witch" and had grown so accustomed to her daily reconnoitering that they had ceased trying to catch her. Impressed by the *Gordon*'s speed, Mason persuaded the government to charter the vessel on October 8 for $10,000 to carry them to Nassau or Havana, where they hoped to connect with a British mail ship. In honor of the new assignment and in keeping with a popular counterintelligence tactic, the owners obliterated the ship's name and painted on *Theodora*. Richmond papers for several days proclaimed the diplomats' impending departure. The sudden sailing of the *Nashville* contributed to the deception. While the United States Navy scrambled madly to assemble a pursuit force, Mason and Slidell made ready to depart.[10]

On a dark rainy night, Mason later wrote, "such as the enemy thought no sinner would be abroad in," the *Theodora* slipped down the coast for three miles in silence with lights extinguished, keeping the captured Fort Sumter between her and the blockading squadron. Despite a heavy rain, the two commissioners (with Slidell's wife and three children, his secretary George Eustis and his wife, and Mason's secretary James E. Macfarland) sat on deck waiting out the run. Mason and Slidell tossed their cigars overboard before passing Sumter. The rainstorm muffled the engine and masked their movement so well that they passed within a mile and a half of the squadron's lights. The four Union vessels never saw the *Theodora*'s dark hulk hugging the coastline. Three or four miles beyond, the steamer put to sea and made for Nassau by the outer passage.[11]

The voyage proved as uneventful as the agents hoped. A strong breeze blew up the next day, and though the sea was calm, the ship's rolling in long, heavy swells nauseated every passenger but Mason, who continued to eat heartily. The vessel reached Nassau on Monday, October 14, at 4:00 P.M., where pilots who boarded the ship reported that no regular transport service connected Nassau and St. Thomas, the departure point for the British line. Since mail steamers came no closer than Havana, the *Theodora* put off for Cuba, cruising for some eighty miles over the shallow, clear water of the Bahama Banks. At daybreak on October 16, running short of coal, they espied the coast of Cuba, eight to ten miles away. A steamer steering westwardly midway between them and land suddenly swung about and made for the ship. Certain that it was friendly, the *Theodora* ran up the Stars and Bars and turned to meet her. The two vessels closed slowly, shutting off steam a hundred yards apart.

Slidell and Eustis went on board the strange ship and discovered it to be a Spanish coast guard cutter. The commander greeted the pair civilly and agreed to escort them as far as Cardenas, assuring them that no Federal steamers were near. They reached the Cuban port about 2:00 P.M. Complications in clearance prevented approval for disembarkation until the next day, when they landed without customs inspection. A few Yankee captains in port raged at the *Theodora*'s Spanish escort, but the governor and leading townsmen offered every courtesy and supplied the ship with coal. Because they had just missed the steamer for Cádiz, the party accepted a wealthy landowner's invitation to visit his sugar and coffee plantations, letting the *Theodora* sail on to Havana. The Confederates were happy to find refuge from the hot weather and mosquitoes.[12]

The party left on October 22 to travel overland to Havana, a pro-Southern stronghold; the ladies of the city had already presented the *Theodora* with a large silken Confederate flag. When Yancey and Rost had arrived in April, they had been royally received by the British consul, Joseph T. Crawford, who had presented them to the captain-general and governor of Cuba, Don Francisco Serrano, and arranged a tour of a British war steamer. Mason and Slidell now enjoyed similar treatment. The afternoon following their arrival Crawford conducted the agents to the captain-general's office in the Plaza de Armas. The Confederate consul, Charles J. Helm, regarded Serrano as "our warm, ardent friend," and Serrano told Helm that "my heart and soul are with you in your struggle for independence." Despite such sentiments, Serrano let discretion and prudence govern his conduct; he refused to receive Mason and Slidell or any other Southern diplomats in his official capacity, but only as "private persons." Satisfied with their reception, the envoys calmly awaited the British mail packet *Trent*, which operated between Veracruz and the Danish island of St. Thomas, the connecting point for British steamers running to Southampton. Slidell and Mason sipped claret and laughed about their escape. Having run the blockade successfully, Mason wrote to his wife, "everything else is plain sailing, because under any foreign flag we are safe from molestation."[13] Mason did not reckon on a Union naval captain who had in mind a different sort of voyage for them.

Across the island at Cienfuegos, the U.S.S. *San Jacinto* rocked gently with the swell. Launched in 1850 at the Brooklyn navy yard, the Federal screw steamer was a first-class sloop-of-war mounting twelve guns, but she was not the Union's best. A former commander had found her "a very inefficient vessel," slow, defective in propeller and shaft, with a battery of the lightest class, eight-inch shell guns. Attached to the African Squadron, the ship had spent twenty months cruising up and down the west coast of the Dark Continent searching for slavers, but had had little luck. She had left the Angolan port capital of St. Paul de Luanda on August 10, 1861, temporarily commanded by Lieutenant Donald McNeill Fairfax, bound for the island of Fernando Po. Captain Charles Wilkes had assumed command at Fernando Po under orders to bring the vessel home to participate in the attack on Port Royal, South Carolina. With characteristic flamboyance, Wilkes had told his son that he was going to the "white man's graveyard" to bring back the whole squadron.[14]

Explorer and author, as well as naval officer, the sixty-three-year-old Wilkes had had a distinguished, if somewhat controversial, career. He was, biographer Geoffrey S. Smith noted, a transitional figure between the old navy of wood and sail and the future navy of steel and steam. A dilettante in science, with little respect for scientists (or anyone else), he had developed an interest in astronomy and, during his supervision of the Navy's Depot of Charts and Instruments, had built the government's first observatory. Never doubting the nation's great destiny, he had been an early advocate of the rapid charting of coastal waters and overseas exploration to secure his country a commanding position in world commerce. As a lieutenant, Wilkes won command in the summer of 1838 of a six-vessel United States Exploring Expedition whose objectives were to protect American whalers, promote commerce, and expand scientific knowledge. Although the "Ex. Ex." would be hailed as the federal government's "crowning achievement in scientific research" for this period, the assignment brought ambivalent personal results. During the four-year, 85,000-mile voyage, Wilkes surveyed 800 miles of the Oregon Country coast and compiled convincing evidence that the United States should claim a northern boundary beyond the forty-ninth parallel in order to control the magnificent waters of Puget Sound and the Strait of Juan de Fuca. He charted some 280 islands in the South Pacific with such accuracy that the Navy used his maps during World War II. Among all the data that Wilkes and a team of scientists gathered, his map of a 1,500-mile unknown coastline proved the most startling, for it revealed that far to the South in a frozen hell of ice and bitter cold lay a new continent, Antarctica. However, a British explorer, James Clark Ross, disputed Wilkes's charts and statements, declaring that he had sailed over his landfalls, while a Frenchman, Dumont d'Urville, claimed prior discovery. Wilkes returned home to public indifference and a court martial brought on by high-handed conduct as commander.[15]

Despite his adventurous life and New York origins, Wilkes was not one of those legendary Yankee shipmasters, "hard, cheery old boys; salt in their talk . . . with everlasting anecdotes of icebergs, cargoes, and close-reefed topsails."[16] Unpopular among both officers and men, he was cocky, headstrong, aware of his abilities, and blind to his imperfections. Sailors thought him impossible. A taskmaster devoted to duty, he expected as much from others, demanded slavish obedience, and overreacted when he felt his position challenged. In the course of the expedition to Antarctica numerous clashes occurred with enlisted men. Before leaving Valparaiso, Wilkes ordered two disorderly crew members lashed well beyond the normal penalty of twelve blows. When three marines would not reenlist at Honolulu he placed them in irons and flogged them until they agreed. In an era when naval officers served as roving diplomats, Wilkes showed a fondness for gunboat diplomacy, and in the Fiji Islands he burned a village after its inhabitants stole some expedition property. He later burned two more villages and killed over fifty Malolo cannibals in revenge for the murder of two officers, including his nephew. Only when the survivors crawled before him to beg forgiveness did the slaughter cease. Convicted by court martial in 1842 of illegally punishing bluejackets but acquitted of all other charges, he escaped with a public reprimand.

Captain Charles Wilkes
Reproduced from the Collections of the Library of Congress

Until the outbreak of the Civil War, Wilkes labored on arranging the expedition's huge specimen collection and supervising the writing of scientific reports, all the while brooding over the actions of an ungrateful government. His capacity for self-pity knew no bounds and he instinctively shifted blame to others. Lincoln's secretary of the navy, Gideon Welles, found him able but lacking judgment, "very exacting towards others, but . . . not himself as obedient as he should be." When the rebellion erupted Wilkes was ordered to the Norfolk navy yard to command the *Merrimac*; however, before he arrived, authorities scuttled her to prevent capture. Wilkes then helped burn the yard. He saw little action thereafter. Quick-tempered, resentful of criticism, he longed for the glory of a naval hero. It would not be denied him again.[17]

Charles Wilkes took command of the *San Jacinto* on August 28, 1861, and, ignoring his orders to proceed to Philadelphia, commenced a month-long cruise of the African coast in search of Rebel privateers, especially the C.S.S. *Sumter* commanded by Raphael Semmes, which had captured ten Yankee merchantmen in South American waters, but was reported everywhere. He reached Monrovia, Liberia, on September 12; on September 25, he reached St. Vincent in the Cape Verdes, where he learned from newspapers that Confederate commerce raiders were having a field day in the West Indies. He set course for the Caribbean. The *San Jacinto* touched at St. Thomas on October 13 and found the U.S.S. *Iroquois*, Commander James S. Palmer, and the U.S.S. *Powhatan*, Commander David D. Porter, already in port. Palmer and Porter had cruised the Caribbean for months, trying to sink privateers. They grumbled that "the sympathy of the West Indies is with the Southern cause." British and French governors alike treated Union warships and Confederate privateers as vessels of "equally legal belligerent powers." Wilkes tended to agree, having heard rumors that Great Britain was allowing Southerners to build and outfit ships in her ports.[18]

The British brig *Spartan* arrived in the afternoon with welcome news. Mistaking her for a Yankee vessel, the *Sumter* had boarded her six days earlier near Rio de Janeiro, shortly after burning the *Joseph Parke* of Boston. Contravening orders of the secretary of the navy, Wilkes directed Palmer and the *Iroquois* to Maranham, 1,000 miles away, to intercept the raider should it coal there; the *Powhatan* would take a southern route. Before leaving St. Thomas, Porter and Wilkes were dinner guests at the home of the American consul where Wilkes reportedly bored everyone with a monologue devoted to the well-known deeds of the Exploring Expedition. The next morning, October 14, the *San Jacinto* adopted the *Iroquois'* former order of search and prowled the Windward Passage to Jamaica, Grand Cayman, and Boca Grande, reaching Cienfuegos on October 23. Wilkes took on coal, and read in Cuban newspapers that the *Theodora* was in Havana waiting for Mason and Slidell, who were traveling overland. The *San Jacinto* weighed anchor and hurried to intercept the ship on her return to Charleston. Wilkes arrived in Havana at the end of October to discover that the *Theodora* had escaped the Union navy again and that the commissioners planned to leave for St. Thomas on the *Trent* on November 7.[19] With no trophies for his unauthorized, two-month hunting cruise, Wilkes began to see Mason and Slidell as consolation prizes.

Deciding that he needed information, Captain Wilkes and his officers called on the United States consul-general, Robert W. Shufeldt. A fifteen-year navy veteran, Shufeldt had most recently served in the merchant marine on the New York–Havana–New Orleans run and had tried to open a transit route across the Isthmus of Tehuantepec. After tilting most of the summer with Serrano over illegal Confederate captures of Northern vessels within Cuban waters, he had become ill with yellow fever and been forced to return home. Weeks passed before he could resume his post. By then Mason and Slidell were promenading in the Plaza de Armas and Wilkes was knocking on his door. Shufeldt took the Union officers to interview Serrano, because he knew Serrano had met the Confederate agents. The governor hastened to assure Wilkes he had "little respect" for the gentlemen and dismissed Slidell "in terms of derision." After the meeting with Serrano, Shufeldt debated with Wilkes the legality of seizing the men from a foreign mail ship. The consul-general could find no precedent in numerous international law books, and thought it "would seem to be a violation of the rights of neutrals upon the ocean." But Wilkes, impressed by the Confederate commissioners' importance and grasping at legal straws, resolved to intercept the vessel anyway. Shufeldt secretly notified the State Department of the captain's decision, noting it might deserve "more favorable consideration" than he first thought, if only because the *Trent* was not a public vessel. He had not tried very hard to dissuade Wilkes. A few days before the capture, the wife of the British consul-general, Mrs. Crawford, called on the Shufeldts. Eventually she remarked to the diplomat that it was rumored the *San Jacinto* had left port to seize Mason and Slidell. "Did you ever hear of any thing more ridiculous Mr. Shufeldt?" "No Madam," he replied, "never heard any thing so ridiculous in my life," and made a very low bow.[20]

Wilkes's decision to remove the Confederate commissioners from the *Trent* deserves close attention. How he strained to rationalize the capture! He pored over authorities on international law, scrutinizing neutral rights and responsibilities. Books by Sir William Scott, Henry Wheaton, James Kent, and Emmerich de Vattel littered the desk of his cabin. Wilkes thought he had the power to capture vessels carrying enemy dispatches, but was not sure he could remove the commissioners for, as he wrote, they "were not dispatches in the literal sense, and did not seem to come under that designation, and nowhere could I find a case in point." However, the captain concluded that since they were "bent on mischievous and traitorous errands against our country," they were "the embodiment of dispatches," subject to arrest if they had no United States passports. Having not yet reached their neutral destination, they held no diplomatic immunity. He saw his way clear to capturing them and knew "of no act that would so effectually nonplus their diabolical scheme."[21] It was a novel theory and a good example of quarter-deck justice, but for all his homework Captain Wilkes did not find a single precedent to support the dubious enterprise; subsequently, neither could anyone else.

Because the rebel agents had given no sign of panicky departure and the *Trent* was not due for several days, Wilkes resumed pursuit of the *Sumter*, by now the object of an intense Union search. On the afternoon of November 2 he headed for the northern coast of Cuba, where he found some excitement. At 8:00 A.M. the next day, twenty miles from Matanzas lights, the French brig *Jules et Marie* sighted a steamer coming head on. The French captain ordered a gun fired and the flag hoisted, but drew no response. A few minutes later the *San Jacinto* collided with the French ship, causing much damage. Wilkes sent a repair party on board and towed her most of the way to Havana before cutting the tow line over the French captain's protest.[22]

In no mood to waste time with the disabled brig, he feared that without assistance he could easily miss the *Trent* on its way from Havana to St. Thomas. The *San Jacinto*'s presence might also have led the British consul, who doubled as booking agent for the mail company, to suggest evasive action. Therefore, after leaving the *Jules et Marie*, Wilkes set a southerly course to deceive the agents and any sympathizers, but after nightfall headed for Key West, reaching port on November 4. There he hoped to find the *Powhatan* or other ships to help patrol the Bahama channels through which the *Trent* was expected to pass. The only two vessels in port were the U.S.S. *Huntsville*, undergoing repair of hull and boilers, and the bark *Kingfisher*, whose captain would not deviate from orders and accompany the *San Jacinto*. Wilkes allegedly confided his plan to Lieutenant Fairfax, who thought it might produce an Anglo-American war and begged Wilkes to consult William Marvin, judge of the United States District Court for the Southern District of Florida, in Key West. If Fairfax ever made such a plea, Wilkes ignored it; he left Florida on November 5, after taking on bedding and other supplies for the comfort of his prospective prisoners. At Sagua la Grande on Cuba's northern coast, he sent Lieutenant K. Randolph Breese ashore to seek information regarding the *Trent*'s schedule from the American consul, James H. Horner, as prearranged with Shufeldt. By now, November 6, Shufeldt had learned the mail ship's time of departure and had sent Horner a cryptic telegram: "Lo veré en la tarde del día seis manden como dirigido en mi carta del veinte y nueve" ["I shall see it in the afternoon of day six. Forward as directed in my letter of the 29th"]. Having received a letter from Breese but not Shufeldt, the consul surmised that Shufeldt was on the *San Jacinto* and wanted to see him in port. Horner arrived after

Breese had returned to the ship, and did not learn the telegram's meaning for another two days. Not receiving the message, Wilkes steamed ninety miles east to the middle of Old Bahama Channel, and waited at its narrowest point of fifteen miles across.[23]

On November 7 at 8:00 A.M., the bulky R.M.S. *Trent* nosed out of Havana with a valuable cargo: $1,500,000 in specie and sixty passengers, among them the Confederate commissioners burdened with "several thousand segars." Flying the pennant of the Royal Mail Steam Packet Company, the paddle-wheeler was part of a fleet that had plied Caribbean, Mexican, and South American waters for twenty years; the fleet operated under mail contract with the Admiralty and, though the ships were not armored, they were built to carry large-caliber guns so that they could act as naval units in time of war. The *Trent* had served as a troopship and towboat during the Crimean War, but now carried only two six-pound brass signal guns to herald arrival and departure from port. Her captain and mail agent, officers in the Royal Navy, were assigned to the *Trent* because they had not demonstrated sufficient ability to advance through the Senior Service.[24] Duty aboard a mail ship in peacetime was normally uneventful so the two men expected a routine voyage.

While the *Trent* steamed down the Cuban coast, Wilkes tacked back and forth along the edge of the Great Bahama Bank, seeking information from other ships regarding the *Trent*'s time of departure. His men boarded two Spanish vessels but learned nothing so, to be safe, Wilkes ordered Fairfax to ready the second and third cutters. At 10:30 on a beautiful Friday morning, November 8, the crew saw a bark to the east and a schooner to the north. At 11:40, the sailor aloft sang out, "Sail ho!" Lieutenant Breese, on deck, asked direction. "Off the port bow, sir." At this point, Wilkes called the officers into his cabin to inform them of the plan. Because he suspected a few were rebels at heart, he acted somewhat impulsively and put them under arrest until the commissioners were captured. Soon the crew detected a cloud of black smoke and, ignoring mess call, watched the funnel grow. Out of its base emerged the spars, hull, and finally the full body of the British mail steamer *Trent*.[25]

Abreast of Paredon lighthouse, 240 miles from Havana, the passengers and crew of the mail ship sighted a steamer 5 or 6 miles away in the Bahama Channel, 10 miles from the Cuban coast. Captain James Moir remarked that it appeared to be a warship bent on mischief, since it was not displaying colors. A mile away, the *Trent* raised a British ensign at the peak mast and the Royal Mail Company pennant at the main. The vessel showed no identification. The *Trent* steamed on. Suddenly, at 1:05 P.M., the warship fired a blank and raised the American flag. The *Trent* raised her flags again and continued on course at reduced speed. By now the two ships were so close that the *Trent's* passengers could see the other vessel's ports open, guns run out, and crew at stations.[26]

At 1:17 the *Trent* closed to less than 300 yards and showed no intent of heaving to; the *San Jacinto* fired a pivot gun shell across her bow, 100 yards to leeward. Moir slackened speed and shut off steam. Moving over to the railing he called, "What do you want?"

"We'll send a boat aboard," the *San Jacinto* answered.

Most of the passengers were on deck amidship and watched a cutter leave the American vessel and come round the *Trent's* stern. Seeing the crew armed with guns and cutlasses, Mason told his secretary to take the Confederate dispatch bag, containing public papers, credentials, and instructions, to the mail agent, Commander Richard Williams, and ask him to lock it up. A few minutes later, Williams told Mason that he had locked the bag in the mail room and would personally deliver it to Yancey, Rost, and Mann in London.[27]

Lieutenant Fairfax, accompanied by Second Assistant Engineer James B. Houston, Boatswain H. P. Grace, and several armed sailors, pulled alongside the *Trent* in the second cutter. Wilkes had instructed his executive officer to demand the steamer's papers, clearance from Havana, and passenger and crew lists; to take Mason, Slidell, Eustis, and Macfarland prisoner and bring them to the *San Jacinto*; and to seize the *Trent* as a prize of war. Although Wilkes did not expect resistance, he gave Fairfax permission to use force in bringing over the diplomats, their possessions, and dispatches should the men prove obstinate. Families were welcome to join them, and Fairfax was to procure any "necessaries or stores" to ensure their comfort.[28]

The instructions to Fairfax seemed to cover any eventuality, but the lieutenant had his own ideas about how to handle the situation. He was determined not to irritate the commissioners, the passengers, or the captain "lest it might occur to them to throw the steamer on my hands, which would necessitate my taking her as a prize." He still feared an international incident and had resolved to disobey orders if it would diminish the consequences. Fairfax told the boatload of marines to remain alongside "until it became necessary to show some force," an alternative he expected as he climbed on board. The *Trent*'s first officer accompanied him to the quarter-deck. Captain Moir, surrounded by passengers, greeted him courteously but cooly, then protested the *San Jancinto*'s manner of heaving him to. Fairfax countered by requesting the passenger list and said he had reason to believe that Mason and Slidell were on board. Moir refused to show documents. What would happen, he asked, should he decline to surrender the men if they were on his ship? Fairfax replied that "his orders were to take the ship in case of necessity." The *Trent*'s captain retorted that he opposed "any thing like a search of his vessel." Only force would extract Mason and Slidell, who, he admitted, were indeed among the passengers.[29]

Hearing his name mentioned, an elderly man stepped forward and said, "I am Mr. Slidell; do you want to see me?" Mason also approached the group. Fairfax again identified himself and his mission. At the lieutenant's request, Mason pointed out Macfarland and Eustis. All four men protested their arrest and refused to leave the *Trent* voluntarily. By now the passengers, many of them Southerners, realized what was happening. They howled with rage and someone yelled, "Throw the damn fellow overboard!" Fairfax asked Moir to keep order and warned the passengers that "a heavy battery was bearing on them" and would be touched off if they attacked him or any man of the boarding party. Moir managed to calm his charges. But hearing the commotion, Houston rushed on deck from the cutter and found Fairfax surrounded by a throng. He returned to the boat and brought back Boatswain Grace and six or eight heavily armed marines. Moir objected, and Fairfax ordered the men to remain in the gangway. Meanwhile, the *San Jacinto* lay 200 yards off the port beam, tampions removed from her guns.[30]

Fairfax and the commissioners resumed their debate on whether the latter would go peaceably. Although Moir scarcely opened his mouth, Commander Williams, the mail agent who had hidden the Confederate dispatches, interrupted constantly. Whenever the conversation lulled he blustered: "In this ship I am the representative of her Britannic Majesty's Government, and in the name of the Government I protest against this illegal act of piracy which you would not dare to attempt on a ship capable of resisting such aggression." Fairfax ignored William's litany, refusing to have contact with anyone but Moir, and sent Houston back to the *San Jacinto* to report the presence of Mason and Slidell and the need for force to remove them.[31]

Mrs. Slidell asked Fairfax who commanded his ship and he answered, "Your old acquaintance, Captain Wilkes." She replied that when the damaged French brig, *Jules et Marie*, had reached Havana, the commanders of two French men-of-war had become furious. "Really," she smiled, "Captain Wilkes is playing into our hands!" Mason politely told her to keep quiet.[32] No one was going to wreck an opportunity to embroil the United States and Great Britain in war.

While Mrs. Slidell nettled Fairfax, Lieutenant James A. Greer put off from the *San Jacinto* in the third cutter, accompanied by Third Assistant Engineer George W. Hall, Paymaster's Clerk Robert G. Simpson, Master's Mate Charles B. Dahlgren, a sergeant, a corporal, six marine privates, four machinists, and a boat crew of thirteen. Another boat followed to carry the commissioners' baggage. Grace met Greer with an order from Fairfax to bring the marines up to the cabin, to keep some men on guard, and to ready the boat crews to board if needed. Greer deployed his men and cleared the space outside and forward of the cabin. Then he sent Engineer Hall into the cabin where Mason and Slidell had withdrawn to pack.[33]

Inside, Fairfax was still trying to persuade the commissioners to leave without creating a scene. "Gentlemen," he said, waving toward the reinforcements, "I hope you will now go with me."

Mason replied, "I have only to reiterate what I said at first. I will not leave the ship unless compelled by force greater than I can overcome."

Fairfax took hold of Mason's coat collar and shoulder, calling to several Union officers, "Gentlemen, lay your hands on Mr. Mason." Hall grabbed Mason by the collar.

Mason chirped, "I yield to force."

"Under protest, Mr. Mason, under protest," piped Commander Williams.

"Yes," droned Mason, "I yield to force under protest, and will go."

Fairfax walked the Virginian to the door and transferred his hold to Lieutenant Greer who, with Hall, escorted him to the third cutter at the port gangway. Mason's secretary, unaccompanied, came out shortly and joined his employer.[34]

Returning to the cabin, Fairfax approached Slidell's compartment; the diplomat's eldest daughter, Matilda, stood in the entrance, arms stretched to each side of the door frame, while her parents remained inside. She refused to let Fairfax pass. They argued loudly enough for passengers and crew to distinguish a woman's voice, but not specific words. Slidell's daughter, one witness observed, was "in the enjoyment of an aggravated attack of hysterics." The *Trent*'s purser later described graphically, and imaginatively, how she stood

MISS SLIDELL ON THE RAM-PAGE.

"I say, with my hand on my heart, that Miss SLIDELL, in her agony, did Strike Mr.
FAIRFAX Three Times in the Face. I wish that her Knuckles had Struck me in the Face."
[*Vide* Commander WILLIAMS's *Account of the Seizure of* MASON *and* SLIDELL.]

Courtesy of *Harper's Weekly*

"with flashing eyes and quivering lips," resolved to defend her father. Commander Williams's account excelled even the purser's. Miss Slidell, he would tell a dinner audience five weeks later, was in the cabin with her arm about her father's neck and vowed she would accompany him to prison. When Fairfax tried to coax her away, "in her agony" she slapped him three times with her "little knuckles" but not with "the vulgarity of gesture which has been attributed to her." (Among his auditors there must have been a groan, which Williams followed with brave words straight out of mid-Victorian chivalry: "I wish that Miss Slidell's little knuckles had struck me in the face. I should like to have the mark forever.") Fairfax afterward stated that Williams had based his account on the fact that Matilda had brushed against him when the ship rolled unexpectedly.[35]

The passengers, more confused than ever, milled around, talking.
"Did you ever hear of such an outrage?"
"These Yankees will have to pay well for this."
"This is the best thing in the world for the South."
"England will open the blockade."

"We will have a good chance at them now."

"Did you ever hear of such a piratical act?"[36]

Houston, one of the San Jacinto's engineers, came to Lieutenant Greer and said he thought there would be trouble. Greer sent him to ask Fairfax if he needed help. Just as the engineer returned with an affirmative, a yell went up: "Shoot him!" At that, Greer and the marines charged into the main-deck cabin, thrusting passengers aside. In a memorandum that Williams subsequently wrote to the British Admiralty, he swore that the soldiers advanced with fixed bayonets, and in his notorious dinner speech he assured the audience that "I had just time to put my body between their bayonets and Miss Slidell," saying, "Back you_____cowardly poltroons."[37]

As the marines advanced, Slidell jumped through a stateroom window into the cabin. Matilda screamed. Fairfax ordered Greer's marines back to the gangway and arrested the commissioner. Since force had been applied to Mason, Slidell insisted that only considerable force would remove him. Fairfax and Hall collared Slidell and delivered him to Grace and Houston, who took him to Greer's boat. As Slidell climbed over the side, he called to his wife, "Good-bye, my dear, we shall meet in Paris in sixty days." Fairfax then brought Eustis to the boat.[38]

In an official protest six days afterward, Captain Moir claimed that before the boarding party left the Trent, Fairfax had demanded that Moir board the San Jacinto, but that he had refused to leave unless taken by force. His allegation does not square with what probably happened; Fairfax had gone out of his way not to antagonize the captain. When Moir had complained that the San Jacinto was crowding him into shoal water, Fairfax had hailed the ship to keep more to windward and in mid-channel.[39] The last thing Fairfax had wanted was to have Moir give up the Trent. Perhaps he had made a belated attempt to carry out his instructions, but no other account supports Moir's story.

By 2:00 P.M. Greer delivered the commissioners and their secretaries. He returned with an extra boat to transfer the baggage. As consolation, Moir sent the commissioners "some dozens of sherry, with pitchers and basins, and other conveniences for the toilet." At 3:20 the Trent stood to the eastward. Ten minutes after the Trent got under way, the San Jacinto hoisted its boats and headed northwest. The families of Slidell and Eustis, who had declined Captain Wilkes's offer to join the prisoners, sailed on to St. Thomas and transferred to La Plata, arriving in Southampton on November 27 with news of the capture.[40]

Wilkes had instructed Fairfax to take possession of the *Trent* as a prize, after removing the four Confederates. Disobeying orders, Fairfax returned with all his men. It would have been improvident, he argued; the *San Jacinto* intended to support Admiral Samuel Du Pont's attack on Port Royal, South Carolina, and detaching a prize crew would weaken the Union vessel, inconvenience innocent passengers (particularly a large number of women and children), and injure distant merchants by delaying transmission of the *Trent*'s mail and specie. Citing these reasons in a report to the secretary of the navy, Wilkes approved his executive officer's suggestion to let the *Trent* proceed, and commended his conduct. Wilkes was convinced that he had treated the British ship generously; he believed that he could have seized it on two counts: resisting lawful search, and carrying enemies of the United States. He was right on the first point. Emphasizing his concern for the passengers' welfare, he had decided "to sacrifice the interests of my officers and crew in the prize, and suffered the steamer to proceed, . . . considering I had obtained the important end I had in view, and which affected the interests of our country and interrupted the action of that of the Confederates." It had been, he observed proudly, "one of the most important days in my naval life."[41]

Even as Wilkes was overhauling the *Trent*, three Union warships were scouring the Atlantic for the *Nashville*, the Confederate vessel on which the commissioners were thought to have taken passage for Europe. However, the orders of the Union captains did not authorize them to interfere with the agents if they were sailing under a neutral flag. Wilkes's removal of Mason and Slidell, therefore, could hardly be called standard procedure for the American navy. The United States had always championed the principle of freedom of the seas, viewing any infringement of its commerce as a challenge to national honor.

Although Wilkes was aware of his country's traditions, he apparently had decided that the agents' importance justified violation of principle. Only a fortnight had passed between learning of their presence in Cuba and welcoming them on board the *San Jacinto*; Wilkes had not had enough time to sail to Hampton Roads, telegraph to Washington for permission to carry out his plan, and return to the Bahama channel. Having served on distant stations, Wilkes had given some thought to the problems and responsibilities of a naval officer unable to communicate quickly with superiors:

> He is cut off from counsel and advice. He has no access to jurists and publicists, whose learning and experience might

guide him in safety through the labyrinths of the difficult and embarrassing questions of domestic and international law, which often bewilder and perplex him. He is bound to decide for himself, decide promptly. There is no time for investigation, scarce for reflection. With the orders from his Government in his hand, and the rules and regulations before him, he must act on the instant. He must take the responsibility.[42]

In the *Trent* incident, Wilkes had neither used discretion nor followed intuition. He operated under a distorted interpretation of international law, and clearly had doubts about the correctness of his decision, doubts that Shufeldt must have reinforced; yet, Wilkes stubbornly persisted. He had acted, and he insisted on taking full responsibility.

After leaving Old Bahama Channel, the *San Jacinto* ran through Santaren Passage and up the southern coast from St. Augustine to Charleston, the commissioners' departure point a month earlier. Wilkes arrived too late to take part in the successful expedition against Port Royal, but his capture of Mason and Slidell almost smothered news of Admiral Du Pont's victory. The latter certainly deserved praise. The Union force had taken the finest natural harbor on the South Atlantic coast; proved that heavily armed, steam warships could silence shore-based guns; and helped raise Northern morale at a critical time. Du Pont appreciated the public relations value of Wilkes's act, but other naval officers viewed Wilkes as a dangerous glory-hunter willing to advance his career at the nation's expense.[43]

With only a half-day's supply of coal, Wilkes put in to Hampton Roads at 2:00 P.M. on November 15. At Fortress Monroe on Old Point Comfort, the *San Jacinto* hurriedly took on 100 tons of coal. There were rumors of a possible attempt to rescue the prisoners during the night, and Wilkes was ordered to keep his crew alert. Before leaving he telegraphed Secretary of the Navy Welles his intent to proceed to New York and sent Commander Alfred Taylor, former commander of the *Saratoga* of the African Squadron (and suspected by some in the navy of disloyalty), ahead with dispatches.[44]

The *San Jacinto* left on November 16, after Wilkes permitted Mason to send a letter to his wife through the Confederate lines at Norfolk. Calm weather prevailed during the day, but it was raining when they arrived in the Narrows that evening. Off Highland Lights, sometime between 5:00 and 9:00 P.M., Wilkes interrupted the commissioners' game of backgammon to say they would not land at New York. A city steamer had brought an order from Secretary of State William H. Seward to take them to Fort Warren in Boston Harbor. Wilkes did not tell them the government had changed their destination to prevent a mob from taking the envoys. As with the Hampton Roads rumor, Wilkes thought the idea preposterous; however, the message had been delivered by United States Marshal Robert Murray and his deputy, who had orders from the secretary of state and the secretary of the navy to accompany the warship to Fort Warren and to let no one else on board.[45]

The barometer fell and winds buffeted the *San Jacinto* so badly for the next two days that she had to put in to Newport for coal. Depressed by the weather, the Confederates asked if they could remain in Rhode Island. Welles telegraphed the ship to continue on course, because Newport lacked a prison. Although Mason and Slidell had been rebuffed, they were not being badly treated. During the rough voyage, they had dined at the captain's table and occupied his cabin bed while Wilkes had slept on a cot. At Fortress Monroe the ship's purser had surprised them by paying the bill for some barrels of oysters they had ordered. The commissioners had been allowed to smoke on the quarter-deck, play whist all night if they wanted, and ignore the lights-out call. At Newport, Wilkes put in a stove and cut a hole in the cabin roof for the pipe. Throughout the voyage the commissioners found that prison life for diplomats could be pleasant.[46]

The *San Jacinto* left Newport on November 21 at 11:30 P.M. An expected gale did not materialize, but fog forced the ship to put in to Holmes's Hole, Massachusetts, the next morning. When the settlement learned that Wilkes had captured Mason and Slidell, small boats raised flags, a shore battery was fired, and a delegation waited on Wilkes with congratulations and supplies. It was a portent of the celebration to come. Wilkes stayed just long enough to pick up a pilot, and on November 23 the *San Jacinto* rounded Cape Cod and anchored off Boston Light. Wilkes decided to postpone the transfer of his prisoners until morning, "the night being very dark and a severe storm ahead."[47]

Somewhere out there in the gloom lay Fort Warren, the Confederates' new quarters. Situated on George's Island, it guarded the main entrance to Boston Harbor. The pentagonal granite-hewn fortress, surrounded by a ditch thirty feet wide, faced the sea with a large battery of heavy guns. The impressive redoubt was, however, weak.

Ammunition consisted of thirty rounds borrowed from another fort. Powder was too low even to salute the governor on visits. Weak and undermanned, the fort had four companies to guard 800 Confederate and state prisoners when the *San Jacinto* arrived.[48]

At 11:00 A.M. on November 24, Mason, Slidell, Macfarland, and Eustis, accompanied by Fairfax and an army lieutenant, climbed over the *San Jacinto* into the steam-tug *May Queen* for the last leg of the journey to prison. To one observer Slidell appeared dejected, while Mason seemed lighthearted. Before leaving the ship they thanked Wilkes for having "uniformly been treated with great courtesy and attention." As a last favor Wilkes allowed the Confederates to count their thousands of "segars" as part of the luggage, thus bypassing customs.[49]

A strange little procession then wound its way along the quarter-mile path from wharf to fort. Marshal Murray and Slidell led the column, followed by Fairfax and Mason, while deputy Sampson escorted Eustis and Macfarland. Officers and police from the fort brought up the rear with two carts of baggage, including assorted brandies, liquors, and Scotch ale. When the prisoners reached the gate an officer called the commandant, Colonel Justin Dimmick, out of church. He found the prisoners waiting in his quarters while theirs were being scrubbed; meanwhile, Marshal Murray searched their trunks for secret instructions. After surrendering all their money but twenty dollars each, the Confederate diplomats and their secretaries were incarcerated in a room eighteen feet square. Wilkes, in the meantime, after getting a receipt for his embodied dispatches, weighed anchor and reached Boston navy yard at 2:00 P.M. where he and his crew were paid, and the *San Jacinto* was taken out of commission.[50]

2.

Welcome to Wilkes!

MORALE IN THE NORTHERN STATES had plunged so low by the fall of 1861 that news of the seizure of Mason and Slidell brought as great an effect as a military victory. During the euphoric days of April 1861 tens of thousands had rushed to join the Union armed forces, confident that they would make short work of the secessionists. But European recognition of Confederate belligerency, the humiliating defeat at Bull Run, and the North's inability to mount an effective blockade had crushed hopes of a quick triumph and convinced many that the Republic was drifting. Northerners yearned for good news, for a sign that their cause was not lost. Word of Du Pont's success at Port Royal restored faith in the navy and considerably cheered the downcast public, but Wilkes's capture of the Confederate commissioners electrified the country. "About the first show of *action* we have had," an American diplomat exulted, "& God knows we need something to show that we are in Earnest in this war."[1] Overnight the mood turned joyous, if tempered by uncertainty about British reaction.

As soon as Wilkes stepped off the *San Jacinto* on November 25, Boston greeted him with open arms. The city had prepared a celebration, and a *Transcript* reporter had composed a poem:

Welcome to Wilkes! who didn't wait
To study up Vattel and Wheaton,

But bagged his game, and left the act
For dull diplomacy to treat on.
. . . .
Rather than let them slip, twere well
That precedent should bear transgression,
    And as for points of law—why Wilkes
Made sure of nine—in flat possession.[2]

Officials greeted Wilkes at Long Wharf and conducted him to a reception at Faneuil Hall where, despite a severe storm, a crowd of two to three thousand heard Mayor Joseph M. Wightman commend the captain's "sagacity, judgment, decision, and firmness." Overwhelmed, Wilkes replied modestly, "I have only to say that we did our duty to the Union and are prepared to do it again." The people cheered wildly, and so many pushed forward to shake his hand that his fingers were blistered for two weeks.[3]

Captain Wilkes also received many congratulatory messages from Union sympathizers. Some correspondents cheered him for capturing "a brace of devils." Others inquired after his autograph or a daguerreotype likeness. One writer nominated him as a candidate for the next presidential election. A few people sent gifts, including "a copy of a Patriotic Song" and a bottle of Madeira drawn from a flask allegedly intended for Slidell. Phineas T. Barnum, a sharp businessman, invited Wilkes to visit the American Museum in New York to see "many interesting curiosities," and to become, perhaps, an attraction to rival his latest acquisition, "a most remarkable dwarf."[4]

On the day following the reception, Wilkes attended a banquet at Revere House sponsored by local merchants who wanted "to put a *stimulant* into the Navey [*sic*] officers who have not so far shown so much 'snap' as we had hoped to see." When the 150 guests had eaten their fill and given Wilkes a long, standing ovation, they settled back to enjoy the oratory. The captain said a few words, remarking that he would not have arrested Mason and Slidell "if they could have shown a pass from the General Government." But the guests had not come to hear a naval officer stammer his thanks; inspired by this symbol of long-awaited triumph, they had gathered to see, cheer, and joyously reaffirm the greatness of America. Governor John A. Andrew declared that Wilkes had performed "the most illustrious service" of the war. "Commodore Wilkes fired his shot across the bows of the ship that bore the British lion at its head." Massachusetts Chief Justice George T. Bigelow pointed out that instinct and patriotism were sometimes more reliable than lawbooks, and that Wilkes's action was "in exact and strict conformity" with international law and his duty as an officer. The British government could not make the affair an issue without admitting to its own similar wrongdoing in the past. The United States needed peace abroad, Bigelow said, but "should never buy it at the cost of our own degradation." Fourteen other speakers discussed the matter for five hours. One of them, state Adjutant General Colonel William Schouler, found himself citing Davy Crockett ("Be sure you are right, then go ahead") and Edmond Hoyle ("When you are in doubt, take the trick"). It was a grand affair, and the speakers "seemed to vie with each other in establishing a record from which thereafter it would be impossible to escape."[5]

The question of the legality of Wilkes's act produced an interest in law books. Everyone who could read seemed intent on validating the capture rather than making an objective comparison with other cases. "Before twenty-four hours were over, every man and every woman in Boston was armed with precedents," noted Anthony Trollope, a British novelist touring America. He thought it "pretty to hear the charming women of Boston, as they became learned in the law of nations." One young lady told him, "Wheaton is quite clear about it."[6]

All of Boston supported Wilkes, rejoiced over the discomfiture of his captives, and felt that the legalities of the affair were almost—nay, entirely—in order. Some of the best legal minds rallied 'round the flag. The Dane Professor at Harvard Law School, Theophilus Parsons, was "just as certain that Wilkes had a legal right to take Mason and Slidell from the Trent, as I am that our government has a lawful right to blockade the port of Charleston." The United States District Attorney for Massachusetts, Richard Henry Dana, Jr., author of Two Years Before the Mast and a work on maritime law, The Seaman's Friend, had clapped his hands and "crowed with delight" when he heard the news of the capture. Willing to stake his professional reputation on the seizure's legality, he declared that "Wilkes has done a noble thing and done it well," for the Trent was "a lawful prize."[7]

Edward Everett, former congressman, governor of Massachusetts, minister to Britain, secretary of state, senator, and Constitutional Union Party vice-presidential candidate in 1860, had not the slightest doubt of its legality. He wrote to Secretary of State Seward in Washington that he had found an Admiralty court decision of Lord Stowell, which stated that a belligerent "may stop the ambassador of your enemy on his passage." This dictum became a popular citation. Critics contended that Stowell meant that a belligerent could arrest an enemy's envoy only if the latter were apprehended on the belligerent's territory; however, Everett thought the interpretation argumentative. Appearing before the Middlesex Mechanics' Association at Lowell, he

Charles Sumner, Senator from Massachusetts
Courtesy of the Massachusetts Historical Society

asserted amid cheers that "the detention was perfectly lawful, the capture was perfectly lawful, their confinement in Fort Warren will be
perfectly lawful. . . ." Three weeks later, in a letter to the New York
Tribune, he further argued that the *Trent* was not a public vessel; it
had violated the Queen's proclamation of neutrality; and "the commission of a foreign Minister is a circular dispatch to all concerned."
Privately, he mentioned to his son the case of Henry Laurens during
the American Revolution: in 1780, while en route to The Hague as
minister to the Netherlands, then a neutral nation, Laurens was
removed from a Dutch packet, the *Mercury*, and sent to Britain as a
traitor. Unfortunately, as Everett and others were to learn, the *Mercury* was an American vessel, and the British had acted properly.[8]

The one person in Boston who might have dampened the enthusiasm for Wilkes's deed refused to issue a statement. Senator
Charles Sumner, chairman of the Foreign Relations Committee,
prided himself on experience in international politics, European
friendships, and knowledge of international law. Years earlier, he had

studied law in Europe, expecting to be appointed to the Dane pro-
fessorship; however, he was defeated by powerful men who were
repelled by his reputation as an "outrageous Philanthropist." Shortly
after learning of the seizure of Mason and Slidell, he apparently concluded that they would have to be surrendered. Sumner remained
silent due to his position and his desire to avoid complicating matters
for the Lincoln administration. He believed that he had done his duty
by notifying the State Department of two precedents that might support Wilkes, although one was questionable.[9] Sumner's conspicuous
absence from the Revere House banquet bothered Wilkes; having
heard no word from Washington regarding his act, he began to
wonder if he would receive a decoration or a court-martial. He finally
called on Sumner and forced from him a reluctant admission that he
doubted the government would sustain the capture. Wilkes bristled,
retorting that at least the American people had the "nerve to take a
proper stand." Through all the celebration and justification of
Wilkes's act, Sumner never altered his private conviction that the Confederates had to be freed.[10]

Meanwhile, how the fortunes of Mason and Slidell had turned!
Robert C. Winthrop, former Whig Senator and Congressman, had
spoken with Mason a few months before the war. When, he asked,
would Mason visit Boston? "Not till I come as Ambassador," the
Virginian had allegedly replied. People now satirized Mason's newest
"appointment" as minister to Fort Warren. Winthrop and the
publisher William Appleton sent gifts to the prisoners—wine to
Mason and Slidell, and greatcoats to the imprisoned North Carolina
soldiers. But Bostonians saw such acts as sympathy to treason, and
Governor Andrew accused them of succoring men "in comparison
with whom Benedict Arnold was a saint." The people of Boston were
pleased with the incarceration. Charles Francis Adams, Jr., recently
enlisted in the Union army, took time to gaze at "the low, distant walls
of Fort Warren, surrounded by the steel-blue sea," and reflected that
"those amiable gentlemen were there; and there they would remain! I
remembered the last exhibition I saw Mason make of himself in the
Senate-chamber; and I smacked my lips with joy."[11]

Mason and Slidell lived rather well within the prison walls. To
accommodate them, the commandant evicted nine North Carolina officers from their quarters, carpeted the floor, and refurnished the

rooms. High spirits prevailed as the new prisoners gave cigars to less-fortunate compatriots. Macfarland, accompanied by guitar, sang ballads and opera tunes. Boring everyone with discussions of international law, Mason bet another prisoner, the former minister to France Charles J. Faulkner, fifty barrels of corn (not bales of cotton) that Britain would demand their release. The Confederate commissioners followed a routine. After eating breakfast at 9:00 A.M., they exercised in a 30- by 300-foot area while a servant cleaned their rooms. A steamer from Boston arrived at noon with mail and newspapers. They ate dinner at 3:00 P.M. and exercised again until 5:00. During the evening they visited other prisoners, who included army and naval officers, over thirty Maryland legislators, and Baltimore's mayor and police commissioners. Mason and Slidell did not have to live on the prison rations of flour, bacon, and potatoes; instead, they received such delicacies from Boston and Baltimore as "fine hams by the dozen, turkeys, saddles of mutton, and canvasbacks." They enjoyed "a better daily table than any hotel affords," Mason boasted to his wife in London, "and whatever wine or other luxuries we choose."[12]

When Wilkes finally departed Boston its residents found life less interesting, but he visited other cities along the route as he slowly made his way to Washington. Arriving in New York City on Sunday, December 1, he found that civic groups still considered him a popular attraction, although his presence was overshadowed by a spirited four-way contest for the mayoralty. He received an enthusiastic welcome at the Historical Society on December 3, and was inducted as an honorary member. President Luther Bradish, in a spirited address, stated: "It is, sir, your prerogative to make history; ours to commemorate it." The assemblage agreed with Bradish that Wilkes's deed deserved "one of the fairest pages in the bright annals of American history"; Wilkes replied modestly that he had done nothing worthy of that page.[13]

New York welcomed Wilkes with many other festivities. A reception committee of three aldermen and two city councilmen called on the captain at his room in Brevoort House on the afternoon of December 4; they came to discuss the next day's events and to present him with a "handsomely engrossed copy" of some complimentary resolutions passed by the Common Council on November 18, when it first heard of the capture. On Thursday morning, December 5, Wilkes was honored at a reception at City Hall. Wearing a dark cloak over undress uniform and sword, he stepped from the carriage and entered the mayor's office to exchange courtesies with the recently defeated incumbent, Fernando Wood, followed by a formal welcome in the Governor's Room. The Common Council surrounded Wood and Wilkes in a semicircle as the mayor told the captain he had acted like a statesman in his capture of the diplomats. Placing his left hand on a table, Wilkes said a few words of thanks; he then positioned himself near a statue of Washington to receive a crowd waiting to shake his hand.

"Commodore, I am honored by shaking your hand."

"You do the country great honor."

"God bless you for what you have done."

One old gentleman said, "Commodore, you must catch us Jeff. Davis next time," to which Wilkes replied, "I am afraid Jeff. is too sly to get caught so easily."

Wilkes's sojourn in his home town continued to be a smashing social success. Immediately following his reception at City Hall, the district grand jury waited on him and Wilkes said he hoped "they would not sentence him to the penalty of making a speech." They accepted his wishes, and Wilkes repaired to his hotel room. A few days later the Wilkes family visited Gurney's gallery, where the captain had several "imperial portraits" taken of him in full uniform.[14]

For almost three weeks prior to Wilkes's arrival, the *Trent* incident had been a major topic of conversation in the city. Every day newsboys in Central Park shouted the latest trivia: "Here's The Extra *Tribune*, *Herald*, *Times*—full account of the capture of 'Slidewell and Massing.' "[15] New Yorkers quickly snapped up the papers, hanging on every detail of the escapade.

Wall Street, however, had not participated in this sweeping euphoria. A concerted bear attack on November 16 drove stock quotations down sharply, with a consequent advance in exchange in London. The decline was brief; soon, prices advanced broadly on heavy volume after many traders decided that international law sustained Wilkes and that the worst consequence would be a public apology to Britain. But the market remained uneasy, and on November 20 it fell, hammered by bears who discounted the anticipated news from England. Heavy decline in foreign exchange, with francs and the pound sterling in great demand, caused observers to accuse brokers and bankers of treason. Ominously, California gold began to flow from San Francisco to London to avoid capture on the New York route in the event of war. The stock of companies particularly sensitive to an Anglo-American conflict, such as Panama rails or Pacific Mail Steam, fell as much as 9 percent, while domestic rails dropped an average of 8 percent during the last half of November. Inevitably, by the end of the month, the market had been oversold and exchange rates weakened. Although it took only a moderate demand to raise prices, full confidence did not return. Some financiers grew tired of Wilkes's role as the public hero, and grumbled about his frequent, ostentatious strolls down Wall Street. Other businessmen welcomed his presence and found ways to capitalize on his fame; a hatter ran an advertisement proclaiming:

> Hurray for Capt. Wilkes!—the gallant commander of the San Jacinto will be the most popular man in the country this week; and next to him will come our indomitable friend KNOX, whose new Winter Hats for gents and Caps for Young America are Fashion's great victories for the season.[16]

Captain Charles Wilkes had finally found glory. He was the man of the hour, perhaps not on Wall Street, but in other parts of New York and the nation.

Despite confidence that the seizure was legal, Mayor Wood worried that enough doubt existed to disturb the city's commercial and financial operations. He took special measures to cover any difficulty. To calm apprehensions, he asked Caleb Cushing for his opinion of the capture's legal aspects. Cushing had been a member of the House of Representatives, the Massachusetts General Court, and the state senate; a brigadier general in the Mexican War; an associate justice of the Massachusetts Supreme Court; United States attorney general; and permanent chairman of the 1860 Democratic National Convention in Charleston and Baltimore. For twenty-five years he had studied foreign policy and international and Admiralty law, and he had served on the House Committee of Foreign Affairs. As commissioner to China, he had negotiated the Treaty of Wanghia in 1844. An expansionist who considered naval and military preparedness as "the right arm of diplomacy," Cushing was an aggressive nationalist and Anglophobe whose writing ability had made him an influential publicist. His strong ambition, cynicism, and willingness to switch political loyalties made him appear to critics as devoid of moral principle, "a Prodicus or a Gorgias in the days of Socrates," according to John Quincy Adams. A recent convert to the Republican party, Cushing now served as legal consultant to Lincoln and Seward.[17] If he could not dissipate the small cloud of pessimism and anxiety hanging over the scene, no one could.

Cushing had already given considerable thought to the matter and decided in favor of Wilkes. Shortly after learning details of the seizure, he might have sent an opinion to Secretary of State Seward. Now he answered Wood's query with a thirty-page letter to nine newspapers and thirty-two persons, including Wilkes and Assistant Secretary of the Navy Gustavus V. Fox. Averring that he wanted to put the *Trent* affair on its "proper footing" of international law and public right instead of national passion, the renowned lawyer commenced by listing matters not at issue: impressment, right of search, arrest of persons on foreign territory as fugitives from justice, "fresh pursuit" of a public enemy, seizure of enemy dispatches, and arrest of military persons. The *Trent*'s status as a mail packet entitled it to no special privileges, he said. The "true and only tenable grounds" for the seizure hinged on Mason and Slidell being diplomatic ministers of the insurgent government. Writers of *"positive law"* accepted Stowell's doctrine justifying the stoppage of enemy ambassadors, and Captain Moir's alleged ignorance of the ministers' identities did not lessen their liability to seizure. The diplomats were not immune to seizure merely because the *Trent* was proceeding between neutral ports. Cushing disposed of the contention that the seizure took place in Spanish territory by saying that international law no longer recognized the Bahamian intra-insular channels as closed seas under exclusive jurisdiction of neighboring lands. Any other nation, even Great Britain, would have acted as had Captain Wilkes, Cushing concluded; Wilkes was "amply justified" by international law.[18]

The trouble with the arguments of Cushing and others was that they were based on a British interpretation of international law traditionally unacceptable to the United States. As U.S. Attorney General, Cushing had written in 1855 that British doctrines of maritime rights were often "in conflict with prevalent notion in all the rest of Europe. Of course, those doctrines are not entitled to conclusive authority as law with us."[19] Passion, expediency, and poor judgment seemed to have infected almost everyone.

It all seemed so contrived, this frenetic celebration of the capture of two men, an early Christmas and late Fourth of July rolled into one demented patriotic binge. There was something desperate in the public jubilation, the willingness to magnify all things great and small about the capture and to minimize or ignore the dangers. Wilkes's fans were loyal, if nothing else. Hostile to criticism of his coup, the majority of Northerners hardly worried about the British reaction. Two arch-traitors had been apprehended; the vessel carrying them had been sent on its way. What if Wilkes had broken a few rules? Any hurt feelings in England could be soothed with an apology, but there would be no need to surrender Mason and Slidell. After all, Wilkes had done no more than follow British maritime practice. And so it went.

Washington had pulsed with excitement when word of the capture first arrived. Although the diplomatic corps was in a furious flutter, according to the British correspondent Russell, officials and private citizens alike were pleased. Volunteer officers, staying in Willard's Hotel and about to take up winter quarters at the outskirts of the city, declared they would "throw off their uniforms" if Mason and Slidell were given up. A small group at the War Department, including Secretary Simon Cameron and Governor Andrew, had been present at the delivery of the telegram: "Slidell & Mason were taken prisoners and are now at Fort Monroe." It was great news, and Cameron led the cheering. Almost immediately Attorney General Edward Bates satisfied himself that the government of Britain would not take offense; he considered it lawful to remove the men and believed the ship subject to confiscation. "The law of Nations," he concluded, "is clear upon the point." While the War Department was resounding with cheers, Bates sent a letter to a United States Marshal at Wheeling asking if Mason "stands indicted for treason *or other crimes*, in your Court. If not, he ought to be, if the testimony can be procured."[20]

But already there was unease within the Lincoln administration. Members of the cabinet (other than Cameron and Bates) had no difficulty restraining their enthusiasm. At the earliest stage of the affair Secretary of the Treasury Salmon P. Chase, it was rumored, regretted Wilkes did not capture the vessel. Postmaster General Montgomery Blair privately denounced the act as "unauthorized, irregular, and illegal," and suggested that Wilkes be ordered to take Mason and Slidell to Britain and deliver them to the government.[21]

The man who could issue the orders to send the Confederate commissioners on their way to London, Secretary of the Navy Gideon Welles, outwardly showed no reaction as he weighed the consequences of the capture and speculated on how his opinion, favorable or unfavorable, would affect the course of the war. Welles was not one to make snap decisions; this trait saved him in a city that fed on intrigue. He had begun his public life as editor of the Hartford *Times*

Gideon Welles, Secretary of the Navy
Reproduced from the Collections of the Library of Congress

and had held several state offices in Connecticut. Once a Jacksonian Democrat, he split with his party over slavery, helped organize the Republican party, became its gubernatorial candidate in 1856, and headed his state's delegation to the 1860 convention. An also-ran for the presidential nomination, he fell into the New England slot for an appointment in the Lincoln administration. Naval officers habitually complained that secretaries came into office "uninformed as to the condition of the navy, ignorant of its wants and usages"; so they were not overly excited about the appointment of Welles, who, despite having served as chief of the Bureau of Provisions and Clothing in 1846–1849, lacked knowledge of the department and had to master it quickly under the most trying circumstances. The New York political boss, Thurlow Weed, had opposed his nomination. Weed suggested to Lincoln that he stop off in a coastal city on his way to Washington to select an attractive figurehead from a ship's prow; Weed would then cover it with an elaborate wig and whiskers and mount it over the entrance to the Navy Department, where it would be as serviceable as, and less expensive than, Welles.[22]

Although Secretary Welles's personal appearance and manner made him a target for humor, they concealed a shrewd, determined mind. His streaming white beard and ill-fitting wig invited such nicknames as "Rip Van Winkle," "Father Neptune," "Marie Antoinette," "the Old Man of the Sea," "Father Welles," "Methuselah," "Jonah," and "that old Mormon deacon." Stories abounded of Welles impersonating a dying sailor's grandmother, of planning to introduce Noah's ark into the navy, and of sleeping so long that four-year-old recruits would finish their terms of service before he awoke. He was ridiculed as a distracted, incompetent old fogy, but Welles fooled them all—the politicians, the cartoonists, and the smart set. His ability for organization transformed the department into a model of efficiency and economy, which magically created and maintained a huge, well-armed navy. Fiercely loyal to Lincoln and the Union cause, Welles resented England's recognition of Confederate belligerency and tested the British government's patience for four long years with a liberal interpretation of belligerent rights and a willingness to back zealous naval officers who overlooked the niceties of international law.[23] He trod a thin line between patriotism and provocation, and constantly bewildered the British, who believed he did not know when to reef his sails.

Two weeks passed after the arrival of Wilkes and his prisoners in Boston before Welles penned an ambivalent congratulatory letter. The captain, he said, had rendered a great public service and merited the department's "emphatic approval," but the forbearance exercised by Wilkes in not capturing the *Trent* "must not be permitted to constitute a precedent hereafter for infractions of neutral obligations." The secretary's remarks displeased some contemporaries, who criticized him for fanning popular approval, encouraging other officers to emulate the act, and curtailing Lincoln's options regarding repudiation. Welles had considered all these arguments before writing to Wilkes: years later, he defended his letter on the grounds that a long period of peace and observance of neutral rights had led many naval officers to doubt their authority and to hesitate to exercise the right of search, detention, and capture of offending neutral ships. He further contended that, for the morale of the Navy Department, he could not have taken a step that would deter officers from discharging their duties; it would have been "impolitic" to condemn Wilkes's initiative while trying to stimulate other commanders' aggressiveness. Still, he resented being forced into the role of administration spokesman on this controversial issue.[24]

The most important reaction to the seizure had to come from President Lincoln and Secretary of State Seward. A week after the

diplomats had run the blockade, Seward had asked Welles's opinion
of an offer from a Baltimore man to arrest all Confederate agents in
Europe and return them to the United States. Incredibly, Welles had
seen nothing wrong with the plan, as long as the government was not
compromised. Upon learning of the capture, Seward, according to
Welles's account published years later, approved of the act and was
"elated." The United States' government, Seward supposedly remarked, "could not think of delivering them up." Yet when reporters
called at the department they learned that the secretary was home with
a cold, unavailable for comment. Welles described Lincoln as being
filled with doubts, misgivings, and regrets. As the city cheered outside
his office windows, Lincoln allegedly remarked to two visitors, "I fear
the traitors will prove to be white elephants."[25]

From the outset it was clear to Lincoln that if he publicly
repudiated the capture, he might damage the war. Conversely, if he
bestowed his blessing on it he would destroy any possibility of
maneuver if the British government were to demand the prisoners'
release. The United States could not afford to alienate the world's
greatest maritime power, thereby offering the Confederacy an ally.
Somehow Lincoln had to extract the country from its predicament
without demoralizing public opinion and jeopardizing national honor;
yet, he had to avoid insulting Britain. Popular feeling was running so
high that the slightest miscalculation could have precipitated an international showdown. Lincoln decided on a policy of delay, leaving
the next move up to the British.

How deep, in fact, was the public enthusiasm for Wilkes and his
daring deed? Was the Lincoln administration really justified in its caution? To measure public opinion is a difficult task. In this case, it cannot be measured by merely the exultant welcome Wilkes received personally. Comments and opinions recorded in contemporary
newspapers must also be considered. A century ago, the press did not
always reflect popular feeling; often, newspapers were more ex-
pressive of the editors' political sympathies, and intended to persuade
or lead rather than merely to inform. The American newspaper of the
Civil War era, "a cross between a county newspaper and a penny journal," devoted much space to eye-catching advertisements, confined its
lead articles to practical comments, and reveled in headings, italic em-
phasis, and detail. American readers of 1861 could choose among

POLICEMAN WILKES, noticing by the last Number of *Harper's Weekly*, that the well-known Rogues, MASON and SLIDELL, were about to Pawn some of their late Employer's Property at Messrs. *Bull, Crapaud & Co.'s* Shop, kept a bright look-out for'ard, and nabbed them in the nick of time."

Courtesy of *Harper's Weekly*

5,200 papers, 450 of which were dailies. However, only New York City periodicals circulated throughout the country, whereas daily papers from other parts of the nation rarely sold in New York. Even so, the New York press no more reflected American public opinion than did London newspapers mirror British popular views, and neither wielded much influence with their governments.[26] In 1861, Northern papers were full of accounts of defeats and of ponderous military movements that seemed without purpose. Wilkes's bold act rescued editorialists and writers from the autumn doldrums, furnishing copy and extra sales for weeks on end. Almost with one voice the Northern press echoed public opinion regarding the grand event, and the complications likely to arise, declaring with "throats of brass" that Mason and Slidell would never be surrendered.

New York City papers had rushed to the defense of Wilkes. The *Times*, organ of the moderate faction of the Republican party, had supported the Lincoln administration before the *Trent* incident, but remained more friendly toward Britain than did other journals. Now it praised Wilkes's act as prompt, energetic, and patriotic, "in strict conformity with the principles of international law," and declared that the feat would not disturb Anglo-American relations despite "a chorus of vociferous howls" from the Tory party. The *Times* assured its readers that, even if the British government decided to redress national honor by force, it would not provoke a collision with the United States until Canada had been adequately prepared, and the onset of winter had rendered military movement impossible for six months. Horace Greeley's *Tribune*, which backed the administration as well as women's rights, abolition, prohibition, and a host of isms, grandly insulted the Confederate agents in the characteristic style of the period. Mason was a "degenerate son" with a "brain composed of the muddiest materials," while Slidell was a "sly, cautious, dark unscrupulous traitor" noted for his "furtive glances and sinister visage." Quoting from the British proclamation of neutrality of May 1861 to prove that the *Trent* had disobeyed orders and jeopardized its neutral status, Greeley defended Wilkes's act as being "in strict accordance with the principles of international law . . . and in strict conformity with English practice"—language that became a familiar litany throughout the crisis. The *Tribune* expected no trouble with England and even hoped for a British demand for the diplomats' surrender, since it would mean that London had accepted a liberal interpretation of neutral rights. The conservative and notorious New York *Herald* was probably the most widely circulated paper in America; it was also read frequently in Europe, where people regarded it as a government organ despite its constant criticism of Lincoln and the Republicans. It expected the administration to disavow Wilkes's proceeding, apologize, and promise never to do it again. However, even the *Herald* believed that surrendering Mason and Slidell was out of the question.[27]

Newspapers across the country from Massachusetts to Missouri agreed that Wilkes, by removing Mason and Slidell from the *Trent*, had done nothing worse than to follow an obnoxious maritime custom of Britain; that the act involved Britain made it all the more gratifying. The Philadelphia *Sunday Dispatch*, among the first journals to report the capture, carried an article the day after Wilkes stopped at Fortress Monroe. Beyond "surly growls and indignation," the *Dispatch* predicted, the British government could scarcely protest the right of search, "a good old English practice." Britain's exercise of that right had done America more damage in the *Chesapeake* incident of 1807, and the United States had not gone to war. Representing the views of many editors, the Philadelphia *Inquirer*, showing exceptional prescience in analyzing conditions, argued that Britain would not go to war even for cotton because it would have a "ruinous effect" on manufacturers and trade, and would give France a free hand in the

Eastern question. A Harrisburg paper, the *Pennsylvania Daily Telegraph*, lauded Wilkes as a "faithful patriot and public servant" whose forbearance in not capturing the *Trent* should please the British. The Washington *Evening Star* and the Boston *Daily Evening Transcript* expressed the opinion generally held in the North that the *Trent* had violated international law by carrying enemies of the United States on a hostile mission, documenting their assertions with dubious cases. The Detroit *Daily Advertiser*, the St. Paul *Pioneer and Democrat*, and the St. Louis *Daily Missouri Democrat* all agreed that British precedent and international law justified Wilkes's act. If Captain Wilkes had made a blunder, the Milwaukee *Morning Sentinel* stated, let it be "promptly righted," but if the *Trent* had violated neutrality, or if any custom or law justified the capture, "let us stand by the act of Wilkes, though all the guns of Europe frown on us."[28]

Newspapers of Civil War times relished technical detail, and analysis of the Wilkes affair became ever more intricate, if less illuminating. The Cleveland *Morning Leader* felt that Wilkes had exceeded his authority and that the government could apologize for the abrupt manner of seizure, but should not return the commissioners. The *Leader* reported that it was surprised and gratified to discover in several books on maritime law, a mass of evidence in favor of the act. The Cleveland *Plain Dealer* declared that the *Trent* should no more be allowed to help the South than the *Caroline* was permitted to aid Canadian rebels during the 1837 rebellion; since the *Trent* had violated the proclamation of neutrality by conveying belligerent ambassadors and their dispatches, "we are ready to accept [Britain's] apology and renew our assurances of amicable feeling and good neighborhood." The Cincinnati *Daily Commercial* also believed that the *Trent* had risked condemnation for carrying enemy dispatches, and cited the Stowell opinion to justify the seizure. A few newspapers, such as the Cincinnati *Daily Enquirer*, warned readers not to let their enthusiasm for the capture blind them to the policy's inherent dangers about which "grave doubts . . . will force themselves upon the cautious and discreet."[29]

West of the Mississippi most newspapers offered a moderate view. The Dubuque *Herald* concluded that the seizure would probably lead to war, although the British government would be acting inconsistently to complain of such an act. The *Herald* philosophized that the whole business of the right of search and seizure "might as well be settled now as at any future time." Lamenting that people were quoting Wheaton's opinions out of context, the newspaper argued that the Union's refusal to recognize Confederate belligerency meant that, in the case of the *Trent*, it could only consider the question, "has it the right to arrest a political criminal on the high seas, found on board a neutral ship under a neutral flag?" The *Herald* recommended that the administration cite British precedents in strictly analogous cases, such as the Laurens capture. The *Freedom's Champion* of Kansas, which carried a quotation from the late Henry Clay at its masthead ("It is better to be Right than President"), rejoiced that some men were willing to "take the responsibility and act decisively" when a case arose not covered by instructions. The Sacramento *Daily Union* expected Washington to disavow the capture, but retain those "traitors of the deepest and blackest character." A quick glance at the elementary works on international law did not show that Wilkes had committed an indiscretion.[30]

Northeastern newspapers were divided in their views of the capture, but not because of the section's exposed condition. Residents of Portland, Maine lived in a sensitive location, the eastern terminus of the Grand Trunk Railway, the best route from Canada to the Atlantic, a natural objective for British attack. Moreover, Portland's fine harbor was defended by only three forts, which were little more than earthworks and lacked artillery. The Portland *Eastern Argus*, nonetheless, did not expect the capture of Mason and Slidell to lead to "serious complications" with the British government, unless the latter desired war. It justified the seizure by citing British principles of maritime law, and a dictum set down by the French international lawyer Laurent B. Hautefeuille that a belligerent could remove from a neutral vessel any party in the service of an enemy. Taking note of other newspapers' defense of Wilkes through citation of previous British outrages upon the United States, the Albany *Atlas and Argus* warned against the disastrous consequences of British intervention in the Civil War. "Is it wise to seize this occasion for acts of retaliation?" Americans could not afford to "belie all our own declarations of national law, and cast contempt upon the noblest chapters of our own history." While the government might not decide to release Mason and Slidell, it was necessary to "disclaim frankly all pretensions to a right of search and seizure such as this." The unrelenting discussion in the press of international law amused W. H. Russell, the London *Times* special correspondent, who soon tired of "the ideas hammered on a thousand clanging anvils—a pin beaten into foil."[31]

Although editorial opinion differed on whether Wilkes had repudiated American tradition and broken international law, and some papers actually suggested that the Lincoln administration apologize, very few Northern newspapers called for surrender of

Mason and Slidell, even though the agents were no great catch. It was unlikely that the Confederate envoys' activities would have materially affected the war's outcome or the success of American diplomatic activities in Europe. Beneath its belligerence the public undoubtedly recognized this fact. But the campaigns of the past several months had had almost no effect on the rebellion, causing Northern despair; then, the sudden, dramatic capture of Mason and Slidell seemed to mark the beginning of the end to the national nightmare. In Northern minds the two men quickly passed from the status of diplomatic agents to amulets—living proof that the Confederacy was not invulnerable.

The Confederacy was pleased by the *Trent* affair for totally different reasons. Almost immediately, Southern editors understood the opportunity provided by Wilkes's action: removal of Mason and Slidell from a British ship carried the possibility of war. Southern newspapers even began to describe Wilkes's act as an attack upon civilization. Scarcely able to control its enthusiasm, the Richmond *Enquirer* declared that Britain would find it morally impossible to accept the "open, palpable disgrace" against its flag. The paper had visions of Abraham Lincoln "eating dirt," and Northern armies retreating before British redcoats. Lincoln would be ruined, the Richmond *Examiner* said, because the seizure proved Washington's desperate imbecility. The diplomats were more useful, the *Enquirer* believed, in Fort Warren than in Europe. The Atlanta *Southern Confederacy* called the act "one of the most fortunate things for our cause." The Nashville *Patriot*, a champion of King Cotton, decided that Britain would do nothing but roar. Two papers in New Orleans reveled in the possibilities. The *Bee* called the seizure the act of a "disgraced Government" and then confidently asserted that the Union would not surrender; it could not decide how Britain would react. It said the incident would force London to define a policy toward the Union, and on Christmas Eve concluded that Britain would recognize the South and break the blockade. The *Picayune* kept more to international law, sure that Britain would protest Wilkes's failure to take the *Trent* into port. It did not see how the Washington government could surrender the men without confessing to cowardice.[32]

Joy in the South would have been incomplete without the literary immortalization of Matilda Slidell who, according to the regional view, had struck a blow for Southern womanhood, independence, and good manners when she slapped Lieutenant Fairfax. The Confederacy had its first heroine:

> Ho, gallants, brim the beaker bowl,
>   And click the festal glasses, oh!
> The grape shall shed its sapphire soul
>   To eulogize the lasses, oh!
> And when ye pledge the lip and curl
>   Of loveliness and glory, oh!
> Here's a bumper to the gallant girl!
>   That smote the dastard Tory, oh!
>
> A bumper, a bumper,
>   To loveliness and glory, oh!
> A bumper to the gallant girl
>   That smote the dastard Tory, oh!
>
> Our boys are fighting East and West,
>   Our women do not linger, oh!
> They take their diamonds from the breast,
>   Their rubies from the finger, oh!
> They send their darlings to the war
>   Of honor and glory, oh!
> They've all the spirit of a man
>   To smite a dastard Tory, oh![33]

In Richmond the members of the Confederate cabinet reacted enthusiastically to news of their envoys' capture. Secretary of War Judah P. Benjamin thought the seizure "perhaps the best thing that could have happened." In his first annual message to the Confederate Congress on November 19, President Davis allotted a paragraph to the *Trent* incident, saying that the United States claimed a "general jurisdiction over the high seas" and violated the "rights of embassy" by seizing Mason and Slidell while under British jurisdiction. Secretary of State Robert M. T. Hunter, who regarded the seizure as a "flagrant breach" of international law, instructed his London representatives to protest. The capture sent Southerners scurrying to their law books, but by late December people were growing weary of technical discussion, and on Christmas Day the Richmond *Enquirer* dismissed the topic by speculating that Lincoln would submit to any indignity rather than fight Britain. Government officials still expected the crisis to end in war and a few advocated Confederate neutrality after British recognition, despite the advantage of having Britain as an ally. But Robert E. Lee cautioned his wife not to count on the United States fighting Great Britain. "We must make up our minds to fight our battles and win our independence alone. No one will help us," he wrote.[34]

King Cotton certainly could not help. The South had decided to coerce foreign recognition by inducing a cotton famine in Europe. Since April, Southern planters, cotton exporters, and citizens' committees had prevented cotton from leaving the South, establishing almost a total embargo. Zealots had burned cotton, ploughed under fields, and recommended against planting a crop in 1862. France experienced a shortage by September 1861; however, Britain enjoyed a surplus of several hundred thousand bales. The Confederate Congress never proclaimed an official embargo, fearing that it would alienate the powers. Instead, they withheld the trump card for play at a critical moment.[35] But in the fall of 1861, Richmond exercised no influence over London and could not take advantage of England's anger by threatening to impose an official cotton embargo unless England declared war on the United States. Confederate officials, then, could only express shock at the violation of neutral rights, offer to cooperate with the Royal Navy against Union forces, and long for a third Anglo-American war. They hoped, and waited.

Wilkes's deed had been done, and the initial Northern reaction positive. It was clear in November of 1861 that President Lincoln would have public opinion behind him if he chose to support Wilkes. People were in a mood to give short shrift to the captain's critics and to savor the insult to Great Britain, even if it meant that the Union faced a possibly serious foreign emergency. A British journalist reporting from New York was incredulous that the prospect of raising the Union blockade and imposing a British cordon around the Northern coast did not abate popular emotion. The North could hold its own, he was told, because the Federal army would overrun the South before the Queen's forces could strike. Union naval officers, too, were astonished that people would clamor "so loudly to go to war with the English at a time when we could scarcely comply with the demands made on us to perform the proper blockade duty."[36] Had the whole country taken leave of its senses?

Clear-thinking Northerners found it monstrously bizarre that such an inconsequential event as the capture of Mason and Slidell could somehow create a full-blown crisis in Anglo-American relations.

Their confidence in the legality of Wilkes's act and the ability of the Lincoln administration to deflect British anger stemmed from the optimistic hope that mighty Britain would overlook this violation of its sovereignty. And yet, by December, after all the welcoming of Captain Wilkes, the consulting of law books, and the marshaling of precedent, the silence from Europe was deafening, a matter of concern to even the boldest Northerners. The Atlantic cable of Cyrus Fields had gone dead, its connections fouled by sea water, making necessary the transatlantic passage of news by steamer. It took approximately twelve days for word of America's reception of Wilkes to reach Europe, and then the British government had to react and the news of its reaction then had to pass back again, perhaps with a lapse of two weeks. Americans of the North and South were aware of this; in a sense, their rejoicings and speculations had been in vacuo. Britain's actual reaction was now imminent. Almost as in a theatre, the talking and conversation of the audience, even of the boxholders, began to die down to a murmur; the lights began to dim in the house, and the curtain quivered slightly. Then, with a rush, it began to open.

3.

Britain and America in the Secession Crisis

CONTACTS BETWEEN THE BRITISH and American governments in the quarter-century prior to the Civil War had seldom been pleasant. A series of problems had arisen with numbing regularity—caused by the Canadian rebellion, boundary disputes in Maine and Oregon, the American effort to acquire Texas and California, clashes over control of Central America, and British recruitment in the United States during the Crimean War. Such clashes had occurred in the Western Hemisphere because the United States rarely took interest in other parts of the world. British officials had learned that proximity, dishonesty, and determination to win caused the Yankees to be "most disagreeable fellows" on any American question, and concessions to "such ingenious Rogues" led only to trouble. It would be "like propitiating an animal of Prey by giving him one of ones travelling Companions. It would increase his Desire for similar Food and spur him on to obtain it."[1]

Although war had threatened on more than one occasion (especially over Central America), public opinion, European conditions, and opposition in Parliament had restrained British leaders who wanted to deal summarily with those "Vulgar minded Bullies" in America. More important, the prime minister in 1861–1865, and leading politician of the era, Lord Palmerston, believed that peace and commercial ties should be the basis of British policy.[2] The two govern-

47

ments had managed to patch up differences, if not eliminate them, and had even taken steps toward friendship, as evidenced by the Reciprocity Treaty of 1854 and the military and commercial cooperation in East Asia. In the years following the Crimean War, with no major issue to disrupt relations, both peoples discovered a kindred spirit of sorts.

When Queen Victoria sent the Prince of Wales on a triumphant tour of British North America in 1860, both America and Britain seized upon the occasion to celebrate their new-found cordiality. Traveling under the title of Baron Renfrew, the prince realized, after he had been in Canada only a short while, that the people of the United States would be disappointed—if not affronted—unless he paid a visit. Although most Americans had never seen royalty and freely criticized the institution as undemocratic, decadent, and useless, they fell over each other to honor the future Edward VII as he crossed the international boundary and proceeded slowly through the North during the fall of 1860. Not since the visit of the Hungarian revolutionary Louis Kossuth had the country staged such demonstrations. Crowds turned out in every city, frantically waving handkerchiefs and hats, while torchlight processions of volunteer fire brigades illuminated the prince's path. He shot prairie hens in Illinois, bought a fast trotting horse in St. Louis, saw thousands of pigs roaming Cincinnati streets, and shook hands with the last survivor of Bunker Hill. His Highness had to endure almost endless visits to factories and inspections of colleges, and attended many civic balls, where local beauties competed for his attention. President Buchanan pledged America's friendship, and Prince Edward planted a chestnut tree at George Washington's tomb. "It seemed, when the Royal youth closed in the earth around the little germ," a London *Times* reporter testified, "that he was burying the last faint trace of discord between us and our great brethren in the West." In New York City a half million people lined Broadway to catch a glimpse. Later, he visited Barnum's American Museum and saw the giant woman, the "negro turning white," the living skeleton, the "what is it?," the Aztec children, and numerous wax figures. Some people grew tired of the "royal imp" and grumbled that the "Hope of England" was "a bore of the first order," but they were a minority. The Americans had proved to no one's surprise that they, as much as their English cousins, were "a spectacle-loving people."[3]

Amazed at the exhibition of friendship, members of the royal party thought it heralded a new day in transatlantic relations. The colonial secretary, the Duke of Newcastle, who accompanied the prince, remarked that people everywhere seemed "mad with enthusiasm and overflowing with intense delight." He attributed the phenomenon to a "personal love of the Queen" and a "rapidly growing affection for England." Lord Lyons believed the outpouring indicated the sentiments of the American people toward Britain. Politicians, he hoped, must now realize that they could no longer seek popularity by attacking the mother country, and perhaps Englishmen would now abandon "unfounded prejudices concerning the feelings, manners and habits" of Americans. Queen Victoria, who possessed some of those prejudices, was astonished at the reception, and lost no time thanking President Buchanan and expressing hope for continued friendly relations.[4]

Although the extravagant display accorded the Prince of Wales pleasantly surprised his family and advisers, British subjects who had spent time in the United States expected nothing less of its crude, but sensitive, citizens. English travel books commented on the "almost morbid anxiety which Americans feel for the judgment of England." After talking with an American for only a few minutes a British visitor was invariably asked, "What do you think of our country?" Foreign guests in every land had undergone similar experiences, but the Americans seemed motivated by more than polite curiosity. The ubiquitous British traveler perceived national differences in the tone and manner of the question. Whereas the French might ask the question "with a supreme conviction that it was morally impossible you should *not* like France," and the English might ask "with absolute indifference whether you like England or not," the Americans would give the impression that they would be hurt if the respondent were to show the slightest distaste, particularly if the critic were English. Commentators from other nations could be as censorious as they wanted, and the American people would shrug. Let the British press and public make slighting remarks and the people of the United States would become furious; yet, praise for things American was often viewed as condescending or patronizing. It was a dilemma for British travelers, who, knowing the American tendency to "conjure up slights" where none was intended, came to dread being asked their impressions. One Briton, straining to compliment his interrogator's country, was rewarded with the retort, "Well, now, I declare I know'd it; we air a great people, and bound to be tolerable troublesome to them kings."[5]

The desperate longing of Americans for British approval—deny it as they would—suggested that they were still trying to prove that the United States was no longer a colonial appendage, but a sovereign, free, independent nation worthy of Britain's respect. The brag and bluster, the cockiness and pugnacity, barely concealed what a later generation would describe as an inferiority complex. If some visitors recognized Americans as "not yet quite sure of the firmness of their footing," many more were not as understanding.[6]

Americans had reason to question British attitudes toward them; as Lord Lyons noted, popular beliefs tended to rest on a bedrock of unfavorable, often groundless, prejudice. While some Britons thought well of the United States—and lauded its high literacy rate, humane laws, small standing army, and the practicality and generosity of its people—offensive opinions still dominated public thinking. British travelers, who were generally well-to-do, did not differentiate between Northerners and Southerners except by attributing to them varying degrees of rudeness. Worse, British novelists, most of whom had never visited the United States and were ignorant of its geography, history, and people, rarely missed an opportunity to demean. "I never yet saw an American to my taste," commented a character in Daniel Madden's *Wynville*. "If educated, they are self-sufficient—if uneducated, coarse; but invariably disagreeable." Such influential periodicals as the *Saturday Review* and the London *Times* contributed misinformation by emphasizing the worst aspects of life in the American mobocracy, the disadvantages of which were apparently infinite.[7]

Critics thus found little to admire in the quality of American life. They dismissed the country's enormous wealth, bustling cities, public education, vast railroad network, and extensive factories with the observation that it all produced "a feeble national character, no political faith, no corporate virtues." Rampant infidelity and habitual divorce, scurrilous newspapers and mean politicians, "the grossest superstition" and strange religions, "inordinate love of gain" and sweeping intemperance shrank in comparison to "universal suffrage," which "tramples everything down to a dead level." Bemoaning the filthy custom of chewing tobacco, Charles Dickens called Washington the "headquarters of tobacco-tinctured saliva," leaving it to others to suggest that the spittoon, not the eagle, should be the emblem of the United States.[8]

The national spirit of boastfulness admittedly irritated British visitors. One Englishman remarked to a Southerner that Providence had evidently chosen the two nations to civilize the world. "Two nations!" exclaimed an eavesdropper. "Guess there's only one, stranger; goin' to annex that island of yourn one of them fine days; don't know how little Vic will like that, but got to do it, and no mistake about that." It was this bumptiousness, this attitude that Americans could "turn their hands to a'most anything, from whippin' the universe to stuffin' a mosquito," that sorely tested British patience. The resentment gave rise to all manner of apocryphal stories about America—of the child who, when asked to name the first man, answered George Washington, and, upon being corrected by a friend who suggested Adam, pleaded that "he did not know that he was to take account of foreigners"; or of the schoolgirl who drew an incomplete map of Europe and, when reminded by a classmate that she had left off Great Britain, was defended by her teacher, who said it was unnecessary to show islands. The editor of the *Economist*, Walter Bagehot, caught the essence of British upper-class attitudes toward the United States when he wrote that the American "low vulgarity, undefinable but undeniable has deeply displeased the cultivated mind of Europe." In a word, Americans lacked polish and, under their present system of mob government, they were unlikely to develop the good breeding characteristic of a great people.[9]

British officials and members of the ruling class scorned the United States but did not underestimate its capacity for international mischief. Americans were regarded as touchy, unpredictable, and dangerous; their natural combativeness seemed exacerbated by the tendency of political parties to make partisan capital out of problems with foreign governments, in order to strengthen the party's reputation for "Americanism" among voters. The American government's habit of "showing their teeth abroad" made all unsettled questions a matter of concern to British leaders, who believed it "prudent to strike the Iron while it is hot, and to make good the settlement of any one Point which they may agree to settle, while they are in the mood to do so"; otherwise, undecided issues could "lead unexpectedly to fatal Results." On subjects in which agreement seemed unlikely, the best policy was to tie the Americans up in "civil negotiations for some indefinite period." Dealing with American officials had inured the British to their irresponsible habits, and understanding the reasons for their behavior did not render it more acceptable. There was always danger that politicians would overexcite the public and lose control of a situation if Britain refused to back down during a dispute. Negotiations with the United States, then, tended to be a matter of "great delicacy"; the British concentrated on using "very temperate, but very firm language," knowing that the fate of imperial possessions in the Western Hemisphere might hang in the balance.[10]

The rumblings of secession, beginning shortly after the election of Lincoln in November 1860, raised the level of anxiety among British officials, who feared that American politicians might divert domestic unrest by stirring up foreign difficulties. Anglo-American relations would be determined by how the Lincoln administration responded to

Lord Lyons, British Minister to the United States
Courtesy of the National Maritime Museum, London

the threat of secession and by the value it placed upon international friendship. News from America, especially the British minister's estimates of the situation, was eagerly awaited in London.

Her Majesty's minister to the United States, Richard Bickerton Pemell, second Lord Lyons, a twenty-year veteran of the Foreign Service, had occupied the British legation in Washington since April 1859. He had served as an attache in Athens before being transferred to Florence to be secretary of legation. A shy, quiet man, he was given neither to boisterous conduct nor to delight in worldly pleasures, which he accepted only from a sense of duty. Prudent, attentive to proprieties, and always aware that he represented the Queen, he was perhaps the most reserved diplomat in Washington; as befitted his judicial turn of mind, he listened more than he talked. Many Americans, and not a few of his countrymen, found Lyons unattractive and cold. The two great English liberals, John Bright and Richard Cobden, no friends of the upper class, believed the times demanded that the British envoy in Washington be "a man of mature judgment & large experience." Bright considered Lyons unqualified, and Cobden rashly dismissed him as "a Lord without any antecedents." Fearing the worst results from his appointment, Bright predicted that difficulties might arise between Seward and Lyons, "the one acting not with good temper, & the other incompetent for the delicate business of his position."[11]

The minister had flaws, but he was not incompetent and he was at least as qualified as his recent predecessors. More important, he enjoyed the full confidence of his government, which, in the early months of the Civil War, relied upon his opinions for an understanding of American intentions. Unfortunately for relations between the two countries, Lyons's dispatches produced deep unrest and a sense of impending disaster within the London cabinet, and persuaded high civilian and military officials that war with the United States was almost a certainty.

Lord Lyons had arrived in Washington during the final throes of the sectional crisis, and observed the Americans as they ripped and tore at each other in Congress, in newspapers, and on city streets. A kind of madness had possessed the people, a suicidal urge that threatened to destroy not only themselves but everyone at hand. The presidential election had intensified sectional fears as the South looked into the future and saw itself bereft of slaves, reduced to a satellite of the North. The inability of Lincoln and the Republican party to do serious damage to Southern social institutions did not lessen talk of secession; by December of 1860, South Carolina was preparing to leave the Union. Aware of the national propensity to patch up domestic discord with a foreign quarrel, Lyons warned his government to afford neither side a pretext for claiming British support. Statesmen, he said, believed that a "contest with England dangerous and unprovoked as it might be, would be the only means . . . of producing an adequate excitement" to end the secession crisis. The incoming administration, therefore, might "not be indisposed to try the effect of a haughty and overbearing tone towards England, if occasion could be found for a dispute."[12] The minister's apprehensions did not surprise or frighten the Foreign Office at this prewar stage, because long ago it had come to view Britain's role as a scapegoat for American domestic troubles as just another hazard of international politics.

Lyons's apprehension about the policy of the Lincoln administration increased when the president-elect chose Seward to head the State

William Henry Seward, Secretary of State
National Archives Photo No. 111-B-1281

Department. The minister lost no time in briefing the foreign
secretary, Lord John Russell, on Seward's past, and likely future, conduct. Seward, he feared, would be a "dangerous" foreign minister
because he had always treated Anglo-American relations as "good
material" for political capitalization. Lyons claimed that Seward had
even told him that England would "*never* go to war" with the United
States.[13]

To Lyons, Seward was typical of American politicians, men of
"second rate station and ability, who aim at little more than at divin-
ing and pandering to the feeling of the Mob of voters." Indeed,
nothing in Seward's experience had prepared him for the State Department. As a young attorney he had drifted into politics, the common
path for lawyers desiring the respect accorded to other professions,
and had passed through six political parties in thirty years.[14]

Lyons's commentaries actually were far from the mark. Seward's
political odyssey did not reflect a lack of principle as much as it
reflected his changing attitudes and responses to local pressure, and

the amorphous nature of early nineteenth-century American politics. To the horror of political cronies, Seward often declared that he cared nothing for party names, and he liked to say that politics was "the sum of all the sciences." Elected governor of New York in 1838, he enjoyed two terms that marked him not only as a reformer-spender interested in national reputation and higher office, but as a wily politician who helped introduce the scheme of "pipe laying," an organized system for manipulating votes. After leaving the statehouse, he returned to private law practice and mended political fences by campaigning for Whig candidates. Such perseverance was rewarded in 1848, when voters sent him to the Senate; there he gained fame overnight through his ability to coin a snappy phrase. His invocation of a "higher law" than the Constitution against slavery made him appear in Southern minds as the "archdemon of an infernal throng."[15] In the North his fiery talk won him an undeserved radical reputation, which contributed to his loss of the Republican presidential nomination in 1860. He had to settle for secretary of state, admittedly the favored bureaucratic route to the White House, but still a consolation prize.

Prior to entering the State Department, Seward had compromised his position with a history of chauvinistic statements on foreign policy that gave an unflattering impression to foreign observers. Abusive, antimonarchical sentiment, much of it gratuitous, radiated from his speeches. He rarely missed an opportunity to goad European powers and encourage revolution. Whether presiding over meetings of Irish repealers or calling for lenient treatment of exiled Irish patriots, he insisted that his government show kindness and charity to freedom fighters. The occasion of Kossuth's visit prompted Seward to declare that "this republic is, and forever must be, a living offence . . . to despotic powers everywhere." Sooner or later, he said, "a struggle between the representative and the arbitrary systems of government" must take place in Europe; such rhetoric left no doubt as to where he thought America should stand. Over two decades, Seward's freewheeling language persuaded the British that he was an aggressive, opportunistic nationalist. His devotion to the cult of manifest destiny, the belief that the United States would absorb contiguous territories to extend the blessings of American liberty, implied that he would give European monarchs no rest as long as they retained possessions on the North American continent. The American population was "destined to roll its resistless waves to the icy barriers of the north, and to encounter Oriental civilization on the shores of the Pacific." Since Canada was already "half annexed" through the process of political gravitation, he professed himself "content to wait for the ripened fruit which must fall." Although Seward never advocated force to enlarge the national domain, his well-known desire for Canada was a source of constant worry to British officials, who did not believe that his baser impulses could be restrained once he became secretary of state.[16]

Although Seward, like many politicians, had established a mild record of baiting Britain, he rarely went to extremes and he privately reassured those who worried about his aims. The explanation he provided Lyons regarding his past behdvior toward England was typical of his style—firmness in public, conciliation in private. As governor he had refused to release a British subject, Alexander McLeod, who was charged with complicity in the death of an American during the *Caroline* raid; however, he secretly assured the Tyler administration that McLeod would be pardoned if convicted. On another occasion, when asked by Virginians how he could use truculent language in advising New Yorkers to frustrate Southern efforts to recapture runaway slaves, he allegedly dismissed his remarks as being necessary for the benefit of voters, but added "surely we ought to be able to understand each other better over a dinner-table!"[17]

The difficulty most persons faced when dealing with Seward was knowing when to take him seriously. He possessed a double personality, Henry Adams observed, "political and personal; but complex because the political had become nature, and no one could tell which was the mask and which the features." In an unguarded moment Seward admitted, "I am an enigma, even to myself," a comment fully supported by contemporaries. One observer praised his "ill-disguised contempt for party obligations and popular applause," while another said he believed in "majorities, and . . . nothing else." Before he took office his political mentor Thurlow Weed counseled that success depended on cultivating a manner and style pleasing to the public. Seward's faithful adherence to that advice over the years convinced detractors that he was a "low, vulgar, vain demagogue," but those who came to know him better invariably admitted that he was "a man of higher faculty" than they supposed. A State Department clerk, proud of his intuitive powers, finally gave up trying to unriddle the secretary. Seward was incomprehensible, he concluded, "and the more so when seen at a distance."[18]

If Seward's enigmatic nature confounded people, his seemingly impulsive outspokenness often made for interesting conversation. W. H. Russell, the London *Times* correspondent, found him "a subtle, quick man, rejoicing in power, given to perorate and to oracular utterances," and a lover of jokes. A raconteur with few peers in the capital, Seward, all agreed, talked like a book, "fertile in illustration, happy in anecdote, and 'death' on words." His conversations, young Henry Adams marveled, would inspire a cow with statesmanship.

Speaking slowly in a thick, husky voice, he would hold forth behind a haze of cigar smoke and fix a hard blue-gray eye on the nearest face. His manner outraged many who did not know him. Seeing humor in odd situations, he could not understand why his audience sometimes failed to respond. He relaxed at parties, became garrulous when drinking champagne or brandy and water, and expected people to listen to him without spreading tales. The secretary's party behavior soon led to ugly rumors. Enemies swore that he drank "like a fish" from a "black bottle" (containing, in fact, only tea) kept in his office; that friends had to ring the doorbell for him after an evening's entertainment because he was incapable of handling the task himself; and that "when he was loaded, his tongue wagged," spilling state secrets to all who listened. Liquor did encourage his natural loquacity, but Seward was no alcoholic, and while his fiery remarks raised more than one eyebrow, he never compromised national security. He was, gossips despaired, "the most confidential man" in Washington. On one occasion, when a woman asked him to divulge a state secret, he replied, "Madam, if I did not know I would tell you." He loved to play with his inquisitors. "What can you do with a man who leads you to a remote corner of a room and, in the most deferential manner, tells you nothing in a low, confidential tone?" lamented a victim.[19]

Seward's most disturbing trait was his penchant for seemingly rash statements, volcanic eruptions heavy with promise of calamity for erring nations, that set foreign capitals buzzing and their ministers, accustomed to the cautious, correct reticence of European courts, into hasty retreat. "There's no shake in him," exulted an admirer. "He talks square up to the mark and something beyond it." Although friends urged him to "disguise his sentiments," the secretary found it nearly impossible.[20]

Sometimes, Seward's free-wheeling conversation had dangerous repercussions; a significant indiscretion occurred during the presidential campaign of 1860. The occasion was a gubernatorial dinner honoring the Prince of Wales during his visit to Albany in mid-October. There, according to the Duke of Newcastle, the then-Senator Seward allegedly stated that "he should make use of insults to England to secure his position in the States, and that I [Newcastle] must not suppose he meant war. On the contrary he did not wish war with England and he was confident we should never go to war with the States—we dared not and could not affort it." Stunned, Newcastle rallied that "there was no fear of war except from such a policy as he indicated and that if he carried it out and touched our honor he could some fine morning find he had embroiled his Country in a disastrous conflict as the moment when he fancied he was bullying all before him." Although another guest remembered Seward making playful conversation with the royal party, no one could verify the exchange.[21]

The story reached the American minister to Britain, Charles Francis Adams, the following July. He dismissed it as banter after Seward's "peculiar fashion" or a "mistake founded on a bad joke," having heard Seward make similar remarks when "he had no idea of the misinterpretations of himself to which he was giving rise." After first denying the tale, Seward finally offered an explanation, in fact several explanations, over a year later. In the course of the evening, Seward related, he had apologized to Newcastle for not joining Prince Edward's party in Boston or New York. Politics made it prudent for him as a Republican not to appear friendly toward the British; such a friendship might provide proslavery Democrats an opportunity to muddy the presidential contest with appeals to Anglophobia, and divert public attention from the real issue of human freedom. "Well," Seward shrugged, "they all understood it." Apparently, Newcastle did not understand; some months later, recalling the substance (but not the tone) of the remarks, he warned the governor of Canada that the new secretary of state's "*first* idea is that we should swallow all the insults he pleases to cram down our throats and that he will establish his own power and representatives amongst his Rowdies without the danger of War,—but his *second* idea . . . is to prepare the minds of the mob for war with England if the result of the quarrel with the Southern States should render an inroad into Canada a measure of political advantage" to him.[22]

Whatever Seward had said that night in Albany was obviously susceptible to misinterpretation and, as Weed dryly noted, it would have been wiser not to "play with edged tools."[23] At first glance the whole affair appeared to be one of those minor, predictable events in the life of any politician. But frequent repetition of the story, and widespread acceptance of Newcastle's interpretation, damaged Seward's reputation in England and hampered settlement of the *Trent* crisis.

Considering Seward's quirks, perhaps the president-elect should have chosen a less flamboyant individual for the State Department. Many British questioned the appointment. What they could not understand was that Seward had not been named because of special experience (limited to a year on the Senate Foreign Relations Committee) or, least of all, because of any need to satisfy Anglophobes; instead, Seward's appointment was intended to heal divisions within the Republican party. British observers tended to regard Seward's accession as the triumph of American demagoguery. A stream of flippant remarks from the incoming secretary about the fate in store for Confederate sympathizers abroad did nothing to allay fears that American policy had fallen into the hands of a madman. The gloomy secession winter of 1860–61, jangled by the din of a collapsing nation, seemed a perfect setting for his lunacy.

Seward established a poor relationship with the Washington diplomatic corps even before taking office. The Newcastle story undoubtedly made the rounds of Washington quickly, serving to warn foreign dignitaries that contact with Seward could prove to be a memorable, even unpleasant, adventure. Soon, the capital was buzzing about his latest harangue to the minister from the Republic of Bremen, Rudolph Schleiden, in late January 1861. The hapless envoy had suggested on the day of Louisiana's secession that the Morrill tariff bill would raise duties considerably, and might induce European commerce and governments to support the South. Rolling his eyes heavenward, Seward shocked the diplomat: "If the Lord would only give the United States an excuse for a war with England, France, or Spain, that would be the best means of reestablishing internal peace." To be certain the message reached "Eu-rope" (as he pronounced it), Seward related the conversation a week later to Lyons, the British minister, adding that it would give him much pleasure if a European power aided South Carolina because then he would "pitch into" the offending nation and be joined by the seceded states, healing the Union. Lyons concluded that Seward viewed foreign relations as levers for manipulating public opinion, and that Northern politicians had no stomach for a civil war. Their advocacy of such nonviolent tactics as terminating postal service and foreign trade to Southern states apparently was intended to make secession unpopular, but was conceived without consideration to the overseas reaction. Leading Republicans, Lyons wrote Russell, were "on the look-out for a foreign dispute, in the hope that they should thus be able to divert the public mind from home-quarrels, and to re-kindle the fire of patriotism both in the North and in the South."[24]

The British minister was nearly right about Seward's desire to end the secession crisis at any cost. After the presidential campaign, he had returned to Washington imbued with the conviction that he alone could prevent dissolution of the Union. In fact, he accepted appointment to the State Department only because he dared not "leave the country to chance"; he was afraid to leave the capital for even three days, lest the nation disintegrate in his absence. He held scant respect

for the president-elect, who supposedly had adopted a pose of
"masterly inactivity" and left party leadership to Seward. Before the
new administration took office, or Seward accepted a post, he compared Lincoln to a hereditary monarch and portrayed himself as leader
of the ruling party with "actual direction of public affairs." Lincoln, he
told everyone, wanted him to be prime minister. The situation did not
escape the notice of foreign diplomats, and was not helped by
Lincoln's confession to Schleiden, "I don't know anything about
diplomacy. I will be very apt to make blunders." Not long after the in-
auguration, other cabinet members began complaining of Seward's
tampering with their departments, running to the President several
times a day, and summoning them at odd hours to confer with Lincoln
and himself about their work. Seward boasted to the British minister,
"I can touch a bell on my right hand and order the arrest of a citizen of
Ohio. I can touch a bell again, and order the imprisonment of a citizen
of New York, and no power on earth, except that of the President of
the United States, can release them. Can the Queen of England do as
much?"[25] Lyons's early warning that Seward would be a "dangerous
Foreign Minister" appeared to have become a chilling reality.

The burden of devising foreign policy for a disunited nation did
not mellow the secretary of state. Now that his position placed a
premium on persuasion and confidence, he continued to act as if
Washington diplomats were local politicians and their governments
rival parties. Within a month of taking office he was snorting like a
war-horse at the smell of gunpowder. Events made Seward almost
desperate. The tragic failure of a Washington Peace Conference to for-
mulate a compromise, the seizure of Federal arsenals and other public
property by secessionists, and the shaky position of Fort Sumter in
Charleston Harbor threatened to undo his strategy of avoiding open
conflict by taking actions that would underscore the impracticality of
secession. He sought to close Southern ports, not by instituting
blockades (legal only in time of war), but by stationing vessels off the
coast to collect duties under the guise of enforcing revenue laws. The
subject came up at a dinner in late March given by Lyons after which
he, Seward, and the French and Russian ministers fell into conversation. Lyons commented that the revenue measure would force other
governments to recognize the Confederacy or accept interruption of
commerce. Seward, apparently having "drunk quite a bit," exploded.
European involvement in American affairs was the best thing that
could happen, he declared, and "if the Union was dissolved, not a
government in Europe would remain standing." As Seward became
more violent and noisy, Lyons turned away to speak to some ladies.
Subsequently, the British minister advised London not to be quick to

rebuff the Confederate commissioners then on their way to Europe. Even though international law and custom dictated that rebels not be recognized until they had established their independence or conquered the existing government, Lyons believed that too strong a rejection would encourage violent policies in the North.[26]

The secretary of state's outburst indicated the strain under which he had operated for the past months as he tried to function as a one-man save-the-Union committee. "The majority of those around me are determined to pull the house down," Seward had said in February, "and I am determined not to let them." His threats against European nations had been calculated to deter intervention and buy time. Exhausted from his labors, and frustrated by lack of progress, he was approaching his limits. Anything could set him off, but he was not ready to give up. What the administration needed most, he decided, was a plan that would seize the initiative, reverse the tide of secession, and preserve the Union. Sympathetic powers had to be warned about aiding the Confederacy, or else the United States would find itself in a foreign war and possibly lose the South forever.[27]

While Seward was forming new proposals, an event occurred that added urgency to the taut domestic crisis. In defiance of the Monroe Doctrine, Spain annexed Santo Domingo on March 30, 1861, and, with French encouragement, was preparing to take Haiti. The next day, Seward drew up a memorandum entitled "Some Thoughts for the President's Consideration" and delivered it to Lincoln on April 1; it has been often described as "Seward's April Fool's Day Madness," or his foreign war panacea. Seward channeled months of agony into this remarkable manifesto, which suggested such sound strategies as defending all Gulf Coast forts, recalling the navy from foreign stations, and establishing martial law at Key West. But Spanish actions in the Caribbean, coupled with European reluctance to discourage the South, led him to recommend some ridiculous moves as well. He suggested that Lincoln demand explanations from Spain and France and, if the explanations proved unsatisfactory, convene Congress to declare war. Britain and Russia should then be asked to explain their probable course in an American civil war. Agents should be sent to Canada, Mexico, and Central America to invoke a spirit of independence against European intervention. If the president lacked the fortitude to follow such policies, Seward implied, he would do it for him.[28]

Although Lincoln pigeonholed Seward's suggestion for a foreign war or wars, and the matter was never raised again, the content of the memorandum leaked. The British minister guessed almost immediately that Seward viewed the Spanish occupation of Santo Domingo as the "question with a Foreign Power, for which he has been on the look out." It made sense. A conflict with Britain would be catastrophic for America's commerce and puny navy, whereas war with Spain would be safe and might lure Southerners to trade independence for the long-coveted territories of Cuba and Puerto Rico. Even though the Americans were concentrating their ire on Spain, Lyons worried that since no one in the cabinet was knowledgeable about foreign affairs, but all possessed "overweening confidence in their own strength," a misstep might place the two English-speaking nations on a collision course. The best chance of keeping the Americans within bounds, he advised his government, was to be very firm and to act "in strict concert" with France.[29]

As word of Seward's fulminations spread through Washington, observers wondered what had happened to the secretary; even his old radical reputation and penchant for colorful remarks did not explain this latest sally, which raised disturbing questions. The chairman of the Foreign Relations Committee, Senator Charles Sumner, decided that the shock of losing the presidential nomination had unbalanced his old adversary, while others, impressed by Seward's political sagacity, which spanned decades of party and sectional turbulence, sought deeper reasons. "He's a precious foxy old man," explained a young friend, "and tells no one his secrets."[30]

Seward may have seemed irrational to Sumner and the diplomatic corps, but method, not madness, inspired him. He believed that two factors would deter European intervention in the Civil War: Union victories, and a manifest willingness to declare war upon any nation siding with the rebels. Such an outlook assumed that foreign powers were so dependent on Southern cotton, so resentful of the Morrill tariff, so antagonistic to the United States, that at the first opportunity they would advance the cause of Confederate independence. The secretary instructed Union diplomats to inform their host governments that if the latter determined to recognize the South, those nations should simultaneously "prepare to enter into alliance with the enemies of this republic." Seward never considered the possibility that Europe might adopt a wait-and-see attitude, postponing the question of intervention until a more appropriate time. When, in the autumn of 1862, the British and French did seriously contemplate interference, the battle of Antietam and Russian opposition made them reconsider. Seward was convinced that his well-known volatility, inexperience, and unpredictability could produce a sophisticated psychological warfare to discourage meddling by the great powers. When Charles Francis Adams attempted to gloss over Seward's bellicosity, the secretary of state warned, "you could do no greater harm, than by inducing an opinion that I am less decided in my intercourse with the British minister than I am reputed to be or less determined to maintain the pride and dignity of our Government."[31] Seward gambled that no government would risk war, and that European nations could not submerge their rivalries long enough to act in concert.

The tactic began to show almost immediate results, but in ways unforeseen by Seward. In mid-April 1861, the British minister, an unhappy recipient of Seward's attention, feared that peace could not be maintained. The danger of an irrational move by the Americans forced Lyons into more frequent contact with Seward, and he was unsure of how to handle the secretary. Lyons believed that if he tried to be pleasant, Seward might take it as a sign of weakness. If Lyons adopted an unyielding position, Lyons might provoke an outburst. The minister came to dread his meetings with Seward.

Canada provided material for the first Anglo-American trouble. Although people in British North America had sympathized with the plight of the Lincoln administration during the secession winter, and possessed an abolitionist bias, they would not violate neutrality by agreeing to sell weapons to the North (a request that Britain saw as a way to make Canada defenseless). Nor did they appreciate discussion in American newspapers of annexing Canada to compensate for any loss of Southern territory. The French Canadians opposed amalgamation because they feared it would threaten their religion; other Canadians criticized American national character, political corruption, and the general democratic malaise.[32]

The Canadian situation worried the State Department. Interpreting the British policy of strict neutrality as pro-Confederate, Seward feared that Canada might serve as a base for rebel raids across the Northern boundary. He persuaded the cabinet on April 12 to approve appointment of a special secret agent to Canada, Massachusetts Congressman George Ashmun, who was instructed to report on public opinion, to keep political feelings favorable toward the Union, and to uncover Confederate agents. The attack on Fort Sumter temporarily occupied everyone's attention, but a few days later the New York *Herald* broke the story of Ashmun's mission, forcing Seward to rescind the appointment. Ashmun remained in Canada, collecting information and meeting Canadian officials, who used him as a conduit to the Lincoln administration. Meanwhile, unaware of Ashmun's recall and informed that not one but two secret agents had been dispatched to determine if Canadian public opinion favored annexation, Lyons protested the "very irregular proceeding." Seward denied that any agent had been sent, but two months later he told Lyons that Ashmun had been instructed to "ascertain the feeling in Canada with regard to fitting out privateers on the St. Lawrence." Lyons considered

Seward's actions in the affair consistent with his character.[33] The
Ashmun mission, however necessary, was an amateurish affair that
hardly fitted Seward's reputation as a political wizard. Poorly conceived and ineptly executed, it served to heighten British suspicion.

Seward's tardy explanation of Ashmun's mission coincided with
another fiasco involving Canada. Reports reached the State Department in late April that the steamer *Peerless* had been purchased by
Confederate agents at Toronto for service as a privateer. Before
Seward could investigate, Governor Andrew of Massachusetts, angry
over Canada's refusal to sell arms to his state, urged the governor-
general of British North America, Sir Edmund Head, to prevent
passage of the *Peerless* down the St. Lawrence. Without proof of the
Confederate purchase, Head naturally rejected Andrew's suggestion.
Seward summoned Lyons and told him that, regardless of any protest
Lyons might register, he would order American naval officers to seize
the *Peerless* as soon as he received information proving its sale to the
rebels. To be told that his objections, no matter how soundly based on
international law, would be disregarded was neither pleasing nor acceptable to the British minister, who viewed the exchange as another
indication of the administration's "arrogant spirit and disregard of the
rights and feelings of Foreign nations," and of Seward's "carelessness
and precipitation." As it turned out, the *Peerless* had been bought by
agents of the Washington government, unbeknown to Seward.[34]

In the retrospect of a century and more, one must conclude that
the secretary pushed too hard with his war of nerves. Lyons's initial
dismay turned to fear and then contemptuous anger as he sought ways
to accommodate American demands. Although his actions often
struck fear into the heart of Lyons, Seward did not succeed in frightening the British government, nor did he improve relations with Canada.
His maladroit negotiations, bumbling attempts at espionage, and dis-
dainful attitude toward international law so alarmed Lyons that for
the next seven months the British minister denounced him in almost
every dispatch, and led his government to interpret every disagreement
with Seward as a prologue to war.

The shabby treatment that Lyons suffered at the hands of Seward
did not dispose the minister to think kindly of his tormentor or of the
government he represented. Lyons decided that Seward's high-handed
conduct and violent language probably were not intended to instigate

war with England, but to make political capital at home; the secretary seemed to have so little appreciation for the strength of European powers. Lyons had even less confidence in Lincoln and the other cabinet members, who were "if possible, still more ignorant of Europe, and some . . . much more violent" than Seward. Keeping on good terms with the American government would be difficult because the administration's supporters, "the ignorant mob of the North," constantly "urge it on to violence." He advised the British government to pursue a policy of "strict neutrality."[35] He was not advocating that Britain cooperate with the Confederacy, but believed that the best way to insure Union respect was to introduce uncertainty into Anglo-American relations. It would involve finesse, dexterity, and probably caution; the Americans might perceive a slight where none was intended.

Lyons became increasingly gloomy; finally, by the third week in May, he reached some pessimistic conclusions about the nature of the American government. His opinion of the United States had fallen as he watched the Lincoln administration fumble the secession crisis. His meetings with the secretary of state, punctuated by threat of war, had so irritated him that he had to exercise control of his temper. Finally, after complaining about Seward for months to the Foreign Office, the minister erupted in a massive thirty-nine-page dispatch (no. 206 of May 20, 1861) that marked the nadir of his dissatisfaction.

The lengthy dispatch went right to the point. "The possibility of a war between Great Britain and the United States," Lyons wrote, "is a subject so painful that it is but natural to shrink from the consideration of it." Despite the absurdity of the United States wishing a foreign war while engaged in a civil struggle, "the conviction has forced itself upon my mind, that it may be impossible to deter this Government from offering provocations to Great Britain, which neither our honour, nor our interest will allow us to brook." The situation had become too serious to be treated with palliatives. Referring to three of Seward's published instructions to Adams, written largely for public consumption and published before they reached London, Lyons said they only hinted at the violence in the conversation of Seward and supporters, and in the inspired, surreptitious newspaper articles. More than mere idle bluster, Seward's language was evidence of underlying causes that could lead to even more high-handed acts. Seward had underestimated the war's gravity, falsely predicted its duration, and lost the confidence of his party; finally, he had seen his peace policy toward the Confederacy overruled by the cabinet. He was trying to regain popularity by advocating violent moves that would allow him to seize control of the war faction. The secretary had always "regarded the Foreign Relations of the Country as safe materials from which to make, (to use his own phrase) political capital at home." The president and other cabinet members, "wholly ignorant" of foreign affairs and incapable of leadership, shared Seward's attitude toward Europe; moreover, in the *Peerless* case, they apparently supported his "Bravado against England for Party purposes." With the United States so dependent upon customs duties to pay the expenses of government and prosecution of the war, the administration had to realize that war with England or France would lead to imposition of a blockade and termination of that source of revenue. Yet this and other considerations might not inspire the Union to abandon "the reckless course upon which it has entered." Another explanation must account for the government's truculence.

The stridency of Seward's language and the boasting and arrogance of the Lincoln cabinet led Lyons to conclude that American officials believed that "under no provocation will England or France go to war with the United States." Northerners looked upon Canada as Britain's weak point. Lyons reminded his government that Seward, while campaigning for the presidential nomination in 1860, had advocated the annexation of Canada to compensate for loss of Southern territory, and had counted on Irish secret societies, especially in New York, to organize an invasion force. The Lincoln administration was hoping that European complications would render an Anglo-French expeditionary force impractical, and that the two nations might go to war, or for some other reason be unable to cooperate on the American question. Northern trade might also hold greater attraction for European merchants than Southern cotton. These convictions of the Washington government had to be shaken, Lyons warned, or Europe could expect trouble.

The minister had spent much time considering ways to disabuse Washington, and narrowed his list to four courses. First, American statesmen and politicians should be convinced that European powers had a point beyond which they would not tolerate insults. London must express its "absolute inflexibility of purpose," and remember that the smallest concession to bullying would be "a fatal encouragement." Second, preparation for war was the best safeguard against being driven into one. The danger was "sufficiently imminent" to warrant placing Canada in a "complete state of defence," and reinforcing squadrons in the West Indies, Atlantic, and Pacific. Third, Britain should act in concert with France. Although it would be "absolute madness" for the United States to risk war with both nations, Lyons did not rule out the possibility, given the willingness to antagonize Europe by cutting off cotton. Finally, he viewed "effectual resistance" by the South, no matter how repugnant to British sympathies, as a "last source of security" to Europe because it would absorb Union energies and resources. Although he did not advocate military aid for the Confederates, he saw no reason to discourage them by rejecting their emissaries. If British officials believed, as did Lyons, that war with the United States was likely, they would do well to follow his recommendations.

In dealing with Seward and other government officials, Lyons declared, he had tried to "smooth difficulties and to prevent unpleasant questions arising" by skirting dangerous topics and commenting carefully. By refusing to give Seward opportunity to use strong language and by avoiding personal altercation, he had managed to preserve a superficial calm, but "difficult questions must soon arise." British subjects stood in danger of being wronged by the blockade and abused by civil authorities, while party politics could inspire violent conduct. Lyons realized that no one outside the United States and unacquainted with American leaders would believe they held such misconceptions about Europe. Nevertheless, he assured the foreign secretary that his number 206 gave a "faithful and by no means exaggerated representation of things as they exist here."[36]

Lyons had exaggerated. If Seward presented problems, so did the British minister. The public was not clamoring for war with Britain or France. Although the North was irritated by Canadian detachment, it was not angry at England; word of Queen Victoria's proclamation of neutrality of May 13 had not yet crossed the Atlantic. And by his Machiavellian portrait of the secretary, Lyons showed ignorance of Seward's public record; he had not always played politics with foreign relations, and he exploited them no more than other politicians. The source of Lyons's information on Seward's desire to lead the "war party" is not clear, but his relationship with Senator Sumner, a political foe of the secretary, may have influenced his attitude. Hardly a model of rationality, and addicted to bombastic pronouncements, Seward often spoke carelessly to the wrong people, yet his actions did not merit the interpretation offered by the British minister.

At about the time Lyons wrote his doomsday dispatch, Seward penned his dispatch number 10 to Adams in London. Like the British minister, Seward had reached a critical point in his view of Europe and the Civil War. Dispatches from American legations suggested that Britain and France were almost ready "to try and save cotton, at the cost of the Union." His efforts to save the Union had apparently been

rejected. "I am a chief reduced to a subordinate position, and surrounded with a guard," he complained to his wife. It upset him to
know that monarchists were cheering the collapse of the United
States, happy that the first government to recognize new republics
"could now be paid in its own coin." He worried that European nations, especially Britain and France, would take advantage of the
plight of the United States by granting recognition of Confederate independence. It was no secret that Lyons had said as much to several
diplomats in Washington.[37] If Europe recognized the Confederacy,
the Union would be forced to declare war on the interfering powers,
insuring a permanent division of the country. Seward held no illusions
about American military invincibility. The United States could never
defeat the combined armies and navies of the Confederacy, Britain,
and France. An eleventh state, North Carolina, had just seceded;
recognition of the growing Confederacy seemed imminent unless he
could warn the great powers. Apparently, his remarks to foreign
diplomats had made little impression. To insure that they were aware
that he spoke for the administration, he gained cabinet approval for a
stern admonition to the British government, the cornerstone of any
European front.

Seward's instructions to the American minister in London began
on a somber note. "This government," he wrote, "considers that our
relations in Europe have reached a crisis in which it is necessary for it
to take a decided stand, on which not only its immediate measures,
but its ultimate and permanent policy can be determined and defined."
Less than three weeks earlier, the British foreign secretary, John
Russell, had informed Adams's predecessor that he was willing to
meet unofficially with Confederate envoys, and that the British and
French governments had agreed to follow a common policy on
recognition. Since Seward believed that any kind of communication
might be construed as recognition, he instructed Adams to have no
contact with the British government as long as it pursued that policy.
"British recognition would be British intervention to create within our
own territory a hostile state by overthrowing this Republic itself." The
United States would not allow recognition of Confederate belligerency
to pass unquestioned, and expected the British to respect a properly
enforced blockade. Seward realized that complications arising from
the Civil War might result in hostilities between the United States and
"one, two, or even more European nations," but Britain, not the
United States, would be responsible. "War in defence of national life is
not immoral," he wrote ominously, "and war in defence of independence is an inevitable part of the discipline of nations."[38] At

Lincoln's insistence Seward expunged his most inflammatory language, marked the instruction confidential and not for communication, and indicated that Adams should be guided by its spirit; yet, Seward did publish it, for all the world to see, in the annual *Diplomatic Correspondence* series he initiated in the autumn.[39]

Relations between Britain and the United States, although rarely congenial, had been deteriorating since Lincoln's victory. Foreign officials looked to Lincoln for clues to policy, and disliked what they saw. Virtually all cabinet choices were politicians, many having campaigned for the 1860 nomination, and they seemed more accustomed to trading votes and jollying county commissioners than solving national problems. The new secretary of state's remarks, no matter what their motive, raised questions in European chancelleries. But within the diplomatic corps, only Lyons believed that Seward sought a foreign war. The exposed position of Canada undoubtedly affected the British minister, but it does not explain his reaction. Although Lyons had become accustomed to the American tactic of bluff and bluster, he could not cope with it in Seward, and had criticized him since the presidential campaign. After Seward assumed office, the minister turned dispatches and private correspondence into diatribes, unable to discriminate among what was said, meant, and worth reporting. Introspective by nature, inclined to view himself as a sentry at the gates of peace, Lyons kept his temper even when he felt insulted, but his complaints about Seward put the British government in a dangerous frame of mind. Months later, when the *Trent* affair burst upon the scene, Lyons's dispatches and the atmosphere they generated were a prime reason for the escalation of a naval incident into an emergency.

4.

The Summer
of Discontent

LINCOLN'S PROCLAMATION OF BLOCKADE raised the issue of whether Britain would respect it. Traditionally a blockade, however poorly enforced, had been accepted by neutrals, but the Declaration of Paris (1856), signed by most of the powers, spoke of "effective blockades." The Union, in 1861, lacked sufficient ships for an "effective blockade." Nevertheless, flying squadrons or lone warships cruising in the sea lanes might capture unsuspecting merchantmen sailing to Southern ports, unless their home government warned them. British officials anticipated the commissioning of Confederate privateers and Union efforts to eradicate them, the destruction or confiscation of neutral cargoes, and other numerous indignities. Additional problems besieged England, including the maintenance of diplomatic relations with both the Union and Confederate governments, development of alternative sources of cotton, protection of British commerce on the high seas, and prevention of an invasion of British North America.

Queen Victoria's proclamation of neutrality was announced on May 13, 1861, a week after Foreign Secretary Russell informed the House of Commons that despite President Lincoln's intention of treating rebel privateers as pirates, humanity and impartiality dictated a different course for Britain. The proclamation benefited the United States by establishing British acceptance of the blockade, by preventing the equipment of warships in British ports, and by forbidding Britons to engage in unneutral activities. However, the proclamation also benefited the South; by establishing recognition of Confederate belligerency, it apparently placed the Southern states on an equal footing with the Union. The latter aspect of the proclamation precipitated a roar of disapproval from Northerners, who had no patience for the intricate arguments of international law that justified the British action.

Northerners criticized the neutrality proclamation as a hasty, if not hostile, act; how, they wondered, could Britain side with slaveowners? Richard Henry Dana, Jr., lamented that the moment the first gun was fired, "before we have had time to begin to collect our militia to suppress the insurrection . . . England *makes haste* to proclaim her *neutrality* (!) between the two 'belligerents,' & unnecessarily declaring the insurgents entitled to all the rights of 'belligerents.' " This "hasty recognition," argued Massachusetts lawyer George Bemis, was nothing more than a move to "throw protection over Confederate privateers and their crews, and to aid the rebel cause with contributions of English volunteers and English naval armaments and equipments." Others later claimed that England's moral support equaled a 200,000-man rebel army and prolonged the war two years. "The good people of England owe to us their good wishes," Senator Sumner protested. "We are fighting the battle of Civilization, & their public men & newspapers should recognize & declare the true character of the conflict. It is not necessary that Emancipate should be openly on our flag. . . . And yet this wicked Rebellion has found backing in England." John Lothrop Motley, the United States minister to Austria expressed the public attitude best when he wrote a member of the British cabinet, "Men did not wish assistance. They would have scorned material aid. But they did expect sympathy." Instead, "there came denunciations of the wickedness of civil war—as if the war had not been forced upon the Government. . . ."[1]

It is difficult to imagine how Britain could have avoided declaring neutrality and recognizing Confederate belligerency once Lincoln had proclaimed a blockade, although Lincoln's proclamation apparently had little bearing at the time on Britain's decision. The issue for Northerners came down to definitions of *public war*, *civil war*, and *insurrection*. Rejecting the term *public war* (a state of armed hostility between nations or sovereigns), the United States at first recognized only a state of insurgency, and expected foreign governments to do no more; however, international law did not then provide for "recognition of insurgency" as a means to confer international rights and obligations. Although nations could specify privileges for insurgents, those privileges did not automatically flow from law. Granting belligerent rights to the Confederacy did not constitute moral support

PUNCH, OR THE LONDON CHARIVARI.—July 6, 1861.

NAUGHTY JONATHAN.

"YOU **SHAN'T** INTERFERE, MOTHER—AND YOU OUGHT TO BE ON MY SIDE—AND IT'S A GREAT SHAME—AND I DON'T CARE—AND YOU **SHALL**
INTERFERE—AND I WON'T HAVE IT."

*The United States Throws a Temper Tantrum Over the British
Proclamation of Neutrality*
Courtesy of *Punch*

for the rebellion and censure of the parent government; instead, it constituted recognition of a material state of war. The rebellion's
magnitude made the term *civil war* more applicable, a fact eventually
conceded by the Lincoln administration. In any event, proclamation
of a blockade rendered the whole argument academic, because such an
action could be taken only in a state of war; technically, by proclaiming a blockade, Lincoln himself had recognized Confederate
belligerency.[2]

The British government and people resented the "unreasonable"
anger of Northerners at the neutrality proclamation, and the expecta-
tion that England would support the Union cause. Was Britain supposed to deny the existence of war, hang rebel sailors, and ignore
Confederate armies just to avoid being charged as "allies and patrons"
of slavery? The British public saw little to commend either the North
or the South, and shared the view of Lord Russell that the "struggle is
on the one side for empire, and on the other for power." A permanent
division of the "great bully of the world" would remove the threat to
Canada, encourage respect for international law in both sections, and

Charles Francis Adams
Courtesy of the Massachusetts Historical Society

lead to broader commercial freedom in the South and greater social freedom in the North.[3] The British government really did not care what the Americans did to each other as long as they respected neutral rights; but the timing of the neutrality proclamation aroused even greater resentment in the North because Charles Francis Adams, the new American minister, arrived in Liverpool the same day, and thus was given no opportunity to forestall the act. It seemed as if designed.

When Adams arrived in London the first news he read was Britain's recognition of Confederate belligerency, hardly an auspicious beginning for his mission. Adams was, in Lincoln's words, "Seward's man," not the President's, having supported Seward for the Republican presidential nomination in 1860. He had accepted appointment to the Court of St. James's despite reelection to Congress, and seemed likely to follow his father and grandfather into the presidency. The new minister was reserved, logical, and intelligent, with a mind that "worked with singular perfection, admirable self-restraint, and instinctive mastery of form." His character, molded in part by two years at an English boarding school, was admirably suited to British taste. When London society, enamored with Confederate pretensions, treated him with frosty reserve, Adams became "a little colder and a little more reserved."[4]

Adams undertook to do what he could with the neutrality proclamation, and on May 18, 1861, discussed it at Russell's country house nine miles from London. Adams found Russell as austere and proper as himself, which is probably why he impressed Russell as "calm and judicious." Russell heartily disliked Americans (although they did not know it). One of the few British leaders who favored the Confederacy, he had advocated mediation of the Civil War and liked to compare the South's cause to the Greek Revolution of the early 1820s. He had taken part in public affairs since entering Parliament at the age of twenty-one, and had risen to become leader of the Whigs, colonial secretary, prime minister, and foreign secretary—trading the latter post back and forth with the present prime minister, Palmerston, since 1846. Along the way he had acquired numerous enemies among the Conservatives, including the acid Benjamin Disraeli, who once remarked of Russell, "If a traveler were injoined that such a man was leader of the House of Commons, he may well begin to comprehend how the Egyptians worshipped an insect." Shy for a politician, Russell offended people with his aloof, haughty manner and disturbed foreign courts with his blunt messages. Adams found him "by no means a demonstrative man" and could detect "no symptom of any emotion in his countenance." Russell showed no emotion at all as he patiently listened to the American state his government's position.

Their initial encounter did not go well, but it could have been worse if Adams had followed instructions and "demanded" explanations of British behavior. He began by asking if Britain intended a policy that would "widen if not make irreparable" the sectional breach. Russell coolly replied that his government had no such intention and was not disposed to interfere in any way. Assuring Russell that the Lincoln administration had not meant to impute such a desire, Adams said that any manifestation of sympathy for the so-called Confederacy, such as the neutrality proclamation and the language used by officials when discussing it in Parliament, would be interpreted as an attempt to make the separation permanent. When Adams asked Russell to clarify his remark about being willing to meet with Confederate agents, the foreign secretary refused to promise that his government "would not at any future time, no matter what the circumstances might be, recognize an existing State in America." This reply led Adams to conclude that the State Department might take offense and recall him.[5]

Lord John Russell
Courtesy of the Massachusetts Historical Society

Subsequent conversation revealed Russell as a tough, shrewd advocate. When Adams continued to object to meetings with the Confederate envoys, Russell reminded him that both France and Britain customarily received revolutionaries—whether Poles, Hungarians, or Italians—and such actions did not imply recognition. As for America's ill-founded complaint about the neutrality proclamation, England intended to be entirely neutral and would not hang Confederate seamen as pirates.[6]

Like so many Americans, Adams could not understand the advantages of the proclamation, and became resentful. He later reminisced that he "never could hold any other opinion but this, that if that government had been actuated by a desire to effect the disruption of the United States without taking any step to compromise its neutral position, it could not have hit upon a more safe and . . . effective line of action than it did to attain that purpose." He regarded the proclamation as premature and believed that it would have aroused less anger if it had been announced at a suitable time and with notice, yet he realized that the Tory cabinet had to contend with the vagaries of

domestic opinion. Adams fluctuated wildly in his estimate of British
public opinion regarding the Civil War. Although his reception on arrival seemed to indicate that England generally held a pro-Confederate
bias, within a month he was writing home that the "great body of the
people and very much the largest proportion of the press do sym-
pathize with us." Britons told him they wanted to be neutral, and that
the proclamation of neutrality signified no hostility. Adams believed
the decided "amelioration of sentiment" had been brought about by
the Union's military preparation and the British government's realiza-
tion that the proclamation had been construed to mean more than intended. And yet, by mid-July, Adams detected signs of uneasiness as
the cotton supply allegedly dwindled. He could not help believing that
the "secret wish of almost all classes is to see us permanently divided,"
even though many people who held that attitude "would feel very indignant if it should be imputed to them." What distressed him the
most was the mixture of ignorance, indifference, and distrust he encountered. People did not seem to understand Americans or their
politics, and persisted in viewing the Civil War as the result of sectional jealousies rather than slavery.[7]

Adams was also disturbed by strange instructions from the State
Department, especially Seward's "bold remonstrance" of May 21,
which arrived on June 10. It was "so arrogant in tone and so extraordinary and unparalleled in its demands" that the government seemed
"almost ready to declare war with all the powers of Europe." Unable
to understand Seward's motivation and intent, Adams kept faith that
his patron was "calm and wise," while other members of the legation
came to believe that Seward meant war.[8] Where it would all lead,
Adams did not know, but of one thing he was certain: unless the Lincoln administration convinced the British government it wanted
peace, and unless Seward made some effort to dissuade British officials of his hostility, war between Britain and the United States might
erupt.

Relations with the United States had never been easy, but life in
the British legation in Washington during the summer of 1861 was
especially hectic. Employees were supposed to be at work by nine,
have a quick lunch of sandwiches and lemonade at their desks, and
work straight through until after seven in the evening. Then they
would race down the street to Willard's Hotel, a hot, noisy place

noted for its huge meals and the mob of placeseekers and politicians who crowded its smoky lobbies. British visitors detested its atmosphere and rambling architecture, but it was close to the legation, and, much to Lyons's dismay, the secretaries and clerks acquired the habit of gulping down cocktails before hurrying back for dinner at eight, after which they often worked at the Chancery until midnight or one in the morning.[9] Eventually no one seemed to notice the routine, perhaps because other legations tended to follow the same schedule.

Anticipating that his government would recognize Confederate belligerency, Lyons expected Northerners to denounce the proclamation, but he was unprepared for the "violent explosion of wrath" from press and public. He found the outcry based on misapprehension of British intent, and ignorance of international law, and he was not amused by such satirical verses as:

A very queer thing is this English neutrality,
Crying, "Fair play," but yet helping one side;
It would be all O.K. if 'twere only reality,
And it could have been so had she but tried.

The ugly tone of popular criticism blended with the "arrogant language" of the Lincoln administration, which Lyons believed had shown "a disposition to have recourse to highhanded acts." He warned the commander of the squadron on the North American and West Indian station, Vice Admiral Sir Alexander Milne, that a Union naval officer might be tempted to seek "popular applause by violent proceedings against Great Britain," and that the American government lacked courage even in peaceful times to punish such acts.[10]

Lyons believed the proclamation might have shaken the confidence of the president and other politicians, although he still viewed Seward as a dangerous adversary. Finding it difficult to keep Seward "within the bounds of decency" even in social situations, Lyons resolved to "scrape on" for a while with the rest of the diplomatic corps. But by late May he intensified his warnings that, no matter how preposterous the notion, the United States might attempt war with a great power; the most probable target would be Britain, about which it was easiest "to excite the American mob." Since only preparedness would deter an attack, he again recommended that Canada, the West Indies, and British territory on the Atlantic and Pacific coasts be placed in a "complete state of defence."[11]

In the misunderstanding between Seward and Lyons, nothing was perhaps more worrisome to Lyons than the position of Canada. He could never forget that during the presidential campaign Seward had advocated annexation of Canada to compensate for loss of the South, and the poorly defended Canadian border offered perfect opportunity. Lyons sought any information that would hint at invasion plans. In early June the consul in New York, Edward M. Archibald, seemed to confirm Lyons's fears by forwarding a tale by one George Manning, "a gentlemanly sort of man," who allegedly had overheard a three-cornered conversation on Friday evening, May 31, involving a Scotsman named Sinclair, one of Seward's sons, and a physician whom Manning had come to consult. The men discussed purchase of several newspapers in Quebec to propagandize for annexation, Secretary Seward having agreed to finance the scheme from the secret service fund. The movement would have its headquarters in Buffalo, but the conspirators would be British subjects to avoid embarrassing Washington if they failed. A Canadian merchant, Hamilton Merritt, would become territorial governor, and an individual named Woodruffe would serve as secretary of state for the province when America annexed it. One of the three conspirators read a letter from the British fishery commissioner, Moses Perley, recommending that the cabal get in touch with a former American consul in Canada and chief promoter of the 1854 Reciprocity Treaty, Israel Andrews, to advance a similar plot in New Brunswick. According to Manning, Sinclair said he was afraid the British government would send troops if it suspected the United States, but Seward's son argued that only carelessness would betray them.

During the conversation, Manning read a letter from Seward that he found on a table. In the letter, Seward gave instructions for annexing Canada by popular agitation, but cautioned the ringleaders not to implicate him and to be prepared to shoulder responsibility, suggesting that documents be kept in Buffalo, Niagara Falls, or Lewiston. At about this point the doctor discovered that Manning had been eavesdropping, but released him without a promise of silence.[12]

Lyons retold the tale to Russell, commenting that he had "only too much reason to believe that Mr. Seward would see with pleasure disturbances in Canada." The minister passed the story to Governor General Edmund Head, who did not believe it; he revealed to Lyons that in 1856, after Seward had made a violent anti-British speech, Manning had visited Head in Toronto with "*a story of exactly the same kind*," although that conversation took place in a Washington hotel where Manning was calling on a lady. When Manning's "cock-and-bull story" reached the Colonial Office in London, officials chuckled at how easily the New York consul had allowed himself to be duped. That no one except Lyons gave it a second thought was a measure of Lyons's singleminded obsession with Seward.[13]

For Lyons, worry was the order of the day, and another uncertainty arose as he contemplated the assembling of a new Congress on the Fourth of July. Speaking with several politicians during visits to Washington, he reported the Republican party in "a state of mind so utterly unreasonable as to border upon frenzy." He sent a coded telegram to the Foreign Office: "No new event has occurred, but a sudden declaration of war by the United States against Great Britain appears to me to be by no means impossible, especially as long as Canada seems open to invasion." It seemed to him that Seward, Congress, and the public all shared a delusion that they could "conquer the South with one hand and chastise Europe with the other." Congressmen would vie with each other in the use of violent language and the advocation of violent conduct toward Britain. Newspapers were preparing the public by accusing England of anti-American actions and stressing that the British had more to fear from a war than the Americans did. Lyons doubted that cabinet members had already decided on war, but he expected that they would if it became necessary to maintain their positions. He foresaw three ways in which a conflict might occur. Americans did not like to declare war without some excuse, so they might close the Southern ports by act of Congress instead of blockade, and seize upon British protests. Secondly, the Lincoln administration might decide to accept Southern secession and try to channel popular wrath into a foreign war. Finally, at the close of the rebellion, a large American army would be "ready and eager for an invasion of British North America." However hostilities might arise, Lyons recommended a speedy, vigorous prosecution of the war to minimize damage to the American economy, limit destruction of privateers, and prevent development of the vast American military potential.[14] He believed that the best means of deterring the Lincoln administration was for the British and French governments to work together, but this was easier said than done.

It was natural that cooperation between England and France would originate with Lyons and his French counterpart in Washington, Henri Mercier, since they had to deal with the State Department on a daily basis and could judge prospects better than their governments. They had consulted on American issues before the attack on Fort Sumter, and both believed that Seward and the American press, as part of a campaign to divide their countries, had made every effort to praise France at the expense of Britain; this situation seemed to continue even after Paris recognized Confederate belligerency, and saucily told the United States that it was the last government to "have a right to complain of the recognition of a revolutionary government." Having witnessed some Sewardian outbursts, Mercier regarded the secretary of state as "definitely beside himself," a demagogue "who can sail only on the sea of popular emotion and who always [tries] to stir up passion in order to exploit it." Mercier worried that when he and Lyons jointly urged the United States to adhere to the Declaration of Paris, it would provoke an "outbreak of anger from Mr. Seward and even lead to some violent proceeding on the part of the Government."[15]

With some trepidation, the two ministers approached the State Department on the morning of June 15, 1861. They entered the drab, two-story brick building through a side door on Fifteenth Street, and made their way upstairs to Seward's office, from which they were ushered into the office of the assistant secretary. A few minutes later Seward entered and, seeing the ministers together, said, "No, no, no. This will never do." Declining to see the diplomats together, he said he preferred to receive their instructions unofficially, and did not think that two European powers "ought to consult together upon the course to be pursued towards a great Nation like the United States, and announce that they were acting in concert on the subject." Although Lyons and Mercier assured him it was common practice in Europe, Seward was not mollified. He conducted Lyons into his outer office and invited Mercier to dinner that evening, but he accepted a copy of the French minister's instructions.[16]

Seward's meeting with Lyons was brief. He read the minister's instructions notifying the United States of the proclamation of neutrality and asking adherence to the Declaration of Paris, which bound signatories to abolish privateering, to employ effective blockades, and, with exception of contraband of war, to exempt from capture an enemy's goods under a neutral flag and neutral goods under an enemy flag. Unwilling to admit that the rebels possessed belligerent rights, and annoyed that the British government would take this method to call attention to the declaration to which he had offered American accession six weeks earlier, Seward refused to take notice of that document or any other statement recognizing Confederate belligerency unless forced upon him; thus, he adopted the policy of the "averted glance." Regarding French recognition, he wrote to the American minister in Paris, "We have declined to hear that. We have not heard it." He had no doubt that the Anglo-French action was based on the "assumption of a certain degree of probability of success by the insurgents." While describing his meeting with Lyons in a letter to Adams several days later, Seward politely declined the "generous and friendly" mediation that had appeared in Lyons's instructions. With an eye to publishing his message, Seward dropped an ominous warning:

The fountains of discontent in any society are many, and some lie much deeper than others. Thus far this unhappy controversy has disturbed only those which are nearest the surface. There are others which lie still deeper that may yet remain . . . long undisturbed. If they should be reached, no one can tell how or when they could be closed. It was foreign intervention that opened, and that alone could open, similar fountains in the memorable French revolution.[17]

Aware of Lyons's unfavorable opinion, but unaware of how far British fears had advanced, Seward explained to Adams that he had never meant to be "intentionally offensive," but had refrained from expressing dissatisfaction to Lyons regarding almost everything the minister had said. If bad feeling existed, it was based partly on Anglo-French recognition of Confederate belligerency, without which "the disunion sentiment would languish and perish within a year." Seward was having second thoughts. Brooding about his past, he subsequently came close to apologizing for his brusqueness; he wrote to Adams that no matter how other people might have misunderstood him, "it had been an earnest and profound solicitude to avert foreign war that alone has prompted the emphatic and sometimes, perhaps, impassioned remonstrances I have hitherto made against any form or any measure of recognition of the insurgents by the Government of Great Britain."[18]

Seward then called Lyons to the State Department to speak of friendship. He surprised the minister by claiming credit for saving Anglo-American relations. By refusing to acknowledge Britain's recognition of Confederate belligerency, Seward said, he had been able to insert the section in Lincoln's message to Congress on July 5 about foreign powers respecting the sovereignty and rights of the United States. Then, destroying the effect of his remarks, he painted a distressing picture of the havoc American privateers would inflict on the commerce of any European power that fought the United States.

Seward seemed incapable of moving Lyons to friendship, or even to reassessment. The minister was caught in the web of his own misunderstandings. Lyons perceived that Seward was trying to say that he was a peaceable man, but that he could not "lessen his means of usefulness" by opposing public sentiment, which foreign ministers should remember when judging him. Lyons told Russell that Seward had had a change of heart because his insolent foreign policy had failed. But Lyons had to admit that the secretary of state "may be opening his eyes to the real danger of war with England." Seward even advised Lyons in August not to submit a written objection to closure of rebel ports because, having the "air of a threat," it might have "an unfortunate effect"; it was ironic that this advice came from the man who specialized in threats. The British minister urged his government not to curtail its defense efforts.[19]

After the beginning of the war Lyons's dispatches slowly created a sense of impending disaster within the British government. Officers who had awaited news of the rebellion, and its effect on neutrals, concluded that the Lincoln administration, especially its secretary of state, posed a danger to national interests. The minister's dispatches, composed chiefly for Russell, achieved a wider circulation; they were read by the cabinet, the diplomatic service, and military and civilian personnel stationed in the Western Hemisphere, and became a staple of conversation in drawing rooms throughout London.

Officials discussed Seward's bluster and debated the best course. As early as May the permanent undersecretary in the Foreign Office, Edmund Hammond, a cautious man, dismissed Seward as wholly unfit, a man who sought to impose by swagger instead of respect. Sending copies of Lyons's reports to the minister in Paris, Lord Cowley, at about the time Russell was proposing a common policy on recognition, Hammond said he would not be surprised if the United States tried to "redress the balance by appropriating our Possessions in the North." The Lord Privy Seal, the Duke of Argyll, who supported the Union cause, nervously informed Senator Sumner of the extreme uneasiness concerning Seward, which was founded more "on things said than on things yet actually done." Many feared that Seward had "got it into his head that the English people can't and won't take offence at anything the American government may do to their ships or their people." The home secretary (and soon-to-be secretary for war), the scholarly and dispassionate George C. Lewis, told everyone about Seward's anti-British sentiment; although he feared Seward, he could not believe that the secretary would be so insane as to declare war against England.[20] Fear of Seward spread like a communicable disease.

Although Lyons's recommendation for military preparedness seemed theoretically sound, British officials agreed that the actual task would not be easy. Vice Admiral Sir Alexander Milne, commander of the squadron on the North American and West Indian station, a forty-year veteran of the Royal Navy, had spent much time in American waters. He possessed tact, administrative experience, and a vast knowledge of international law and foreign policy. His squadron occupied a weak position, charged with defending Canada, the British West Indies, and other island groups; protecting British merchant ships from maltreatment by blockaders; and maintaining contact with British consular officers in the warring sections. Milne commanded fourteen vessels. The core of his squadron, the flagship *Nile* and the *St. George*, were 90-gun line-of-battle ships that displaced more than two thousand tons and carried crews of six hundred. Blasting away point-blank at enemy craft, these behemoths relied on sheer weight of iron to sink opponents. But they were backed by only two 21-gun corvettes, the *Cadmus* and the *Jason*; seven sloops; two gun-vessels; and a gunboat.[21] In a sudden war with the United States, Milne's squadron would fare badly.

Milne took every precaution to avoid antagonizing the United States. The blockade and Britain's neutrality proclamation prompted him to issue the following instructions to his officers on protecting British commerce: exercise the "strictest neutrality"; respect the blockade and report any weaknesses to the blockading squadron; protect British vessels from privateers; report to Milne on foreign ships met each month, as well as the blockade's strength; use care when approaching unlighted American coasts; do not enter Southern ports except to protect British lives; do not search Union or Confederate merchant ships; and prevent British subjects captured as privateersmen from being treated as pirates.[22]

The admiral's fears were continually reinforced by Lyons who, in a private and confidential letter of June 10, informed Milne that a sudden declaration of war by the United States was possible. If circumstances prevented Lyons from sending a coded telegram, he would telegraph the following message: "Could you forward a letter for me to Antigua?" Milne prepared for this possibility by sending out an order to Bermuda, to cruisers on the coast, and to senior officers: "Be on your guard and prepared. States may declare war suddenly." He pleaded with the Admiralty for more frigates and corvettes. He complained about territorial defenses. Antigua had none; Jamaica had unserviceable guns, rotting gun carriages, corroded shot, and damp powder; and the Barbados, Bermuda's southern coast, St. John, New Brunswick, the Great Lakes, Newfoundland, and the coal mines at Pieton and Cape Breton all needed protection. The Admiralty drew up orders for the *Diadem* and another frigate, and followed with other vessels; by September, Milne commanded twenty-five ships mounting 509 guns, with 6,506 officers and men. The Admiralty refused any line-of-battle ships because their departure would weaken some other fleet, cause additional expenses, and mean desertion of more sailors at Halifax.[23]

Britain also had to guard against aggression by stronger, more dangerous nations than the United States. They could not fully trust France, despite Anglo-French cooperation on American issues, and, in early 1861, there were rumors that the Russians, their old adversaries from the Crimean War, had formed "some secret understanding" with France.

It was fortunate for the United States that the British suffered from an exaggerated concern for French ambition. The British government distrusted the French as much as it feared American irrationality. Although they appreciated French deference over the American question, they realized that France was interested in acquiring Indochina, building the Suez Canal, conspiring over Italian destinies, and erecting a puppet government in Mexico. Palmerston thought it "unreasonable to expect honesty in a Portuguese or a Frenchman." On one occasion a Frenchman, meaning to be gracious, said to him, "If I were not a Frenchman, I should wish to be an Englishman," to which Palmerston replied, "If I were not an Englishman, I should wish to be an Englishman." The underlying fear was that Napoleon III might seek to enlarge his empire at the expense of Britain. After Napoleon annexed Nice and Savoy in March 1860, Palmerston turned even more suspicious. "The Emperor's mind seems as full of schemes as a warren is full of rabbits," he observed, "and, like rabbits, his schemes go to ground for the moment to avoid notice or antagonism."[24]

The British policy of maintaining a navy as strong as the combined fleets of France, Russia, and the United States had become difficult after the Crimean War. During that conflict the British army lost some of its luster, while the French navy proved to be Britain's equal in everything but size. Thrilled at the showing, the French public approved greater naval expenditures, and naval officers who once feared war with England gained confidence. According to British intelligence the French were stockpiling coal in the West Indies. "It is quite clear," Palmerston morosely concluded, "that the French are getting ready to attack us on many foreign stations." London's concerns were exacerbated when Napoleon allegedly declared in January 1861, "I desire and will make every sacrifice to maintain friendly relations with England, but if public opinion in France . . . should render a rupture necessary, I will make war on England with such vigour and such means as shall at once put an end to the affair."[25]

The British government established a special committee to monitor French shipbuilding. The committee reported in 1859 that although Britain led slightly in steam line-of-battle ships, France floated considerably more steam frigates and was constructing 4 shell-resistant vessels ("ironclads"), and Britain had none. The French navy, which allegedly consisted of 461 ships carrying 12,520 guns, would probably surpass Britain's in quality by the summer of 1862, and in quantity a year later. Visions of England's "pasteboard end" navy blown to splinters led to a recommendation that the Royal Navy be expanded in every category—especially ironclads—regardless of cost; otherwise, the Admiralty warned, "we should commence a war with France at a greater disadvantage than at former times." To meet the challenge to the three-power standard and close the "ironclad gap," the Admiralty increased its ironclad program from 1 ship in 1859 to 15 by August 1861, and stopped building large wooden vessels entirely. The latest information, however, indicated that France would have 6 ironclads ready by the spring of 1862, and another 10 by the end of the year. What the British government did not know was that French officials were recommending 45 ironclads in addition to 11 armored floating batteris.[26]

Britain simply could not allow France superiority at sea. Armed with an ironclad fleet, Napoleon could seize control of the English Channel (which Frenchmen perversely called "the Sleeve") and stage an invasion of England. British fears of an attack stemmed from the construction of great naval bases at Dunkirk and Cherbourg; unlike the building yards at Brest l'Orient and Toulon, these new bases seemed destined to serve as naval and military assembly areas. French steamers were judged capable of transporting an army of 60,000 men with a month's provisions and equipment. To secure the nation against invasion, a Royal Commission proposed additional land fortifications and ironclad harbor-defense vessels. At the same time, artillerists were developing guns that could pierce eight-inch armor plates and destroy any ironclad.

Naval protection of British possessions by Milne's squadron, however, would not resolve the major problem of defense in the Western Hemisphere—the protection of Canada from a land invasion by American troops. The long frontier from the Great Lakes to the

Atlantic lay open. Canada's poor roads and water routes, too close to the border, were weakened by an intricate American network of roads, railways, and canals that seemed to converge on the boundary. When London officials had planned the defense of Canada after the War of 1812, they allotted two armies of 5,000 regulars each to defeat an invading force of 8,000 but by the summer of 1861 an expected invasion army of 50,000 to 200,000 would encounter only 4,300 British regulars (2,200 in Canada, the rest in the Maritime Provinces) and 5,000 volunteers, whose "military ardour exhibited itself only on gala days and in drawing pay." They had available only 7,000 Enfield rifles and 10,000 antiquated muskets. The Great Lakes positions could be reinforced by sending small wooden vessels loaded with soldiers up the St. Lawrence River and through a set of canals, but such passages were too easy to interdict and were frozen solid in the winter. Since no British gunboats could pass American batteries on the St. Lawrence to reach the Great Lakes, the U.S.S. *Michigan* remained secure as the only war vessel on the Great Lakes; control would fall to the Americans. The Canadian frontier was "less an obstacle than an invitation to attack." Why, then, did the British government worry about territory that could not be defended and had been considered since 1815 "a millstone round our necks . . . scarcely worth the expense"? The conquest of Canada, Palmerston declared, would be "a heavy blow to the reputation of England both for sagacity and strength," and such a blow must have seemed impermissible in view of France's burgeoning navy and estimated 900,000-man army.[27]

The difference of opinion in the British cabinet over sending reinforcements to Canada depended on the extent to which each member feared Seward or, rather, placed the most credence in Lyons's dispatches. Russell, Palmerston, and Newcastle advocated strengthening defense; others, despite their low opinion of the "vapouring, blustering, ignorant" Seward, doubted that he would be so rash as to attack Canada in the midst of a civil war. The prime minister found Lyons's information "very unpleasant," and did not think it "at all unlikely that either from foolish and uncalculating arrogance and self-sufficiency or from . . . Calculation Mr. Seward may bring on a Quarrel with us." Although Russell doubted that the United States would attack Canada, he did favor quietly sending three battalions to the provinces to deter irritating conduct. Palmerston perceived the battalions more as a foundation upon which to build an army of militiamen and volunteers. Newcastle agreed that Seward's "unscrupulous and bullying conduct" posed a danger, and that only a "bold front and a show of preparation" would prevent attack. The

HOW THEY WENT TO TAKE CANADA.
" For the outrage offered in the Queen's Proclamation, the United States will possess itself of Canada."—New York Herald.

Courtesy of *Punch*

time of greatest threat, he and many others believed, would occur at the close of the war when politicians might dispatch to Canada the swollen regular army, "composed of the scum of all nations— Germans—Irish and others who fear neither God nor man—who are imbued with hatred of all Government and whose aspirations are for a 'Red Republic.' " Nevertheless, Newcastle argued that the evaluation of Seward's outrageous actions must take into account the "hyper-American use of the policy of bully and bluster."[28] Argyll, Lewis, Chancellor of the Exchequer William E. Gladstone, and First Lord of the Admiralty the Duke of Somerset agreed with Newcastle's evaluation and opposed rushing into preparations for war.

Debate ran through the summer and into October, and ultimately resulted in a policy of token reinforcement. In May and June of 1861, three infantry battalions, a field battery of artillery, and 8,000 rifles with ammunition were sent to Canada. The first group crossed the ocean without fanfare, but the second contingent—consisting of more than 2,000 officers and men, almost 500 women and children, and scores of horses and assorted supplies—was loaded on the largest ship afloat, the 700-foot merchantman *Great Eastern*, which was five times bigger than any other vessel. A money loser since her maiden voyage a year earlier, she had a voracious appetite for coal, which the government could afford for only one charter. On the voyage to Canada, her thirty-year-old captain drove her as if pursued by the "Flying Dutchman," slowing for neither icebergs nor a Cunard liner, and crossed the Atlantic in a record eight days and six hours. After remaining two days in Quebec to disgorge passengers and cargo, the ship dropped down to New York where over 140,000 people paid a dollar each to tour one of the world's modern wonders.[29]

The *Great Eastern*'s voyage was an impressive display of speed and daring, the sort that appealed to the imperial crowd, but more cautious members of Parliament questioned the sending of troops in "hot haste in a very ostentatious manner" and worried that the United States would interpret it to mean war. The Foreign Office naturally did not mean to provoke a war crisis, and carefully explained the movement to Adams when the American minister came calling. It was, Russell said, only a "proper measure of precaution" since few soldiers were stationed in British North America, and the United States "might do something"; that "something" had already been indicated by the *Peerless* and Ashmun incidents, not to mention certain projects being fomented by the New York Irish. Refusing to be unduly alarmed by the matter, Adams rejoiced that Anglo–American relations were "gradually returning to a more friendly condition." Although Adams anticipated better times ahead, by July the British prime minister, troubled by Lyons's latest dispatches, was becoming more apprehensive; he began to argue that before ice blocked the rivers, the government should raise its Canadian forces to not less than 10,000 men complemented by artillery, because "our dear friend & ally at the Tuileries" would not help if Britain were "singled out for attack."[30] But the cabinet did not agree with Palmerston on additional reinforcements until news of the *Trent* incident reached London, and then Canadian defense forces increased rapidly.

Palmerston and other bulldog officials always felt that an inverse relationship existed between British preparedness and American bluster, that the sending of troops had a "wholesome effect" on the tone and temper of men "who have no sense of Honor and who are swayed by the Passions of irresponsible masses." They earnestly believed that one could never be too careful when dealing with the United States because it was "quite impossible for European Ingenuity to foresee the Countless Tricks and subtleties upon which the North Americans might contrive to pick a quarrel with us if they wished or thought it for their advantage to do so."[31]

Great Britain's relations with the United States, troubled for months by alarms and diversions, received another blow in early August when news arrived of the Union debacle at the battle of Bull Run on July 21. The London *Times* description of the panic-stricken retreat of Northern soldiers did much to inflame anti-British passions throughout the North. The British sarcastically dubbed the battle "Yankees' Run" and "the Bull's Run Races," and *Punch*, a popular magazine, published the satirical verse:

> An English Bull's run calls aloud to beware
> Of his horns, ever prompt to assail,
> But a Yankee Bull's Run is another affair;
> And creates most alarm by its tail.

Confederate commissioners in London chose this opportunity to petition Russell for recognition of Southern independence, but the cabinet would not depart from its policy of nonrecognition. Unaware of the rebel overture and the British denial, the American legation saw little to cheer. Adams found that Bull Run drastically changed public opinion in Britain; division of the Union was now regarded as a fait accompli. The British people, he said, having "little mercy for weakness physical or moral," were pleased with Union misfortunes and believed that since the North would never subjugate the Confederacy, "the only thing to do is to recognize the necessity of a new government."[32]

In late August, Adams informed Russell that, after months of negotiation, the United States had decided not to sign the Declaration of Paris, an instrument designed to protect the rights of neutrals, and based on principles advocated by the United States as far back as the American Revolution. The State Department would not agree to the provision abolishing privateers unless all private property not contraband of war was exempt from capture. Russell regarded this action as new evidence of Union perfidy; he commented bitterly to Palmerston: "It all looks as if a trap had been prepared. And I am not sure that Seward, when he finds we will not walk into it will not blow up the coals again as a last measure to maintain himself." Russell then recommended strengthening Milne's Bermuda squadron.[33]

Russell's unease increased when he learned a few days later that the United States wanted to expel a British consul for engaging in unneutral conduct while stationed in the South. The origins of this incident lay in the period of uncertainty of May 1861, when Britain had issued the proclamation of neutrality and sought additional means to shield British commerce from the ravages of privateers. When Russell had instructed Lyons on May 18 to work for Union adherence to the Declaration of Paris, he had also asked him to initiate discreet talks with the Confederate government on the same subject. Russell then suddenly withdrew the order, but Lyons had already asked the consul in Charleston, Robert Bunch, to handle the matter. A veteran of seventeen years in the foreign service, the senior British consul in the Southern states had been serving as a middleman between the Confederate government and the Foreign Office for some time before receiving Lyons's request. Although the British minister had told Bunch to discuss this issue only through the governor of South Carolina, Francis W. Pickens, Bunch could not reach him and instead consulted a respected lawyer and former diplomat, William Henry Trescott, who eventually made contact with Jefferson Davis. The Confederate president would have preferred that the British government negotiate with Southern envoys in London (an implicit recognition of the Confederacy), but agreed to submit the question to Congress for consideration. The Confederate Congress accepted the Declaration of Paris on August 13, excepting only Article I, the provision abolishing privateers.[34]

There the matter might have rested had a freak accident not occurred. The day after the Confederate Congress accepted the declaration, secret service agents in New York City arrested an ex-British merchant and naturalized American, Robert Mure, as he was preparing to board a ship for Liverpool carrying a sealed bag from Bunch to the Foreign Office. It contained about two hundred private letters, one of which claimed that the consul had taken the first step toward Southern recognition. The American government demanded Bunch's recall, charging him with conducting an illegal negotiation with the Confederacy, issuing an irregular passport to Mure, and allowing Mure to carry enemy letters. Russell would not recall Bunch for obeying orders. He reassured the State Department through Minister Adams that "Her Majesty's government have not recognized and are not prepared to recognize the so-called Confederate States as a separate and independent State," but would continue to treat them as a belligerent. It bothered him that Seward had not also demanded the recall of the French consul in Charleston, Belligny de Saint-Croix, who had cooperated with Bunch in the negotiations. But Belligny, unlike Bunch, had not discussed the matter with private citizens or tried to evade the newly introduced American passport system. Seward would have ignored even the British consul's role in the affair, in keeping with his policy of the "averted glance," had Bunch not become involved with Mure, a situation impossible to overlook. Although the State Department revoked Bunch's exequatur, the consul stalled his departure until February 1863, hoping in vain that Seward would relent.[35]

The British government viewed the Bunch affair as one more indication of the Lincoln administration's desire to manufacture an excuse for war. Lord Russell was not appeased when Lyons wrote that Seward had apologized for the dismissal of Bunch, and seemed to be "taxing his ingenuity" to avoid a quarrel with Britain and simultaneously remain on good terms with violent partisans. Russell did not attach much importance to the explanation, because he believed that Seward was so slippery he might change his tone by the next session of Congress in December. Regarding Bunch's dismissal as a perfect example of Seward as a "bully & coward," Russell tended to agree with Undersecretary Hammond that Seward was determined to "pick a quarrel" and break diplomatic relations. "I scarcely know how to deal with such a man," he told Palmerston. The incident convinced both Russell and Palmerston that they should send more troops to Canada and further strengthen Admiral Milne's squadron; they saw the Americans as a "swaggering bullying set of men, and the mere knowledge or belief that we are vulnerable in Canada might lead them to venture out of their Depth" on almost any matter under discussion. But there were more serious matters at stake than the security of British possessions. No man, Palmerston said, blasting economizers like Gladstone, "with half an Eye in his Head, or half an Idea in his Brain could fail to perceive what a lowering of the Position of England in the world would follow the Conquest of our North American provinces by the north americans, especially after the Bulls Run Races."[36]

The rest of the cabinet opposed sending additional reinforcements. Although everyone regarded Seward as "the very impersonation of all that is most violent & arrogant in the American Character," and agreed that he and his colleagues were "disposed to quarrel with us at any *convenient* moment," no one but Russell and Palmerston viewed the Bunch affair as a harbinger of war. Majority opinion held that the United States would have to concentrate all its attention on defeating the South, and could not afford to "divert all their warlike tendencies to Canada during the next 7 or 8 months." Canada was safe until spring unless the Union army chose to attack in the winter, repeating the horrors that befell Napoleon's invasion of Russia. The entire cabinet, except for Palmerston and Russell, believed that the present body of soldiers in Canada adequately demonstrated that England intended to protect it, that enough troops to defeat a strong invasion force could not be shipped before winter, and that sending any more might frighten the Americans into launching a preemptive attack. Neither the opinions of the prime minister and foreign secretary, nor pleas from Canada for an additional 100,000 stand of arms and artillery, moved the War Department or the Colonial Office. The London *Times* ably summarized the views of most cabinet officers when it lamented, "We can sweep the Federal fleet from the seas, we can blockade the Atlantic cities; but we cannot garrison and hold 350,000 square miles of country."[37] The Canadians were on their own until May.

The Bunch affair, as Henry Adams observed, was certainly "a pretty to-do," but it was not the war crisis imagined by Palmerston and Russell. Anglo–American relations had been rather calm since June; so calm, in fact, that at the height of the controversy over Bunch's activities, the American minister had reported that popular feeling, which fluctuated with news from America, had reverted nearly to the favorable condition existing before Bull Run. The policy of neutrality seemed to have gained wide support, despite efforts to tilt opinion in favor of the Confederacy and to represent Americans as being anti-British.[38]

Just as the ill feelings generated by the Bunch affair began to subside, Seward raised them again by publishing a circular on October 14 addressed to the governors of states on the eastern seaboard and the Great Lakes. Secessionists were trying to involve Europe in a war with the United States, Seward wrote, and, although prospects were less serious than at any other time, he recommended that ports and harbors on the ocean and the Great Lakes be put in a condition of complete defense. The circular's message, and the manner in which it was issued, aroused criticism on both sides of the Atlantic. The Philadelphia *Inquirer* called the "sudden and public" method of warning the governors a "grave error." If the frontier really stood in danger, *Leslie's Illustrated Newspaper* declared, then authorities should have been told quietly, not through "an ill-considered but characteristic piece of humbug and clap-trap." The London *Times*, dismissing it as an attempt to make political capital, sneered that Seward could have chosen a better way to make a quarrel.[39]

The secretary's motives for issuing the circular were not clear. Perhaps he had meant to warn London that the United States had noted Canadian reinforcements and the strengthening of Milne's squadron, and did not intend to be caught off guard, especially after the London *Times* had suggested that more soldiers were on the way.

The New York *Times* speculated that the circular had been aimed at France, Spain, and England, who were preparing to invade Mexico on a debt-collecting expedition. When the French minister, Henri Mercier, appeared at the State Department to discuss another matter, Seward commented that the United States would "resist to the last gasp any attempt of the European powers to interfere" in the contest for cotton or for any other reason. His recent circular, he said, was fair warning that the country "would be ready to resist any attempt to dictate to it." After listening to Mercier's account of the interview and hearing bewildered Americans speculate on the circular, Lord Lyons decided that the secretary probably wanted "to convey an impression that the Government was ready to act with vigour towards Europe"; perhaps, Lyons suggested, it was no more than a show of energy by Seward to protect "his personal position in the American political world" and to pacify popular displeasure over the proposed European foray against Mexico.[40] Whatever Seward's purpose for issuing the port circular, he succeeded in stirring up another tempest in Anglo–American relations.

The British cabinet, divided in its counsels, scarcely knew what to make of the Lincoln administration and its erratic secretary of state. Union forces so far had been unable to defeat rebel armies, and the blockade had proved ineffective; nevertheless, the United States government conducted foreign policy as if no nation, or nations, would stand against it. With the world's largest navy and the support of France, Britain should have felt secure. But the British expected almost daily an American declaration of war or, at least, a suspension of diplomatic relations. Each government mistrusted the other. The United States was convinced it had caught England trying to recognize Southern independence. England, fearful of a Union move against Canada, helped to create that impression by reinforcing the North American fleet under Milne "in hot haste" and fortifying the border. Prime Minister Palmerston had adopted a fatalistic view of relations with the United States. "The only thing to do," he told Russell, "seems to be to lie on our oars and to give no Pretext to the Washingtonians to Quarrel with us, while on the other Hand, we maintain our Rights and those of our Fellow-Countrymen."[41]

5.

Outrage on the British Flag

ANGLO-AMERICAN RELATIONS HAD FRAYED by November 1861, and the chances of improvement became more remote with each passing day. The two governments, regardless of the misconceptions that each harbored, did not deliberately antagonize each other. Despite all the alarm of the previous summer—threat of retaliation, shipment of troops, fortification of borders—Britain and the United States had managed to work out, or ignore, most of their major differences. None contained the peculiar mixture of ingredients necessary for brewing a war. Since the American Revolution, relations between the nations had deteriorated to open hostility only once—in June 1812, when the United States declared war over British failure to respect neutral rights. Although clashes had occurred over trade with the British West Indies, disputes over the Oregon and Maine boundaries, and control of Central America, neither government had considered such differences violations of vital interests. In the fall of 1861 events were conspiring to end this situation.

Following the Bunch incident, and even before its conclusion, new trouble threatened a rupture in diplomatic relations. About two weeks before Secretary Seward revoked Bunch's exequatur, Mason and Slidell sailed for Europe from Charleston, the site of the British consul's alleged misdeed. The British government learned of the departure in mid-October, and expected the envoys to arrive shortly

94

thereafter. The possibility existed that Mason and Slidell would not reach their destination; according to reports, an American warship was waiting at Southampton to intercept them.

The information available to British officials was partly correct, but exaggerated. Union officers had ordered three warships—the *Curlew*, the *Connecticut*, and the *James Adger*—to pursue the C.S.S. *Nashville*, the ship on which they believed Mason and Slidell had taken passage, but only the schooner *James Adger*, Captain John B. Marchand commanding, had instructions to follow the *Nashville* across the Atlantic. The eight-gun *Adger*, a wooden sidewheel steamer with three masts, was not much of a warship; it had once served on the passenger run between Charleston and New York. After leaving New York on October 16, the *Adger* was tossed by gales on the Newfoundland banks and forced to put in at Queenstown on October 30 to take on coal. Marchand cruised a few days off the Breton coast before running for Falmouth to make repairs and acquire more coal. When the Union warship reached Southampton on November 6, Marchand learned that Mason and Slidell had landed in Cuba. The next day, he went to the legation in London to seek information. Although Adams could not help, the minister told Marchand that his instructions justified remaining overseas to capture such privateers as the *Gladiator*, a screw steamer recently equipped in London as an arms-carrying blockade-runner, which had departed that day for Bermuda or Nassau with hundreds of cases of rifles, cannon, and munitions. Captain Marchand did not interpret his orders that broadly and sailed the *Adger* home a few weeks later; therefore, he missed the *Nashville*, which burned the American ship *Harvey Birch* off the English coast.[1]

Marchand's inquiries and mission did not pass unnoticed by the Palmerston government, which tended to exaggerate the importance of the *Adger*. Although the cabinet had learned of Mason and Slidell on October 15, no one worried about the Confederates' capture until the *Adger* steamed into Southampton. Its arrival, officials reasoned, was not coincidental. Having suspected for over a week that the Southern agents might board a West Indian mail ship at Havana for the last leg of their voyage, and aware of three Federal warships pursuing the *Nashville*, Foreign Office personnel guessed that one of the vessels was the *Adger*, coaled and ready for sea. They feared that Marchand, having missed the *Nashville*, would apprehend Mason and Slidell before they entered British waters.[2]

England had not acquired an empire by letting other nations seize the initiative, and the Palmerston government had no intention of doing so now. Rather than wait for an incident, the prime minister asked Hammond to study the hypothetical situation of an attack by the

Adger on the West Indian packet. In a message to Crown law officers on November 9, Hammond requested advice on the right of an American warship to halt and board the vessel; examine papers and open mail bags; remove Mason and Slidell or seize their credentials, instructions, and dispatches; or put a prize crew on board. He asked if a British warship would be justified in preventing her capture. Meanwhile, in case the law officers decided that the Federal warship had a right to search the steamer, Hammond suggested to Palmerston that the government circumvent such action either by stopping the vessel at Cork to take off passengers and mail, or by escorting her up the Channel.[3]

During the American Civil War, the most important duty of the law officers in London was to advise the Crown on international legal questions arising from that conflict. A standard, simple procedure guided officials. The department seeking advice on a particular subject usually sent the law officers copies of dispatches, letters, and other related documents, with a cover letter asking for a legal opinion. Rarely, as in Hammond's query on the West Indian mail packet, did a department "define or limit the points on which advice was wanted," or attempt to separate questions of policy from questions of law. The law officers, in turn, based their opinions on British and American practice in former wars, decisions by their courts, and historical (rather than *theoretical*) treatises on international law.[4] The government always seemed to want an opinion immediately.

While law officers studied the questions posed by Hammond, the cabinet assembled for several hours on Tuesday morning, November 11, to decide what they could "properly do" about the cruiser at Southampton. The meeting was attended by Palmerston; Lord Chancellor Richard Bethell; Home Secretary Sir George Grey; First Lord of the Admiralty Somerset; and Dr. Stephen Lushington, judge of the High Court of the Admiralty. Hammond substituted for Russell, who was ill with a severe cold. Informality prevailed as the group sat around a large table and thrashed out the issues. Although Palmerston and Russell disliked consulting the cabinet on foreign policy, the prime minister showed no sign of irritation. Speculating on the same questions that had occurred to Hammond, the cabinet debated whether the *James Adger* would be acting within a belligerent's rights by stopping and searching the mail steamer, whether it could seize Mason and Slidell without capturing the ship, and whether it would be legal and proper for a British warship to intervene.[5]

All these matters were highly technical, and although several cabinet members had studied law, they deferred to Lushington and

Bethell. Almost eighty years of age, Lushington had served as an Admiralty judge for twenty-three years, during which he had extended the court's jurisdiction, preserved the independence of the Admiralty, and achieved an eminence second only to the greatest Admiralty jurist in English history, Lord Stowell. An ardent reformer and supporter of the church and a forceful speaker in Parliament, he possessed a reputation for decisions seldom appealed and rarely reversed, yet his worst fault was judicial inconsistency. Lord Chancellor Bethell (titled Lord Westbury), although by rank the highest judicial officer of the Crown, was less distinguished than Lushington; a "dapper little man," he walked like a bird, "with a slight poising and repoising of the head, which kept time with the motion of the feet." Specialists in law believed that Bethell was inclined to brush aside judicial opinion; rely on common sense; and reach decisions by, if anything, "a few elementary rules of law"—a phrase he was fond of using when about to reverse a predecessor. Bethell enjoyed telling the government when it erred. Once asked for an opinion on British retaliation for the *Arrow* incident in China, he said the government was wrong in wanting to defend the ship, and warned of arguments the opposition might use in Commons. "We all thought it very evident," Argyll recalled, "that, were it not for his office, it would give him immense pleasure to take the part of leading counsel against us."[6] During discussion of the *James Adger*, Lushington and Bethell agreed on the important points, and Bethell explained them to the cabinet.

Bethell lived up to his reputation as a devil's advocate in handling the *Adger* problem. Speaking slowly, pronouncing each syllable as if a separate word, he set out the legal points with an unusual regard for precedent. According to principles of international law established by Lord Stowell and "practiced and enforced by us," he told the cabinet with a slightly irritable voice, a belligerent could stop and search any neutral vessel that was not a warship. If an American cruiser found a mail steamer on the high seas and suspected her of carrying not only commissioners but enemy dispatches, it might stop and search the packet and either take out the commissioners, their dispatches and credentials, or seize the packet and carry her to New York for adjudication. In such a case, Bethell and Lushington advised the government not to allow a British warship to intervene.[7]

Palmerston nodded, remarking only that if the packet "is to be stopped searched and captured it is better that this should not be done in the Presence of a non interfering English ship of war." The cabinet determined "to do no more than order the *Phaeton* frigate to drop down to Yarmouth Roads and watch the proceedings of the American

within our three-mile limit of territorial jursidiction, and to prevent
her from exercising within that limit those rights which we cannot
dispute as to belong to her beyond that limit." The mighty Royal
Navy, it appeared, could do nothing to prevent the mail packet from
being molested; this frustrating position irritated Palmerston, whose
first impulse was "always to move fleets and to threaten our opponents, sometimes on trivial occasions, on the details of which he
had not fully informed himself by careful reading."[8] He soon received
a legal opinion more to his liking.

The Crown law officers had been well aware of the seriousness
with which the government viewed the alleged mission of the *James
Adger*, and of the consequences that might result from their opinion.
Therefore, they had spent the better part of three days pondering the
questions posed by Hammond before they advised Palmerston on
November 12. Queen's Advocate John D. Harding, Attorney General
Sir William Atherton, and Solicitor General Sir Roundell Palmer
agreed with Bethell and Lushington on many small points, but did not
agree with the two men on whether Mason and Slidell could be taken
off the ship. The rights of belligerents established under maritime law
allowed the Union warship to halt and board the mail steamer and examine papers and the contents of general mail bags; the only papers
they were forbidden to violate were those contained "in any Bag or
Packet addressed to any officer of Her Majesty's Government." If the
Americans discovered enemy dispatches or other evidence proving the
West Indian steamer had violated British neutrality, they could put a
prize crew on board and take her to a United States port for adjudication. But, the law officers emphasized, the Union captain could *not*
remove Mason and Slidell, "leaving the ship to pursue her voyage."
Certain conditions, they said, would justify the mail packet and cargo
being conveyed to a Federal port; but, in the interest of humanity, the
warship "might, however, and, in our opinion, ought, under the circumstances, to put onshore at some convenient Port Passengers and
their baggage not being contraband of war." A British warship would
not be justified in preventing the search and seizure, because the case
was "not one of such character as to justify resistance by force."
Whether documents found on board constituted contraband of war,
or whether they were "protected either by the nature of the con-
veyance or by the character of the persons to whom they [were] addressed," were, they admitted, questions unresolved in international
law and dependent on the decision of the captor's prize court.[9]

The law officers presented an interesting dilemma. The British
government now had two legal opinions agreeing that an American

warship, presumably the *James Adger*, could stop and search the mail streamer and, if she carried enemy dispatches, seize her, put a prize crew on board, and carry her to an American port. Opinions differed on whether the Americans could remove Confederate diplomats and convey them to the United States. Historians disagree as to what Bethell and Lushington really said in cabinet; most authors have accepted James P. Baxter's hypothesis that Palmerston misunderstood them, because, so the theory goes, they would not have sanctioned removal.[10] However, it is unlikely that the prime minister would have erred on so critical a point. Lushington and Bethell undoubtedly based their oral opinion on Britain's own record of removing sailors from neutral ships during the French Revolution and Napoleonic Wars. When Palmerston ignored their advice and based government policy on the written opinion of the law officers, he was making the correct, not expedient, decision. The mere fact that Bethell and Lushington were also attorneys did not place them on an advisory level equal to the law officers, even though some historians, thinking that the law speaks for itself and that lawyers can agree on its interpretation, have insisted that Palmerston, rather than Bethell and Lushington, made a mistake. The important point is that Harding, Atherton, and Palmer never wavered in their conviction that Mason and Slidell could not be removed from the mail packet, and it was their opinion that formed the basis of policy toward the *Trent* violation.

Having secured a legal opinion against seizure of the commissioners, the British government turned to diplomacy with Minister Adams, hoping that he would discourage the *Adger*'s captain from performing his alleged mission. The American diplomat looked out his bedroom window on the morning after the cabinet meeting, November 12, to see London shrouded in fog. He had visited the Russian Embassy the previous evening, and expected to spend the day working on routine business; however, when he arrived at the legation, he found a note from Palmerston requesting "a few minutes conversation . . . today at any time between one and two." Shortly after lunch Adams rode off in a carriage to Cambridge House, 94 Picadilly, the prime minister's London address. One wonders what passed through Adams's mind as he was met at the door and escorted into the presence of the man who Victor Hugo once said "belonged a little to history, but much more to fiction."[11]

Palmerston had always shown a flair for the dramatic. Despite a reputation for being a dandy in his youth, he had been a lord of the Admiralty at twenty-three and secretary at war shortly thereafter; subsequently, as foreign secretary in two cabinets, he acquired

Lord Palmerston
Courtesy of the Massachusetts Historical Society

notoriety as a warmonger and international busybody. His provocative instructions to British envoys earned him the nickname
"Firebrand," and a piece of German doggerel illustrates the point:

> If the Devil has a son
> Then he's surely Palmerston.

Internationally, Palmerston was disliked for the same traits that
endeared him to the English, who, as Gladstone noted, always had "a
sneaking kindness for a lord." A supreme nationalist, he considered
Britain's interests paramount, avoided ties with any nation, and
always worked to maintain a balance of power. "We have no natural
enemies—no perpetual friends," he said, keeping an eye on France,
Russia, and the United States. Morality had no place in his foreign
policy. He was the prime minister who won the Crimean War; he was
the diplomat who thought warships, cannon, and engineers made the
best peacemakers. In many ways his attitudes resembled those of his
American nemesis, Seward, and neither man was as dangerous as

foreigners seemed to think. But taken together, Palmerston and Russell constituted a formidable pair in British foreign policy—Robin Hood and Little John, according to the wife of George Lewis; "those two dreadful old men" to Queen Victoria. The American minister faced no easy task in dealing with them, singly or together.[12]

Palmerston received Adams alone in the library and launched into a monologue interlarded with *hums* and *ers, ohs,* and *ahs,* pausing frequently to keep his false teeth from falling out. A United States warship, the *James Adger,* he said, had stopped at Southampton to take on coal and supplies, after which the captain had gotten very drunk on brandy and moved his vessel down to the river's mouth as if to sail. It appeared that he might have orders to watch for the West Indian steamer expected November 14, and meant to remove Mason and Slidell. The prime minister would not speculate on America's right to such an act, leaving that exercise to legal experts, but he did think it would be "highly inexpedient in every way [Palmerston] could view it," especially since one or two more Confederates in Britain would hardly "produce any change in the policy already adopted." Seizure would offer no "compensating advantage" and would "occasion more prejudice than it would do good."[13]

Adams interrupted Palmerston when the latter turned to another topic. He privately felt that the prime minister "had taken for granted" the American intention, and that the prime minister lacked confidence in "our principles of action" because he had tried to convince Adams of the act's inexpediency rather than impropriety. Adams asked Palmerston on what he based his belief that Marchand intended to seize Mason and Slidell. Slightly surprised, Palmerston replied it was his "impression derived from the fact of the arrival of the U.S. steamer just now and the coincidence of her preparation to start again within the period assigned for the approach of the gentlemen in the West India steamer." Adams answered that he had read Marchand's orders, and they did not mention interference with any British vessel; rather, they directed capture of the *Nashville,* which the captain had missed, and he was now refitting his ship for the return voyage. The minister said he had urged Marchand to seize the blockade-runner *Gladiator,* which had sailed from London carrying arms for the Confederacy under the British flag "with scarcely any pretense of concealment," if Marchand were to find her beyond national jurisdiction. Would not this be all right? To seize the *Gladiator,* Palmerston remarked, would be "a delicate business." Regarding the half-hour session as productive, the prime minister thought that Adams had offered a "very satisfactory explanation" for the presence of the *Adger.*[14] The cabinet, it seemed, had overreacted and troubled the law officers for an opinion of a situation that now appeared more hypothetical than ever.

While the meeting may have temporarily satisfied Palmerston, it did not please Adams; the minister left Cambridge House with a low opinion of his host, or so one might conclude by reading a private appraisal of the talk written some years later. Palmerston's attitude had irritated him. Puzzled by the report of Marchand being drunk, Adams investigated, and discovered it a fabrication by the people of Southampton. He decided that Palmerston's statement was "prompted by the anxiety of the rebel emissaries here who from a dread of such a [sic] insult instigated their friends . . . to make these slanderous representations to him."[15]

Actually Palmerston had not meant to be abrupt. He could have allowed the matter to drift until Russell recovered from his cold, but by then Marchand might have acted, forcing the British government to protest or retaliate. Although he had received Adams's remarks with apparent equanimity, he continued to have doubts about the mission of the Union warship, and communicated them to his colleagues. Russell, in particular, became concerned; he later wrote to Lyons that, although Adams may have been sincere, "we are not quite out of the wood."[16] His fears were confirmed a fortnight later, when the merchant ship *La Plata* arrived, with word of the Confederate envoys' capture.

Life in the American legation had been singularly depressing since the proclamation of British neutrality in May. The Adams family had discovered that the position of minister did not guarantee entry into London society, and may have been a barrier. They had not regretted their isolation during the early summer months, because the regularity of Anglo-American disagreement made for strained conversation at any party. By August, with the lessening of tension, the Adamses began to look for entertainment, and discovered that London generally shut down during the hot season; Parliament, public officials, social butterflies, royalty, and the fashionable set all fled the city, and resorts, libraries, galleries, and theaters closed. Whole blocks lost their residents, throngs of carriages no longer clattered through the cobblestone squares, and shuttered windows looked down on empty streets.[17]

The calm ended with the Bunch incident. Business returned to normal for the legation as the London *Times* and other papers fired editorial broadsides, and the American minister once again became a familiar sight at the Foreign Office. The legation staff, sensitive to public criticism, expected the British government to sever diplomatic relations and perhaps declare war any day. In an attempt to reduce tension, Adams offered at the Lord Mayor's annual banquet in early November some pacifying remarks concerning diplomacy, "one of the great inventions of modern times." In ancient ages, he said, quarrels between nations were followed by war, whereas in "modern times" negotiation "always precedes war, and very often averts it." His purpose, Adams declared to resounding cheers, was to "continue and perpetuate the friendly relations" between Britain and the United States. After hearing his "highly complimentary" speech, the London *Times* wished that "America could speak more frequently to us by the mouth of her Minister, and never at all in the tone common to her press and her Secretary of State."[18]

But shortly after noon on November 27, the legation received a telegram from Captain Britton, confirmed by Reuter's News Agency, that according to the captain of *La Plata*, recently docked at Southampton, a Union warship had removed Mason and Slidell from the *Trent*. The legation's three secretaries "broke into shouts of delight." They were "glad to face the end," Henry Adams wrote. "They saw it and cheered it! Since England was waiting only for its moment to strike, they were eager to strike first." But the dour assistant secretary of legation, Benjamin Moran, considered the consequences and doubted that any advantage had accrued to the North, noting in his diary that "the act will do more for the Southerners than ten victories, for it touches John Bull's honor, and the honor of his flag."[19]

The American minister was out of town, having left two days earlier to visit Fryston Hall in Yorkshire, the house of the poet and member of Parliament, Richard Monckton Milnes, who, despite pro-Union sympathy, could "see no gleam of good in anything American." On the third day of the visit they had ridden out in the rain to inspect the ruins of Pontefract Castle, the murder scene of Richard II. As Adams walked through the wicket gate he heard a clatter of hooves. The rider sprang from the saddle and produced a telegram from Moran: "Mason and Slidell have been taken forcibly from British steamer *Trent* by the U.S. ship *San Jacinto* in Bahama Channel." Turning to the others he said quietly, "I have got stirring news." The tidings reinforced the rain as a damper on further festivities, but although the minister "had little relish left for further diversion in the country," he declined an offer of immediate transport back to his office; London was the last place he wanted to be. At dinner he took his mind off the *Trent* by arguing United States tariff policies with some

Huddersfield manufacturers, but his wife felt miserable, sensing the other guests were "provoked at what had occurred, friendly as they were." The Adamses returned to London the next day, arriving about 6:00 P.M. at King's Cross Station.[20]

Wilkes's act had made the legation the center of unwelcome attention. When Moran went to mass at the French Chapel in King Street on the morning of November 28, members of the diplomatic corps asked him if Britain and the United States would go to war. He refused comment and after services hastily left for the legation, where he found John Bright, the liberal member of Parliament and friend of America, deploring the incident. A note arrived from Russell, requesting an interview with Adams at 2:00 P.M.; Moran drove to the Foreign Office to tell the undersecretary, Austen H. Layard ("Mr. Lie-Hard" to his political foes), that the minister could not keep the appointment. The legation was busy that day as American visitors milled about, throwing the place into turmoil. The incompetent first secretary, Charles L. Wilson, chattered with Henry Adams, and Moran thought they made some very indiscreet remarks to strangers about the *Trent* business.[21]

When news of the seizure broke on the exchanges, London funds fell 1 percent, the price of saltpeter rose, and at Lloyd's war risks of five guineas were demanded on vessels from New York. Troubled investors did not know whether to believe what they read, and consequently vacated their positions in railroad securities, driving down consols so steadily that a major firm intervened toward evening and bought enough to support the market. On the Liverpool exchange, where the American consul could not set foot because of insults,[22] someone posted a placard advertising a meeting at 3:00 P.M. in the cotton salesroom:

OUTRAGE ON THE BRITISH FLAG—THE SOUTHERN COMMISSIONERS FORCIBLY REMOVED FROM A BRITISH MAIL STEAMER.[23]

At the appointed hour a crowd filled the room, buzzing that Adams should be sent his passports, and ultimately approving a resolution calling on the government to "assert the dignity of the British flag by requiring prompt reparation for this outrage." Two men arose to condemn the meeting, urging the group to consider the matter "calmly and dispassionately" because it would be "impolitic and unjust" to push the government into a headlong course. A third man tried to reason along similar lines. Cooler heads eventually amended the resolution, striking out the phrase "by requiring prompt reparation for this outrage." The meeting disbanded, and afterwards many older merchants on the exchange said privately that it had been premature. An American consular official described Liverpool as more agitated than it had been when the Bank charter was suspended in the Panic of 1857, but he also reported that the indignation meeting did more good than harm, since every influential man disapproved of it.[24]

London crackled with anger. "The people are frantic with rage, and were the country polled," an American wrote Seward, "I fear 999 men out of 1,000 would declare for immediate war." He did not see how Palmerston could resist the pressure, because the opposition would topple him if he hesitated to defend British honor and had driven him from the office on other occasions for being less "Palmerstonian" than the people. Before the *Trent* incident, British public opinion afforded only slight sympathy for the South, but now support grew all over London; even the "staid and sober" men of the Reform Club reacted angrily to the news. A member of Parliament declared that, if the insult were not atoned for, he would recommend that the British flag "be torn into shreds and sent to Washington for the use of the Presidential water-closets." The consul in London told Seward that merchants "talk openly & speculate on the fortunes that will be made, with the Northern ports blockaded, Northern ships driven from the sea & Southern trade open." Diners in restaurants picked at their Yorkshire pudding and conversed only about the incident, in the "most violent" language. Late in the evening rumors circulated that Adams had been given his passports, and orders had been issued for seizure of American ships in British ports.[25]

Although excitement diminished over the next two days, financial indicators continued to fall and patriotic spirit rose as the public rallied around the Union Jack and proposed solutions. At Lloyd's a lower war risk of twenty shillings was being paid for vessels coming from New York. Consols dropped another 2 percent on the report that the government was ready to send large reinforcements to Canada. Several volunteer reserve units sent letters to their commanding officers: "we are ready to fulfill our engagement and protect the honour of our flag, our good Queen, and country, whenever called upon to do so." Letters urging war dominated Foreign Office mail. A popular view held that the United States was courting war so that it could abandon the South and make up the loss with Canada. Another view held that the Americans probably had a secret accord with France, since the Yankees were too smart to "go to war with us *for nothing.*" Others suggested that the government break the blockade or order warships on foreign stations to intercept and capture or destroy the *San Jacinto*. A Glasgow man proposed that the Channel fleet rendezvous at Bermuda, and that the government embargo war materials and consider recognizing the South, if France could be "induced to join us."[26]

It would be a mistake to calculate British public opinion on the basis of what appeared in newspapers, or to assume that the government worried about what "the man in the omnibus" thought. Newspapers were read principally by the educated classes and circulated in such public places as taverns, hotels, and coffeehouses. Serving more as the organs of parties and factions than as sources of information for the public, the papers had some effect on political opinion, but only negligible effect on cabinet officers. Such officials released information to select journals, notably the London *Times*, to manipulate the views of the so-called "Upper Ten Thousand." Historians who rely on the *Times* as a barometer of public opinion—who believe that "when the *Times* took snuff the rest of England sneezed"—are according it influence it never possessed in the 1860s, except among a small portion of the upper class. Although other newspapers exercised some influence without having access to government leaks, not one could be described as an index to popular sentiment.[27] Despite all limitations, the editorial opinions expressed in English newspapers offer a more representative view of Britain's reaction to the *Trent* crisis than do minutes and memoranda of the cabinet.

Typical of the moderately indignant view taken by the press toward the seizure was that expressed by the *Times*. Long before the *Trent* crisis, its editor, John T. Delane, had compromised his journal by a close connection with Palmerston, who passed word of policy in return for support, an arrangement that had led Prince Albert to mock the paper as "that worshiper of truth." The *Times*, which could not always be counted on to adhere to the government line, remained calm in the wake of the capture of Mason and Slidell and saw a paradox between British reaction and policy, for "we have ourselves established a system of International Law which now tells against us. In highhanded, and almost despotic manner, we have in former days claimed privileges over neutrals which have . . . banded all the maritime Powers of the world against us." Although precedents could be cited for the right of search, the *Times* felt that past wrongs should not rule the world, explaining: "We were fighting for existence, and we did in those days what we should neither do nor allow others to do, in these days." Jurists, not naval officers, should decide if the two Confederates were contraband. The *Times* warned that people should not overreact, even though they may "regard the act in the worst light, as a confirmation of the indications so long given by Mr. Seward of his desire to involve this country in a collision at any cost." The *Times* could not believe it was "the fixed determination of the Government of the Northern States to force a quarrel upon the Powers of Europe."[28] Without mentioning a word about sending the minister his passports or staging a military demonstration for the benefit of the United States, Delane's editorial contrasted with the loose talk in pubs and clubs.

The papers soon were reporting the Crown law officers favorable to the United States, and discussing the intricacies of international law and Anglo-American custom. The London *Star* declared Wilkes had acted "upon principles which have always been asserted by his own Government, frequently exercised by ours, and are probably inseparable from maritime warfare." The *Star* believed only the right of search, not seizure, was in question. The *Economist* predicted that the Federal government would defend the capture by claiming that Mason and Slidell were contraband of war and that the United States had merely imitated Britain's practice of impressment. It urged readers not to be swayed by error, declaring that "The honour of England is tarnished by the ill-treatment of our guests; the securing of our commerce is impaired by the violation of our vessel." The *Morning Post*, reportedly the organ of Palmerston, said the *San Jacinto* had a right to search the *Trent* and seize contraband of war, but the removal of four passengers who lacked official status was "not according to international law." The insult was most gratuitous and if it proved to be "unwarranted by the code of nations, it [would] not only be deeply felt, but duly resented." If British law officers were to rule the capture as legal and proper, they would have trouble persuading Britons to accept it, the Manchester *Guardian* predicted.[29]

Some journals saw Yankee devilry around every corner. The London *Standard* feared the outrage was "but one of a series of premeditated blows aimed at this country . . . to involve it in a war with the Northern States." It speculated that this was the last card Seward had to play, and that he meant to combine forces with the South to drive the British out of Canada. The *Times* agreed it was only "the last and most offensive" in a series of insults, and saw no reason why Britain should continue its rigid neutrality while British industry stagnated because of an ineffective blockade. Other papers refused to view the incident as part of a plot. Certain that no government would defend corsair practice, the London *Examiner* believed that Wilkes had removed the men on his own initiative and that Washington would repudiate him. The *Saturday Review* agreed that the act probably had not been committed to insult Britain, but even if it were legal, it remained "unnecessary, discourteous, and an exaggerated application of vexatious power." Although the *Star* decided that the American government had ordered the seizure, it saw no deliberate insult and no substantial wrong "because these Confederate Commissioners were to all serious intents belligerents sailing under a neutral flag." Moreover, the *Star* urged that it was time to revise policy concerning the rights of belligerents and neutrals.[30]

Not every part of the realm reacted angrily. In Ireland, people showed extravagant joy. Meetings sprouted, and the largest assembly, organized by moderate nationalists and chaired by the Celtic leader The O'Donoghue, was held in Dublin at the Rotunda on December 5. Placards covered the walls, declaring: "War between America and England—Sympathy with America. Ireland's opportunity." The assemblage cheered when speakers extolled American friendship and speculated on the likelihood of war. "God send it," someone yelled, and anyone who suggested that Washington surrender the diplomats was shouted down. The group resolved that Ireland could not be indifferent to war. But the Fenians and the the two rival nationalist organizations used the *Trent* episode in their battle for popular support; they cared little about American problems. Liberal and conservative Protestant unionists agreed that England would have to declare war if America did not atone for the insult. Other Dublin residents petitioned Russell to have the dispute arbitrated.[31] The British government paid little attention to the stir in Ireland because, although a majority of Irish sympathized with the United States, they would not necessarily act as fifth columnists in the event of war.

Underneath the newspaper opinions and popular outcry, there were few hard facts. The British government was desperate for accurate information, and Commander Williams, mail agent of the *Trent*, was the only official witness. He had raced to London from Southampton on a special train and spent hours with the Admiralty, with Layard at the Foreign Office, and with the prime minister. After the briefing, Palmerston wrote Layard that "It would be well that a search be made to see whether any similar case has ever happened by sea, and what cases have happened by land of Persons going on a diplomatic mission being seized on neutral Territory." Several cabinet members were out of town, and Palmerston had to wait for their return. In the meantime, he got in touch with Secretary for War Lewis to see if the Canadian militia had been sent the small arms and guns he had insisted on months ago.[32]

Feeling among political leaders both within and outside the government was running against the United States. Critics reiterated their suspicions regarding potential American aggression toward Canada, while skeptics began to have second thoughts. "There can be no doubt," Palmerston told Lewis, "that Seward is actuated in his Conduct towards us by the Belief that Canada is insufficiently defended; while he treats the French with great Respect because they have no vulnerable Point, but have a fleet which could do the Northerns mischief." Lewis did not think the American government would disavow Wilkes, but he contended that Britain should not be satisfied with anything but the surrender. "The present state of affairs," he replied to Palmerston, "seems to me to be inevitable war." Lord Clarendon, a former foreign secretary who maintained ties to the cabinet, had no doubt the outrage was "a deliberate and premeditated insult." Since the outbreak of the Civil War, Seward had been "trying to provoke us into a quarrel and finding that it could not be effected at Washington he has determined to compass it at sea." Although he abhorred war, he worried about the figure "we shall cut in the eyes of the world if we tamely submit to this outrage." The reaction of France had to be considered, but the government "ought not to show either too much or too little anxiety" about Napoleon.[33]

British leaders faced a tortuous decision. A mild reaction might embolden the United States and arouse French scorn, while a strong one might cause a war that would injure British commerce and drain treasury receipts designated for the naval race with France. Yet to Palmerston, the hazards of peace always seemed greater than the dangers of war. When he asked for advice from the foreign secretary, Russell replied, "The United States government are very dangerous people to run away from." At an informal meeting of cabinet members at Downing Street on the morning of November 28, the prime minister allegedly walked into the room, threw his hat on the table, and swore, "I don't know whether you are going to stand this, but I'll be damned if I do!"[34]

Wary of legal complications, Russell asked the law officers to comment on the *Trent* outrage. Harding, Atherton, and Palmer informed the government, in keeping with their previous opinion, that

"the conduct of the United States officer . . . was illegal and unjustifiable, by international law." Even though the *San Jacinto*
"assumed to act as a belligerent," the *Trent* "was not captured or carried into a Port of the United States for adjudication as Prize;
and . . . cannot be considered as having acted in breach of international law." Therefore, the government would "be justified in requiring reparation for the international wrong which has been on this occasion committed."[35]

Russell continued to move cautiously. Having raised one false
alarm about the Union warship *Adger* and been lectured by Adams, he
edged toward the problem of the *Trent* by seeking information from
the American minister before the cabinet meeting. Soon after returning to London, Adams was asked to come to the Foreign Office at
1:45 P.M. on the afternoon of November 29. The old building in
Downing Street was a dingy place with "a sort of crusted, char-
womanly look"; it was the only public department where employees
could smoke in the offices. In the anteroom Adams met the Russian
minister, Baron de Brunnow, "a tall man, with an intensely ugly but
very shrewd face." Brunnow expressed regret at the "misunderstanding" and offered his services, personal and official, in restoring
relations. Thanking him, Adams passed into Russell's office, and met
with Russell for only ten minutes; all the foreign secretary wanted to
know was whether Adams had information that would be useful at the
2:00 P.M. cabinet meeting. Unsure how much authority Wilkes
possessed, Adams said he knew no more than what he read in the
papers; then, at Russell's request, he repeated what he had said to
Palmerston two weeks earlier about Marchand's instructions. Adams
privately thought it was fortunate that the *Adger*'s presence at
Southampton had prepared the British government for another incident involving international law, but the situation looked ominous.
The minister returned to the legation feeling that "all opportunity for
further usefulness in my present capacity threatens to be soon at an
end," and told Moran they would probably not be there a month. "On
the whole," he confided to his diary, "I scarcely remember a day of
greater strain in my life."[36]

At the cabinet meeting that afternoon, the British officials reacted
angrily when the law officers and the Admiralty advocate, international law scholar Sir Robert Phillimore, told officials of the seizure's
illegality. Hammond regretted that the fleet on the Atlantic station
had not intercepted the *San Jacinto*. The Duke of Argyll viewed
Wilkes's act as "one of inconceivable arrogance and folly," and
despaired that a democratic government would ever acknowledge

Queen Victoria and Prince Albert
Courtesy of the Massachusetts Historical Society

itself as wrong. "I am all against submitting to any clear breach of International Law." Palmerston did not say much, but later described the seizure to Queen Victoria as a gross outrage and violation of international law. Doubting Mrs. Slidell's report that the *San Jacinto* had acted on its own, the prime minister suspected that the warship had communicated with New York prior to the seizure.[37]

Earlier, Palmerston might not have briefed the Queen and Prince Albert, now his cooperation mattered less; they had secured their own sources within the government to relay cabinet discussion. Encouraging dissent within Palmerston's administration, the Prince Consort differed constantly with the prime minister and took charge of organizing opposition to his policies. An important ally was Chancellor of the Exchequer Gladstone, whose clashes with Palmerston over defense expenditures had long interested politicians. Gladstone rode out to Windsor Castle for dinner that evening to report the cabinet proceedings; as usual, he irritated the Queen, who complained that "he speaks to me as if I were a public meeting." Gladstone reported that the cabinet had reached no decision, possibly because a government opponent, John Bright, had urged them to postpone action until Monday, December 2, by which time Adams might have word from Washington.[38]

But Gladstone had underestimated Palmerston's willingness to force the issue into the open. Shortly after the cabinet meeting, the law officers' decision had been leaked to the press, probably by Palmerston. The news instantly affected the stock market, with consols falling 1 percent below the previous day. In the afternoon they rallied, when buyers decided that the Cunard steamer due Sunday might bring an American disavowal. Wilkes, people said, was a secessionist who had tried to precipitate war, and it was rumored that Adams had stated that the Washington government could not have authorized the act. Adams thought he saw the government's hand in the *Times* leaders on November 29 and 30. The first, he believed, broke ground for a concession, but public anger influenced the second editorial, which disregarded precedents and appealed to authorities on the law. This "violent and arrogant" editorial of November 30, he believed, let loose the dogs of war. He was disgusted with the law officers for denying his government the right "to take out persons when they did not take papers and things." Great Britain, he rasped, would have been "less offended if the United States had insulted her a great deal more." He took a long walk in the evening, trying to lose his worries in the labyrinth of London streets.[39]

The cabinet's apprehensions increased with reports of large American purchases of saltpeter. The transactions were coincidental, in no way a prefiguration of war, but the British government had no way of knowing. At the outbreak of the Civil War, the War Department in Washington had less than 2,000 tons of saltpeter, a six-month supply dating from the Mexican War. American gunpowder manufacturers could secure some saltpeter in their own country, but had to buy most of it from India. Military need exceeded all projections and, by the fall of 1861, imports were becoming insufficient for gunpowder production. The diminishing supply of saltpeter, coupled with fear that sympathy for the Confederacy might cause England to abandon its cash-and-carry policy, led the navy to authorize Lammot Du Pont to sail for London in early November. Between November 19 and 23 he acquired all the saltpeter for sale in Britain, nearly 2,300 tons, and contracted for another 1,000 tons from India. Du Pont began loading his cargo at London, Liverpool, and Grennock on November 28, the day after the British government learned of the *Trent* incident.[40]

Du Pont's purchases, abnormally large, could not fail to attract attention. Palmerston heard about them on November 27, a few hours after *La Plata* docked at Southampton, when a Treasury agent reported that American authorities had purchased 3,000 tons in London that afternoon and arranged to ship out 1,000 the next day for New York. The agent asked, "Cannot Govt. by an order in Council stop these shipments of warlike stores?" Another agent notified him that the United States had purchased 2,000 tons in London and 1,000 in Liverpool, driving up the price by six shillings. This brought the total Union purchase to more than a year's supply, and the rapid purchase and shipment within three days looked "as if the Federal Government, having decided on a rupture with this country, was desirous of first laying in a supply." At the Foreign Office the purchases seemed more than coincidental. "I wish the saltpetre to be stopt," Russell informed Layard, "if it can be done by an order of the Treasury or the Customs." The next day, British police searched one of Du Pont's chartered vessels, the *Cornelius Grinnell*, and the dockmaster forbade her captain to take on any more saltpeter. The London *Times* told its readers that "the intention of offering an outrage to England . . . was the cause of the hasty despatch of this extraordinary order."[41]

American agents were also buying arms. Forced to compete with private individuals filling orders for the War Department and state governments, Union buyers had encountered obstacles in the purchase of first-class arms, unavailable at any price on the open market. Russell learned that a Sheffield arms manufacturer was handling an order for the American government for "*cast steel guns. 76 inches long & 10 inch bore.*" One of the firm's salesmen had returned on the last steamer from the United States with larger orders. Decrying these purchases and the shipment to the United States of 100,000 firearms designated as "hardware," the *Times* called for measures to "prevent this breach of neutrality in favour of the Northern belligerents."[42]

There were certain complexities about these arms and munitions purchases. A Foreign Office inquiry led the Queen's advocate, Harding, to offer the disturbing opinion that existing laws did not permit the government to ban exportation. The Foreign Enlistment Act of 1819 was "limited to enlistment of men or equipping or augmenting the force of Ships for the service of belligerents." The neutrality proclamation of May 13, he said, "does not forbid the exportation of anything."[43] Prohibition of contraband exports would have to be achieved through other means.

Evidence of massive Federal purchases continued to pour in from Treasury agents watching the major ports and, although some reports duplicated previous information, the prospective loss of critical war supplies worried officials. Palmerston probably decided after the cabinet meeting of November 29 to call another council the next afternoon. Since a war with the United States was possible, "would it not be an act of folly amounting to absolute Imbecillity to let those who may soon be our enemies . . . go on extracting from our warehouses and workshops the means to make war, against us?" There were also important political considerations. "If our men were shot down by Rifles made by us, and with gun Powder supplied by us," Palmerston shuddered, "should we not as a Government be laughed to scorn as unfit to conduct the affairs of the Country." An embargo would not only cripple the North's ability to make war, he told Russell, but "lessen the Probability of their risking a Rupture." It would be "a good political warning to Seward & C. of which they would not justly complain, but which would probably be understood." Palmerston either brought up the subject at the November 29 meeting (instead of waiting another day as planned), or—more likely—appealed to the Queen; by royal proclamation of November 29, the Crown (with the advice of the Privy Council) did "order and direct that . . . all gunpowder, saltpetre, nitrate of soda, and brimstone, shall be, and the same are, hereby prohibited either to be exported from the United Kingdom or carried coastwise." The ban also affected pending shipments to Russia, Italy, and the Confederacy.[44]

Although the embargo stymied Du Pont's efforts, the American minister to Belgium, Henry S. Sanford, transferred all his government funds from London to Paris banks and, fearing that the United States would exhaust its meager saltpeter reserves, quietly began to investigate the markets at Antwerp, Hamburg, and Bremen. He decided to ship as many arms and barrels of saltpeter as possible without quibbling over prices or shipping rates. In late November the steamer *Congress* left Antwerp with a large shipment of arms, but when stormy seas forced it into Southampton, British authorities would not let it leave. Sanford soon learned that the departure of another Antwerp vessel, the *Estella*, chartered to carry 350 tons of arms and 20 tons of saltpeter to New York, was prevented by the British consul in Antwerp. Freight rates surged and shipping companies charged extortionate amounts. On Christmas Eve, Sanford dispatched the *Saxonia* from Hamburg with 800 tons of guns and saltpeter, arranged to ship another 25,000 guns and 140 tons of saltpeter on the *Melitia* from

Antwerp, and planned to smuggle more guns out of England by packing them in crockery casks and providing "a good fee" to the customs officer. As December drew to a close, Sanford curtailed his purchases so that he would have enough money to equip privateers if war broke out. Although he had shipped most of the contraband without authorization, he believed the crisis justified his action, and Lincoln later commended his initiative.[45]

Having secured a legal opinion, tested the political waters, and banned export of war material, the British government could turn again to the *Trent* question. Lamps burned late at the Foreign Office, as clerks and subordinate officials endeavored to meet demands for information. Russell spent the morning of November 30 working on a dispatch to Lyons that set forth the government's view. Leading off with a brief account of the circumstances, he concluded that removal of Mason and Slidell was not justified because the *Trent* was "pursuing a lawful and innocent voyage." Her Majesty's Government was "unwilling to imagine" that the Lincoln administration would not "of their own accord be anxious to afford ample reparation," which included liberating the prisoners, placing them under British protection, and offering an "apology for the insult to the British flag."[46] The curt tone of Russell's draft made it seem an ultimatum.

Russell submitted two dispatches for approval to the afternoon cabinet meeting, and spirited discussion ensued. Granville wanted to make it as easy as possible for the United States to retreat honorably. Gladstone objected to the second dispatch, which called for Lyons's departure seven days following Seward's receipt of the dispatch, if the United States did not comply with the terms. He urged the government to hear what the Americans "had to say before withdrawing Lyons for I could not feel sure that we were at the bottom of the law of the case or could judge here and now what form it would assume." The cabinet overruled him. Lewis was certain that Washington did not order the capture, but thought the Americans would refuse reparation. However, he exclaimed, "It seems incredible that Seward can seriously desire" a war with Britain. Russell was not happy with cabinet amendments, and complained to Palmerston that they made "my American dispatch badly told & weakened the statement of our case considerably."[47]

Russell's dispatch still had to run the gauntlet of Royal opinion, which proved to be more of a problem than he had expected. In all matters of government, Queen Victoria usually sought the advice of Prince Albert, relying heavily on his knowledge, judgment, and writing ability. Whenever Russell sent a dispatch box containing a poorly worded message, Albert never returned it with a curt rejection, but, following a procedure outlined by Clarendon, concentrated on what was "good and proper" in it and suggested alterations. Russell invariably accepted the changes. Fourteen persons had already proposed emendations in this latest dispatch by the time it reached Windsor Castle on the evening of November 30, and the Prince Consort was almost too ill to add his own. Chronically ill, he had inspected the new Staff College and Royal Military Academy at Sandhurst on November 22 in a cold, driving rain, and returned to the castle exhausted and chilled. Instead of staying in bed he went to Cambridge the following day to visit the Prince of Wales, whose brief affair with an actress had turned his father into an insomniac. By the morning of December 1 a combination of fatigue, chills, and sleeplessness, aided by the unsanitary castle drains, had brought on an attack of typhoid fever; Albert ignored his condition and rose from bed at 7:00 A.M. to revise Russell's dispatch. Within an hour he had composed a memorandum stating that although the Queen approved the drafts she thought the main part, which intended for communication to the American government, was "somewhat meagre." Looking "very wretched" and unable to eat, he brought the memorandum down to breakfast for the Queen's perusal. When he handed the paper to his wife he said that "he could scarcely hold his pen while writing it." Victoria was as angry as her ministers at "the American outrage" and approved the government's decision, but, like her husband, worried about what might happen if the United States refused Britain's demands; the Americans, after all, were such ruffians.[48]

The changes Albert suggested were incorporated. Wilkes's deed, the revised dispatch stated, was "an affront to the British flag and a violation of international law." The British government was willing to believe that Wilkes did not act "in compliance with any authority" or, if he had been so authorized, that he greatly misunderstood his instructions. American officials "must be fully aware that the British Government shall not allow such an affront to the national honor to pass without full reparation, and Her Majesty's Government are unwilling to believe that it could be the deliberate intention of the Government of the United States unnecessarily to force into discussion . . . a question of so grave a character." The British nation trusted that the American government would "of its own accord offer to the British Government such redress as alone would satisfy the British nation, namely the liberation of the four Gentlemen . . . and a suitable apology for the aggression which has been committed."[49]

The revision changed the tone of the dispatch, removing the menace implicit in the peremptory list of reparations. Albert had not altered the demands of apology and surrender, but had rephrased them in a way that would not insult the American government.

Russell's second dispatch of November 30, which was intended only for Lyons, escaped Albert's criticism. It instructed Lyons to allow Seward seven days to study the terms of Britain's demands. If, after seven days, Seward did not answer the first dispatch or agree to comply, Lyons should leave Washington for London, taking all legation members and the archives, and direct the consuls to continue discharging their duties unless prevented. Despite the tone of ultimatum, Russell was willing to bend; he directed Lyons to report the facts and remain at his post if he "should be of the opinion that the requirements of Her Majesty's Government are substantially complied with." In that event, Lyons should send a copy of America's answer, regardless of content, to Admiral Milne and "inform him whether . . . there is a probability of any aggression on Her Majesty's ships or territories before the answer of the U.S. shall be received in London." The minister was naturally expected to pass on information to the governors of Canada, Nova Scotia, New Brunswick, Jamaica, Bermuda, and other possessions in the Western Hemisphere. Both dispatches went out on the *Europa* from Queenstown on December 1.[50]

While the British government deliberated over the dispatches, Yancey, Rost, and Mann, the Confederate envoys already in England, were not idle. As soon as the West Indian steamer arrived with Mason's and Slidell's papers and dispatches that Commander Williams had concealed, the envoys composed a protest to Russell against "this act of illegal violence," maintaining that the proceeding violated international law and was unjustifiable under any treaty between Britain and the United States. They did not dispute that Mason and Slidell were liable to seizure, but the liability was a judicial question best decided by Admiralty courts. Seeking only to lay the facts before the British government and to claim for the imprisoned commissioners their just protection under a foreign flag, they hoped Her Majesty's Government would restore the men to the deck of a British vessel or take them to the port for which they had paid passage. Two days later the envoys followed their protest with a legal brief. Submitting a list of the forty-five vessels, including the *Nashville* and

Theodora, which had run the blockade in the last seven months, they deemed the list "conclusive evidence that this blockade has not been effective and is therefore not binding." They claimed that it was the sort of paper blockade outlawed by the Declaration of Paris of 1856.[51]

The three representatives decided not to press for recognition of the Confederacy, preferring to wait until Britain received an answer to the demands for an apology and reparation. Nevertheless, Mann wrote Confederate Secretary of State Robert M. T. Hunter that recognition would not be delayed much longer; he claimed that an hour after the cabinet had decided its course, a friend of his who was close to Palmerston had furnished details. This assertion was surely more valid than that of his son, who remembered the prime minister and Mann standing before a map of the United States, plotting grand strategy against the North. When, a year later, Mann looked back on the preparations for war, he exulted, "The British officers met me like brothers, conversed with me like brothers. I already esteemed them as allies." But when Russell answered the envoys' protests on December 7, he continued Palmerston's policy, avoiding official communication for the present.[52]

Despite mounting international tensions, life in London had to go on, even within the American legation. Any winter in London was a severe trial, Henry Adams reflected at this dismal moment in his country's fortunes, but the month of December 1861, he afterward wrote, would have "gorged a glutton of gloom."[53] Young Adams was disgusted with London society:

> Supposing you are invited to a ball. You arrive at eleven
> o'clock. A footman in powder asks your name and announces
> you. The lady or ladies of the house receive you and shake
> hands. You pass on and there you are. You know not a soul.
> No one even looks at you with curiosity.[54]

British balls were "solemn stupid crushes"; state dinners were "dull, heavy, lifeless affairs." The *Trent* affair made him feel worse. He wrote his brother in the Union army that "we are dished, and . . . our position is hopeless." Great Britain meant to make war. "Do not doubt it. What Seward means is more than I can guess. But if he means war also, or to run as close as he can without touching; then I say that Mr. Seward is the greatest Criminal we've had yet." Having given the American minister no warning, the government seemed "almost to have purposely encouraged us to waste our strength in trying to maintain the relations which it was itself intending to destroy." He was ready to take up his "old German life again as a permanency."[55]

For once, young Henry Adams was justified in his pessimism. The long summer of Anglo-American discontent and the Union's military humiliation that climaxed with the rout at Bull Run had been bad enough, but the *Trent* incident promised a disaster. Although Henry and his fellow secretary had shrieked with joy on hearing the news, the gravity of Wilkes's act had become evident within a day or two, as they observed the movements of the British government and felt the tremor of enraged popular opinion. Charles Francis Adams knew nothing about the affair, and took some comfort in the belief that Wilkes probably had not seized Mason and Slidell by order of the administration. But even without an Anglo-American war, which the elder Adams regarded as inevitable, confidence between the two nations had been destroyed. "Ministers and people now fully believe it is the intention of the [American] Government to drive them into hostilities." The minister's morale had plummeted so that he no longer cared whether he remained in London, and he worked feverishly to complete routine legation business before being recalled.[56]

Events were moving rapidly. The law officers' opinion had been widely disseminated and few people expected the United States to apologize. England had to prepare for war, or risk having the Americans overwhelm their forces in the Western Hemisphere before Russell's dispatches crossed the ocean.

6.

Preparation

IN THE WINTRY DAYS OF DECEMBER 1861, as thick fog rolled in from the sea, the thoughts of Britons turned from the fate of vessels on the storm-tossed Atlantic to the tempest brewing with the United States. It was difficult for the English to understand why the Lincoln administration, which professed friendship with all nations, seemed determined to provoke a crisis over the wanderings of Confederate diplomats. The American secretary of state especially baffled observers, who daily scanned the accounts of the British minister, reporters, and private correspondents for the new evidence of Seward's hostility. A war with England made no sense for the Union cause, but then nothing had ever made any sense in the topsy-turvy world of Anglo-American relations. British officials had given up trying to diagnose the malady affecting their cousins across the sea.

Although the cabinet in London had decided to protest the seizure of Mason and Slidell, it hesitated to begin preparation for war without reviewing the circumstances leading to the commissioners' removal. Overreaction might force the unpredictable Union government into a move that would hurt both nations. But whatever was to be done had to be done immediately, or all the effort to reinforce Canada against invasion would be futile because of the onset of winter.

The cabinet met again on December 4 to discuss the *Trent* affair. At each member's place lay a seven-point memorandum that set forth the apparent facts of the seizure. The *San Jacinto*, the document began, did not encounter the *Trent* in the "usual way," but had left Havana *"for the express purpose of waylaying* and making an hostile attack upon the British vessel." Union officers had halted the ship with an unnecessary and dangerous act of violence "accompanied by an offensive display of force." They had not searched the *Trent* in the ordinary way, but had demanded passengers and then removed them. The American captain had neither charged the mail steamer with violating laws of neutrality nor referred to instructions from his government. It was an invariable principle, so the cabinet document read, that a belligerent could not use any violence against an unresisting neutral ship, except to bring the vessel before the belligerent's nearest tribunal; neither goods nor persons on board the ship could be touched *"save after trial and sentence by a competent Court."* A belligerent violating this principle committed a hostile act. Since Her Majesty's Government had discovered nothing that offered reasonable cause for a Union complaint, the attack had to be considered as being of the most wanton nature. Britain must be able to communicate with the Confederate States, and must be permitted to treat citizens of each belligerent equally, and to protect them while under the British flag. Any British requirements of the Northern government were no less than would have been demanded of the South.[1]

Cabinet members wondered if the seizure had been designed by Washington to drive Britain into war. Palmerston did not say much during the meeting, but it was evident that he doubted that Britain would receive a reasonable reply from the Americans. The Washington government, he told the Queen, was not guided by reasonable men. However, he believed Britain had all the advantages. The Federals would humiliate themselves and bring honor to Britain by complying with the demands, he said, and if they refused, Britain could harshly punish them. Fearing that war would result if the "exiled Irishmen who direct almost all the Northern newspapers" succeeded in goading the American masses, he thought it a proper time for Lyons to propose to Federal authorities that, in case of hostilities, neither government should issue letters of marque.[2]

The rest of the cabinet tended to agree with Palmerston's gloomy assessment. Gladstone, a foe of big military budgets, rarely allowed panic to lead to military buildup because he would have to defend extra expenditures, but the Mason and Slidell matter worried him more than the naval race with France. The American government, he said, would "probably have sense enough to avoid absolute refusal but not

courage enough to do the right thing"; therefore, Lincoln would propose arbitration and insist on choosing the arbiter. Doubting that
Wilkes had acted on orders or that the United States wanted to fight,
Gladstone believed that an uncertain future justified military preparation; although such preparation would be expensive, it would hardly
be provocative. His willingness to abandon economy in the *Trent*
crisis indicated his concern for British security as well as his lack of
sympathy for the United States; he believed that the Civil War was not
a struggle for freedom, but an "immense mischief, not merely to
democratic but to all liberal and popular principles."[3]

The seizure convinced skeptics of a design on Canada. Although
War Secretary Lewis had disapproved of England's former practice of
impressment and thought it resembled the *Trent* outrage, he knew of
no Admiralty decision that justified the capture. Respected by colleagues for his prudence, sound judgment, and scholarship, he
wielded influence within the government and helped tilt doubters
toward a stern policy. In the present crisis the Palmerston cabinet
would survive a political attack, he decided, because people would approve military preparation if war broke out; moreover, if Lincoln surrendered the Confederate commissioners, the public would think that
the British government's action had caused it.[4]

Speculation at the Foreign Office regarding Washington's ulterior
motive had not lessened after a week of analysis, and Undersecretary
Hammond expressed the common attitude when he called the *Trent*
affair "a premeditated scheme to force us into collision." Irritated by
Minister Adams's assurance that dispatches would soon arrive from
Washington, he suspected the American of trying to postpone British
measures. Lord Lyons's account of Northern reaction had led him to
conclude that Britain could employ intimidation to avoid a rupture.
Hammond advocated announcing in British newspapers that six heavy
frigates were ordered to Bermuda, with an equal number to follow;
this news might convince Americans that a large convoy would escort
artillery already en route. The prospect of war was not hypothetical,
he believed, because no American statesman possessed sufficient
patriotism "to sacrifice himself to save his country."[5] The only uncertainty remaining involved choosing the best measures for protecting
British possessions.

Before the government could dispatch frigates in the ostentatious
manner proposed by Hammond, it was necessary to close the
loopholes in British neutrality law that endangered national security.
Customs supervision on the docks was so lax that a Liverpool merchant claimed he could ship the saltpeter as sugar and all the arms as

hardware; such lack of control was being exploited by Northern agents. Palmerston believed that the failure to embargo weapons put Britain in a defective position and that the government had committed an act of folly, which he could not defend, by "abundantly supplying with arms to attack us that Party which we have Reason to expect will before long be our enemy." Businessmen's arguments that an arms embargo would throw the gun trade into foreign hands were cobwebs. Swayed by Palmerston's logic, Queen Victoria issued a proclamation on December 4 that prohibited arms, ammunition, military stores, and lead from being exported or carried coastwise.[6]

The seriousness with which the government viewed the *Trent* incident was demonstrated by creation of a special War Committee of the Cabinet, composed of Palmerston, Somerset, Newcastle, Granville, Lewis, Russell, and the commander-in-chief, the Duke of Cambridge. Standing committees had been established on only three occasions: during the Crimean War, in response to the Indian Mutiny, and in 1859 to buttress Palmerston's campaign for a stronger defense against the French. The latest committee, whose decisions had to be approved by the cabinet, concentrated on protecting Western Hemisphere possessions (notably Canada), and reinforcing Admiral Milne's squadron. Expecting that any potential conflict might evolve into a gigantic, if brief, repetition of the War of 1812, officials aimed at control of the seas and occupation of Maine to counteract any invasion of British North America, but did not count on much success until the spring of 1862.[7] No one suggested postponing preparation for war until Washington had responded to Russell's demands; a show of force was considered necessary to guarantee compliance. The British government took to heart the aphorism of Frederick the Great that "diplomacy without armaments is like music without instruments."

Once the cabinet had agreed upon military action, and the Queen had forbidden export of virtually all war materials, Britons focused on ways to defend British North America against invasion, and on preventive and retaliatory moves to compensate for weakness in Canadian armor. A captain of the Royal Engineers in Canada, William Halt Noble, suggested measures for the provinces. The Admiralty, he said, should station warships in the St. Lawrence off Quebec to allow the commander-in-chief to detach garrison troops for fighting the invader, and leave to recruits the task of defending the city with the aid of naval gunners. Noble reported that the dockyard buildings at Isle aux Nois in the St. Lawrence were in a state of decay, and that both Fort Lennox and a naval arsenal at Penetanguishene were being used as juvenile reformatories. The Ontario shore defenses lay open, except

Kingston at Fort Massasanga, and ships ascending the St. Lawrence would have to run American fire for a hundred miles. But the United States border had some weak points also, which, if exploited, might lessen the danger to Canada. An unfortified naval arsenal at Sackett's Harbor in New York, which contained thirty tons of gunpowder and cannon, could be taken. He deemed it necessary to seize three other American forts once war broke out: Fort Champlain at Rouses Point, to secure Montreal from a southeastern attack and to interrupt communications between New York City and Ogdensburg; Fort Niagara, to assume command of the western end of Lake Ontario; and Fort Mackinaw, to control Lakes Huron and Michigan. Noble also advocated the capture of Michilimackinac Island. He expected all fighting to occur in the Niagara peninsula along the Welland Canal, a Canadian artery uncomfortably close to the United States.[8]

The inspector general of fortifications, General Sir John Fox Burgoyne, was an expert on the strategy of defense and a veteran of the Napoleonic Wars, the War of 1812, and the Crimean War. He anticipated a desultory conflict complicated by marauding parties. Rather than a thin line of British soldiers along the southern border of Canada, he advocated "district arrangements of the local forces," whose duty would be to converge on points under attack. He believed that Federal forces at Port Royal, South Carolina, at the mouth of the Mississippi, and at other outposts on the Gulf Coast should be swept away, but he doubted if British troops in strength could attack the North from the sea. He asserted that only an invasion of Maine from New Brunswick should be attempted, because it would allow direct communication with Canada. He anticipated that the Union's rail net could allow quick movement of troops against an invader. Some coordination of British attacks could be expected, he believed, with those of the Southern armies, but he opposed large-scale cooperative expeditions against Northern ports.[9]

The British government also sought the advice of England's foremost military theoretician of the period, Colonel Patrick L. MacDougall, whose respected *Theory of War* expounded the views of Jomini, the Archduke Charles, and Major General Sir William Napier. Attached to the Royal Canadian Rifles, MacDougall had served in the Crimea, participated in the unsuccessful assault on the Redan, and commanded the Staff College at Sandhurst for its first four years. He had stated in *Theory of War* that it was essential to place "in a certain position at a certain time . . . a body of troops *in fighting order* superior to that body which your enemy can there oppose to you," but as he pondered the situation of Canada he must have realized the hollowness of such advice. There was no doubt in his mind that the United States had staged the *Trent* incident. A war would provide an excuse for not defeating the Confederacy; a winter campaign against Canada promised successes because British reinforcements could not arrive until spring. Viewing the Royal Navy as the key to victory, he advocated blockade of Northern ports and capture of the American navy, to be followed by mediation of the Civil War; this strategy depended on the infantry being able to hold a 200,000-man invasion force. Since British forces could not defend the frontier, he suggested that they concentrate around large cities and the Welland Canal, as well as Fort Malden at Amherstburg, which was then serving as a lunatic asylum. The few thousand English soldiers would have to rely on recruitment of 75,000 volunteers—"backwoodsmen, armed with their own rifles"—who could be attached to every regular regiment and "act as the pioneers of the army." Believing that a strong faction in Maine favored annexation to Canada, MacDougall agreed with Burgoyne's recommendation to invade and seize Portland, as well as to occupy Sackett's Harbor on the New York side of Lake Ontario. Such tasks looked easy on a map, but they violated another of MacDougall's rules that an army's route of march "must be sheltered by its own frontiers or by some natural obstacle throughout as great an extent as is possible."[10]

War Secretary Lewis expected the Americans to try something desperate, such as a dash on Montreal. He favored sending four militia regiments and two artillery batteries to Halifax, and advised conditional orders for seizing Portland, provided military and naval forces at Halifax could safeguard the venture. Having instructed the elite Horse Guards to send staff officers to help organize the Canadian militia, Lewis recommended, in the event of an impending or actual invasion, seizure of Fort Fairfield in Maine, a few miles across the border on the Aroostook River, and access roads to the upper St. John River. Troops in New Brunswick and at Halifax should then proceed to Riviere du Loup.[11] He was one of few officials to advocate preventive raids against the United States and to recognize the necessity of controlling transportation and supply points.

Home Secretary Sir George Grey concurred with Lewis's suggestions for the defense of Canada, thinking it probable that the American government would refuse to make proper reparation and would authorize an attack on the Welland Canal, the area between Prescott and Cornwall, or Montreal. He suggested that British troops forestall attacks by seizing Portland, which threatened the Grand Trunk Railway's terminus; otherwise, American control of the Grand

Trunk would force British troops to undertake an arduous overland trek, inadvisable for medical as well as military reasons. British control of Portland would allow enough time to reinforce the Canadian interior. Although Grey favored a surprise attack, he disliked sending out cavalry and horse artillery before war appeared inescapable, and saw no reason to incur large expense and to risk men and material just to make a show of strength.[12]

The government's focus on taking Portland to safeguard the Grand Trunk's terminus coincided with the November visit to London of a Canadian delegation seeking aid for an intercolonial railway. A rail connection between Halifax and Rivière du Loup would link up with the Grand Trunk, diminish Canadian dependence on American transportation, and foster a new sense of colonial pride. But the proposed route lay uncomfortably close to the border, while the Grand Trunk ran south of the St. Lawrence between Montreal and Quebec. The existing and proposed railways would be nearly impossible to defend, and British skepticism was heightened by the Canadian government's refusal to spend more than slightly over 1 percent of its 1860 budget on defense. Only Newcastle showed interest in the railroad project, and he wrote emotional letters and arranged interviews with Palmerston; however, the prime minister shooed the Canadian delegates on to Gladstone, knowing he disliked subsidies and believed that the colonists should do more to help themselves. The group was ready to admit defeat when word of the *Trent* affair opened doors. "I suppose *now* they will succeed in getting their hands into our pockets," grumbled Richard Cobden, a liberal politician and foe of big spending.[13]

At the War Office, Lewis was in no mood to economize; he threw his support behind the railway and asked the delegation what Canada intended to do about the potential threat of American aggression. The Canadians promised to fight, but complained: "we cannot fight with jack-knives; and there are no arms in the country. You have failed to keep any store at all." At Lewis's urging, the delegation drafted a memorandum warning that the seven American railroads running to the border could deliver 100,000 men for use against principal cities before Canada could concentrate its meager forces. Construction of an intercolonial railroad, they argued, might prevent a war because it would make surprise attack impossible and a protracted war doubtful. How could they go back with a refusal, they exclaimed, and ask the population to arm? The argument seemed sound, particularly in the context of alarm over an impending American attack. Yet the chancellor of the exchequer refused to be rushed into a decision, and saw the railroad as "a source of new demands for defence rather than an instrument of power."[14] The future of the intercolonial railway, whatever its military and commercial benefits, would not be settled until spring. Meanwhile, the Canadians had to manage with what they had, and hope that enough British regulars would arrive to forestall an invasion.

Despite reluctance to pour money into another railroad, cabinet members and military advisers agreed that it was necessary to take some action before receiving the American answer. Troops should go to Canada to prepare to seize strategic points in the northern United States, either by surprise or in reaction to an outbreak of hostilities. Although no one advocated an invasion, as in the War of 1812, many advised occupation of ports along the southeastern and Gulf coasts. Unfortunately, wisdom acquired on the battlefields of Europe had little application in a region as sparsely settled as Canada. The British government knew that increasing regular forces by a few thousand would have no effect in the event of war, and that the overland route to Canadian forts and cities could be severed whenever the Americans chose. Officers and civilians proposed tactics that would be successful only *if* the Union army continued its incompetent performance, *if* the St. Lawrence froze late, *if* the Canadian militia fought well, *if* enough weapons and military supplies could be sent—*if*, *if*, *if*.

Discussion of the most effective ways to defend Canada did not mean that the government viewed war as inevitable; London worried only that the Lincoln administration, under Seward's prod, might accompany a negative reply with an act of war. Cabinet secretaries, advisers, and former officials continued to analyze the seizure, comparing it to Britain's past conduct to determine if anything could absolve the American government of wrongdoing. The weakest part of the case, Clarendon and others confessed, was "our having so often claimed the right to the *same sort of thing*." They pored over memoranda on the arrest of Lucien Bonaparte off Caligari, the case of the *Maria* (1799), Spanish detention of a mail packet (1855), removal of a Mexican pilot from a British vessel by a French warship (1838), British search of the American *Peggy* (1798), and capture of Garibaldian volunteers by the Neopolitan government. Gladstone concluded that the American case was "juridically so exceedingly bad, that I cannot but believe they will avoid refusal and for the present at least avoid war." Argyll shared Gladstone's aversion for war, but worried that, if the *San Jacinto*'s action passed unchallenged, it would encourage European governments to seize their rebels trying to escape on British ships. "Ours is the cause of all neutral nations," agreed Gladstone.[15]

After receiving numerous opinions, the Cabinet finally agreed that it seemed necessary to reinforce Canada. Although Newcastle was a capable colonial secretary and fancied himself an expert on British North America and its people, his knowledge consisted of statistics, public information, and scattered impressions from his single visit in 1860 with the Prince of Wales. Nine days after learning of the seizure, he warned Canada's new governor general, Viscount Charles Monck, that Mason and Slidell would probably not be surrendered and that war would likely result, with "Seward at the helm of the United States and the mob and the Press manning the Vessel." Seeing the crisis as a golden opportunity to induce Canadian subjects to bolster their defenses, he told Monck not to wait for a declaration if Lyons left Washington; instead, he should call up regiments and build gunboats, taking care that some sneaking fellow did not cross the border and burn the three steamboats Monck had recently sent to Kingston. Montreal might be defended most effectively, he said, by fortifying Victoria Bridge with guns from Quebec. If the provincial government could raise 100,000 militia and hold out until spring, London would provide Enfield rifles and officers of the Horse Guards. Winter would limit assistance to a few regiments, blockade of Northern cities, and destruction of the Union navy. Newcastle arranged for two regiments to leave for Quebec immediately, and marked another with artillery for St. John to protect the Metis Road connecting New Brunswick and the rest of Canada; the troops would have to use this route rather than the border road. Because there was no rail connection from Halifax, he decided to open another road via Matapedia, between the St. Lawrence and the Bay of Chaleurs. As an afterthought, he reassured authorities in Newfoundland that they had nothing to fear except Yankee privateers, and he would send a battery of artillery to defend St. John's harbor against any vessel rash enough to come within range.[16]

In the first week of December, troops began boarding ships for Canada. The destination was Halifax, a naval base and a magnet for Confederate agents seeking supplies. Among the earliest vessels to leave was the Cunard screw steamer *Melbourne*, a slow, unseaworthy, condemned transport of the Crimean War that may have been pressed into service because it could sail immediately. The ship took on board 2 batteries of Armstrong guns, several howitzers, 30,000 stand of arms, and 2,500,000 minié rifle balls; the troops on board were E battery, 4th brigade, Royal Field Artillery, which had marched behind the regimental band from Woolwich to the arsenal. The quartermaster corps, whose duty was to prepare a reception for thousands of troops to follow, traveled with them even though they had asked to be sent out on a ship leaving later but arriving sooner. Crowds cheered along the route of march, and families thronged the dock on the afternoon of December 7 as the ship cast off to a flutter of caps, handkerchiefs, and applause. But gloom reigned on board ship. "Do not be in the least surprised if you hear of us all being made prisoners of war before the end of February," an officer wrote morosely. The decrepit *Melbourne* took almost a month to reach Halifax. The soldiers disembarked and tramped through the streets of the "quaint, ricketty little village," past brightly dressed Indian squaws, and went into hastily prepared quarters to rest for the long overland journey by road and rail. Taking a different route, the quartermaster staff traveled on a mail steamer to Boston, passed through Customs uninspected after removing military labels from baggage, and continued to Montreal.[17]

After departure of the *Melbourne*, followed by the *Australasia* and the *Niagara*, a lull in sailings ensued as the British government frantically recalled men from leave, encouraged the naval reserve to be ready and to prepare to pardon any returning deserters, assembled mountains of supplies, commandeered the ships of mail companies as troop transports, and ordered completion of a hospital for reception of wounded. The home secretary appealed to Florence Nightingale for advice on sanitary arrangements, and instantly accepted her recommendations on clothing (buffalo robes instead of blankets), transportation, food, and care of the sick and wounded. Chatham dockyard hummed with activity greater than that experienced during the Crimean War, as 4,000 mechanics and workmen struggled to refit vessels for service; yards at Portsmouth, Sheerness, Woolwich, and Devenport received orders to hire hands and prepare ships without delay. No one in the cabinet thought that Britain could strengthen Canadian defenses to repel an American army before springtime, but the government could not pursue a dilatory course and yet claim to have protected the empire; so the troops sailed and arsenal workers labored to increase the province's supplies, although everyone in authority knew the task, if not hopeless, was extremely difficult.[18]

By mid-December military movement had gathered momentum and troops began to depart regularly. On the morning of December 18, 1,800 Grenadier and Scots Fusilier Guards left Southampton on board the *Parana* and the *Adriatic*, the latter a recently purchased American side-wheeler that still had a Stars-and-Stripes painted on the paddle box. As the ships passed the C.S.S. *Nashville*, the Fusilier Guards band struck up "I'm Off to Charleston." Two days later, the *Magdalena* departed with 1,000 men, and the *Asia* departed with 470 men; they were followed over the next two weeks by *Cleopatra*, *Calcutta*, *Victoria*, *Canada*, *Hibernia*, *Adelaide*, and *Peru*, all loaded with soldiers and supplies. Only the *Persia* ever reached its Bic Island destination. Some were forced to turn back—the *Adelaide* after losing a cylinder lid, and the *Victoria* (which never did make North America) for additional coal after consuming too much fighting a hurricane (which sank the storeship *Trojan*). Canadians were amazed that the *Persia*, having come so far, did not continue up the St. Lawrence to Rivière du Loup, where fine facilities awaited. Instead, only a portion of her cargo and passengers were unloaded at Bic; then, according to her captain, she was forced by closing ice to race for safety. Even if the river had been navigable, as local inhabitants claimed, the *Persia* would have had to dodge islands and submerged rocks without the aid of lighthouses, which were extinguished for the season. The other ships changed course for Halifax and St. John, losing a ten-thousand-pound premium for not landing at Bic. The reinforcements raised the numbers of British troops in Canada, the Maritime Provinces, and Newfoundland to 924 officers and 17,658 men—11,000 fewer than Lewis had proposed. With these forces and the Canadian militia, Britain expected to hold off an American invasion of 50,000 to 200,000 men anticipated within two months.[19]

Travel by steamship in the mid-nineteenth century could be a dangerous adventure. It was during this period that the "bon voyage" party originated, a tearful occasion when loved ones assembled in the passenger's "coffin-like cabin" to exchange farewells; upon safely reaching the destination, passengers customarily presented the captain with a silver plate for preserving their lives. The unfortunate soldiers and their dependents who crossed the Atlantic in the winter of 1861 faced hardships scarcely considered by the festive crowds cheering them on their way. Some transports departed so hurriedly that tons of unsecured stores, arms, and accouterments posed a menace to the seasick, cramped soldiers. The ships were rigged to carry sail for emergencies. Ironclad vessels also habitually leaked around loose plates. Storms lashed the vessels, saturating officers and men; snapping spars; carrying away lifeboats; ripping the bridge, longboat, and sails; and forcing destruction of horses. The experience of being pitched and tossed across the Atlantic was enough to make ruddy-cheeked young soldiers ignore their general's advice to drink milk instead of rum, if they were actually able to keep anything in their stomachs. Of the 11,376 officers and men belonging to guard, infantry, garrison and field artillery, military train, and engineer units that reached Canadian shores in varying states of nausea, over half marched off their ships into the maw of a blizzard and crowded into sleighs for a freezing, seven-day trip to the interior.[20] Almost all arrived after the *Trent* crisis had been resolved peacefully.

Canadians trembled at the prospect of invasion. They were not afraid to fight, but they were simply outnumbered, outgunned, and outsupplied. Seeing no way out of an unpleasant situation, they grimly set about preparing for a war they could only lose. "The cry of war rings throughout the land," the Toronto *Globe* wrote. "At the corner of every street, you hear the excited discussions as to the Mason and Slidell outrage, the next news from England, the erection of forts, and the probabilities of 'a fight with the Americans'." Political and linguistic divisions that normally affected Canada vanished in the crisis; Irish, French, and English, laboring and upper classes, rallied "to arm and do their duty by the old flag." Newspapers urged readers not to contribute to Northern temperance lecturers and called for an embargo on hay to the United States. The sight of a Federal uniform provoked jeers of "Bull Run!" and renditions of "Dixie" in saloons. When word of British demands reached the Montreal Exchange, merchants and leading citizens cheered and practically suspended business. Quebec students began organizing a military company, merchants proposed a Rifle Association, the Aurora Snow-Shoe Club laid plans for a military company, and all counted on Generals January and February. In mid-December, the Victoria Volunteer Rifles gave three cheers for the Queen, their commander, and Mason and Slidell, and three groans for the Yankees and Captain Wilkes, and then worried that other Canadians would accidentally shoot them if they wore the proposed colors of gray and red, identical with the uniform of the Vermont regiments. Two hundred men on the St. Gabriel Locks organized to fight, as did four hundred employees at Grand Trunk Railway stations. "War, war; we hear nothing but war," complained a woman, while another Canadian, exulting in the heady atmosphere, averred, "We were at once Canadian and British."[21]

Outrage and unity manifested themselves in Canadian newspapers, regardless of each paper's stance toward the Union or grievances against the Crown. The most widely read and influential paper in British North America was the Toronto *Globe*, organ of the Reform party and supporter of the Union cause. Although the *Globe* saw no possible justification for the *Trent* affair, it anticipated a long legal battle rather than war; Seward, it stated, would "easily find points upon which to hang an argument," and the matter would end in a verdict of "nobody hurt." The American people, despite their fondness for "blowing" about foreign policy and their approval of Seward's antipathies, "must be taught to show a decent and proper regard for the feelings and rights of other nations." The *Globe*'s rival was the Toronto *Leader*, unofficial organ of the provincial government, and advocate of the Confederate position. The *Leader* called the arrest of Mason and Slidell a "wanton, unprovoked, and utterly indefensible insult to the British flag," a perversion of international law, and a blow to British authority. It believed that a war with the United States might benefit Canada, which stood to gain a winter seaport, the territory of Maine, and all American lands west of the Mississippi down to the forty-fifth parallel.[22]

Other Canadian journals reacted similarly, taking potshots at the secretary of state and lecturing the American people. The Ottawa *Citizen* reflected on Seward's past offensive conduct, which it believed could not be disassociated from the incident; furthermore, it saw in the *Trent* imbroglio an opportunity to teach the Americans, "a proud, and withal a self-conceited" people, the lesson that sooner or later "they [would] have to learn,—to respect the rights of others while paying a due regard to their own." Whereas the *Globe* anticipated a peaceful resolution, the Halifax *Morning Chronicle* feared that the United States, after so much boasting, would find it impossible to recede with honor. The Montreal *Gazette*, an early proponent of the Confederacy, agreed with many of the British that Seward wanted to fasten a quarrel on Great Britain so as to obtain a pretext for abandoning the attempt to conquer the South. Although the *Gazette* admitted that Canada could offer only slight resistance to a nation with half a million men under arms, it expressed the hope that throughout Canada there were not "ten lily-livered, snivelling creatures willing to disgrace their manhood and the honor of the sires who begot them" by shrinking from war.[23] The appeal was reasonable, if emotional, but the editor of the *Gazette* soon realized that patriotism alone did not substitute for trained soldiers.

Where would the Canadians find the tens of thousands they needed? In late 1861, Canada and the Maritime Provinces contained 625,000 men of less than forty years of age, but had enrolled only 5,000 regulars and 5,500 poorly disciplined militia (about a fifth of which had been organized). Although the militia dated back to the days of New France, and old laws required universal service, officials had long grumbled that the colonists did not understand that self-government and self-defense went together. The commander of Her Majesty's Forces in British North America, Sir Fenwick Williams, described as a man who in a siege would eat his boots before surrendering, recommended calling out as many volunteers as he could arm. Although he had scant respect for the usefulness of volunteers, and would have preferred to increase the regular troops, he believed that the Canadian government would not pay for enough dollar-a-day men to meet the danger. Monck refused his request to call out volunteers, because he believed that such action might antagonize Americans near the border, and laws dictated that volunteers be called out only in case of war, invasion, or insurrection. MacDougall, the military theoretician, believed that an officer "should look on his men as a good sportsman regards his horse, and take care that they are always 'fit to go for a man's life,' " but the active militia of Canada was not fit to go for anything except the kegs of whiskey furnished at drills. Kingston, with a population of 13,000, had 3 weak rifle companies, from which 17 men turned out for a drill. Toronto, population 46,000, had 400 to 500 riflemen on the rolls, and 61 came to drill. Hamilton, population 19,000, had 140 active riflemen and 40 for drill. On December 2 the government of Canada decided to raise the volunteer force to 7,500, but knew it would have to borrow at least 2,000 arms from imperial stores. Although the volunteer concept had always appealed more to town than country, large numbers of recruits had never materialized, and the *Trent* crisis, while stimulating short-term interest, did not noticeably improve efficiency. Thousands of recruits, some only fourteen years old, answered a call to arms, but monotonous drilling with the heavy Enfield rifles was often so long that the men felt "as lop-sided as a pig with one ear," and they soon became disillusioned. They worried that the crisis would end before they had "smelt powder," yet they did not relish campaigning in sub-zero temperatures.[24]

On December 20, General Williams decided to begin drilling a company of 75 men in each battalion, about 38,000 soldiers, of the aptly titled Sedentary Militia. Untrained and undisciplined, they showed up in all manner of dress, with belts of basswood bark and sprigs of green balsam in their hats, carrying an assortment of flintlocks, shotguns, rifles, and scythes. Their officers, prefacing orders with "please," recoiled in horror as formations of the backwoodsmen zigzagged on command to wheel to the left. Such antics did not disturb Governor Monck, who thought he could have 100,000 men in arms by April if Britain would only supply weapons. The regular army in

Canada had a mere 25,000 longarms, of which 10,000 were smooth-bores, and in the Maritime Provinces, the army had 13,000 rifles and 7,500 smoothbores; in both regions, the Sedentary Militia possessed a total of 200 rifles. As the chilling absurdity of Canada's situation penetrated the minds of the public, uncertainty replaced the former braggadocio. "With God's blessing," the *Globe* prayed, "we shall not yield an inch of our soil to an invader."[25]

Knowing that it would take more than heavenly intervention to compensate for decades of neglect, officers struggled to rebuild forts, or at least to give them the appearance of strength. The fort at Isle aux Nois and the navy base at Penetanguishene were being used as juvenile reformatories, while Fort Malden at Amherstburg served as a lunatic asylum. Toronto works were ludicrously weak, Montreal had only a few guns, and Fort Erie and the celebrated Quebec citadel were in-capable of resisting modern artillery. Williams and a colonel in the Royal Engineers embarked on an ostentatious tour of Canadian forts in November and December; the tour irritated Monck, who lamented that it was "difficult to keep before [Williams] . . . that we are not at war" and that preparation might provoke an American reaction without strengthening anything. Williams's tour confirmed existing reports; forts were either decaying or nonexistent, and the amount of necessary remedial work was stupefying. At Toronto and Kingston he proposed earthworks with heavy ordnance, and allocated two hun-dred men for extending and strengthening them. A new ten-gun bat-tery was to replace the rusty cannon overlooking the Grand Trunk Railway tracks, wharf, and channel, and a Royal Artillery officer ar-rived to instruct men in its use. Williams wanted to blow bridges over the St. Lawrence and, in the event of attack, close Toronto by sinking ships. Desperate moves were necessary.[26]

The key to checking any overland aggression against Canada was control of the Great Lakes; America would have to invade with the navy, because the prospect of attack on American cities would tie down part of the army. The first lord of the Admiralty, the Duke of Somerset, thought that no threat to Canadian ports on the Great Lakes existed, because British gunboats could annihilate the single American warship on Lake Ontario and the 100-gun vessel lying in lakeside stocks since 1813. Still, Somerset expected the United States to equip some ships, and he suggested that a naval officer assist the provincial government to prepare some gunboats to leave at short notice for the Great Lakes when winter ended.[27]

There was something pathetic about British and Canadian ef-forts. Canada had always been a hostage to friendly Anglo-American relations. Although British North America had filled a place in the imperial system, it had not warranted active defense; dangers in that part of the world had seemed less threatening after resolution of the Maine and Oregon questions. Forts decayed or had been turned into reformatories and asylums, volunteers and militia had replaced regulars; and Britain had not even bothered to station the single warship allowed by the 1818 Rush-Bagot Agreement. Canada had clearly fallen victim to political apathy.

British plans for war with the United States rested on a touching faith in the ability of the Royal Navy. Officials based grand strategy on previous Anglo-American conflicts. In the innermost sanctums of 10 Downing Street and the Foreign Admiralty, and War offices, where grave and bearded men sat around heavy oak tables and discussed distant territories, it was as if time had stood still since the French Revolution, the Napoleonic Wars, and the War of 1812. The voices of Wellington and Nelson still echoed in those musty chambers, with no one to contradict their ghostly whispers.

Statistical comparisons made it easy for makers of policy to be sanguine about a maritime war. Britain did have a large numerical advantage, for the navy comprised 856 vessels, of which 700 were steamers. Two-thirds of the fleet armament was concentrated on 16 warships. Home waters were patrolled by 46 vessels carrying 1,500 guns, and 68 tenders averaging 3 guns each. Most of the ships fell into three classes of reserves. The Royal Navy floated 80 line-of-battle ships ranging from the massive 131-gun *Royal Sovereign*, *Prince of Wales*, and *Duke of Wellington* to the 72-gun *Wellesley*. There were over 20 ships in the 60- to 70-gun class, about 40 50-gun frigates, almost 90 ships carrying between 22 and 50 guns, over 300 steamers with less than 22 guns, and 185 gunboats with 2 Armstrong cannon.[28]

Outnumbering its American counterpart by more than three to one, not a terribly large advantage for an attacking force, the Royal Navy counted on a series of lightning blows to win the day. Somerset planned a blockade of eight major ports and five secondary ports. The navy could not patrol the long Northern coast, but by concentrating outside large coastal cities with fairly good harbors, it could prevent the entry of all but the smallest ships. Combinations of line-of-battle ships, frigates, sloops, and gunboats could bottle up each of the thirteen ports. Boston, New York, and the Chesapeake region would attract the heaviest forces. Baltimore, Washington, Norfolk, and Boston would each be patrolled by seven vessels led by two line-of-battle ships. Fifteen vessels were to blockade New York's southern approach and Long Island Sound. Portland rated five ships; Delaware Bay, four; and Portsmouth and Port Royal, two apiece. Penobscot Bay, the Kennebec River, Cape Ann, Cape Cod, and Nantucket Shoal would receive complements. Presumably, sixty-eight vessels could handle the blockade, which would be much easier to maintain, Somerset decided, if Spain allowed Britain a coaling station at Havana.[29] Having no intention of fighting its way into American ports and being raked by shore batteries, the Royal Navy foresaw no difficulty in movement along the North American coast.

Admiral Milne would supervise the blockade. His force, apart from the ships designated for blockade duty, did not seem overwhelmingly strong, even though it was the largest on station since the War of 1812. At the beginning of the crisis, he commanded twenty-five ships carrying over 500 guns and 6,500 men. The *St. George* and the flagship *Nile*, 90 guns each, led the force, and Somerset allocated an additional six steamers to Milne on December 1. Three of the new ships carried only 5 or 6 guns, but the *Sanspareil*, 70 guns, and the *Conquerer* and the *Donegal*, with 99 apiece, lent an air of authority. Five days later Somerset marked for American waters the *Hero* and the *Agamemnon*, with 89 guns each; the *Aboukir*, with 86; and the *Emerald*, with 51. Double gangs worked around the clock, seven days a week, to fit out the ships. Thirty vessels were placed in readiness, including the 51-gun *Shannon* and *Euryalus*, and the *Sutlej* prepared to leave with *Devastation* and *Geyser*. Seven gunboats stood ready at Portsmouth to depart at an hour's notice. On December 6 Somerset telegraphed the commander at Malta to send two of his most efficient line-of-battle ships to join Milne at Bermuda, the base for Carribbean and South Atlantic operations. In contrast to his grudging reinforcement over the past summer, the urgency that now drove Somerset was evident. Additions eventually boosted Milne's force to some forty vessels mounting 1,273 guns, but it was still an inadequate fleet in the admiral's eyes.[30] London papers claimed that Milne commanded more ships than composed the entire Union navy. He was, in fact, outnumbered six to one, although the American navy was very old, had fewer ironclads, and contained many converted merchantmen.

The Admiralty did not expect Milne's West Indies squadron to blockade any ports except Key West and Tortugas; the main objective of the fleet was to chase blockade-runners and harass coastal cities. In the event of war, prior to blockading or attacking Northern ports, Milne was to loosen the Union's grip on the South by destroying the blockades and, "without directly cooperating with the Confederates, enable them to act & to receive supplies." Somerset recommended that as soon as Milne destroyed the Union blockade, he should secure a Southern port where ships could obtain coal. The admiral would have to stop Union supply ships at sea to prevent the United States from reinforcing its vessels in the Pacific via the railroad across Panama. There was always danger that Milne would not learn of hostilities until after the Lincoln administration had taken steps to neutralize his fleet. Assuming that Lyons would demand his passports and the United States would begin war without a declaration, Somerset suggested that Lyons direct Milne to take reprisals without waiting for orders, especially if the Americans committed warlike acts and laid an embargo on British shipping.[31]

Although Milne had been freed from blockade duty, he had been given responsibilities that did not lighten his burden. If he had sought to carry out all his duties—blockading Northern ports, attacking naval vessels, protecting British possessions and trade routes in the Atlantic and along South America—American warships would have destroyed his thinly spread blockade forces piecemeal. After considering alternatives, the admiral decided to attack American blockading squadrons north and east of Florida with fourteen ships, while Commodore Hugh Dunlop would strike to the west with eleven vessels. The remaining British ships would serve as a weak protective force for the British Carribbean. Milne had already decided to accompany the combined expedition of British, French, and Spanish warships against Mexico, but the Foreign Office advised him to send a subordinate officer wtih no more than one line-of-battle ship and two frigates, because the new crisis demanded his presence in the Atlantic.[32]

When Milne had suffered his first Lyons-induced war scare in June of 1861, he had described for London's edification the indefensibility of Bermuda, the West Indies, and other possessions in the Carribbean. The warning had failed to move his superiors to action, and now it was virtually too late.

Plans for the anticipated war with the United States continually revealed the extent to which Britain expected to fight the American Revolution and the War of 1812 again. The government worried about swarms of privateers destroying the merchant fleet. Officials brooded over the legend of John Paul Jones and, imagining how buccaneers might dart in and out of Scottish ports, suspected that American vessels were already steaming toward Pentland Firth in preparation to declaration of war. Aberdeen, Firth of Fourth, and Firth of Tay seemed likely targets. Because war with the United States had traditionally developed into a duel of large proportions, Somerset ordered a line-of-battle ship and two smaller ships to Gibraltar to protect gold ships and merchantmen plying Mediterranean and Atlantic waters.[33]

Likewise, British naval officers everywhere began to worry. Rear Admiral Sir Thomas Maitland, commander-in-chief of the Pacific Squadron, had been directed to defend trade and territory from Valparaiso (his former headquarters) to Esquimalt in British Columbia (his present base of operations, which lacked both a garrison and artillery); he considered his fleet of only a dozen ships inadequate for the task. The five warships stationed at Vancouver relied for repairs on the American dock at Mare Island in San Pablo Bay, north of San Francisco. During the autumn of 1861, the 6-gun surveying ship *Hecate* ran aground and was convoyed to Mare Island, where she remained throughout the *Trent* crisis. Another vessel, the gunboat *Forward*, needed boiler work. British Columbia and the disputed San Juan Islands were defended by two hundred Royal Engineers and Royal Marines; fortunately, in the event of war they would face even smaller American units in Oregon and Washington territories. Governor James Douglas advised Maitland to attack Puget Sound and push inland to establish posts on the Columbia, violating the Oregon Treaty of 1846. Knowing that Union privateers would be fitted in San Francisco, Maitland planned a blockade of the port, although he realized that he would have difficulty maintaining it. However, the American navy in those waters posed little threat because it consisted of only one or two small revenue cutters.[34]

Although it failed to send adequate reinforcements to Maitland, the British government did not dismiss the Pacific theater's importance, and worried that an American army might destroy the handful of British soldiers before additional forces rounded Cape Horn. A quicker route to the Pacific seemed necessary. The Americans managed the Panama Railroad, which crossed the jungles of Central America; Somerset wondered if Britain could seize it without alarming other powers. Unsure of treaty rights in the region, Russell decided to ask Washington to respect the neutrality of the Panama transit, as guaranteed in the Clayton-Bulwer treaty of 1850. American hesitation would justify seizure of the ports at both ends. He instructed his representatives in Panama to inform the local diplomatic corps and the governors of Panama, United Columbia, and New Granada that Great Britain would stand ready "at all times to act in concert with them to maintain the neutrality of the Panama Railroad." Russell ordered Lyons to inform Seward that Her Majesty's Government trusted that no attempt would be made to seize the railroad because "force [would] be met by force."[35]

If units of the Royal Navy in the Atlantic, Caribbean, and Pacific had attempted to carry out all their orders, they not only would have failed, but also would have exhausted themselves trying. Perhaps the British government was never serious about going to war over Mason and Slidell; perhaps the Americans were not the only ones who could play the game of "brag," a version of poker.

The long wait for messages to cross the Atlantic caused the British government to worry about all sorts of real and imaginary problems. Grasping at scraps of information, rumor, and foreign gossip, officials energetically investigated the wildest story and tracked down the most asinine speculation, trying to anticipate all contingencies but succeeding mainly in frightening each other.

The British believed the Washington regime capable of anything. Palmerston feared an American privateer would kidnap Queen Victoria, and stopped fretting only after the War Office assured him that an 800-man battalion stood guard a few miles away. He then worried that Washington would evade Russell's demands by taking Mason and Slidell to the Virginia border and turning them loose. Bethell suggested that the United States might claim it lacked jurisdiction, as in the McLeod incident of 1841; in which case, it might transfer Mason and Slidell to the custody of criminal law, or offer to release the prisoners to Britain pending decision by a prize court, as if the *Trent* had been taken into New York.[36]

Palmerston also related to Queen Victoria a rumor about the former general-in-chief of the United States Army, Winfield Scott, then visiting Paris in search of medical relief from dropsy and vertigo. Scott reportedly had said that the Lincoln cabinet had "deliberately determined upon and ordered" the seizure; foreseen that it might lead to war with Britain; and commissioned him to ask France "to join the Northern States in a war against England," and to offer Napoleon the restoration of Canada, formerly lost in the Seven Years' War.[37]

The story about Scott's alleged remark spread so quickly, even to the Confederacy, that the general issued a public denial, but privately told friends that Washington had ordered capture of the commissioners dead or alive if found on a rebel ship. The American consul in

Paris, John Bigelow, was so troubled that he discussed the matter with
a republican member of the Chamber of Deputies, Louis Antoine
Garnier-Pagès, who suggested publishing a letter to refute the rumor
and explain Wilkes's act. Shortly thereafter, Bigelow met with the
American minister, William L. Dayton, and two special agents and
political allies of Seward, Archbishop John Hughes and Thurlow
Weed, to frame such a document for Scott's signature. In the letter,
which appeared in *Le Moniteur Universel* on December 4, Scott
denied having said that the Lincoln administration ordered seizure of
Mason and Slidell, especially since at no period in American history
had British friendship been more important, or the United States "in a
condition to make greater concessions to preserve it." He further
stated that England certainly should neither question the right to
search commercial vessels suspected of transporting contraband, nor
complain of an act for which her own naval history offered numerous
precedents. Scott doubted that the British would make trouble over
the *Trent* not being taken into port, and assured readers that friendly
relations between the two countries were not in danger. Despite the
letter's optimism, Scott sailed for America on December 11, intending
to make available his knowledge of the Canadian frontier in the event
of war, but his hasty departure only sparked another rumor that he
had received an urgent dispatch from Washington.[38]

While waiting for Seward's answer, the Foreign Office spent
much time speculating on what it would be. Everyone expected
Washington to try to circumvent British demands. Russell worried
that Lyons might mislead or antagonize Seward, or that Seward would
somehow trick him; therefore, he advised Lyons in private letters to
prepare Seward for the demands before their presentation, and to ask
him to propose a course of action. At the next meeting Lyons should
read the dispatch and, if Seward asked the consequences, say he
wished to "leave him and the President quite free to take their own
course," and that he desired "to abstain from anything like menace."
Nevertheless, he was to assure Seward that the British government
wanted "a plain Yes, or a plain No to our very simple demands . . .
within seven days of the communication of [Russell's] dispatch." With
communication between the two countries taking twelve to fourteen
days, Lyons might receive the November 30 dispatch by mid-
December and notify Seward of its contents between December 18 and
20; this would provide Seward with a December 27 deadline for reply.
Russell decided to press Washington, because "devices for avoiding
the plain course are endless, & the ingenuity of American lawyers will
seek perhaps to entangle you in endless arguments on Vattel, Wheaton

& Scott." If Seward surrendered the Confederate prisoners and avoided making a direct apology, Britain would be satisfied, but an apology would not suffice, and Lyons would have to come home if the secretary refused to release the men. Russell believed that "the best thing would be if Seward could be turned out and a rational man put in his place."[39] Lyons dispatches had worked well; they had convinced Russell that the American secretary of state was so unpredictable, so blinded by ambition, that not even a threat of war could bring him to his senses.

All of Britain's military and naval preparations had been undertaken to place the nation in an advantageous position to attack or retaliate against American aggression, to defend weak territories, and to satisfy public outrage. Officials had once believed that the Lincoln administration would reject Russell's demands, but later decided that Washington, after a certain amount of procrastination, might eventually release the prisoners. The British government could accept nothing less, Russell told Lyons, because the *Trent* affair amounted to more than a disagreement over neutral and belligerent rights. It had become a question of national honor, and woe to any politician who shrank from its defense.

7.

"Waiting
for an Answer"

AFTER ALL THE PREPARATION, British officials could do nothing but
wait a long month for the American answer. Uncertainty gnawed at
the government as it appraised popular reaction, trying to calculate
the annoyance, pique, anti-Americanism, and confusion that marked
public opinion. Every cabinet member realized that public fury would
not remain at fever pitch, that people would perhaps come to value
peace over national honor.

Citizens continued to speak about the capture. At the Adelphi
Theatre in the Strand, a large Confederate flag billowed in the breeze
beside an American flag wrapped tightly around its staff. A cab in Oxford Street displayed on its panel the crossed flags of the Confederacy
and Great Britain, over the motto "Unum." Small boys sold miniature
Rebel banners. During intermission at Covent Garden an actor read
from an evening paper that the government had decided to exact reparation, promoting cheers and a chorus of "God Save the Queen." At
Evans's an entertainer sang about the *Trent*, how the Yankees were
used up, and why Britannia would rule forever, all to the pounding of
pint-pots on the tables. King's College advertised a course on international law to begin December 12.

Rumor abounded: Mason and Slidell had been hanged; the *War-
rior* was preparing to bring back Lyons; Palmerston favored war;
America had received a forty-eight hour ultimatum. Mrs. Slidell was

telling everyone that Lieutenant Fairfax had laughed at the suggestion of retaliation, and said "Oh, John Bull would do as he had done before, he would bark, but not bite." Naval Reserve units declared their patriotism, as did the Sunderland detachment, which resolved to "shed the last drop of our blood against any nation that dares to insult our gracious Queen or national flag." The group marched through town to the beat of a drum, carrying a large banner that declared, "Ready, aye ready!" Most Britons agreed with the writer William Thackeray that "the attitude of the nation after having its a—— kicked was notably forebearant."[1]

Businessmen and politicians advised the government on which actions to take to injure the United States most effectively. An official of the Black Ball Steamship Line suggested that all American merchantmen be seized before they could transfer to British registry. The Manchester Chamber of Commerce asked the Foreign Office if American ships bound for Britain and carrying British property would be allowed to enter and leave British ports; the government refused comment. A member of Parliament advised the Foreign Office to secure a treaty with the South before declaring war. Another declared to his constitutents that if America refused to meet Russell's demands, the Royal Navy would sweep Yankee vessels from the sea. The Persian vice-consul at Liverpool wanted to sell a 1,340-ton screw steamer adapted for carrying troops and horses, and another individual proposed transporting 30,000 men across Canada for £300,000.[2]

Meanwhile, the British press had turned to rational discussion of belligerent rights and English precedents. The *Edinburgh Review* continued to view the seizure as an act or war, but granted that the United States and Britain had changed positions on neutral rights. The editor believed all vessels carrying a government mail officer should be immune to search, despite absence of such protection in international laws. *McMillan's Magazine* agreed that it was time to call an international conference to revise and codify maritime laws for belligerents and neutrals, and lamented that "every dove is turned into a raven" because America had failed to make amends. Even the London *Times* saw no reason to assume the inevitability of British military triumph or the unsullied correctness of the English position. Although it noted that the undergunned and overage United States naval vessels contained scarcely "a dozen worthy antagonists" for British warships, it cautioned that if the Americans "will do little, they will do that little well." The *Times* conceded that the British were no more immaculate than other people in violation of maritime law, but argued that they had never treated unjustifiable acts as precedents.[3] The editor's ignorance of British practice in no way mitigated his refreshing candor.

The prospect of war no longer titillated most newspapers, which by mid-December had come to see more burden than glory in hostilities. Editors continued to berate Wilkes and the American government, and still desired reparation, but a certain caution appeared as they considered the likely ramifications of war. Agreeing with the *Times*, the *Illustrated London News* saw no reason to "fire up in anger, or to proceed in haste or in harshness to the last fearful arbitrement." The *Spectator* correctly evaluated the position of American journals as "a disposition to condemn Captain Wilkes for recklessness, even while he is exalted for pluck." Although the *Saturday Review* had no respect for the Northern urban "sewerage of Celtic and Teutonic nationalities" and considered Wilkes's act a monstrous outrage, committed in the sly, rapacious, and aggressive spirit of past American maneuvers, it saw no point in war. Many papers expected France and the cotton spinners to profit, American privateers to cover the seas, and maritime insurance rates to double, they did not expect that any significant land campaigns would develop. The prospect of an alliance with the Confederacy disturbed the London *Examiner*, which believed that to ally with the slavocracy "would not be for the honour of England." People must give the Americans a chance to surrender.[4]

Some periodicals advocated neither arbitration nor concession, but wanted either to humiliate the American government or to defeat it in battle. They saw the *Trent* affair as a clear violation of international law and national sovereignty. Dedicated to defending British honor, *Punch* castigated American perfidy in tasteless, if humorous, cartoons and verse. The first in a series of sketches during the crisis carried the caption, "LOOK OUT FOR SQUALLS." A portly British sailor, towering over a seedy, unkempt American naval officer with a brace of pistols in his sash and a cigar between his lips, admonished him, "You do what's right, my son, or I'll blow you out of the water." Another cartoon, titled "A BAD CASE OF THROWING STONES," portrayed John Bull warning an American admiral: "Now mind you sir—no shuffling—an ample apology—or I put the matter into the hands of my lawyers, Messrs. Whitworth and Armstrong" (manufacturers of cannon for the government). Verses lauded Britain as an asylum for the world's exiles and described the United States as an overgrown puppy with which John Bull had lost patience:

Remember in time the old tale of the showman
　Who his head in the mouth of the Lion would sheath,
Till with lengthened impunity, bold as a Roman,
　He seemed to forget that the Lion had teeth.[5]

PUNCH, OR THE LONDON CHARIVARI—December 7, 1861

LOOK OUT FOR SQUALLS.

Jack Bull. "YOU DO WHAT'S RIGHT, MY SON, OR I'LL BLOW YOU OUT OF THE WATER."

Courtesy of *Punch*

Throughout December, *Punch* persisted in its disdain toward the "Untied States." The magazine's editors could not understand how anyone could forget the affront to honor, and even slightly consider letting the Americans escape. To remind readers that the Lincoln administration had been given time to reach a decision, *Punch* ran a cartoon entitled "WAITING FOR AN ANSWER," which portrayed Britannia clad in helmet and armor, leaning against a cannon and casually holding the lanyard. Two weeks later, *Punch* published "COLUMBIA'S FIX," wherein Columbia asked, "Which answer shall I send?" as she sat on the ramparts of a fort overlooking the sea, with the eagle of war perched on her arm and the dove of peace clutched to her breast. The accompanying text carried the verse:

And still in doubt doth COLUMBIA stand,
A bird and an answer on either hand;
For War,—the Eagle with eyes a-glow;
For Peace—the Dove, with her plumes of snow.
But Peace or War should the message be
'Twill find them ready across the sea.[6]

PUNCH, OR THE LONDON CHARIVARI.—December 14, 1861.

WAITING FOR AN ANSWER.

Courtesy of *Punch*

Editors thought they had received an answer to Britannia's demand when Lincoln's annual message of December 3 arrived without any mention of the *Trent*. Some papers believed this a sign, but attacked the message as discursive and colloquial, poorly arranged and even more poorly expressed, "conceived in the same low moral tone and executed with the same maladroitness" of preceding American state papers. They criticized Lincoln's reference to foreign relations as "morbidly sensitive and disagreeably defiant." Speculating that the president had decided to let the course of events determine his decision, the *Times* accused him of abandoning the vessel of state to "drift helpless before the gale of popular clamour."[7]

All this discussion might have contributed to further unrest in British financial circles, which had already been whipsawed by rumor. Consols fell another 2 percent, to a rate comparable to the first years of the Crimean War, while other securities averaged declines of 4 to 5 percent. The *Times* called this an extraordinary movement since war had not yet been declared, and feared the public would view such

PUNCH, OR THE LONDON CHARIVARI—December 28, 1861.

COLUMBIA'S FIX.

Columbia. "WHICH ANSWER SHALL I SEND?"

Courtesy of *Punch*

financial developments as indications of imminent hostilities. Speculators began closing accounts, forcing prices down to a plateau. Reacting whimsically to any news, the market moved spasmodically and remained weak because of speculative movements and the large floating supply of stock in dealers' hands. The railway market, as well as colonial and foreign securities, declined; American issues went into a tailspin. The seizure of Mason and Slidell had caused a panic on the Liverpool cotton market, as the possibility of an end to the Gulf blockade dropped prices nearly two pence per pound, making it unprofitable to import large quantities from India and Egypt. Investors displayed reluctance to take extended positions in any commodity except land and homegrown wheat, which advanced steadily against the bear market. In a blend of cynicism, anxiety, and clairvoyance, the exchange emphasized the most pessimistic outlook, expecting the North to stage a new act of aggression even if the present crisis passed.[8]

A small but important movement for peaceful resolution of the crisis now appeared and gained support from a variety of interests.

Although many Britons held the "pestilent, vulgar and insolent democracy" of the United States in low repute, an alliance with the slaveholding South seemed immoral. When Mason and Slidell were viewed as representatives of slavery, the affront to honor took on new meaning. Others believed hostilities with the United States would be "a civil war—a fratricidal war—a war with our own children." "These people," Anthony Trollope wrote, "speak our language, use our prayers, read our books, are ruled by our laws, dress themselves in our image, and warm with our blood." A war with the States would be "an unloosing of hell upon all that is best upon the world's surface." Peace advocates spoke of the "slack work, low wages, and dear food" that war would bring the laboring class, which would also be called to furnish tens of thousands of men to "be slashed with swords, and stabbed with bayonets, and torn by shot, and thrown into the sea, or an undistinguished mass of carnage, heaped together in some pit upon a distant battle-field." Shippers and merchants, who had already seen insurance rates soar, envisioned destruction of the maritime fleet by American privateers, and anticipated an end to lucrative transatlantic trade; such concerns led them to wonder if the Lincoln administration should be given more time. "Is our flag of so recent invention, with so poor a history, enriched with so few memories of glory, that it will be dishonoured by a short and dignified delay?" A growing number of people thought not. Although advocates of peace resented Wilkes's action, they could not view it as a cause for hostilities. Peace rallies blossomed in Scotland. Several large public meetings in Lancashire soon resolved for government mediation. In Liverpool, people did not want war, neglected preparations, and found hope in "every idle telegram and . . . every imperfect rumour" of a peaceful solution. A Lancashire member of Parliament, W. E. Forster, won the support of 2,000 constituents when he urged arbitration and suggested that the Union be given a grace period for passions to cool, after which the Americans would probably make reparation, but not an apology. A meeting in Brighton, attended by two members of Parliament, agreed that the affair arose from misinterpretation of international law, and adopted a unanimous resolution that the dispute be referred to a neutral power.[9]

Two other members of Parliament, John Bright and Richard Cobden, made themselves odious to the "Rule Britannia" crowd. Known as spokesmen for the United States in Parliament, they admired Americans, corresponded with them, and lauded their policy of nonintervention in Europe. Palmerston disliked Bright and Cobden for having "run a muck [sic] against everything that the British Nation respects and values—Crown, Aristocracy, Established Church, Nobility, Gentry, Landowners" and for having "laboured incessantly to set class against class, and the Poor against the rich."[10] The government was not surprised to learn that the two liberals were trying to rally public opinion against war with America.

Bright had antagonized the establishment throughout his long opposition to a church rate, the Corn Laws, capital punishment, and imperialism. His resistance to the Crimean War had won him the nickname "John Muscobright" and Palmerston's scathing analysis that he reduced everything—including liberty and independence—to the question of pounds, shillings, and pence, and would vote against defenses if it were cheaper to be conquered. Bright's pro-Americanism irritated critics who resented his "strange hallucinations" about the quality of American presidents, educational systems, and finances, compared to British institutions. Having made the Civil War a test of the English Radical creed, he aroused intense hatred and probably did serious, if unintentional, damage to the cause of the United States. "If I had my way, I would blow President Lincoln from a mortar with a bombshell, and, if there wasn't wadding enough," declared a conservative, "I'd ram John Bright down in after him."[11]

Loathing the diplomatic service as "a gigantic system of relief for the aristocracy," Bright had no confidence in the ability of the Foreign Office to bring a peaceful end to the *Trent* affair. He had resented the seizure of Mason and Slidell and had hoped for ample retaliation, but as the nation prepared for war he attempted to defuse public anger. He opened his campaign on a cold night in December with a speech to his Rochdale constituents that lasted one hour and forty minutes; in the speech, he reminded the audience that Britain had not observed friendly and cordial neutrality in the Civil War because she was not accustomed to being neutral. He would not deny that the seizure was impolitic, regardless of legality, but he believed that the United States would make reparation for the action if American lawyers condemned it. Although Palmerston and Russell had argued that the seizure was another example of Washington's desire to pick a quarrel, Bright disagreed; he doubted the Lincoln administration had authorized the capture. Do you believe, he asked, that any government fighting a formidable insurrection "would invite the armies and fleets of England . . . to render it impossible that the Union should ever again be restored?" Accidents could happen in any war and Britons should not let bloodthirsty journalists turn them against their former countrymen. What could be more monstrous than "before we have made a representation to the American Government, before we have heard a word from it in reply, [we] should be all up in arms, every sword leaping from its scabbard and every man looking about for his pistols and his blunderbusses?"[12]

Journalistic reaction to Bright's speech was predictably hostile. Newspapers ridiculed him as the "Great Infallible," and accused him of attacking the national interest. "Mr. John Bright has appeared as *amicus curiae* in the court of Mr. Justice LYNCH," the Manchester *Guardian* said, "and summed up the case, as usual, against his country." The London *Times* treated Britain's "political shrew" tolerantly. A devil's advocate was a useful institution, it declared, and people should rest assured that nothing else could be said against the nation. Never missing an opportunity to snipe at an old adversary, *Punch* reacted with a poem:

> Keep some fight, for the Yankees, JOHN BRIGHT,
>   JOHN BRIGHT
> Keep some fight for the Yankees, JOHN BRIGHT;
>   To their wrong if they stand,
>   And reject our demand,
> And declare CAPTAIN WILKS [*sic*] in the right,
>   JOHN BRIGHT
> If they vote CAPTAIN WILKS in the right.[13]

Richard Cobden, who had worked with Bright against the Corn Laws and the Crimean War, joined the crusade for tolerance by speaking to public meetings, writing vigorous letters to be read at gatherings he could not attend, and corresponding with notables at home and abroad. Although he thought peace could be preserved only by arbitration, he recommended other courses to his influential friend in America, Charles Sumner: free Mason and Slidell; stipulate that Britain abandon the old code of maritime law; exempt private property from capture at sea by armed government ships; exempt neutral vessels from search or visitation; and abolish privateering and blockades. Wishing the United States to release its prisoners and agree to the Declaration of Paris, he suggested that Washington raise the blockade before Europe did, and recognize Southern belligerency in order to gain "*a standing ground on the Trent affair.*" Perhaps, he wrote half-seriously to a Manchester merchant, the "wisest course would be to leave open their prison door by mistake and let them run." Although Cobden never said so publicly, he believed that a compelling factor for peace was Anglo-French reliance on American grain.[14]

Convinced that parliamentary declamations and letters to newspapers would have negligible effect on the nation's course during the

Trent crisis, Cobden viewed public meetings as the best way to press the government. They should advocate arbitration instead of peace, he said, because the latter might imply submission. Critics of Bright and Cobden charged that they had "done their best to bring about war by trying to make the Yankees believe that their offence was slight." The two men were careful not to leave that impression, and always cautioned American correspondents that England was in an ugly mood. When Bright approved Cobden's strategy for protest assemblies, the latter began to think about "a permanent society for the sole object of applying the Resolution of the Paris Congress, in favor of Arbitration to all cases of misunderstanding as they may arise." How, he asked, could the government spend millions for protection against France, yet rush into an American war, giving Napoleon III a free hand in Europe. "Might we not be justified in turning hermits," he sighed, "letting our beards grow, and returning to our caves!"[15]

If Bright and Cobden were in the fore of the arbitration movement, the churches followed closely. On the Sunday following reception of the stirring news, ministers of several churches and chapels had mentioned the insult to the British flag and the necessity of vindicating national honor, while their congregations applauded the government. Yet, religious spokesmen lost no time exerting their influence on the behalf of peace, and reminding Christians of their duty. The publisher of the *Protestant Layman*, James Frazer, implored Lord Russell "as a Christian statesman" to use every possible effort to "avoid so dire and dreadful a calamity as a war with our own flesh and blood in America." Both the Confederacy and the Cottonocracy of Britain, he wrote, would do anything to involve the Federal government in war with another country and facilitate the export of cotton, thus the false cry of indignation, "redress-revenge-war." Nonconformist churches worked to reverse belligerent opinion. When the Evangelical Alliance, an amalgam of Dissenters and Churchmen, called a meeting at Exeter Hall, four thousand members came to pray for peace. A few days later at a general assembly of the three major Dissenting denominations in London, resolutions condemning war and favoring arbitration passed unanimously. The Committee of the Peace Society asked all Christian denominations in England to "throw the oil of Christian love on the rising waters of strife." The Board of Congregational Ministers in and around London and Westminster suggested arbitration, while the Baptist Union of Great Britain and Ireland and the Congregational Union of England and Wales presented peace memorials to Russell in person.[16] A stream of petitions flowed into the Foreign Office.

The Society of Friends drew up a memorial at the London Meeting for Sufferings on December 6 and 9. One of the memorial's promoters, Jonathan Pim of Dublin, had suggested settling the dispute by referring the question of neutral and belligerent rights, particularly limits on the right of visit and search, to a congress of maritime powers. Although the London body did not adopt Pim's call, it incorporated arbitration in the memorial, which was signed by forty-one persons and presented to Palmerston and Russell on December 9. The memorial asked that, in the event of an unsatisfactory American reply, the government refer the dispute to arbitration, rather than declare war. The Friends indicated they did not approve of all Northern activities, even in regard to slavery, and would use their connections to encourage brethren on the other side of the Atlantic to lobby peacefully with state legislatures.[17]

Hope for the memorial having a "sedative effect," of lessening the pressure on the government, went unfulfilled. Palmerston refused to send a delegation to the Meeting for Sufferings, and showed no sign of being affected by the petition, or even of having read it. The Friends could always pray for the spiritual guidance of the prime minister, but some churchmen, remembering his past refusals to appoint days of prayer for the harvest or relief from cholera, doubted it would do any good; the prime minister seemed to view Heaven as a foreign power.[18]

The government did not welcome journalistic discussion of legal technicalities and Britain's maritime conduct; efforts to rally sentiments against war; or petitions and memorials of religious and peace groups, all of which pressed the Palmerston cabinet. Officials were not as afraid of peace as they were apprehensive that conciliatory feeling would not only lessen resolve to defend honor, but encourage the Lincoln administration. Cabinet members began to wonder if they had misjudged opinion and acted precipitately.

Amazed at the public transition from anger to deliberation within two weeks, the foreign secretary decided that if the Americans refused to surrender the commissioners in a "reasoning, & not a blunt offensive answer," London should give them another opportunity. "I do not think the country would approve an immediate declaration of war," he told Palmerston.[19] If the antiwar movement continued to attract advocates, the administration would have to enter the public discussion of international law to attempt to explain how the *Trent* affair violated maritime precedents established by Admiralty courts, but not always followed by British governments. The most difficult task involved defending the demand for Mason and Slidell, while simultaneously refusing arbitration. Uninformed opinion, based on a naive faith in a statement of the facts, argued that a just case would inevitably triumph.

Long after the cabinet had decided to demand the envoys, law officers continued to ransack volumes for cases justifying the seizure. Although War Secretary Lewis could not find such a case, he believed the doctrine advanced by England in 1812 regarding search for seamen in neutral ships "certainly approaches to the act which we now condemn, but it is not identical." Lewis did not agree with Bethell that the Lincoln administration was preparing to meet British demands, and half expected Washington to refer the matter to the czar of Russia for arbitration, a move that would cause all sorts of international and domestic political problems. "They are busy at the Foreign Office hunting up precedents for arbitration very much against their will," chortled a peace activist.[20]

During the last three weeks of December, the Foreign Office and Crown law officers flooded cabinet members with confidential memoranda. A memorandum of December 7 compared the *Trent* incident with four cases spread over sixty years, yet found no holes in the British argument; another of December 14 discussed the arrest of Lucien Bonaparte; a December 26 memorandum treated the Neopolitan government's capture of Garibaldian volunteers, and detention and search of the American ship *Peggy* by a British warship in 1802; the *Hendrick en Alida* and *Caroline* cases were reviewed on December 28 and 30. The *Hendrick* case excited officials because they found a precedent for release of Mason and Slidell. In 1777, during the American Revolution, a Dutch brig had been brought in to Portsmouth because it carried a cargo of arms and ammunition and five military officers commissioned by the colonial army. The Admiralty Court had ruled that the ship and contents were free to leave, since the vessel had been proceeding from one neutral port to another. Lord Chancellor Bethell regarded the case as extremely important; the same principles could be applied in the *Trent* case to support the British position.[21] Still, all this supportive documentation would be helpful only if the case went to arbitration, a situation that the government seriously hoped to avoid.

Legal opinion encouraged prudence, and officials began to consider alternatives to demanding the diplomats' release, including arbitration. Hoping to confront the United States with an ironclad case against Wilkes's action, Hammond asked Crown lawyers if international law recognized a difference between postal packets and other merchant ships. They answered negatively, on the asumption that the mail ship was privately owned and chartered to carry mail. Hammond's query reflected a desire of many officials and advisers to find broad ground, "as little technical, and attorney-like as possible." Argyll disliked precipitating an international crisis over Wilkes's technical violation of international law—removing Mason and Slidell from the *Trent* instead of conveying the vessel and its contents to a Northern port for adjudication; a prize court may or may not have ruled that Moir's resistance to search constituted grounds for seizure. Although forms of procedure constituted the "essence of justice," compliance with proper forms would have eliminated ground for complaint, despite the illegality of the commissioner's detention. Both Gladstone and Russell thought it a mockery for the United States to restore Mason and Slidell, or to free them on parole pending the decision of an arbiter, whose decision might return them to bondage or execution, completing the defeat and degradation of England. If Washington restored the diplomats, Russell was willing to sign a treaty, similar to the Franco-American agreement of 1801, giving up "our pretentions of 1812—& Securing immunity to persons not in arms on board neutral vessels—or to all persons going bonà fide from one neutral port to another." It struck him as a nice compromise, "a triumph to the U.S. in principle while the particular case would be decided in our favor." Russell continued to refuse any mediation while the Confederate agents remained in American custody.[22]

International opinion, so long the bane of British foreign policy, now acquired unusual importance in cabinet strategy. In the old days Britain had never worried about the attitudes of other nations, but the growth of European navies, the increased difficulty of defending the empire, and the economic consequences of war—even with the United States—were horrible to contemplate. Britain's world dominance of the seventeenth and eighteenth centuries had vanished; the Royal Navy, although more powerful than ever, no longer ruled the waves absolutely. Forced to accommodate a new order, the English people had to live with the possibility that old grudges might surface as Eurpopean governments, especially France, saw an opportunity to repay Britain.

Fortunately, the French government never considered taking advantage of the *Trent* affair. Although the war had crimped France's cotton supply, Napoleon III's adventure in Mexico and his desire to use the United States as a counter to British naval and commercial power precluded action. French liberal support of the Union, and opposition to the Second Empire, as well as the danger of the Royal

Navy to Napoleon's ambitions, discouraged moves against Britain. Inclined to adopt a neutral stand, the emperor had the support of his people.

At the outset French opinion seemed against the Washington government. "Till the Seizure of the *Trent* France was with us in sympathy," the United States consul general in Paris, John Bigelow, wrote Seward in early December. "On that subject there is not a live Frenchman that is not against us, not even the Republicans of '48." News of the affair had struck the Bourse like a bomb—the bulls reeling in astonishment, and the bears spreading rumors that Britain and the United States had broken relations and that Adams had received his passports. Funds that had been steadily rising closed down, and the bears went home "uttering blessings long and loud" on Captain Wilkes and the *San Jacinto*. The event dominated conversation in financial and commercial circles; Unionists and Secessionists congregated at café's to discuss the likely results; and on every corner one could hear, "*Grand Dieu! Quel reveil attend ces pauvres gens-là!*" ("Great God! What an awakening awaits those poor people!") Liberals were torn between support for the Union cause and conviction that a principle of international law had been violated. Initial French reaction condemned Wilkes for acting as an Admiralty judge, and the United States as "a Power reckless of the obligations of international law."[23]

Then it became clear that the French were friendly. Reports of the *procureurs généraux*, the Ministry of Justice's legal agents in the twenty-eight Imperial Court districts, provided the best information on how the ordinary citizen viewed the *Trent* affair. Besides serving as public prosecutors-in-chief, these officials were charged with taking accurate surveys of public opinion; their reports to Paris were free of the distortions in newspapers and superior to material collected by the prefects. They revealed a general desire for neutrality in an Anglo-American war, as well as support for French mediation of the dispute. Agents in several towns reported that fear of hostilities had drastically reduced business transactions, although merchants disagreed on whether a war would damage the French economy. But more towns thought a conflict would mean increased profit for the carrying trade if American privateers forced English ships to transfer cargoes to neutral powers. Owners of textile mills in Colmar, having stocked up on winter supplies, feared that war would bring a glut of cotton and depress prices, while colleagues in Besancon trembled at the possible destruction of the American merchant fleet and ultimate control of cotton supplies by England. Only the businessmen of Nancy and Bordeaux demanded intervention to secure cotton and markets.[24]

Concentrating on reaction in the business community throughout France, the reports provided moderate government officials with arguments for peace, and antidotes to belligerent articles appearing in the press.

The opinions expressed in the French press made France seem especially chilly to Union supporters in December of 1861. Although the newspapers did not reflect public opinion, they agreed that the seizure was wrong, but differed on what France's official position should be. Progovernment journals, in keeping with their Confederate sympathies, opposed the Union action. The *Constitutionnel*, which scoffed at the idea of war, argued that because the United States would have seized Mason and Slidell under any flag, there was no reason to sacrifice the Anglo-French alliance, "the pivot of the modern world." Carrying the British connection a step further, *La Patrie* supported the position of the Crown law officers, declared that the *Trent* question was crucial to all maritime nations, and urged that France cooperate with Britain. An article in the *Gazette des Tribunaux,* which was reprinted in London for cabinet use, attacked the seizure and stated that past English conduct had no bearing on the affair because the rights of all neutral powers were affected. The semiofficial *Pays* denied the legality of Wilkes's act and said that the prisoners, who could not be seized as either soldiers or diplomats, would have to be surrendered. It looked to the inevitable collapse of the Union and emergence of the South as an independent nation. The liberal press at first defended the United States, but gradually gave ground. Two Orleanist papers, the *Journal des Débats* and *Revue des Deux Mondes,* could not believe that Lincoln had risked war with an "incomprehensible provocation"; they opposed French involvement against America, fearing that London might seize upon the *Trent* crisis as an excuse to break the blockade. Both the conservative *Correspondant* and the *Débats* called the capture of Mason and Slidell an "infinitely regrettable mistake" but not a crime or a premeditated insult, and accused the *Trent*'s captain of violating neutrality by carrying Confederate dispatches. The *Opinion Nationale, Journal du Havre,* and *Indépendence Belge* also absolved Wilkes of any provocation, but could not justify the act.[25]

Discussion of international law, normally confined to a few experts, became as popular in France as it was in England and the United States. A well-known authority, Laurent B. Hautefeuille, published *Questions de Droit International Maritime,* which circulated widely and eventually reached the British government. Charging the *San Jacinto*'s commander with violating every rule on the right of visit, he said the diplomats could not be considered contraband because they were not in military service of the enemy and were traveling between neutral ports on a neutral vessel. The ship should have been conveyed to port for judgment. Wilkes had acted "contrary to the most elementary and most important principles of international maritime law," he declared, and the seizure constituted "a bloody outrage."[26] Generally supporting the British law officers, Hautefeuille cut to the center of the problem, set forth the issues, and delineated procedures that Wilkes should have followed.

American and British diplomats in Paris reported every scrap of information relating to the opinion of the French government. Conflicting rumors circulated: the minister of marine was "itching" to join England; the Council of State had decided to recognize the Confederacy; the Council of State favored neutrality. Officials and agents of both Britain and America worried about French intentions. Although Paris had supplied 5,000 pairs of boots from army stores to outfit British troops going to Canada, Lord Russell suspected that Napoleon had an ulterior motive. He queried the British minister in Paris, Lord Cowley, who assured him that his suspicion was groundless. Russell was plainly worried that the emperor would attack Austria as a means of securing Venetia and the Rhine. In the past, Napoleon had embarked on foreign adventures to distract the public from problems at home. According to Lord Cowley, Austria was safe because Napoleon faced no domestic crises and Italy did not have the finances to aid such a war. American agents had less cause for optimism. Bigelow feared that if Napoleon were asked to mediate the question, he would insist on reviewing the Confederate cause. An unoffical goodwill envoy, the Catholic archbishop of New York, John Hughes, recommended that Seward ask France to arbitrate, or, failing that, the secretary should persuade the Lincoln administration to give Mason and Slidell fair trial, condemn them to death, commute the sentences, and allow them to leave. Another Union activist, the wealthy capitalist and former minister to the Netherlands, August Belmont, advocated arbitration by Russia, France, or Holland, and predicted that although the verdict would go against America, it would save national honor.[27] In the absence of an official government declaration, the diplomatic corps lived on rumor.

French Minister of Foreign Affairs Thouvenel mercifully put an end to speculation about French policy. After learning of Russell's message to Lyons, he sent Mercier instructions on France's position on

December 3. He began by describing the public feeling of extreme astonishment at an act committed in apparent violation of international law. The French government felt obligated to speak out in the interests of neutral rights and international peace. He stated that France was unable to understand how the Lincoln administration could approve Wilkes's conduct without forgetting America's principles; the diplomats were not liable to seizure as contraband of war because the flag protects all passengers not in military service of an enemy. Moreover, they could not be removed as "bearers of official dispatches of the enemy" because the *Trent* was a neutral ship traveling between neutral ports, nor could they be seized as rebels without violating the immunity accorded sovereign territory. He recommended compliance with British demands and claimed that France had proved its loyal friendship to the United States by revealing its views.[28]

Unaware of Thouvenel's message, the American minister to Paris, William L. Dayton, requested an interview with him on December 6. Thouvenel indicated to Dayton that although the *Trent* affair was England's problem, his government viewed it as a clear breach of international law. Dayton asked if France would go beyond expression of an opinion in the event of war, and Thouvenel replied that although his country would be a spectator, the moral force of its opinion would be against the United States. Thouvenel's words spread through the American community in Paris, prompting Archbishop Hughes to request an interview with Napoleon. Meeting with the emperor, empress, and prince imperial on December 27 for an hour and ten minutes, Hughes implored Napoleon's services as a mediator. The emperor declined, stating that the issue involved national honor and not a material question.[29] The French government had moved carefully in the Anglo-American crisis, refusing to become involved but condemning the seizure in a friendly manner. If other nations reacted similarly, the United States would find itself isolated.

The only continental power likely to oppose Britain and France on the *Trent* issue was Russia, which had been defeated by them in the Crimean War five years earlier. Despite a shaky rapprochement with France, the czarist regime nursed a barely controlled rage against the victors, resented British suspicions of Russian designs on Turkey and India, and sought friendship with the United States. Dislike for democracy did not prevent Russia from viewing the Americans as a commercial and naval balance to the Anglo-French threat, but the relationship rested on common hatred of England. The Russian government, however, could not justify Wilkes's action. When the American minister, Cassius M. Clay, a swashbuckling, knife-wielding Kentuckian, approached Foreign Minister Aleksandr Gorchakov to learn the czar's attitude, Gorchakov answered that no American argument against release of the prisoners would be effective because Britain based its protest on political and industrial reasons, not facts.[30]

Gorchakov encountered difficulty with the British minister, Lord Napier, who reported that although Gorchakov first appeared to regard the seizure as "violent, impolitic & illegal," he hesitated to express an opinion and would probably not analyze the incident unless he considered a ruling an "imperious official necessity." Desirous of preventing war, Napier told Gorchakov that he favored arbitration or mediation by an "impartial, non-maritime Power." After learning that Gorchakov had also rebuffed the French chargé, Fournier, Napier pleaded with Gorchakov for an official opinion. The Russian appeared shaken and answered that he saw no reason to cry aloud on a single alleged infraction of international law when nations daily ignored illegalities, especially since Russia, unlike France, had no motive for rescuing England. He reminded Napier that he, as well as Russian envoys in England and America, had given conciliatory advice to Union, Confederate, and British leaders in the past, but their counsels had neither been sought nor heeded, and he would not "preach in the desert." Finally satisfied that the Russian government would not deviate from strict neutrality, Napier concluded that Gorchakov's "surly isolation" indicated hostility to Britain; he reported to Britain that Gorchakov had no desire to harm the United States, but preferred to see "England suffer, than America thrive."[31]

When the British Foreign Office learned of Napier's meeting with Gorchakov, it rebuked Napier for approaching Gorchakov without official sanction. Appalled by Napier's request for arbitration, Russell said that he should have strengthened Gorchakov's negative opinion of the seizure. Napier had not studied the Paris agreement of 1856, which did not contemplate arbitration of questions affecting national honor. If an arbiter had decided against England, French and Italian flags would have protected passengers on their ships, but the British flag would have safeguarded no one. Reminding Napier of Russia's desire to counteract the Royal Navy with American vessels, Russell openly questioned the minister's common sense. Undersecretary Hammond was equally perturbed by Napier's action. Although Hammond had not opposed Napier's appointment, because it seemed impossible to make mischief in St. Petersburg, he now admitted that he had not understood that a man of Napier's character could be dangerous "even under the most discouraging circumstances."[32] The Foreign Office obviously believed that, through the greatest of luck, Britain had avoided a heavy blow to the appearance of a solid European front it so desperately wanted to show the United States. With Russia neutralized, no other power possessed sufficient prestige to damage Britain's strategy.

Although other nations, including Austria, detested the Confederacy and sympathized with the Union during the Civil War, they would not defend Wilkes. The Austrian government and people identified the Union cause with law, order, and legitimate authority, and viewed the Southern position as rebellion and anarchy; Vienna's leading paper, *Die Presse*, ran articles supporting the Union almost daily. The Austrian mail service would not handle letters carrying Confederate addresses; the War Department speeded delivery of 60,000 rifles from arsenals to the United States; and officials constantly asked the American minister, John Lothrop Motley, for permission to serve in the Union army. Motley anticipated no foreign interference with the war "unless we bring it on by ourselves by bad management, which I do not expect." Two weeks later, he was concerned that Seward would try to avoid dishonor by evading Russell's demands. Living his life "in telegrams," he did not appreciate "gas blowers" who threatened war with England, and he dreaded to see a servant bring in a folded piece of paper on a salver, always picking it up between thumb and finger "as if it were a deadly asp" instead of a telegram. Motley came to abhor diplomatic dinners; everyone discussed the *Trent* "very gravely, looking very wise, & being really very ignorant."[33] As the historian of the rise of the Dutch Republic, Motley feared that he might one day chronicle the dissolution of his own country at the hands of an Anglo-Confederate alliance; therefore, he decided not to push matters by seeking a friendly word from the Austrian government.

The British minister to Austria, Lord Bloomfield, did not suffer as much anxiety as Motley did. His government, unlike Motley's, kept him informed, and the Vienna regime heartily condemned the seizure. When Bloomfield revealed Russell's demands to the Austrian foreign minister, Count Rechberg complimented their moderate terms and stated that he hoped they would be answered in a spirit of conciliation. Austria had its own reasons for encouraging peace between Britain and America: an Anglo-American war would allow France to meddle with Italy and Germany. Bloomfield saw Rechberg again on December 16, and suggested that he inform the United States of his belief in the correctness of Britain's position. Rechberg agreed that world criticism would encourage the Lincoln administration to make reparation and resist popular pressure for war. A few days later he notified the Austrian representative in Washington that Austria believed England had the right under international law to protest the insult and demand satisfaction. The United States, he concluded, should be able to grant the inoffensive demands without sacrificing its dignity.[34]

Prussian statesmen also saw advantages in a peaceful resolution of the crisis, which both diplomats and ordinary citizens feared as being harmful to commerce. The *Preussiche Stern Zeitung* stressed America's military weakness, while local papers claimed that England had proposed to signers of the Paris Declaration that they raise the blockade and recognize Confederate independence. The American minister, Norman B. Judd, former manager of Lincoln's campaign for the presidential nomination, asked the Prussian foreign minister, Count Bernstorff, if the rumor contained any truth. Bernstorff denied that Britain had made such a proposition and asserted that either Britain or the United States had sufficient ground for debate, but neither should blunder directly into war. When Judd asked, "Why dont [*sic*] your government keep the peace?", Bernstorff said he thought that any interference might be misconstrued. The British minister Lord Augustus Loftus, raised the same issue a week later, and Bernstorff conceded that, in the interests of peace, it would be sensible to ask the United States to make reparation; however, he believed that such a message would probably arrive too late for "any practical service." Loftus immediately replied "it [is] never too late to do a good and right act" that might cause Lincoln to reflect on the consequences of refusal. The French minister, La Tour d'Auvergne, added pressure by reading Thouvenel's note to Bernstorff and inviting Prussian cooperation.[35]

On Christmas Day, Bernstorff wrote to Baron von Gerolt, the Prussian Minister to the United States. The dispatch bore resemblance to Austria's. It apologized for not speaking out earlier due to lack of information, and expressed a conviction that England would not set conditions that would offend American honor. Ardent concern for the welfare of the United States, he said, prompted the King to hope for peaceful settlement. But Prussian and Austrian efforts for peace only irritated American officials, who resented advice from "second-class" powers. Seward later remarked that Prussia could do worse than to follow America's general maritime policy. A State Department adviser scornfully labeled the Austrian and Prussian notes as "the kick of asses at what they suppose to be the dying lion."[36]

The newly established Kingdom of Italy, delicately preserving independence against Austrian and Papal hostility, refrained from advising the United States, although the Turin Diplomatic corps and Italian officials unanimously condemned the Condederate agents' seizure. At a reception the American minister, George P. Marsh, asked Foreign Minister Ricasoli if the newspaper accounts that the King had considered mediation were true. Disgusted with the treatment of Italy by the world powers, Ricasoli condemned international congresses and foreign mediations, interventions, and arbitrations; he believed that Italy had never benefited from international meddling and he had no desire to harm America. When Seward learned of Ricasoli's remarks he wrote merrily, "I do not know whether the Baron would esteem it complimentary, but . . . you may say to him that he speaks on the subject very much like an American statesman."[37]

In the Papal States, opinion was divided concerning the *Trent* crisis; the Pope's agents prayed for American capitulation, but other ecclesiastical circles favored war. Some suspected that the United States and France had planned the seizure to draw England into war. The Ultramontane party, an extremist group, assumed that France, after defeating Britain, would reestablish the Italian Confederation with the Pope as honorary president. The cardinal secretary of state, Giacomo Antonelli, symphathized with Union efforts to subdue the Confederacy and hoped that the Union would avoid further hardship by yielding to English demands, which he believed to be in accordance with international law. He told Marsh that Great Britain obviously saw an opportunity to weaken Federal authority, but he suggested that the United States deal with such foreign adversaries after the Civil War had ended.[38]

Across the length of Europe, rulers, politicians, and private citizens disapproved of the seizure. The American minister to Spain, Carl Schurz, found that all Spaniards opposed it, except those naturally hostile toward England, and advised Seward not to depend on any European sympathy. The Spanish minister of state, Calderon Collantes, informed Schurz's first secretary that Spain believed the illegal action of the American naval officer compelled England to protest. Although the Council of Ministers had not yet discussed Spain's position in the event of an Anglo-American war, he thought complete neutrality would best serve Spanish interests. The Netherlands and Sweden held similar views.[39]

International expressions of disapproval pleased the British government, but offended the United States. Lord Clarendon was probably accurate when he remarked that "the Yankees altho [*sic*] they mean to whip all Creation don't like to stand alone in the midst of it." Although most of the protests arrived too late to affect Washington's attitude, they were an impressive display of interdependence and, perhaps, as Elihu Root later observed, of acceptance of a "moral obligation" to preserve "the law through which alone the community can continue to exist."[40] European governments realized that if the seizure of Mason and Slidell passed unchallenged, citizens of any nation could not travel the seas without fear of molestation; thus, they protested Wilkes's act just as in previous times they had seconded American objections to British maritime practices.

Americans residing overseas understood the international reaction and viewed the *Trent* affair as a dangerous blunder, a rip in the fabric of national security that threatened to aid the Confederate cause. The interminable delay of the American response created a period of anxious uncertainty that weighed heavily on Americans thousands of miles from home; ignorant of their country's reaction to the seizure, they were filled with a feeling of utter helplessness as events seemed to spin out of control, and the two nations drifted toward war. When the crisis wore on for two weeks, a month, six weeks, hopes for peace grew slimmer and the possiblility of war less remote. Union agents abroad cast about desperately for ways to avoid hostilities or to place their government in a stonger strategic position.

American visitors to Britain found the American minister quiet and serious during those bleak December days of 1861. Feeling as if he were "perched on the top of a volcano, doubtful at every minute where I may find myself," Adams marveled at the calm confidence of Northerners that Britain would accept Wilkes's action merely because Americans could quote chapter and verse of past British outrages. "Here is all Europe from end to end arrayed in opinion against you," he wrote, "and not a shade of suspicion that you may not be right yet rests upon your brows." Adams privately thought that Great Britain was right in principle but inconsistent, and moaned, "Our mistake is that we are donning ourselves in her cast-off suit, when our own is better worth wearing." The minister's son, Henry Adams, fiercely critical of his friends for deserting the "great principles of our fathers," declared simply, "You're mad, all of you." The American legation was especially disturbed because the State Department had not kept them as informed as some British politicians seemed to be. If his father were to see Lord Russell walking down the street, Henry remarked, "I believe he'd run as fast as he could down the nearest alley." Knowing little more than what he read in newspapers, Adams grumbled that his situation was "becoming very rapidly not merely one of little or no public use but also of some personal embarrassment." The minister might have been less ignorant of developments if he had not forced Henry Sanford to suspend his espionage operations against Confederate agents in Britain at the beginning of the *Trent* crisis because they had attracted public notice and appeared to infringe on Adams's own preserve. Unfortunately, no comparable system existed for collecting information, and American consuls lacked the time to mount a similar, less conspicuous, operation. So Adams continued to fret and tried to complete the legation's ordinary business, expecting diplomatic relations to be severed within a month. He finally begged Seward to send full information, complaining, "I am placed in a predicament almost as awkward as if I had not been commissioned here at all."[41]

In mid-December, Adams finally received a brief message that said that Wilkes had acted without instructions or the government's knowledge, and that since Lyons had refrained from discussing it, Seward had decided to wait for the British reaction. On the same day another note arrived with a list of grievances against Britain. Seward repeated that "without indicating that we attach much importance to it," Adams might say to Russell that Wilkes had acted on his own and freed the government from the "embarassment which might have resulted if the act had been specially directed by us." Urged by two legation secretaries, Wilson and Moran, to read the note to Russell, Adams waited two days before requesting an interview.[42]

Adams's appointment was for Thursday, December 19, at 3:00 P.M. He began by informing Russell of Seward's disclaimer and then tried to convince the foreign secretary that America did not want war, saying that he did not understand how the rumors about Seward had started. Russell referred him to a speech Seward had made in 1860, which advocated the acquisition of Canada as compensation for loss of the South; the British could not ignore Seward's record. Nevertheless, Adams stated, the American government had not authorized the seizure. Russell nodded, saying that he had never thought so, once he had learned of the *James Adger*'s intructions. At Adams's unofficial request, Russell summarized the contents of his November 30 message to Lyons. Adams declared that Seward's statement denying authorization of the capture should pass for an apology; would war result if

Lyons left Washington? Russell answered that much would depend on America's reply to the British demands. Irritated by Russell's coolness, Adams told him that the French government had maintained neutral rights; he could not pay Great Britain the same compliment. He would dispense with compliments, Russell retorted, if the *Trent* affair could be amicably resolved. Adams returned to the legation as depressed as he had been before the meeting. The frosty exchange had proceeded according to his expectations, and seemed to have accomplished nothing; the British government still insisted on the release of Mason and Slidell, and Washington, although it disclaimed responsibility, showed no intention of surrendering its prisoners.[43]

Yet the British position, unknown to Adams, had shifted significantly. Russell had been impressed by Adams's oft-stated belief that Washington would yield on the issue if Britain's tone was "not too peremptory"; therefore, he had instructed Lord Lyons not to insist on an apology if the American government stated that Wilkes's act was unauthorized. The key to overcoming mob influence on the American government, Russell told Palmerston, was for the bankers in the eastern cities to refuse purchase of bonds to pay the expenses of an Anglo-American war. Argyll regarded Seward's message as clearly indicating a "desire to avoid collision—to keep open a door for their own retreat" unless popular passions blocked the way. Lewis was also cheered by the interview. "Seward," he told Gladstone, "does not wish to provoke a war."[44]

The Russell-Adams interview encouraged gossip over the next few weeks. The afternoon following the meeting, Thurlow Weed, who had been working in London as a propagandist for only a few days before the *Trent* crisis, rushed into the legation with news that stocks had gone up on the rumor that Adams had read a peaceful dispatch to Russell. Belief in the rumor was so widespread that the *Morning Post*, a Palmerstonian organ, denied it; but the country eventually learned on January 11 from American newspapers that such a dispatch had been read. The *Post* then accused Adams of suppressing the dispatch so that he and his friends could buy depressed stocks in anticipation of a rise. Of course, there was no truth in the allegation. One man had offered Weed £3,000 for an "intimation" from home, but neither Weed nor Adams engaged in stock-jobbing or other financial deals. Adams concluded that Palmerston, anticipating a refusal of British demands, had deliberately suppressed Seward's note so that he could maintain public excitement until the danger had passed.[45] Actually, popular anger had diminished considerably, and the

Palmerston ministry was trying only to protect national interests in case Seward's message was a trap to induce false security prior to a surprise attack.

While Adams worked through diplomatic channels to soften the blow of the *Trent* affair, Weed worked to change and soften the opinions of the press and influential politicians. Knowing that the British viewed Seward as "the incarnation of hostility to England," he concluded that the incident was a "fit question" to be arbitrated. "It is said, in high places," he wrote Seward, "that you seek war with England because the Rebel War will ruin you; and the suspicion that S[lidell] & M[ason] are in collusion with Wilkes and Fairfax gains ground." This rumor resulted from Fairfax's failure to search the *Trent* for Confederate dispatches. "All England," Weed commented, "is bitten with the 'Honour to the Flag'-phobia." Although Weed had sent a constant stream of letters to the London press and assiduously cultivated influential politicians in a succession of breakfasts, dinners, and other social functions, most of his efforts to present the Union case succeeded only in arousing criticism. "I have ventured into the Lion's Den, and of course got scratched," he remarked philosophically.[46]

Weed soon received an opportunity to work for peace when Russell, taking advantage of his close relationship with Seward, invited him to his house for dinner on December 13. Weed talked with Russell for an hour and a half. He tried repeatedly to persuade Russell to consider a pacific policy, but the latter refused, saying that if the American government had not authorized the seizure "there could be no embarrassment" in yielding to his demands. Russell then mentioned a rumor that General Scott, having suddenly left France, was rushing home at Lincoln's request, presumably to help plan offensive operations against Canada. Weed assured his host that Scott intended to offer his skills for peacemaking, but, if peace proved impossible, he would oversee the buildup of coastal defenses. Russell nodded amiably, appreciating the attempt to allay his fears, but he believed that Weed lacked perspective since he was "not under the harrow." Waving aside Weed's arguments, Russell said it was necessary to have Mason and Slidell in Liverpool or Southampton. After dinner Weed strolled about the grounds with Lady Russell, who, according to Weed's later reminiscences, remarked that ladies "knew nothing of state secrets, but . . . sometimes heard things. . . . The sympathies of the Queen were with our government . . . and [the Queen] would do everything in her power to prevent a rupture with America." Weed inferred that the information came from Russell, because he had seen him speak to his wife before the walk.[47]

Apparently, the royal position was softening. The government's change of heart resulted in part from Prince Albert's continued advocacy of compromise, as well as lessened public anger over the incident. Upper-class Englishmen resented Albert's reserve, his German accent and mannerisms, and even his "damned morality." Still, the prince had worked hard for his adopted country and counseled the Queen on all matters. Victoria relied on him constantly. But in December of 1861, he became fatally ill with typhoid fever. He had had a history of rheumatism, catarrh, gastric attacks, and other ailments, and the constant pain had made him fatalistic. "I am sure, if I had a severe illness," he had once told the Queen, "I should give up at once, I should not struggle for life." By mid-December the chills from the drenching at Sandhurst had worsened and, surrounded by physicians unable to diagnose the typhoid fever until too late, he died on December 14. The nation went into deep mourning. *Punch*, a harsh critic of the Consort, regretted its previous attacks and printed a long poetic eulogy:

> How should the Princes die?
>   With red spur deep in maddening charger's flank,
>   Leading the rush that cleaves the foeman's rank,
> And shouting some time-famous battle-cry?
> . . . .
> Gallant, high-natured, brave,
>   O, had his lot been cast in warrior days,
>   No nobler knight had won the minstrel's praise,
> Than he, for whom the half-reared banners wave.[48]

Under an overcast sky two days before Christmas, a long train of black-plumed horses and mourning coaches carried Albert to a temporary resting place in the Royal Vault of St. George's Chapel. London was still—business suspended, blinds drawn, shutters closed. Flags flew at half-mast and hundreds of churches held services. At noon came the tolling of bells and the long, solemn, reverberating echo of minute guns. And then silence.[49]

8.

The Storm
Passes

NEARLY A MONTH HAD PASSED since Americans had learned on November 16 of the capture of Mason and Slidell. Although this was ample time for the flush of excitement to run its course, the American press still blared defiance and individual citizens showed little concern for British reaction. The wait for news to cross the Atlantic deprived the citizenry of fresh facts to stablize public opinion; rumors and theories spread quickly and gained credibility. Union military reverses seemed to have ended, despite General McClellan's constant drilling; naval operations promised to bring the war home to the Confederacy; and Congress had established a Committee on the Conduct of the War to investigate past sins and to prevent new ones. The country had set about organizing for a long internal conflict, undeterred by the prospect of foreign war.

Day after day in December 1861, Washington was shrouded in fog so dense that people on sidewalks could hear the processions of army wagons thundering over the cobblestones, but could not see even their outlines. Then came a severe frost, a little snow, and a thaw; mud covered everything, hiding holes for unwary carriages, creeping over wheel hubs, and turning Pennsylvania Avenue into a slough rivaled only by the putrid bayou called the Tiber. European visitors had always held a low opinion of the capital. They had called it an "overgrown watering-place," an "architectural conundrum," a "shinplaster in bricks and mortar"; it looked, they said, as if it had been run up in the night "like the cardboard cities which Potemkin erected to gratify the eyes of his imperial mistress on her tour through Russia." The combination of winter mud and evidences of a nation at war now made such harsh criticism seem almost justified. Where else to find such chaos? Bootblacks, newsboys, and street vendors vied with Union soldiers for places to stand on crowded corners. Regiments marched through town, and orderlies galloped down the avenues. Long wagon trains laden with provisions and ammunition trundled along the muddy streets. Surrounded by a cordon of forts and troops, the city resembled a military camp; houses had become hospitals, mounted guards were at every intersection, and cannon were placed at strategic points. Even so, the capital's defenses did not impress foreign officers, who declared they would rather fight outside than within the ring of bastions.[1]

Visitors were drawn irresistibly to the centerpiece of Washington's public architecture, the Capitol. They poured into the rotunda past an ugly column of woodwork hung with "dauby pictures" of the landing of Columbus, the baptism of Pocahontas, the surrender of Burgoyne and Cornwallis, and other notable events in American history. Throughout the building, "wide-mouthed highly decorative iron spittoons" squatted everywhere—in a tight, convenient circle under the dome; throughout the halls; flanking the tribune and Speaker's chair; gracing the presidential chamber; and surrounding the walls of both houses. Tobacco juice stained the floors, walls, and staircases a dull yellowish-brown, testifying to the inaccuracy of Americans. Poor ventilation, oppressive heat, and the stench of sweating bodies in both legislative galleries induced fainting and nausea. Combining the qualities of "a grand California bar-room and a second-rate Paris Café," the House chamber offended foreigners with its low ceiling, gilt and scarlet paint; in contrast, the Senate's plainness and small proportions appeared incongruous. Europeans were unable to reconcile the "tawdry vulgarity of splendor" with the nation's simple republican principles and were even less impressed by the quality of the debates.[2]

The mood of Congress was with Wilkes when it met on the first Monday in December. The members of the House had hardly sat down when the abolitionist clergyman from Illinois, Owen Lovejoy, rose to present a joint resolution thanking Wilkes for brave, adroit, and patriotic conduct. Representative Sidney Edgerton of Maine offered to amend the resolution with a request for the president to present Wilkes a gold medal embossed with suitable emblems and devices. The House defeated the amendment, but passed Lovejoy's resolution and sent it on to the Senate, which referred it to the Committee on Naval Affairs. Two representatives next offered some vindictive resolutions. Schuyler Colfax of Indiana asked that the president confine James M. Mason in the cell of a convicted felon as long as rebel authorities continued to treat Colonel Michael Corcoran, a prisoner from Bull Run, in similar fashion. Moses F. Odell made a motion that Slidell be handled as badly as Colonel Alfred Wood.[3]

When Lincoln sent his annual message to Congress the following day, the galleries were crowded with sightseers driven inside by a bitter, cold wind; the visitors were more intent on avoiding streams of tobacco juice than on listening to the president's words. The message began with a hope that the government had acted prudently toward foreign powers, avoided irritation, and maintained American rights and honor. Recommending that Congress provide for foreign dangers by adopting "adequate and ample measures" for public defense, the president asked members to vote funds to fortify the coasts, Great Lakes, and rivers. After suggesting compensation to owners of the British ship *Perthshire*, which had been unjustly detained, Lincoln commented that "justice requires that we should commit no belligerent act not founded in strict right, as sanctioned by public law." He then presented data from Secretary of War Cameron's annual report, which stated that the government could field an army of over 3,000,000 men in any emergency and "show the world, that while engaged in quelling disturbances at home we are able to protect ourselves from abroad."[4] Lincoln's message never mentioned Mason and Slidell, nor offered any preview to government policy on the *Trent* affair.

On December 4, the portly Canadian minister of finance, Alexander T. Galt, and George Ashmun, the object of the brief diplomatic flurry nine months earlier, had an interesting conversation with Lincoln and Seward at the White House. Galt remarked to the president that Seward's port circular of October 14 had made the Canadian government uneasy. Lincoln nodded, saying that he, but not the cabinet, had supposed it might cause tension. Galt said Ottawa saw the administration's actions and the tone of the press as indicating a desire to molest his country. Answering that the press did not reflect his opinion, Lincoln denied ever hearing a cabinet member express hostile sentiments toward Canada. He pledged as "a man of honor" that neither he nor any of his cabinet had any desire to disturb Britain's rights in North America. When Ashmun interrupted to say that the *Trent* affair might cause difficulty, the president replied vaguely that the "matter could be arranged." Galt assumed that Lin-

coln would not let the incident turn into a quarrel and was cheered by
Seward's statement that he would be glad to see Canada placed in a
defensive posture. "I cannot, however, divest my mind of the impression," Galt wrote later, "that the policy of the American Govt is so
subject to popular impulses, that no assurance can be or ought to be
relied on under present circumstances."[5]

Galt reported the conversation to Lyons, who gave Russell a
garbled version. According to Lyons, Lincoln explained his recommendation to fortify the Great Lakes by remarking, "We must say
something to satisfy the people," and dismissed the *Trent* incident
with the flip comment, "Oh, that'll be got along with."[6]

During this same period a delegation of Baltimore Quakers
visited the White House to present a copy of the London Friends' petition. After a two-hour wait in an anteroom crowded with senators,
congressmen, and military and naval officers, they were ushered into
the president's office. Lincoln rose from a large, easy chair before a
blaze in the marble fireplace and, after shaking hands all around,
listened to their communcation. The Quakers assured him that the
petition would be supported by several Friends in Parliament, among
them John Bright. Lighting up at the mention of Bright, whose photo-
graph hung in his office, the president said, "Those are the first words
of cheer and encouragement we have had from across the water."[7]

An uneasy feeling obviously prevailed. Although most people
believed that British maritime precedent justified Wilkes's act, they
suspected that popular excitement, hatred of the United States, and
desire for cotton would cause Britain to abandon "all her professions
of philanthropy and civilization and humanity and liberation" in favor
of war or suspension of diplomatic relations. "I feel like repudiating
the Archbishop of Canterbury and transferring my allegiance to the
Patriarch of Constantinople," one New Yorker complained.[8]

Submitting the dispute to arbitration became more attractive. On
the evening of December 10, President and Mrs. Lincoln, Lyons,
Seward, and Chase all rode to Camp Pierpont, Virginia, to attend the
wedding of Captain Charles Griffin and Miss Sallie Carroll. At the
reception Lincoln told Senator Orville H. Browning of Illinois that,
according to Mercier, the Crown law officers had declared Wilkes's
act justified by the law of nations; but, he added, there would be no
trouble.[9]

Meanwhile, American officials at every level, like their Canadian
and British counterparts, worried over the condition of Atlantic
coastal defenses. Every available gun was an obsolete smoothbore, no
help against ironclad warships. The largest and most important commercial city, New York, lay open to a hostile fleet. A granite fortress

being constructed on Sandy Hook had barely risen above its foundation, less than 150 inadequate artillery pieces occupied three forts and
two shore batteries defending the Narrows, Fort Schuyler on Long
Island Sound had only a third of its necessary armament, and no
works existed at Gravesend Bay. Because engineers estimated that it
would take years to modernize the defenses of New York City,
authorities decided that the best immediate steps were to throw up
earthworks and close the Narrows with a float of pine timbers.
Civilians recommended shad nets anchored a few feet beneath the surface of the Hudson River and all ship channels, to foul propellers and
keep hostile ships in range of batteries. The New York City Board of
Councilmen urged Governor Edwin D. Morgan to take immediate
measures to organize and equip the state militia. The state adjutant
general asked the War Department to garrison forts on Lake Ontario
and around New York City. However, to maintain the safety of the
capital and other strategic areas, few troops could be moved; New
York would have to rely on the feeble militia. Officials imagined a
fleet of warships sailing up the St. Lawrence to Lake Ontario, from
which they would pass through the Welland Canal to the upper Lakes.
The defense, if heroic, would be futile; harbor and frontier forts
needed repair and lacked arms, the Great Lakes had an improvised
navy of merchant ships, and the available troops were "a raw, hastily
gathered militia" that would have to "encounter the British regulars
seasoned in the Crimea and India."[10]

Pacific coast defenses, especially those in California, were even
weaker than their eastern counterparts. Washington was pursuing a
remarkably negligent course. The western coast was guarded by only
1,200 soldiers, 10 field guns, and 167 heavy artillery pieces, scattered
from Alcatraz Island to Camp Baker, Oregon Territory. San Francisco, the headquarters of the Pacific Fleet, was defended by Spanish
cannon manufactured in 1673. Fort Point and Alcatraz contained
most of the army artillery, 140 guns, but needed twice that number to
be effective; the navy yard at Mare Island was manned by only 34 men
and 89 guns. If the British could break through the harbor defenses,
they would easily capture the arsenal at Benicia. Californians could
not rely on the so-called Pacific Fleet for much assistance. It consisted
of six small wooden warships carrying about 100 guns and less than
1,000 men, which patrolled the coast south of San Francisco; guarded
the $40,000,000 annual cargo of treasure ships; and protected com-
merce from Talcahuano, Chile to San Francisco, a distance of 7,000
miles. One or two vessels were usually either undergoing repairs at
Mare Island or en route to that facility, and two other vessels were
sailing sloops that could not operate in the windless area between the

equator and the Gulf of California. Only two revenue cutters and a Coast Survey steamer could provide support for the beleaguered defenders of San Francisco.[11] Luckily, the Royal Navy on the Pacific station occupied an even worse position; it was no larger than the American contingent and equally as dependent on the Mare Island dockyard for repairs. Operations in the Pacific theater would have brought no glory to either side.

By December 1861, the country's financial structure, which was based on gold, stood in jeopardy. Secretary of the Treasury Salmon P. Chase initially attempted to finance the Civil War through regular taxes and loans. This system had worked well during the Mexican War, but proved inadequate during the Civil War, because expenditures reached astronomical levels, and bankers realized that the gold they loaned to the government would never return to their vaults. When the Treasury issued $50 million in non-interest-bearing "demand notes" after Bull Run, it discovered that merchants, hotel owners, railway agents, bankers, and virtually all other businessmen hesitated or refused to accept them until they were made legal currency for payment of tariffs. In mid-August the banks of Boston, New York, and Philadelphia agreed to a loan of $150 million and, at Chase's insistence, made advances of $5 million in gold coin every six days. By early December much bank capital was tied up in government notes and bonds. Instead of paying creditors and thus putting gold back into circulation, the Treasury accumulated specie to establish a reserve. With the banks' specie reserves dropping, news of Wilkes's action precipitated both runs on gold and such a steep decline in the price of bonds that banks could not sell Treasury notes to refurbish their reserves. Hoarding increased and, when Chase's December report failed to recommend heavy taxes to counter the growing federal deficit, bankers began to talk openly of suspending specie payments.[12] Although the *Trent* affair did not cause the national banking crisis, it contributed to the virtual collapse of a haphazard system of war finance, which depended on public confidence.

Traders on the exchanges became frantic. Word of British displeasure—governmental and public—arrived at long last on December 13, and a weekend of contemplating overseas reports turned bulls into bears. Investors decided that anything—cash, sterling, or commodities—was more sound than American common stocks. A temporary panic broke out in New York on Monday, December 16, and the market rallied briefly at the end when traders agreed that "the possibility of a war was, at the worst, too remote to excite serious apprehensions"; however, bears resumed their attacks two days later. Sterling and bankers' bills on London advanced, as smart money ran for cover. Speculators refused to purchase commercial paper for longer than sixty days. Such commodities as coffee, tea, and sugar, increased in value, along with saltpeter, gunpowder, and other war goods, returning profits of 100 percent to some speculators. "Muskets *is muskets*, now," exclaimed one broker.[13]

Already nervous from the *Trent* episode, Wall Street and other eastern exchanges seethed with rumors that banks had decided to suspend specie payments as a "temporary and precautionary step," and did not grow calmer on the banks' assurances that they saw "nothing in the position of the loans to the government to cause uneasiness." New York banks lost $17 million in three weeks, as large depositors converted their accounts to gold and, because of falling markets and the war crisis, institutions could not sell Treasury notes at home or abroad to replenish reserves. Although nothing short of government intervention could halt the drain of specie from banks, the market rallied when Chase told reporters that the crisis with Great Britain could be peacefully resolved and that "negotiations with the banks were progressing satisfactorily." Thereafter, the investment climate improved steadily, benefiting from the general belief that the Lincoln administration would "do everything consistent with the national honor to avert hostilities."[14]

During these stark days Seward's behavior did little to reduce the tension. He arrived at a White House tea on Sunday, December 15, with a report that the British government had called the arrest of Mason and Slidell a violation of international law and was insisting on an apology and surrender of the men. Doubting that London would do "so foolish a thing," Senator Browning declared that if London wanted to force a war "we will fight her to the death." War, he believed, would cause "a general upheaving" of the nations. The following evening, Seward was among the dignitaries at a ball hosted by Senhor de Lisboa at the Portuguese legation. The historian and diplomat George Bancroft spoke with Seward there, and thought he looked "dirty, rusty, vulgar, and low; [and] used such words as *hell*, and *damn*, and spoke very loud." Later in the evening William H. Russell drifted into a group surrounding Seward and heard him tell the Prince de Joinville that the effects of a war forced upon the United States by Britain would be terrible. "We will wrap the whole world in

OUR ARTIST WAS ON THE SPOT.

The American Reaction to the British Ultimatum
Courtesy of *Punch*

flames!" he exclaimed, perhaps under the influence of brandy. "No power [is] so remote that she will not feel the fire of our battle and be burned by our conflagration." As Russell retreated, shaken by the encounter, another guest took him aside and said, "That's all bugaboo talk. When Seward talks that way, he means to break down. He is most dangerous and obstinate when he pretends to agree a good deal with you."[15]

News of the British reaction not only excited the executive branch, but generated shock waves in Congress; having virtually ignored the *Trent* affair after the initial statements in the House of Representatives on December 2, Congress now plunged into a brawling debate on December 16 and 17. The well-known Ohio Peace Democrat, or "copperhead," Clement L. Vallandigham, offered a resolution that the president "firmly maintain" the seizure, despite any British demand, and that the House pledge full support of the honor of the United States. "The time has now come," said the man who refused to vote defensive measures against the South, "for the firmness of the House to be practically tested, and I hope there will be no shrinking." He drew a quick reaction. William A. Richardson of

Illinois, Reuben E. Fenton of New York, and Samuel S. Cox of Ohio jumped up to oppose the resolve, clamoring for attention. Professing surprise, Vallandigham asked to know "what has caused this change in sentiment? Is it the foreign intelligence of this morning?" In an effort to quash the resolution, Fenton moved to refer it to the Committee on Foreign Affairs. Vallandigham demanded a vote, and Cox somehow gained the floor. An uproar ensued, with Fenton protesting and Vallandigham and Owen Lovejoy demanding recognition. Vallandigham's resolution was eventually referred to committee, by a vote of 109 to 16.[16]

When discussion resumed the following day, Cox argued that the United States never had a "clearer case of indisputable right on the high seas." He hoped the House did not mean to express an opinion contrary to American rights by referring Vallandigham's resolution to committee. Schuyler Colfax retorted that he had voted for referral because, poised as the country was on the brink of another war, it was the duty of a standing committee, not a solitary member, to set forth House policy. Rising slowly from his chair, Vallandigham asked Colfax why he approved Wilkes's conduct. Colfax replied that he had initially considered Mason and Slidell traitors, but now placed them in the realm of foreign relations. "These men will be surrendered before three months," Vallandigham predicted, "in the face of a threat." Colfax scoffed, and Cox said he had too much faith in the sagacity of Seward and the general public to believe they would permit the government, "in a case of clear right, to so dishonor" the American people.[17]

With tempers wearing, Lovejoy attempted to settle the matter by protesting that discussion of Anglo-American relations was out of order. Cox declared that the United States should demand its rights because the *Trent* had committed a hostile act by carrying the diplomats. Another representative, Abraham B. Olin of New York, joined in objection to the debate. Disregarding his colleagues' criticism, Cox then began to speak, lacing his remarks with international law, patriotic appeals, and oratorical flourishes. "I do not understand," he declared, "why it is that an act which has been indorsed [sic] by the Secretary of the Navy, as well as the House itself, should provoke such irritating points of order." The redoubtable representative from Pennsylvania, Thaddeus Stevens, formidable both in appearance and speech, later expressed the feeling of many colleagues when he speculated on the outcome of an Anglo-American war and exulted that "our banner would wave over freemen, and not but republican freemen, from the Gulf of Mexico to the Arctic Ocean, and from the Bay of St. Lawrence to Puget Sound!"[18]

Lord Lyons finally received instructions from a special messenger, Captain Seymour Conway, who reached Boston on December 17, rode as far as Baltimore, and chartered a train to Washington arriving at 11:30 P.M. on the 18th. The minister studied the dispatch (no. 444) overnight, and went to the State Department at 1 P.M. the next day. Seward was at the Capitol, meeting with the Committee on Foreign Relations, so Lyons returned at 3 P.M. At Seward's request, Lyons summarized the dispatch and gave him until the next day to consider the matter and discuss it with Lincoln.[19]

Although Seward promised to have an answer on December 21, he asked if a deadline had been established; Lyons told him "privately and confidentially" that he had seven days. Here, then, was a deadline—an ultimatum. When he returned to the legation, Lyons followed Seward's request, and sent over his private secretary, Edmund Monson, with an advance copy of the dispatch "unofficially and informally"; it was still two days before the date Russell had stipulated for delivery. Seward scanned the dispatch and rushed to the legation. What would happen, he asked, if at the end of seven days he sent either a refusal or a proposal to discuss the issue? "If the answer was not satisfactory and particularly if it did not include the immediate surrender of the Prisoners," Lyons warned, "I could not accept it." On the same day, December 19, Lyons notified Admiral Milne that if Seward's answer forced him to leave, he would take with him the legation secretary, six attachés, and some servants. Although Lyons thought that "naval reasons" should determine the port of embarkation, he preferred Annapolis because he wished to avoid any "fierce excitement" at New York. But, after all, he laughed weakly, "I am not living among savages."[20]

Lyons returned to the State Department on December 21 for the official reading of Russell's dispatch. Seward apologized for not being ready with the American reply; he claimed that he had not found time to study the question. The secretary declined to make a formal request to postpone the dispatch's communication, but said it would be "a great convenience to himself personally" if Lyons would consent to the delay. Since the next day was Sunday, Seward asked if the minister could defer the reading until Monday, December 23. Lyons reluctantly agreed, provided that the secretary would receive him early in the day; he could not allow another packet to sail without sending word to Russell that he had obeyed orders. Seward scheduled an appointment for 10:00 A.M.[21]

Meanwhile, the French minister, Henri Mercier, still following the policy of Anglo-French cooperation in American matters, sought out Seward on December 21 to reveal reports he had received of Washington's worldwide ostracism on the *Trent* question. The only choice open to the American government, Mercier told Seward, was to comply with British demands or go to war. In the event of war, the United States could not depend on any French assistance, despite the "vulgar" rumors circulating about Napoleon's imperial schemes. "Do you think," Seward asked, "that Lyons' leaving would necessarily mean war?" "Yes," the minister replied, and he offered to tell senators and other influential persons that France would have pursued a course identical to England's under similar circumstances.[22]

The administration did not lack for advice during this suspenseful period. Lincoln received many letters from private citizens, as well as suggestions from members of Congress. Belatedly, Senator James R. Doolittle of the Foreign Relations Committee recommended that the government continue corresponding with Britain to postpone delivery of any ultimatum; when demands arrived, the administration should say that it considered the arrest justified, but would refer the matter to arbitration by the French emperor and the Russian czar, and would be willing to join a conference to define the rights of belligerents and contraband of war.[23]

Sumner urged a similar course. Although he agreed with the noted educator, Francis Lieber, that a congress of all Western maritime nations should be called to extract some "canons out of the cloudy realm of precedents," he doubted that such a move could solve the present crisis and believed that "some triumph of our traditional policy with regard to maritime rights" should be associated with any decision about Mason and Slidell. Because Sumner was not sure that Lincoln understood the seriousness of the situation, he explicitly described to him the consequences of war with England: British recognition of Confederate independence; destruction of the Union blockade; a counterblockade of the entire east coast; elimination of the American merchant marine; and free trade between England and the South. When he showed Lincoln letters from Bright and Cobden, who expressed surprise that the United States would ignore its own principles and risk war over a "very trivial incident," Lincoln appeared "much worried & astonished." Sumner then argued that Lincoln should settle the issue as quickly as possible by proposing either the King of Prussia or three learned European publicists as arbitrators. Further delay would paralyze naval and military movements against the South, since the forces might be needed to defend Northern territory from British attack.[24]

The president did not need any prodding from Doolittle, Sumner, or anyone else on the subject of arbitration. After much consideration, he told Browning on December 21 that Russell's dispatch meant trouble. The two men agreed that the moment had arrived for the nations to discuss neutral rights and that a peaceful solution could be found if Britain acted justly. Lincoln then read to Browning a letter that he intended to send as Seward's answer. The note conceded that Britain was entitled to reparation, but stated that the president could not give a categorical answer upon only a "partial record" of the case. Lincoln, the draft read, hesitated to divulge his views without the assurance that the British government would listen, yet his administration neither intended an affront to the British flag nor wanted to force discussion of an embarrassing question. Wilkes had acted without orders, but the United States was not willing to waive "an important, though a strict right" unless Britain could show Wilkes's act wrong or "very questionable," at which time America would make reparation. Any discussion of the *Trent* affair should include collateral issues of Britain's position on the Civil War, together with the relation of Mason and Slidell to the United States, the object of their voyage, the *Trent* captain's knowledge of their mission and its national character, the point of seizure, and precedents and positions assumed by the two nations in analogous cases. Once the British government had submitted the above information, the United States would, if agreed to by Britain, "go to such friendly arbitration as is usual among nations, and [would] abide the award." As an alternative, Her Majesty's Government could determine whether and what reparation was due, provided it did not differ from nor transcend that proposed in dispatch no. 444, and that determination would govern all future analogous cases between Great Britain and the United States.[25]

Lincoln was naive if he thought Britain would agree to his proposals, and probably intended the letter to be more of a delaying tactic than an honest effort to settle the question. With a civil war on its hands, the United States government occupied a weak position. The British government did not have to accept any provision it disliked.

The days were passing inexorably. On Monday, December 23, at 10:00 A.M., Lyons returned to the State Department to read his instructions. When the minister had finished, Seward said he would discuss the dispatch with the president and give an answer without delay. Suspecting that Seward would want some time, Lyons said he would consent to a postponement of seven days only. When Seward requested that such a time limit not be considered as part of the note, the minister indicated he could not risk being reproached for not having given "due warning," and said Seward could do what he pleased with the statement as long as it was clearly understood that it had been made. Worried about the deadline's effect on cabinet opinion, Seward hinted that his problems would increase if he had to announce the time limit. Lyons repeated that it was up to him, since the limit was not part of the written note; however, the deadline would expire at noon, December 30. He avoided making any statement that could be claimed by Seward as rendering the time limit confidential.[26]

Although Lyons personally doubted that the United States would comply with Russell's demands, he suggested to London that, in the interest of Anglo-American relations, "compliance should have as much as possible, the air of having been made spontaneously." The minister expected to have some kind of answer within a week, but thought its content would depend on news from Europe. The American government would make no concession if it thought that France would mediate or that refusal would not cause war, but only a rupture of diplomatic relations. Despite the Lincoln administration's fear of another war, Lyons thought that only the first shot would convince the United States of the dangers. It was time to teach the Americans a lesson for their own good; a reprieve would "lead them on to their ruin," under less advantageous conditions for Britain.[27]

One development that encouraged Lyons was Seward's apparent change of heart concerning how to conduct diplomacy, especially with England. Ten months in the State Department, Lyons believed, had dispelled the secretary's illusions—of a Union party in the South; of the return of the South to the North in the event of foreign war; of his power to frighten Europe with talk of the Union's ability to fight both the Confederacy and foreign powers; and of Anglo-American relations being "safe playthings to be used for the amusement of the American people." Still, he might find it hard to handle unpopularity, and thus refuse to take responsibility for surrendering Mason and Slidell; anything could happen. Although Lyons did not expect the American government to act rashly if he left Washington, he was concerned that the Irish on the Canadian border might launch a filibustering expedition against Canadian canals, and that subordinate officers, when commanding superior forces, might "commit acts of aggression without orders from their superiors."[28]

Meanwhile, Milne had ordered Captain George Hancock to Annapolis with the *Immortalité* to take Lyons to Bermuda if necessary, and to prepare for action in case the American squadron attempted a surprise attack. Lyons had cancelled some Christmas dinner invitations, but decided to renew them after talking with Seward. He could only wait, and hope the administration complied.[29]

The receipt of dispatch no. 444 and the conversation with Lyons proved to be critical developments in the forming of American policy on the *Trent* issue. Seward set out to convince the other members of the administration, including the president, that the American government would have to surrender Mason and Slidell.

Lincoln posed a problem. While not overjoyed with Wilkes's act, he was glad to have the diplomats behind bars, and public demonstrations had testified to the capture's popularity. Seward lost no time in conveying Russell's message to the White House. After hearing the British ultimatum, Lincoln shook his head. "No." When Seward reminded him of the consequence of refusal, Lincoln supposedly said, "No matter. I will never give them up." Seward frowned and rose from his chair. "Then I shall be obliged to ask you, Mr. President, to write the reply to Earl Russell, for the strength of the argument from our own past policy, so far as I can see, is in favor of a compliance with his demands." Lincoln nodded and the secretary left.[30]

A cabinet meeting on Christmas Day decided nothing; discussion turned from the *Trent* to the tripartite expedition against Mexico. Seward stayed after the meeting to resume the argument, but Lincoln was not in the mood, and said:

> Governor Seward, you will go on, of course, preparing your answer, which, as I understand it, will state the reason why they ought to be given up. Now I have a mind to try my hand at stating the reasons why they ought *not* to be given up. We will compare the points on each side.[31]

The next day in Washington was sunny and mild when the cabinet assembled in the State Department at 10:00 A.M., a departure from their normal routine of Tuesday and Friday conferences in the president's office. Seated around an oak table, members listened first to Russell's dispatch and then to Seward's draft answer, which stated that Mason and Slidell would be surrendered. Secretary of War Cameron informed the cabinet that one of his agents, then in Britain to buy soldiers' clothing, had reported that the *Trent* mail agent, Commander Williams, had said that Mason, Slidell, and Wilkes had arranged the seizure at a meeting in Havana. Senator Sumner, present at the cabinet deliberations, next read the letters from Cobden and Bright that had worried Lincoln earlier; they now unnerved the cabinet as well. The correspondence corroborated a rumor that Wilkes had conspired with the two Confederate diplomats, and claimed that the British government was "ready for war if an excuse can be found for it."[32]

The cabinet realized it could not count on French support in a war with Britain. Shortly after the Christmas cabinet meeting had begun, Mercier had arrived breathless at the State Department with a December 3 dispatch from Foreign Minister Thouvenel. The French government, Thouvenel wrote, believed it should speak out in the interest of neutral rights to prevent a possible Anglo-American war. He saw no way in which the Washington administration could approve Wilkes's conduct without forgetting American principles. Mason and Slidell were not liable to seizure as contraband of war because the flag protects all passengers not in the military service of an enemy; they could not be removed as "bearers of official dispatches of the enemy" because the *Trent* was a neutral ship traveling between neutral ports; nor could they be seized as rebels, because such seizure would violate the immunity accorded to a sovereign territory. Admitting his knowledge of the British demands, Thouvenel recommended compliance and claimed that the French government had proved its "loyal friendship" for the United States by revealing its views.[33] While Thouvenel's note was not the only factor in cabinet considerations, it helped demolish hope that Anglo-French rivalry would be America's gain in the present crisis.

What to do? Secretary Chase, rebuffed by New York bankers two weeks earlier in an attempt to float another loan, remarked that Wilkes had "clearly violated" international law and Britain had a right to ask for disavowal of his act and restoration of the diplomats. He was provoked that the *Trent* was "knowingly employed" in violation of the neutrality proclamation and thought Britain could overlook Wilkes's "little wrong" in not seizing the ship. Surrendering the scoundrels, Chase growled, "is gall and wormwood to me." He reluctantly agreed to release the men because more delay would injure Northern commerce and the war effort. Other cabinet members favored surrender for one reason or another. Attorney General Edward Bates, waiving the question of legal right, argued that a war with Britain would mean the triumph of secession, destruction of Union ships in Southern waters, ruin of trade, and bankruptcy of the Treasury. Although he regarded Russell's dispatch as peremptory and unspecific, he believed it would be folly not to accept British conditions. In short, he said, "we *must not* have war with England." Secretary Welles, who had always doubted the legality of Wilkes's act, had not been reassured by the Navy's consultant on international law, Charles Eames, who found many precedents.[34] After four hours, the meeting ended. Mason and Slidell, the cabinet finally decided, would have to be surrendered. The deed, then, was to be undone.

When everyone had left, Seward said to Lincoln, "You thought you might frame an argument for the other side." The president smiled and shook his head, replying, "I found I could not make an argument that would satisfy my own mind, and that proved to me your ground was the right one."[35]

There remained the business of wording the note of surrender. Closeting himself in his office, Seward spent the rest of the day polishing his reply without assistance from specialists in international law, and the final result showed it. The secretary's reliance on argument, his impatience with legal technicalities, and his scant knowledge of maritime law all combined to produce an ineffective paper. He repeated the facts of the seizure as presented by Russell, added some corrections, and affirmed that Wilkes had acted without instructions. After citing ambiguous comments by Vattel ("War allows us to cut off from an enemy all his resources, and to hinder him from sending ministers to solicit assistance") and Scott ("You may stop the ambassador of your enemy on his passage"), he said that "dispatches are not less clearly contraband, and the bearers or couriers who undertake to carry them fall under the same condemnation." Therefore, Mason, Slidell, their secretaries, and the dispatches were *all* contraband of war; further, Wilkes had a legal right to stop, search, and capture the *Trent*, despite its proceeding from one neutral port to another. Seward then spent several pages in a rambling discussion of past practices of condemnation and the question of whether the captor could act as a judge. Contraband vessels, he concluded, must be sent into port for adjudication before Admiralty courts. Now came Seward's complicated exit; having said the capture was legal, he needed an excuse to repudiate it. If Wilkes had *involuntarily* released the *Trent*, he reasoned, the United States would be entitled to keep the prisoners; however, by *voluntarily* freeing the vessel, Wilkes waived America's right to claim the prisoners. Wilkes's "inadvertency" constituted an illegal act for which Britain deserved reparation. He admitted to arguing Britain's case, but said he was "defending and maintaining, not an exclusively British interest, but an old honored and cherished American cause"—opposition to impressment. The American government "could not deny the justice of the claim presented to us in this respect upon its merits. We are asked to do to the British nation just what we have always insisted all nations ought to do to us." Calling Russell's choice of words "guarded language" rarely used, Seward sought to imply that Britain feared a war.

Seward might well have stopped at this point, but because he had other purposes and another audience in mind, he continued. If the

Union's security had required the commissioners' detention, he said, illustrating his contempt for international law, they would not have been surrendered despite their illegal capture. Britain could have the Confederates because the "waning proportions of the existing insurrection, as well as the comparative unimportance of the captured persons" made their retention unnecessary. As an afterthought he expressed appreciation that the two countries had finally settled the fifty-year-old impressment issue. Great Britain could "in no other way so effectually disavow any such injury . . . by assuming now as her own the ground upon which we then stood." The prisoners would be "cheerfully liberated."[36]

The note was a monument to illogic. If he had concluded with his first reason for freeing Mason and Slidell—the voluntary release of the ship—he would have written an ingenuous but acceptable document. By bringing in the unrelated issue of impressment, he muddled the question; the only similarity between impressment and Wilkes's act was that both involved removal of men from foreign vessels. Mason and Slidell were neither pressed into the American Navy nor removed for their alleged status as American nationals. Seward surrendered the men for the wrong reasons, indulging in what Lincoln liked to call the "horse-chestnut" style of argument, a "specious and fantastic arrangement of words by which a man can prove a horse-chestnut to be a chestnut horse."[37]

The Lincoln administration could not claim that it followed a series of prudent moves designed to anticipate any British reaction; unfortunately, federal officials surrendered the initiative almost immediately, behaving like the average American who anxiously awaited the latest news from London. Content to react rather than act, the United States government had placed itself at the mercy of British policymakers and had found them unforgiving. Less than two weeks after receiving news of British preparations, the American government had decided to risk popular disapproval to avoid the greater danger of foreign war. Although the administration should have released Mason and Slidell immediately upon determining the facts of the case, it had postponed the inevitable decision pending word from London. A hastily called series of cabinet meetings and a frantic rummaging through historical records substituted for what should have been a carefully researched investigation of international law and preparation of public opinion in the intervening month between the arrival of the Confederate diplomats and receipt of intelligence from Britain. The difficulty of suppressing a major insurrection, combined with deep financial problems and poor relations with foreign governments, made additional complications unthinkable. Yet Lincoln had seriously considered retaining the men, proposing arbitration, and letting an open sore in Anglo-American relations fester indefinitely. His reluctant concession to Seward's arguments added no luster to the American position.

9.

The Black Abyss

DURING THE *Trent* AFFAIR, Americans and Britons developed a deep
interest in international and maritime law. Book stores could not
stock enough references; lecturers were beseiged with invitations; and
newspapers published letters and editorials comparing the removal of
Mason and Slidell with previous incidents, and studded tedious
discussions with reference to arcane decisions of the eighteenth and
nineteenth centuries. "What a cruel fate of a future historian," a State
Department clerk wrote, "who, if conscientious, will be obliged to
read all these darkness-spreading lucubrations!" No dinner party
lacked for self-styled experts who soon became bores. "Oh, the pity of
it all!" lamented a spectator. "Capt. Wilkes with his instincts and law-
studies *extemporary*, and notion of 'embodied despatches'! To quarrel
about such a man's 'notions'!" The "black abyss of Admiralty
learning" had been sounded.[1]

Naval officers were expected to possess rudimentary knowledge
of international law so that they could act responsibly when deprived
of access to legal advisers. Rather than relying on relevant sections of
civil code, they had to contend with the rulings of prize courts; texts of
treaties, conventions, and other agreements; international custom;
general principles of law followed by civilized nations; and private
works that speculated on how to modify the law. "Diplomacy of the
quarter-deck" or "quarter-deck justice" tended to show little con-

sideration for the rights of others, and its practitioners relied upon government advocates to find a means to legalize their conduct.[2]

Wilkes had waded through the usual potpourri of legal treatises to justify capture of Mason and Slidell. Unable to comprehend how a technical error in procedure could invalidate the capture, the captain felt a "glow of shame" for his country when it yielded to the demands of John Bull, and he described Seward as "a very coward."[3] Ironically, the *Trent* would have been condemned if brought before a prize court.

The *San Jacinto*'s confrontation with the *Trent* raised questions concerning the following neutral and belligerent rights and duties: visit and search, unneutral service, types of contraband, status of mail ships, carriage of military and nonmilitary belligerents, diplomatic privileges and immunities, and carriage of hostile dispatches. United States prize law was based on British Admiralty decisions, but they had been adapted to American circumstances, and did not slavishly follow misconstruction of public law by British courts.[4] Basing their arguments regarding the *Trent* primarily on British prize court decisions, both Britain and America had sought to disprove the allegations of the other. Seward, like the erring naval captain, had asserted that the Confederate commissioners were contraband of war, and dismissed the *Trent*'s neutral points of departure and destination as irrelevant. Russell argued that Mason and Slidell were not contraband, and regarded the vessel's travel between neutral ports as decisive for exempting it from capture. Although the law of contraband was inapplicable, it became the focal point because both countries accepted Wilkes's convoluted reasoning as a basis for discussion. The real issue, that of alleged unneutral service, was lost in the scuffle.

The arrest of Mason and Slidell had brought immediate protests from jurists that Wilkes had violated the privileges and immunities of diplomatic agents. Diplomatic protection was recognized in almost every culture, had been affirmed by international treaty, and sometimes seemed the only immutable element in a chaotic world. Judicial bodies and writers in Europe and America had supported the axiom. A leading reference work, Emmerich de Vattel's *The Law of Nations, or Principles of Natural Law Applied to the Conduct and Affairs of Nations and Sovereigns* (1758), declared that "every sovereign state . . . has a right to send and to receive public ministers" and "a sovereign who attempts to hinder another from sending and receiving public ministers, does him an injury, and offends against the law of nations."[5] Protection of diplomats from harassment in time of war or peace had been accepted for over a century.

Yet an ambiguity existed in the minds of Wilkes, Seward, and other Americans who, without contesting the right of sovereign nations to send and receive envoys, believed that a belligerent could intercept enemy agents. Confusion resulted from misinterpretation of a judgment by the British Admiralty jurist, Sir William Scott (Lord Stowell), in *The Caroline* (1808):

> [P]ersons discharging the functions of ambassadors, are, in a peculiar manner, objects of the protection and favour of the law of nations. The limits that are assigned to the operations of war against *them*, by *Vattel*, and other writers upon those subjects, are, that you may exercise your right of *war against them*, wherever the character of hostility exists: *you may stop the ambassador of your enemy on his passage.* . . .[6]

Seward cited this opinion to justify Wilkes's behavior. He did not realize that Vattel and Scott had meant that ambassadors could be stopped only when passing through territory controlled by their enemies, i.e., "wherever the character of hostility exists."[7] If Wilkes had sought a clearer exposition of Scott, he had only to read James Kent's *Commentaries on American Law*, one of the great American treatises, a copy of which lay on his cabin desk. It stated:

> An ambassador is also deemed under the protection of the law of nations in his passage through the territories of a third and friendly power, while upon his public mission, in going to and returning from the government to which he is deputed. To arrest him under such circumstances would be a breach of his privilege as a public minister.[8]

Both British and American authorities, then, agreed that neutral territory safeguarded a diplomat from interference.

Another point of contention regarding the status of Mason and Slidell rested on the fact that no government had granted de facto recognition of Confederate *independence*, but merely *belligerency*; and, because the commissioners were in transit at the time of their capture, their alleged immunity as "resident" ambassadors of a "sovereign" power seemed questionable. Judge Joel Parker, a "good dry technical lawyer" from Massachusetts who argued always on the narrowest precedents, insisted that belligerents could send only agents, not ambassadors; therefore, he argued, Mason and Slidell could not claim immunity.[9] Other American lawyers said that although the envoys' arrival in the countries to which they were accredited would vest them with diplomatic character and privileges, while en route they must be regarded as "*embryotic* ministers only."[10] Legalists could debate the right of rebellious subjects to diplomatic representation; however, international custom dictated that when a rebellion had grown into a civil war the emissaries of both parties, whether ambassadors or political agents of a quasidiplomatic character, were "clothed with the powers and enjoy the immunities of ministers, though they are not invested with the representative character, not entitled to diplomatic honors."[11] Therefore, the commissioners were bona fide diplomats en route to countries of accreditation, entitled to all privileges and immunities of their office; the Confederacy had established a form of foreign embassy months earlier, by placing Yancey, Rost, and Mann in Europe.

In their zeal to demonstrate that the Confederate agents were not lawful envoys entitled to establish and maintain relations with other governments, Northern advocates overlooked the right of foreign nations to protect their citizens in that portion of North America controlled by the South. Although Europe's unofficial reception of Southern agents offended the United States, it did not violate international law. In *The Caroline*, Scott had written that "the neutral country has a right to preserve its relations with the enemy, and you are not at liberty to conclude, that any communication between them can partake, in any degree, of the nature of *hostility* against you."[12] The Lincoln administration opposed both the stationing of foreign consuls in the Southern states and toleration of Confederate envoys by European governments; yet tradition, necessity, and American precedent contradicted such a position. During the Latin American wars for independence, the United States had received the emissaries of rebellious colonies despite Spanish protests; the government could not now deny similar privileges to the Confederacy. Neutral nations were entitled to unofficial relations with what was, for all practical purposes, a de facto government, and to allow passage of its agents to their capitals by commercial transportation.

Although diplomats remained inviolate when traveling on neutral vessels or through neutral territory, merchant ships on which they took passage carried no immunity from visit and search in wartime. "The duty of self-preservation gives to belligerent nations this right," Kent stated. "It is founded upon necessity, and is strictly and exclusively a war right, and does not rightfully exist in time of peace, unless conceded by treaty." Without the right of visit and search, there could be no right of maritime capture because, as Scott observed, "if you are not at liberty to ascertain by sufficient inquiry whether there is property that can legally be captured, it is impossible to capture." In *The Nereide* (1815), Chief Justice John Marshall similarly ruled that "belligerents have a full and perfect right to capture enemy goods and articles going to their enemy which are contraband of war. To the exercise of that right the right of search is essential. It is a mean justified by the end. This right had been established by such classic authorities on international law as Vattel and Cornelis Van Bynkershoek, and all legal experts acknowledged it.[13]

Did the application of belligerent violence to a British packet constitute a "barbarous, as well as a dastardly and illegal action"? No aspect of the *Trent* incident escaped controversy, including the character of the vessel on which Mason and Slidell took passage. As a ship of the Royal Mail Steam Packet Company running between the West Indies and Vera Cruz, one of several vessels operating under Admiralty contract and subsidized by government funds to carry the mail, the *Trent* lacked immunity from visit and search; however, many Britons believed that, while not a public craft in the sense of a warship, it differed "materially from any private neutral ship, used or chartered for a hostile purpose" and possessed an "essentially public character." Wilkes's critics pointed out that mail packets had been treated as "privileged vessels" in the recent blockades of Mexico, Buenos Aires, and the Dalmatian coast of Austria; furthermore, Article XX of the Postal Convention, which had been signed by the British and American governments on December 15, 1848, protected mail packets from "impediment or molestation" for six weeks following notification of a declaration of war by either nation, and permitted them "to return freely, and under special protection, to their respective ports." During the war with Mexico, the United States had allowed British mail ships to pass through the blockade without hindrance. France claimed the privileges of public ships for its postal packets, and those of Britain were supposedly entitled to similar consideration.[14]

Jurists and government officials agreed with outraged British subjects that mail ships should be inconvenienced as infrequently as possible, but nowhere did any Admiralty decision or international law treatise state or imply that such vessels enjoyed special treatment. American authorities were correct in their view that a mail contract neither changed the character of a merchant ship to that of a national vessel, nor altered the rights of belligerents who, as an act of comity, needed only to treat them "in such a manner as to cause no unnecessary interruption to the postal service of the neutral." When a seaman had sued the royal mail packet *Lord Hobart* in 1815 for back wages, Scott had expressed alarm at the danger that "might . . . [arise] to the public service from the detention of vessels of this kind" as a result of legal action, but he did not rule on immunity from civil procedure or any other process. And, in *The Maria* (1799), he had declared that the right of visit and search of all private ships met at sea was "an incontestable right of the lawfully commissioned cruizers [*sic*] of a hostile nation."[15]

Established principles of international law relating to neutral and belligerent rights had placed Captain Wilkes in jeopardy as soon as he made the decision to inspect the British vessel for evidence of contraband. And such principles clearly protected the Confederate commissioners from interference while traveling on the high seas on a neutral ship to a neutral destination, even though the *Trent* itself lacked immunity from visit and search procedures.

The allegedly rude manner in which the personnel of the *San Jacinto* had conducted the visit and search of the *Trent* aroused great anger among the ship's crew and passengers, as well as the British public, but the uproar betrayed profound ignorance of maritime law. Visit and search by a belligerent warship involves stopping a neutral merchant ship, sending on board a small party, and searching the vessel by examining the ship's papers, questioning persons on board, and inspecting (without opening or removing) the cargo. The procedures employed by the personnel of the *San Jacinto* in overhauling, visiting, and searching the *Trent* adhered to those established by maritime law, and furnished no grounds for objection. Considering the provocation by Captain Moir, the boarding party showed commendable restraint in carrying out what Seward accurately described as a "simple, legal, and customary belligerent proceeding." Moir's protest that Wilkes had heaved him to in an aggressive manner was groundless. According to practice, the *San Jacinto* had simultaneously raised a flag and fired a blank shell to signal the *Trent* to halt. When the British vessel showed no sign of stopping, the Union warship next fired a *coup de sémonce*, or affirming shot, across her bow. Had Moir not responded to the second hailing, a third shot would probably have struck the *Trent*'s rigging. Treaties specified that the warship either remain beyond the range of cannon or halve the range after halting its quarry, depending on sea conditions, the size of the warship, and other factors—a precaution against pirates and renegade privateers. The *San Jacinto* kept well within range, ready to pour in a broadside at the first sign of violence. While the boarding party traditionally consisted of one or two officers and an unarmed crew, the *San Jacinto*'s group included appropriate personnel to navigate the *Trent* after capture, and eight marines to discourage resistance; such a party hardly reflected normal procedure for greeting a neutral vessel.[16] Wilkes's precaution, however, turned out to be justified.

After boarding the *Trent*, Fairfax immediately asked to see the ship's papers and passenger list, a routine request that Moir should have granted. In prize courts the evidence for acquittal or condemnation, according to Wheaton, "must, in the first instance, come from the papers and crew of the captured ship"; failure to produce this information would deprive the belligerent of a basis for judging a neutral's conduct. While authorities differed on the nature and character of the papers required, Kent listed the register, sea-letter, muster roll, logbook, charter party, invoice, and bill of lading as necessary documents. Absence of some of these papers constituted "strong presumptive evidence against the ship's neutrality," he wrote, and concealment "justified a capture, and carrying into port for adjudication, though it does not absolutely require a condemnation." English prize regulations of 1664 and 1672 had equated concealment or destruction of papers with resistance and flight, which were regarded as more dangerous and of greater illegality than transportation of contraband, violation of blockade, or other hostile action. In *The Maria*, Scott declared it to be "a wild conceit that wherever force is used, it may be forcibly resisted; a lawful force cannot lawfully be resisted." By refusing to show his papers to the boarding officer and opposing "any thing like a search of his vessel," Moir imperiled the *Trent* and its cargo.[17] Wilkes could have seized control of the vessel, escorted it to the nearest American port, and initiated prize court proceedings. As for Fairfax's argument that the *San Jacinto* could not spare a prize crew because of an intent to participate in the Port Royal offensive, the Supreme Court had ruled in *The Alexander* (1814) and *The Grotius* (1815) that placing a single man on board a vessel sufficed for capture if the captured ship had no hope of rescue; it was "indicative of an intention to seize and to retain as a prize; and it is always sufficient if such intention is fairly to be inferred from the conduct of the captor."[18] In retrospect, historians should condemn Fairfax, not Wilkes; he not only violated orders, but also ignored a major infraction of maritime law.

The odd part about the incident was Wilkes's twisted rationale for removing Mason and Slidell and allowing the *Trent* to continue its voyage. In his cursory reading of Kent, Scott, Wheaton, and Vattel, Wilkes concluded that a belligerent could seize a neutral vessel for carrying enemy dispatches, a form of contraband, between neutral ports.

HIGHLY INDIGNANT BRITON. "To Harms! To Harms!! Britons Harouse!!!"
MR. BULL. "Hi say, control your just Hindignation. The blarsted Yankees 'av MASON and SLIDELL, you know; but we'll make 'em Hapologize or Fight, you see, for not taking the TRENT, Cargo and all. To be sure we will, by George!"

Harper's *Mocks the British Position on Wilkes's Violation of International Law*
Courtesy of *Harper's Weekly*

As diplomats who had received instructions from their government, the two commissioners were, in Wilkes's eyes, "living" dispatches who carried in their heads what the Confederate Department of State normally would have conveyed in written form to agents already operating in Europe. Like his executive officer, Wilkes really did not wish to seize the *Trent*; he had issued the order only because he knew it to be the proper response, and allowed Fairfax to disregard it. His argument for arresting Mason and Slidell did not concern them as much as the vessel on which they traveled because, even if the Confederate agents were the embodiment of dispatches, neither they nor written dispatches could be removed.

Wilkes may not have seen that the central issue of the whole affair concerned not just the contraband status of Mason and Slidell but also the question of whether the *Trent* had engaged in "unneutral service." By carrying such alleged "contraband," the *Trent* could be judged as committing an unneutral act and, therefore, subject to seizure and

prize court proceedings. Still, the term "unneutral service"—also
known as "accidental contraband," "analogues of contraband,"
"enemy service," and "*l'assistance hostile*"—did not even exist in
Wilkes's time, although Sir Christopher Robinson, a reporter of prize
cases adjudicated by the English High Court of Admiralty, used the
phrase "unneutral conduct" as early as 1808. During the Napoleonic
Wars, British courts established the basis for the law of unneutral service, but the expression did not appear in textbooks until the 1890s. It
covered the variety of serious actions considered as assistance to the
enemy that did not fall into the categories specifically covered by carriage of contraband or breach of blockade. Rulings by the High Court
of Admiralty and the House of Lords applied the concept of "unneutral service" to neutral maritime transport of troops and dispatches
in the direct service of the enemy. Unneutral service differed from the
carriage of contraband because the latter had to be detected en route
to an enemy location; such cases of unneutral service as transmission
of signals might not involve a destination or relate to acts of commerce. Neutral traders who committed such violations acted at their
own risk because they imparted a hostile character to the offending
vessels, relinquished the protection of their governments, and lost the
privileges they normally enjoyed when traveling between neutral
ports. The penalty for carrying contraband was confiscation of the
cargo, whereas the punishment for unneutral service was condemnation of the vessel. The offenses of carrying contraband and engaging in
unneutral service were, as T. J. Lawrence said, "unlike in nature,
unlike in proof and unlike in penalty."[19]

Past British maritime seizures doubtlessly had encouraged Wilkes
and Seward to misconstrue the word *contraband*. Britain's abusive
practice of seizing so-called "contraband of war" in the period prior to
the War of 1812 had enraged neutrals. An exasperated President Jefferson had asked,

> And what is *contraband*, by the law of nature? Either every
> thing which may aid or comfort an enemy, or nothing. Either
> all commerce which would accommodate him is unlawful, or
> none is. The difference between articles of one or another
> description, is a difference in degree only. No line between
> them can be drawn.[20]

The seizure of contraband, and its composition, has always been a
contentious topic in international relations. Although no binding
treaty ever defined *contraband*, most nations in the nineteenth century—including the United States and England—followed the classi-
fication scheme established by the father of international law, Hugo

Grotius, the famed seventeenth-century Dutch national lawyer. There were, he wrote, three classes: articles used mainly for military purposes in war (always contraband); articles that existed only for peaceful purposes (never contraband); and articles that could be used in either war or peace, depending on circumstances (contraband when destined for the military or naval use of a belligerent). Although many nations had concluded treaties that specified the appropriate class for articles, they disagreed with one another; therefore, all efforts to restrict the number and types of contraband articles had failed, leaving the fate of ambiguous items to the discretion of belligerents. Modern writers have termed arms, munitions, and military and naval stores as *absolute contraband*, and ambiguous articles as *conditional* or *relative contraband*, although in practice, warring nations make no distinction, answer to no tribunal, and ignore the protests of neutrals. Basically, *contraband* has traditionally referred only to things or chattels, not enemy persons or papers (both of which are not brought before a prize court), and a ship libeled for carrying the latter must be found guilty of unneutral service in order to be penalized.[21]

The important factor in determination of contraband lies not in the nature of the articles in question, but in their destination; a neutral vessel could be freighting military or naval goods for another neutral power or for a belligerent not at war with the country of the inspecting warship. According to international law, the condemnation of contraband necessitated that visit and search reveal the vessel to have a hostile destination. In such a case, the ship could be seized and brought before a prize court for adjudication. The contraband articles, Scott said, "must be taken *in delicto*, in the actual prosecution of the voyage to an enemy port." Goods destined for a neutral port "cannot come under the description of contraband, all goods going there being equally lawful."[22] And the *Trent* was proceeding between neutral ports.

The American government, then, faced serious limitations when it came to justifying the removal of Mason and Slidell as contraband; they neither fitted into any prohibited category nor had a hostile destination. The carriage of belligerent military and nonmilitary persons, the right to remove them from a neutral ship, and the status of the vessel conveying them had generated much diplomatic discussion by the time of the *Trent* affair. International law allowed belligerents to prevent neutrals from transporting members of an enemy's armed forces, and vessels that did so became liable to seizure and condemnation. The same fate supposedly befell neutral ships that carried dispatches and nonmilitary individuals who had positions that made them likely prisoners of war, or who were going abroad to further the enemy's cause. Yet, as the English Privy Council observed in *The Rebecca* (1811), "No case has ever yet occurred where persons found on board in the employment of the enemy in a purely civil capacity have ever induced condemnation of a ship." Although both the *Trent* and *Rebecca* cases amounted to unneutral service, the neutral vessel did not acquire enemy character unless it had been let out under contract to the enemy's government to convey persons "described as being in the service of the enemy." The number was immaterial, "since fewer persons of high quality and character may be of more importance than a much greater number of persons of lower condition." If the belligerent persons did not travel on the public service at the public expense, the vessel committed no violation by transporting them.[23]

In absence of treaty, nineteenth-century custom did not allow belligerents to remove persons from a neutral vessel on the high seas unless such persons were in the military employ of the enemy, and then they could be taken off as prisoners of war rather than as contraband. "Men present no real analogy to contraband, although they as well as despatches are often spoken of as its analogues," Westlake observed. "Men cannot be forwarded like goods, in pursuance of an intention formed about them by some one else.[24] Nations had restricted the right of removing belligerent persons as early as 1675, and the United States repeatedly had entered into agreements, beginning with the French treaty of amity and commerce (1778), that extended to nonmilitary individuals the protection of the flag of the vessel on which they sailed; this concept was based on the principle that free ships make free goods.

Wilkes knew of this prohibition and thought he could evade it by treating the persons of Mason and Slidell as diplomatic dispatches. The carriage of enemy dispatches ("official communications of official persons, on the public affairs of the government") by a neutral vessel had always struck jurists as a particularly heinous crime. It was more serious even than the smuggling of contraband, because, according to Scott, "in the transmission of despatches may be conveyed the entire plan of a campaign, that may defeat all the projects of the other belligerent in that quarter of the world." The most injurious offense, carriage of dispatches between the mother country and its territories, had been viewed by English courts since 1802 as unneutral service; as Sir Christopher Robinson stated in *Collectanea Maritima* (1801), the British government had admitted as early as 1636 "the right of the French to visit English ships in order to prevent the transportation of their enemies' advices and directions." Since mere confiscation of the article, as in cases of contraband, seemed "ridiculous," the captor normally condemned the offending vessel. A plea of ignorance on the part of the master did not spare the ship if the court believed that he had not exercised proper caution or due diligence in the port where the papers were received, especially if that port were hostile. Moreover, the captor did not have to prove "even by inference that the ship was hired or taken for the carriage of the dispatches. It is enough that they were carried." But if the voyage were to commence in a neutral country and terminate at a neutral port, there would be less evidence to arouse the master's vigilance; in such cases, "some allowance" might be made "for any imposition which may be practiced upon him." Later generations have been inclined to be lenient with mail packets or other vessels that carried mail or dispatches as a matter of business without special remuneration; however, nineteenth-century custom did not provide for special handling, despite eloquent advocacy by the French publicist, Laurent Hautefeuille. Instructions and other documents between a hostile government and its representatives in a neutral country were exempt from seizure because they related to lawful communication between the belligerent and neutral states.[25]

Precedents set by international law and custom did not support the assertions of Wilkes, although they would have supported his seizure of the mail ship. The Trent's voyage between neutral ports protected the vessel and its cargo from molestation; the nonmilitary status of Mason and Slidell made their removal illegal; and, even if one chose to argue the inaccurate analogy comparing diplomats, dispatches, and contraband, the right of neutrals to maintain relations with belligerents served as additional security for the Confederate agents. Yet Wilkes could have seized the Trent legally, and thus detained Mason and Slidell, on grounds other than Moir's refusal to show the ship's papers. When the San Jacinto's cutter, containing Fairfax and an armed crew, had rounded the Trent's stern, Mason told his secretary to take the Confederate dispatch bag to the mail agent and ask him to lock it up. Commander Williams subsequently informed Mason that the bag was secured in the mail room and that he would deliver it to the Southern agents already in London. At that instant, the Trent became guilty of unneutral service, and Moir's ignorance of Williams's action in no way mitigated the offense. The principle had been established in 1808 by Scott's ruling in The Atalanta. In that case, a Bremen ship was captured on a voyage home from Batavia, and a packet of French dispatches was found concealed in a small tea chest of the second supercargo. The court declared that "not to have pointed them out to the attention of the captors, amounts to a fraudulent dissimulation of a fact, which, by the law of nations, he was bound to disclose to those who had a right to examine, and possess themselves of all papers on board." It was, Scott said, "an aggravated case of active interposition in the service of the enemy, concerted and continued in fraud, and marked with every species of malignant conduct." Therefore, the *Atalanta* and its cargo were condemned.[26] An American prize court would probably have cited this case and rendered similar judgment against the *Trent*.

But what would have become of Mason and Slidell if Wilkes had taken the *Trent*? A prize court can proceed only *in rem*—against the ship and cargo, not persons. Dana studied the problem in his edition of Wheaton, and adopted an extra-legal position. "They could not be condemned or released by the court," he wrote. "They would doubtless have been held as prisoners of war by the United States Government." Like many Americans, Dana believed that the two men lacked diplomatic immunity because the Confederacy had not been recognized and its agents meant to obtain aid for an insurrection.[27] If an American court had condemned the commissioners as contraband or remanded them to the custody of the government, Britain would have protested anew and sought satisfaction for violation of its neutral rights and territorial sovereignty. The Lincoln administration probably would have surrendered its prisoners, thanks to Seward's willingness to defuse the situation, but would have had a ship and valuable cargo for its trouble. In the end, the United States was well served by Wilkes's "inadvertency"; Seward could take advantage of the technicality and end the war crisis, claiming he was adhering to old, established American principles.

For all the discussion, the *Trent* affair contributed little to the advancement of international law. Although contemporaries proclaimed that the incident "established the proposition that the ambassador of a belligerent cannot be taken from the ship of a neutral upon the high seas," it actually served only to affirm that principle, which was first propounded by Vattel, given force by Sir William Scott in *The Caroline*, and supported by Kent in his *Commentaries*. Equally irrelevant was Seward's gratuitous assertion that British objections to Wilkes's act indicated repudiation of impressment. There was, as Sir Vernon Harcourt (writing as "Historicus") stated, about as much resemblance between impressment and the removal of Mason and Slidell as between chalk and cheese. The diplomatic status of the Confederate commissioners, and their neutral destination, did not grant them or the *Trent* immunity from interference. If Wilkes had had reason to suspect that the envoys were on a belligerent mission—to sign an alliance for continuance of war—he could have arrested the two men and taken them and the ship before a prize court. The court would have faced the novel situation of proceeding *in rem* against persons.[28] This hypothetical set of circumstances did not occur, and both sides persisted in arguing the law of contraband for a question concerning alleged unneutral service.

The *Trent* affair, then, did not strengthen neutral rights; it neither established a new principle nor expanded an old one. "Its value as a leading case," one publicist wrote, "ranks very low."[29] But developments in the following century demonstrated that the *Trent* affair had left its mark.

The status of mail ships disturbed Anglo-American relations long after settlement of the crisis, and attracted international attention well into the twentieth century. In February 1863, efforts of the Union navy to enforce the blockade led to the visit, search, and subsequent capture of another British vessel, the *Peterhoff*, in the Danish West Indies, on suspicion of carrying contraband. The *Peterhoff*'s captain had refused to send his papers on board the American warship as required, and had ordered some of the papers destroyed. The Supreme Court, on appeal by the ship's owners, later resinded the lower court's condemnation of the vessel, but not of its cargo. However, Chief Justice Salmon Chase stated in 1866 that the captain of a merchant steamer "is not privileged from search by the fact that he has a government mail on board; on the contrary, he is bound by that circumstance to strict performance of neutral duties and to special respect for belligerent rights." The controversy continued until Seward wearily expressed the wish that governments arrive at some regulation sparing neutral mail from interruption and preventing it from being used for unfriendly purposes.[30]

No nation, including Britain, really wanted to excuse mail steamers from search; all nations feared that such a policy might hinder protection against abuse. A British manual of naval prize law published in the 1880s specified that the "Mailbags carried by Mail Steamers will not, in the absence of Special Instructions, be exempt from search for Enemy Despatches."[31] Yet, such policy was not universal. At the outset of the Franco-Prussian War, Paris declared that it would accept the word of the official mail agent on a neutral vessel in regard to the absence of offensive dispatches. Similarly, in 1898 President McKinley declared on the occasion of war with Spain that the "voyages of mail steamers are not to be interfered with except on the clearest grounds of suspicion of a violation of law in respect of contraband or blockade." The Navy Department then instructed blockading vessels that "a neutral vessel carrying hostile dispatches, when sailing as a dispatch vessel practically in the service of the enemy, is liable to seizure, but not when she is a mail packet and carries them in the regular and customary manner." In *The Panama* (1900), the Supreme Court expressly ruled that international law did not exempt a mail ship from capture as prize of war. During the Boer War, the British government asked the law officers if dispatches addressed to the South African Republic by its minister in Europe, and dealing with the conduct of the war, should be treated as contraband, and whether a closed mail addressed by a neutral to an enemy government could be opened on board a German steamer, the *Herzog*, performing regular mail service. The law officers replied that "a good deal of authority" (including Russell's instruction to Lyons, January 23, 1862, which claimed special treatment for mail packets) exempted the dispatches of a diplomatic agent from examination. They stated that even though the "right to examine closed mails for the purpose of finding despatches therein relating to the war has never been excluded by international law," there has been a "marked tendency" of late to extend immunity to such mails that should be opened only "in case of the most urgent necessity." The British government subsequently instructed naval officers not to search such vessels on suspicion only, and to expedite search procedures if they became necessary. But in 1902 both Great Britain and Germany refused free passage of neutral mail steamers through their blockade of Venezuela. When Russian cruisers boarded British and German mail ships and removed mail bags during the Russo-Japanese War of 1904–1905, the State Department protested violation of the Universal Postal Convention (1878), and asserted that "a usage has in recent years grown up to exempt neutral mails from search or seizure."[32]

During World War I, the Allies forced mail ships to enter British ports, whereas the Central Powers destroyed several without warning. Such actions were supposedly prohibited by the Eleventh Hague Convention of 1907. This document declared official and private postal correspondence of neutrals and belligerents inviolable on the high seas, but did not exempt neutral mail ships from the laws and customs of maritime war; signatories agreed to search such vessels only "when absolutely necessary, and with as much consideration and expedition as possible."[33]

The question of whether enemy nationals, civil or military, could be removed from a neutral vessel also disturbed international relations for decades after the Civil War. A naval conference in London in 1908–1909 considered the matter, and Article 47 of the resulting Declaration of London stated: "Any individual embodied in the armed force of the enemy, and who is found on board a neutral merchant vessel, may be made a prisoner of war, even though there be no ground for the capture of the vessel." Although this ruling had been designed as a compromise to save neutrals the inconvenience of having their vessels captured, neturals complained that it amounted to an unwarranted extension of belligerent rights, while belligerents regarded it as too restrictive. The war revealed the inappropriateness of many of its provisions, and belligerents tended to expand the right of removal to categories of persons not covered. The agreement of 1909 never came into force and, although many nations adhered to all or part of it, Britain abandoned it in 1916.[34]

Never was the inviolability of the neutral flag more thoroughly tested, with the possible exception of the Napoleonic Wars, than during World War I. The Central Powers gained an odious reputation for destroying scores of neutral and belligerent merchant ships and their crews and passengers, and the Allies repeatedly violated neutral rights by intercepting vessels at sea and removing certain classes of passengers. United States ships were often the victims of such interference. The American government had never accepted Article 47 of the Declaration of London, and contended that no belligerent had a right, unless by treaty, to remove enemies from neutral vessels without first seizing the vessel and placing it "in prize."[35] In the round of correspondence exchanged among the American, French, and British governments on this subject in 1914–1916, the *Trent* case figured prominently.

American discontent over removal of passengers by the Allies began with a series of violations committed by French cruisers. In November 1914, officers of the *Condé* removed from the American steamer *Windber*, traveling between the neutral ports of Colon and New York, a German-born steward, August Piepenbrink, apparently because he was alleged to be a German citizen. Although Piepenbrink had filed a declaration of intent to become an American citizen four years previously, the British, who received custody of him at Jamaica, would not release him. The State Department cited a statute that granted protection of citizenship to foreign seamen who had filed a declaration of intent and were traveling on American vessels, and declared that there was no "justification in international law for the removal of any enemy subject from a neutral vessel on the high seas bound for a neutral port, even if he could properly be regarded as a military person," which he was not. Secretary William J. Bryan quoted a passage from Lord Russell on the *Trent* case, as well as Thouvenel's note of December 3, 1861. "The seizure of Piepenbrink by the French Government," Bryan concluded, "was clearly contrary to the rule thus announced by that Government." Britain agreed to free him as a "friendly act, while reserving the question of principle involved." But the seizures continued. Several German subjects, suspected of plotting in the West Indies, were removed from American vessels by the French cruiser *Descartes* in 1915. The State Department again pointed out that since the men were "so far as known not incorporated in the armed forces of an enemy of France," removal was "not only an unwarranted invasion of the sovereignty of American vessels on the high seas, but an act of no military value to the Entente powers" and an "intolerable and indefensible interference with American merchant vessels plying between American ports." Although France subsequently released the men, the United States was dissatisfied with the lack of an announcement regarding future French policy, and reminded Paris that the principle of the *Trent* case "denies to a belligerent the right to remove from neutral vessels on the high seas even the paid agents who are not incorporated in the armed forces of its enemy."[36] France, like Britain, refused to admit any such principle.

The case during World War I that provoked the most extensive correspondence arose from removal of twenty-eight Germans, eight Austrians, and two Turks from the American steamship *China* by the British cruiser *Laurentic* in February 1916. The United States protested the action as "an unwarranted invasion of the sovereignty of American vessels on the high seas," and demanded the prisoners' immediate release because they were not members of the enemies' armies or navies. Britain replied that the proceeding was, in a sense, a reprisal for Germany's removal from occupied France and Belgium of all persons liable to military service. Since November 1914 the British Foreign Office had instructed the Royal Navy that enemy reservists on neutral vessels should be made prisoners of war, but Germany had acted only in areas under its control, never on neutral territory. The British argued that the enemies of Britain were plotting warlike and criminal enterprises on neutral soil throughout the world, and the men removed from the *China* had intended to establish an arms-smuggling operation in Manila. "Practical considerations" had changed, and such persons "must be placed within the category of individuals who may, without any infraction of the sovereignty of a neutral State, be removed from a neutral vessel on the high seas." The British dismissed the relevance of the *Trent* case, raised by the United States, stating that it bore no resemblance because Mason and Slidell had been diplomatic agents whose functions did not include "organizing of outrages upon the soil of the neutral country" to which they were accredited.[37]

Washington denied that the prisoners' alleged clandestine, belligerent activity made them subject to seizure on a neutral vessel on the high seas, and reminded the Foreign Office that the United States, not Britain, was responsible for breaches of neutrality in its territory:

> The rule is plain and definite—only military or naval persons may be removed from neutral vessels on the high seas. This rule has been contended for and maintained by the United States for over a century. It was expressly invoked by the British Government and followed by the United States in the *Trent* case, and received the official approval of nearly all of the governments of Europe. It was affirmed by the British Government in its proclamation of neutrality of April 23, 1898, in the Spanish-American war; and recognized in the cases of the *Bundesrath*, *General*, and *Herzog* in the Boer War.[38]

Stirring up an old controversy that the world would not forget, the State Department denied a distinction between the *China* and *Trent* cases. In the *Trent* incident,

> [F]our private persons, enemies of the United States Government, *en route* from a neutral country to a neutral country, not in the military service of their government but bent on the violation of the neutrality of England by granting commissions and dispatching commerce destroyers from her ports, were arrested and removed from a British merchant vessel on the high seas by an American ship of war.[39]

The British government finally agreed in May to release the men, admitting its error with respect to the facts, but admonished that "no general precedent is established and British doctrines in regard to the seizure of individuals of hostile nationality on board neutral ships will be safeguarded." On learning that some of the individuals removed from the *China* were military or naval reservists, the Foreign Office informed the United States that "any future cases shall be discussed on their merits without being prejudiced by the *China*." The State

Department naturally considered such status irrelevant to the principle involved. Several months later, on the occasion of America's entry into the war, London solemnly granted Washington's request that United States warships have the right to remove enemy subjects or agents from British vessels.[40]

Controversy over removal of enemy subjects from neutral vessels continued into World War II, as belligerents—particularly Britain—became increasingly bolder, and neutral rights suffered. In January 1940, a British warship removed twenty-one Germans from the Japanese steamer *Asama Maru* about thirty-five miles from the coast of Japan. Protesting a "serious, unfriendly act," the Japanese government remarked that only persons belonging to an enemy's armed forces might be taken off a neutral ship on the high seas. Again the British government countered that the persons affected were returning home for military service, and cited the Royal Navy's illegalities of the previous war as precedent. Japan refused to admit the validity of Britain's defense, citing the *Trent* case as a clear refutation.[41] Similar violations were committed by Britain against American vessels, but the State Department muted its protests, perhaps because it had begun to see merit in the British practice.

Since 1945, the American government has hardly led the world in support of neutral rights. Indeed the United States naval manual of 1955, *Law of Naval Warfare*, stated:

> Enemy nationals found on board neutral merchant vessels and aircraft as passengers who are actually embodied in the military forces of an enemy, or who are en route to serve in an enemy's military forces, or who are employed in the public service of an enemy, or who may be engaged in or suspected of service in the interests of an enemy may be made prisoners of war. (The removal of any of the categories of enemy nationals enumerated in this article may be exercised by a belligerent even though no sufficient reason exists for the capture of a neutral merchant vessel or aircraft.)[42]

Poor Wilkes! He erred only in being ahead of his time.

10.

The Accounting

THE LINCOLN ADMINISTRATION was relieved to see the *Trent* crisis end. During the period that it dominated public affairs, it disrupted the money markets, revived an ugly Anglophobia, and imperiled the Union cause. The episode probably would have been resolved earlier were it not for the government's fear of antagonizing American public opinion, and the pleasure many officials derived from the imprisonment of Mason and Slidell.

The State Department had to work quickly on the surrender arrangements. The slightest delay could lead to an incident along the Canadian boundary. No one could rule out a foray across the frontier by Irish revolutionaries or a revival of the Hunters' Lodges of the 1830s, which might be viewed by the Royal Navy as a prelude to a general offensive necessitating a preemptive attack.

The surrender note completed, Seward asked Lyons to come to the State Department on December 27. He claimed that he had been through "the fires of Tophet" to get the men surrendered and had appreciated Lyons's great kindness and consideration. The minister asked about arrangements for receiving the prisoners. Overwhelmed with business, Seward asked Lyons to return the following day and to keep the surrender secret until then, when it would be published in the papers.[1]

That evening, while the president went for a long, solitary cruise on the *Pensacola*, Seward held a large dinner at his house on Lafayette Square for members of the House Foreign Affairs and Senate Foreign Relations committees. Built on a lot once owned by Henry Clay and known as the Old Club House, the roomy, brick house had served as the residence of cabinet officers and diplomats. After dinner, Seward ushered his guests into the drawing room, which was decorated with the portraits of reigning European sovereigns and their ministers of state ("my tormentors," Seward called them). He flopped down in a leather chair, lit up a cigar, and announced, "To-day, the order was issued to release Mason and Slidell." The announcement was met by dead silence. Seward looked around expectantly, then read Russell's dispatch of November 30 and his reply, as well as Thouvenel's letter to Mercier and his own answer to the French protest. The chairman of the House committee, the venerable John J. Crittenden, swore vehemently, but all present agreed that the circumstances warranted the release.[2]

Reaction in Congress tended to parallel the feeling of Seward's guests: bitter, but resigned. The general attitude was best expressed in a Senate prayer, which asked for heavenly help "when domestic treason stabs at the nation's heart, and foreign arrogance is emboldened to defeat the public justice of the world." It was, the chaplain said, a day of darkness and reproach, "a day when the high principle of human equity, constrained by the remorseless sweep of physical and armed force, must for the moment succumb under the plastic forms of soft diplomacy." The Senate had resumed debate on the seizure on December 26, before the country had learned of the administration's decision. The genial senator from New Hampshire, John P. Hale, noted for his epithets, led off by branding surrender a fatal act that would reduce the United States to a second-rate power, the vassal of Britain. Sumner accused Hale of making a war speech and of only guessing at British demands; after these brief comments, discussion languished. In the House the topic attracted more attention. On December 30, the sinister-looking Thaddeus Stevens of Pennsylvania, angered by Seward's capitulation, criticized Thouvenel's harsh and dictatorial note as impertinent interference and lamented the lost fruits of an Anglo-American war, which would have allowed the Stars and Stripes to wave from the Gulf to the Arctic, and from the Bay of St. Lawrence to Puget Sound. War with all nations was better than national dishonor and disgrace. For the first time, Vallandigham stated that he, too, would have preferred war. For the first time, he jeered, the American eagle had cowered before the British lion. Benjamin Thomas of Massachusetts vowed that America would gird itself to "strike the blow of righteous retribution" against Britain's "un-manly and unjust" demands. Lovejoy objected to the appropriation of $35,000 for a commission to the London Exhibition of 1862, and declared that he would bequeath to his children an inextinguishable hatred of England. He hoped that after the rebellion had been crushed, Americans would stir up the Irish and English Chartists; encourage revolt among the French residents of Canada; and, with French and Russian aid, despoil Britain of its eastern possessions. Many other congressmen, however, said that the country could not handle another war and should not feel humiliated by a surrender based on lofty American principles.[3]

The emotional remarks in Congress served as a prelude to a Senate address on January 9, 1862, by Charles Sumner, chairman of the Foreign Relations Committee. Sumner's speech filled the seats and galleries. Unable to give a short or extemporaneous address, the senator carefully had written out and memorized his remarks, relying on a rhetorical model, oratorical flourishes, and classical quotations. Sumner lectured his audience, repeating every point, never at a loss for a Latin phrase no matter how inappropriate. Detractors scorned him as an orator—"one of them literary fellows"—and not an accomplished debater. "He works his adjectives so hard," the journalist Edwin L. Godkin remarked, "that if they ever catch him alone, they will murder him." Confident in his self-righteousness, oblivious to all criticism, he made every speech a crusade; in regard to the *Trent* affair, he planned to rescue American honor from Seward's careless defense.[4]

Elegant in tailored English cloth, he rose from his chair at 1:00 P.M. and, tossing a mane of brown hair, began to speak about the "two old men" taken off the *Trent* on a voyage of "treason, conspiracy, and rebellion," despite their "pretended embassadorial character." In a long address interlarded with illustrations from Shakespeare and ancient history, and spiced with Latin phrases, he went over the pre-1812 diplomatic correspondence regarding "the British pretension" to the right of removing men from neutral vessels. Wilke's act, he said, could be justified on "those British principles which, throughout our history, have been constantly, deliberately, and solemnly rejected," but which had undoubtedly led Captain Wilkes to err. He stated that according to American precepts, the *Trent*, although morally guilty, was legally innocent of wrongdoing by offering passage to Mason and Slidell; international law, American treaties, and European governments all agreed that a belligerent could remove only military and naval personnel and that carriage of dispatches did not subject a vessel to capture. Hailing British acceptance

of American principles as a victory of truth, he looked to the day when
the two nations, "equally endowed by commerce, and matching each
other, while they surpass all other nations, in peaceful ships, may
gloriously unite in setting up new pillars, which shall mark new triumphs, rendering the ocean a highway of peace, instead of a field of
blood." Sumner exulted that the "champion of belligerent rights 'has
changed his hand and checked his pride.' Welcome to this new
alliance."[5]

The speech excited Sumner's friends and enemies alike, who
almost universally commended his scholarship. An international legal
authority, Theodore Woolsey, congratulated him on having exposed
Seward's errors and given shape to the *Trent* affair, while diplomats
allegedly viewed the address as "forming a chapter in the law of nations."[6] But Sumner, like his archrival Seward, his other contemporaries, and future historians, concentrated on the irrelevant issue of
impressment and proved the obvious. His superficial address contributed no new chapter to international law, propagated misconceptions about American treaties, and aggravated old wounds. He
followed—not led—public opinion, and revealed himself to be no
better than what he had branded Seward, a politician.

Publication of Seward's surrender note was greeted with
something close to jubilation, despite some dissent and numerous
vows of vengeance against England. People described his dispatch as
courageous and masterly, an admirable analysis of international law,
and a triumph of American principles. Newspapers called it temperate
and ingenious, a victory for defense of neutral rights, more damaging
to the Rebel cause than a hundred defeats, "a hot shot into the
magazine of British diplomacy." Seward was "just about the tallest
man" in the country. Niagara Falls, a guide commented, "are like one
of our great statesmen just now. There's nothing particular about
them when you first catch a view of them; but when you get close and
know them better, then the power comes out, and you feel small as
potatoes."[7] Most Americans breathed a deep sigh of relief when they
realized that the crisis had ended.

The *Trent* affair left a residue of disappointment and anger in
America; people believed that Britain, not the United States, had acted
poorly, and had taken advantage of America's weakened condition.[8]
James Russell Lowell expressed the resentment of many Northerners
over Britain's threatening manner:

> It don't seem hardly right, John,
>   When both my hands was full,
> To stump me to a fight, John,—

Your cousin, tu, John Bull.
Old Uncle S. sez he, 'I Guess
We know it now,' sez he,
The lion's paw is all the law,
Accordin' to J.B.,
That's fit for you an' me![9]

"It was and remains hopeless for us to expect sympathy from England," wrote John Lothrop Motly. "We might as well try to get sunbeams from cucumbers." To a gathering at the Tremont Temple in Boston, the abolitionist orator Wendell Phillips thundered his disapproval of the Lincoln administration's backing down to British demands: "I call it the Apology Cabinet. It is the only Cabinet in the history of the nation whose whole record is a series of apologies." Only a few journals agreed with Phillips, attacking the surrender as a "sacrifice of the National Honor," a "cringing and abject" act, a humiliation. A large number of newspapers, magazines, and private citizens shared the Detroit *Daily Advertiser*'s "bitter determination to be avenged" after the Civil War. They longed for the day when England," wrote John Lothrop Motley. "We might as well try to get States could declare war "upon *general* principles, proclaiming that England must be put down as an enemy to mankind." Others called for a boycott of British goods, high tariffs, a nonintercourse act, and abrogation of the Canadian Reciprocity Treaty.[10]

A few periodicals were able to laugh off the prisoners' surrender. A cartoon in *Harper's Weekly* pictured Jonathan saying to John Bull, standing before Mason and Slidell in prison garb, "Well, Johnny, . . . if you feel like going into that kinder Business, I can let yer have just as many more as you like from . . . Sing Sing!" Seward's remark that he would cheerfully liberate the commissioners sparked more merriment. Mocking Seward, the Philadelphia *Inquirer* said, "We have no cross feeling in the matter! Not we! We do it 'cheerfully.' That is the word. We captured them cheerfully; and we have kept them cheerfully; and now we surrender them cheerfully." The Albany *Atlas and Argus* suggested that Seward's note, if not literal *hara kari*, "would certainly fall under its translated definition of 'Happy Despatch'."[11]

All the critical remarks made the administration wince; it did not want to surrender Mason and Slidell any more than the American people did. A few days after the capitulation, Cameron held a dinner for Lincoln, Seward, Chase, and a few senators, including Charles Sumner. When conversation turned to the *Trent*, Seward said he had "no memory for injuries" and surrendered the Confederate agents in

JONATHAN ON THE MASON AND SLIDELL AFFAIR.
BROTHER JONATHAN. "Well, Johnny, if you want 'em very bad, you can take 'em—and tell yer what, if you feel like going into that kinder Business, I can let yer have just as many more as you like from a little Establishment of mine called SING SING!"

Courtesy of *Harper's Weekly*

good faith. Encouraged by his adversary, Sumner remarked that the administration should convince Britain of its friendship. Lincoln answered simply, "I never see Lord Lyons. If it were proper I should like to talk with him, that he might hear from my lips how much I desire peace. If we could talk together he would believe me." When someone asked how he felt about giving up the men, Lincoln leaned back, laughed softly, and replied:

> I felt a good deal like the sick man in Illinois who was told he probably had n't many days longer to live, and that he ought to make peace with any enemies he might have. He said the man he hated worst of all was a fellow named Brown, in the next village, and he guessed he had better begin on him. So Brown was sent for, and when he came the sick man began to say, in a voice as meek as Moses's, that he wanted to die at peace with all his fellow-creatures, and he hoped he and Brown could now shake hands and bury all their enmity. The scene was becoming altogether too pathetic for Brown, who had to get out his handkerchief and wipe the gathering tears from his eyes. It was n't long before he melted and gave his hand to his neighbor and they had a regular love-feast of forgiveness. After a parting

that would have softened the heart of a grindstone, Brown had about reached the room door when the sick man rose up on his elbow and called out to him: "But, see here, Brown; if I should happen to get well, mind, that old grudge stands."[12]

Seward still had to find a dignified way of handing over Mason and Slidell. Assistant Secretary of the Navy Fox suggested taking the commissioners to Provincetown, forty miles from Fort Warren, to avoid offending Bostonians with the presence of a British frigate. Perhaps, he said, the navy could also avoid embarrassment by allowing a State Department officer to handle the surrender. Seward related the proposed arrangements to Lyons on the evening of December 28. Like Seward, Lyons did not want the prisoners' transfer to cause another affair, but he insisted that it take place in daylight and that the four men go on board a British warship in American waters or travel to an English port in an American vessel. They agreed that the surrender would occur on New Year's Day.[13]

The American government, as it turned out, almost had more trouble in getting rid of the Confederate agents than it had in capturing them. A State Department officer, Erastus D. Webster, and a United States Marshal, John S. Keyes, arrived at Fort Warren on the morning of January 1, 1862, to take Mason and Slidell to Provincetown. Webster insisted that the prisoners leave immediately, but Slidell, who had been ill for several days, replied in "language more forcible than chaste" that he would go when he was ready. After packing, the commissioners said farewell to their friends in their room, since the fort commandant, Colonel Justin Dimmick, did not want them to create a scene while departing. The commandant posted two details on the ramparts to keep the other prisoners off, and then allowed them to watch Mason and Slidell leave only after they promised not to cheer. Dimmick ordered the guard to stand at parade rest and to refrain from saluting him, for fear the diplomats would acknowledge it. The prisoners lined the sallyport and removed their hats as the diplomats walked by. Slidell stopped suddenly as he saw the flooded wharf, and refused to climb on board the tugboat *Starlight* unless a British officer escorted him. Webster, a corporal, and six marines convinced him to board the boat in a manner, Mason huffed, of "designed and marked indignity." At 10:45 A.M., the *Starlight* headed out to sea while the prisoners waved. The tug encountered rough weather on the way to Provincetown—another winter storm was brewing—but delivered its passengers safely at 4:00 P.M.[14]

Lyons had ordered the H.M.S. *Rinaldo* to receive the diplomats as "private gentlemen of distinction" and take them to Britain,

Halifax, or any neutral destination, but not to a Confederate port. That evening, the *Rinaldo* left Provincetown for Halifax and plunged into a severe gale. Waves buffeted the ship for four days, coating everything with ice, damaging the steering mechanism, and sweeping away lifeboats and sails; finally, Commander Hewett gave up and headed for Bermuda to coal. Mason and Slidell left there on January 10 for St. Thomas, where they boarded *La Plata* for England. They arrived in Southampton on January 29, and were greeted in silence by a large, curious crowd.[15]

The surrender had a strange, almost cathartic, effect on the American people. Having lived with the *Trent* affair for six weeks, discussing and arguing the minutiae of international law, they were relieved to put it behind them. Northerners scarcely felt Southern jabs about the "dirt eaters' " pusillanimous, cowardly, obsequious propitiation of the British government.[16] They had convinced themselves that Wilkes had inadvertently violated a national tradition, and that no disgrace attended a surrender based on American principles.

Across the Atlantic the suspense had become almost unbearable. The general public wondered if the Americans would answer Russell's demands with an attack on Canada. The government already had received, of course, an intimation from Seward on December 19 that Wilkes had acted on his own and might not be supported. The Palmerston ministry had suppressed the information and encouraged anti-American newspaper articles in order to maintain public anger as a hedge against one of Seward's tricks. Speculation about war had subsided within the cabinet, since members anticipated compliance. They were pleased, but not surprised, to learn on January 8, 1862, that the Foreign Office had received a telegram at 4:00 P.M. announcing the surrender.[17] The news had a wondrous effect on public morale. Within an hour all London knew it, and as telegraph lines carried the bulletin throughout the kingdom, the bells in St. Peters, Mancroft, Norwich, and other churches chimed with joy. Theatergoers leaped to their feet, cheered, and sang the national anthem. The prices of cotton goods stiffened, consols rose 1 percent, and rates for war risks at Lloyd's declined. The prospect of peace pleased even the *Times*, which criticized Mason and Slidell as "habitual haters and revilers" of Britain, the "most worthless booty" one could extract from the Americans, and asked readers not to cheer their arrival. *Punch* declared that people should abstain from any act that might lead the

PUNCH, OR THE LONDON CHARIVARI—January 11, 1862.

" UP A TREE."
Colonel Bull and the Yankee 'Coon.
'Coon. "AIR YOU IN ARNEST, COLONEL?"
Colonel Bull. "I AM."
'Coon. "DON'T FIRE—I'LL COME DOWN."

Courtesy of *Punch*

North to conclude that Britain sympathized with the South. In satiric gratitude for Wilkes's livening up what could have been a very dreary winter, the magazine asked that Parliament pass a vote of thanks, and proposed giving him a statue, a whittling knife, or a spittoon. Other papers accused the Lincoln administration of yielding not to international law, but to fear of Britain's preparations. A meeting of workers held in London's most populous district resolved that Mason and Slidell were "utterly unworthy [of] the moral sympathies of the working classes" of Britain and urged others to express support for the United States and denounce such pro-Southern newspapers as the *Times*. A few people in England, notably displaced Southerners and the war party, were less enthusiastic. In the best tradition of southern womanhood, Mrs. Slidell and her two daughters promptly swooned when they heard the news, while Confederate agents bemoaned the popular reaction against their cause. Disappointed Englishmen, who wanted to give the Yankees a good drubbing, believed that the settlement postponed war to a time less convenient for the Empire.[18]

Throughout the affair, the American minister had been chafing under the restraint posed by his position. Adams resented not being

PUNCH, OR THE LONDON CHARIVARI.—January 18, 1862.

NAUGHTY JONATHAN.

Mrs. Britannia. "THERE, JOHN! HE SAYS HE IS VERY SORRY, AND THAT HE DIDN'T MEAN TO DO IT—SO YOU CAN PUT THIS BACK INTO THE PICKLE-TUB."

Courtesy of *Punch*

kept informed concerning the administration's every move; he was frustrated by the inability to take action, and he disliked being a target for English wrath. Although he detected a subsiding of popular passion, he had received anonymous letters threatening to burn the legation. The endless, amateurish discussion of international law had provoked him to ask: "And who is Sir William Scott? Why an intense English judge in the most intense period of English tyranny on the ocean, who sat in his court sternly bent on sacrificing every shadow of neutral right. . . ." He was flabbergasted that the American people could adopt "the ultra tory doctrines of the stiffest tory of the present century!"[19]

Shortly after news of the surrender broke, the State Department ended its long silence with Minister Adams. Although the capture had galvanized the "loyal portion" of the American people, Seward wrote, he did not think they could have been united in a "voluntary war" against Britain; it was the wrong time to be diverted from the Union cause. Letting a flash of the old Seward shine through, he reminded the minister that the daily military and naval preparations of the government equaled, if not surpassed, Britain's recent war activity. He thanked Adams for his diligence and sagacity, and assured him that he had been given information as quickly as the department learned it, adding: "I have had to feel my way."[20]

Adams had conflicting emotions about the surrender. Its first effect, he noted, was that the "current which ran against us with such extreme violence six weeks ago now seems to going with equal fury in our favor"; however, he discovered that its solution left an impression of nothing to do and doomed him to remain in "this purgatory" a while longer. Although he rejoiced that Britain had abandoned "one of the most odious assumptions of power over the ocean," he scorned the Crown law officers, who stood ready to "turn their backs on all the musty decisions of their predecessors, and to proclaim a brand-new doctrine, precisely suited to the purpose in hand." Thinking Russell's arguments specious—that if the offense had been greater, the grievance would have been less—the minister conceded that the American government would have done badly if it had sacrificed principle to satisfy a vindictive feeling toward Mason and Slidell. Adams informed Russell of the surrender decision on January 9.[21]

The British cabinet heard Seward's note that same day and decided to accept the prisoner's release, but to ask the law officers for an opinion on the many points of international law Seward raised. Russell acknowledged Seward's surrender in a dispatch the next day, but held out the possibility of comment, and suggested that the American government instruct its commanders not to commit acts "for which the British Government will have to ask for redress and which the United States Government cannot undertake to justify." Seward's surrender on the narrow ground of Wilkes's failure to bring the *Trent* before a prize court had dismayed several cabinet members. Argyll and Somerset feared the principle would bring the two nations to the "point of war every week" if American captains insisted on taking British packets into port for adjudication. In that case, Palmerston decided, any British warships coming across an American warship should force a release, unless the captor could state a prima facie case against the vessel. After all, he had just learned that on December 9 another American cruiser had overhauled a British vessel, the *Eugenia Smith*, while on a voyage from Matamoros to Havana; two Confederates had been removed, and confined in Fort Lafayette.[22]

The law officers' opinion, which they submitted to Russell on January 15, supported the cabinet position. Disputing Seward's contention that Britain had adopted any new principle, they saw "plain and broad distinctions" between impressment and seizure of persons

as contraband of war. No part of Seward's note escaped their
criticism. A neutral had a right to maintain relations with both
belligerents; the *Trent* did not violate British neutrality by carrying the
diplomats or their dispatches; and finally, the *Trent* could not have
been condemned because commissioners and dispatches were not contraband and the ship had a neutral destination. They dismissed
Seward's quotations of Scott as "irrelevant" and warned that illegal
condemnation of the vessel would have vitally affected the "general interests of civilization, and of all neutral and commercial nations."[23]

Everyone in the cabinet recognized the dual necessity of refuting
Seward's doctrines, but moving carefully. With all the "Stowell-
worship" in Britain, they thought it best to answer Seward's points in
order, and to avoid "putting the quarrel of 1812 in the fore ground,"
unless they were prepared to give up impressment. Russell's "anti-
Seward dispatch" of January 23, 1862, drew heavily on the law officers' opinion, but also claimed special treatment for mail packets.
Such vessels, though not exempt from visit and search during war, he
said, were entitled to "peculiar favor and protection." Unnecessary interference with them "would be an act of a most noxious and injurious
character, not only to a vast number and variety of individual and
private interests, but to the public interests of neutral and friendly nations." Great Britain, Russell concluded, "could not have submitted to
the perpetration of that wrong, however flourishing might have been
the insurrection in the South, and however important the persons captured might have been." Relieved to be done with the *Trent* affair,
Russell exclaimed to Lyons, "What a fuss we have had about these
men."[24]

Within the cabinet, only Palmerston could not take part in the
celebration. He was so disabled by gout that he could use neither
hands nor feet, and rumors circulated that he had died. A secretary
read him Seward's dispatch, but the old man, saturated with drugs,
was too drowsy to understand it. On hearing it again, he cheered up,
but advised keeping the Royal Navy and Canadian garrisons ready for
anything.[25]

The Palmerston ministry still had to face parliamentary fire from
the right and left. Although the opposition leader, the Earl of Derby,
approved the government's handling of the affair, he warned against
negotiations on international law. Officials should not forget that
Britain had "a deep and preponderating interest in maintaining the
rights of belligerents; and this country was not one which could lightly
sacrifice the legitimate rights which they now possessed in that
respect." The government's chief gadfly, John Bright, launched an at-

tack on Palmerston, criticizing the "ferocious gesticulation" of his war measures and the violent language of government newspapers. Bright said those actions created a universal impression that the government "either knew war was all but inevitable, or that they intended war, if war could by any possibility be made out of it." He accused the ministry of acting under the mistaken belief that either Seward desired war or that a display of power was necessary to overawe the mob that supposedly controlled the American government. The Palmerston regime, he stated, should have tried all "moderate and courteous means" before resorting to measures that paralyzed world commerce and caused financial loss to almost all classes.[26]

Palmerston went on the offensive, accusing Bright of holding an opinion confined to himself, and reminding him that the American people, Congress, and the Navy Department had approved Wilkes's conduct. If the United States was bound by its principles to release the two men, why did the country tarry so long? Measures to strengthen Canada were not "ferocious gesticulation"; but they were sound moves, designed to prove to Americans that conquest of Canada would not be easy.[27] Palmerston concluded that there was:

> no better security for peace between nations than the conviction . . . that each is capable of defending itself, and that no insult or injury committed by the one against the other would pass unresented. Between nations, as between individuals, mutual respect is the best security for mutual goodwill and mutual courtesy.[28]

Unperturbed by Russell's retort to his surrender note, Seward managed to have the last word, and play what the British regarded as a cheap trick. First, he reminded Russell on February 21 of the debates and conventions concerning maritime war, and said that since Britain seemed so anxious concerning neutral rights, the United States would agree to any melioration of maritime law "even to the most liberal asylum for persons and the extreme point of exemption of private property from confiscation in maritime war." Then, Seward had an opportunity to be ironically helpful. About that time ice blocked the channels on the Canadian coast, and Edmonstone, Allan and Company, agents and part-owners of the Montreal Ocean Steam Ship Company, asked Seward's permission to send through Maine some of the baggage of the British troops en route to Canada. Seward gladly consented to transportation across American territory of all baggage, military stores, arms, munitions, and troops with no exceptions. Lyons erupted when he found out, because it made his country look

foolish. He thought that Seward gave permission "for the sake of making a sensation," but saw no way to decline without appearing
ungracious. Although Lyons eventually told Seward that his permission was superfluous, the damage had been done, and all of America
laughed at Seward's "act of killing kindness."[29]

Many years after the Civil War, on the fiftieth anniversary of the
capture of Mason and Slidell, Charles Francis Adams, Jr., remarked in
an address to the Massachusetts Historical Society that there was "a
discipline, even lesson perhaps, in a remorseless retrospect." But many
Americans, including some historians, have found it nearly impossible
to look back on the *Trent* affair with detachment; instead, they have
shared the feeling of Henry S. Commager who, while admitting the
technical correctness of Britain's position, branded the British attitude
and the demand for war over "a minor mistake" as arrogant and un-
pardonable. It was a familiar refrain, initially sung by the first
historian of the incident, Thomas L. Harris. He considered British
behavior unwarranted and inconsistent with either the "pretended
position of England as a leader of civilization or with the past record
of that country as regards her treatment of neutrals." England, he
believed, had intended to menace the United States at a time when
Americans were already in a deadly struggle and unable to resent
foreign insults.[30]

British preparations for war, which began before the United
States had a chance to release its prisoners voluntarily, did appear to
be rather hasty and indicative of, if not a desire for conflict, at least a
lack of confidence in American goodwill. The history of Anglo-
American relations certainly had not given the British government any
cause to expect friendly treatment; American jealousy of the Empire
was legendary. The two countries had been sparring for several
months over Britain's exercise of neutral rights, and the American attitude struck the British as typically unreasonable, especially in view of
the rumors circulating about Seward.

Having received warnings from Lyons for over a year that Seward
wanted to provoke a war to revive his sagging popularity and make up
for the loss of Southern territory, cabinet officials were understand-
ably edgy by the time of the *Trent* affair. Although the Adamses
believed that their old friend Seward was running a classic bluff, that
his tactic made European nations more careful to avoid giving offense

and helped preserve peace, they saw too late how he had placed the United States at a disadvantage. Seward did force the British government to move more slowly, but he also touched its instinct for self-preservation and created a functional Anglo-French alliance. Great Britain's decision to send more troops to Canada, made before the *Trent* affair led to further reinforcements, underscored Seward's diplomatic failure. British cabinet officers had not expected him to give in so easily on Mason and Slidell, and afterwards questioned the British minister's interpretation. "I do not believe that Seward has any animosity to this country," Russell said. "It is all buncom." Even Lyons had to revise his opinion. When Seward's political foes tried to force his dismissal from office a year after the *Trent* crisis, Lyons worried that his replacement would be "less disposed to keep the peace."[31] It seemed a surprising reversal for the British minister, but, then, Lyons and other officials had begun to understand their nemesis and the government he represented.

Many writers, including Lyons, have thought it fortunate that the Atlantic cable, which was laid in August 1858 but broke a month later, was not functioning in 1861. They believe that a war would have resulted if each nation had been able to receive instant word of the other's reaction.[32] Such reasoning fails to account for the fact that the American government surrendered its prisoners only after learning of the hostile British reaction. It is tempting, but not logical, to claim that the two-week delay in communications gave people time to cool off. Great Britain received word of American jubilation within a few days of *La Plata*'s arrival with news of the seizure. If the Atlantic cable had been functioning, it would have allowed Americans to know how much Britain and the rest of Europe disapproved of Wilkes's act; this might have caused an earlier release of Mason and Slidell. British officials were well aware of the harmful result of slow communications. "I am very much inclined to think that if a submarine telegraph from England to New York, or Portland, or even Halifax were now in working order, the chances of a war would be greatly diminished," Lewis had written at the time. "If war occurs, it will be owing to the Americans committing themselves irrevocally [*sic*], before they know the serious view of the transaction which is taken in England and France." The quick American response to news of British preparations not only underlined the importance of restoring the cable, but also confirmed what many Britons had always suspected. "The moral of all this is very plain and simple," Bagehot observed. "In all future dealings with the American Government, we must ask for what we want courteously but peremptorily."[33]

The *Trent* affair thus came to an end, and the participants turned to other activities. It is interesting to observe their subsequent actions, which were sometimes accompanied by developments that the world describes as success, sometimes with changes of circumstance that brought virtual failure.

The major British figures in the *Trent* affair continued their careers more or less unaffected by the crisis. Palmerston remained at the head of the government throughout the Civil War and, in his last months of power, tried unsuccessfully to settle the war between Prussia and Denmark. At the age of eighty he was still riding horses, a hardy old man if ever there was one. After having been a member of sixteen parliaments, and of all but two of the ministries from 1807 to 1865, he died in October 1865, murmuring, "That's Article 98; now go on to the next." His foreign secretary, Lord Russell, continued in his post after the *Trent* affair and, less than a year after the release of Mason and Slidell, came close to offering British mediation of the Civil War. His failure to stop the *Alabama* from leaving British waters cost the government over £3,000,000 in a great arbitration in 1872. Meanwhile, he had succeeded Palmerston as prime minister, and held the office until June 1866, when his electoral reform bill met defeat. Twelve years later, as he lay dying, Russell said to his wife, "I have made mistakes, but in all I did my object was the public good."[34] Lord Lyons never did take Lincoln's advice to get married, and in February 1865 resigned as minister to the United States, wrongly believing that his health was failing. He went to Constantinople, and shortly thereafter became ambassador to Paris, holding the latter post for twenty years before resigning in November 1887, and dying within a month.

The leading figures on the American side pursued equally eventful careers. Seward developed into a skillful secretary of state and, more than any of his predecessors, wrote dispatches with an eye on public opinion. It was no coincidence that the initial volumes of *Foreign Relations of the United States*, the best annual compilation of diplomatic documents published by any government, appeared during his tenure. He combined the qualities of idealist, realist, and opportunist—an unusual mixture of talents—and established policies that led to the emergence of the United States as a world power in the twentieth century. Easily turning aside all threats of foreign intervention in the Civil War, he convinced the French in 1865–1867 that they should withdraw from Mexico before American public opinion forced the Johnson administration to expedite their departure. An expansionist in an antiexpansionist period, he negotiated the purchase of Alaska in 1867, but was unable to acquire the Danish West Indies, Santo Domingo, or Hawaii. After leaving the State Department, he became the first major American public figure to tour the world. He died in October 1872, helplessly paralyzed, but leaving behind a large record of accomplishment. His political ally, Charles Francis Adams, remained in London until June 1867, rendering more valuable service to the Union. He rose so high in British esteem that the House of Commons cheered him amidst debate on the *Alabama* claims a few months before his departure. He declined the presidency of Harvard upon return to his native Massachusetts, and was briefly considered as the Liberal Republican candidate in 1872. Although afflicted by senility in later years, he lived on until 1886, longer than any other notable in the *Trent* affair except Lyons.

The initiator of the *Trent* affair, Captain Wilkes, was rewarded briefly with the command of the James River Flotilla and the gift of a $1,200 sword from the city of Boston. However, while commanding a special squadron in November 1863, he again disobeyed orders, violating neutral rights; he publicly protested Secretary Welles's version of his action, and was court-martialed and suspended from duty for three years. The war ended before he could return to active duty, but he became a rear admiral on the retired list, living quietly until his death in Washington in 1877.

The two Confederate envoys whose peregrinations had caused it all remained in Europe until the war's end, and discovered that the six-week imprisonment of 1861 was their greatest personal triumph. During the war, Mason cultivated leaders in the Lords and Commons, together with businessmen and journalists, and raised money for the Confederate cause, but he never gained official recognition from the British government. Disgusted with Russell's detention of the Laird rams in September 1863, he abandoned his post and went to Paris, where he stayed until a year after the war. He then sailed for Canada, and returned to Virginia three years later under President Johnson's second proclamation of amnesty. Because his Selma Plantation had been put to the torch by troops of Major General Philip Sheridan, he was forced to pass his final days elsewhere, and died in 1871. During the Civil War, Slidell helped arrange the construction of four corvettes and two ironclads in France, but American consuls prevented their sailing. He negotiated a Confederate loan in 1863 with Baron Emile Erlanger, but so much money was spent to support the bonds on the market that the Confederacy received only slightly over half of the Erlanger issue. Slidell remained in Paris after the war. Although he applied for permission to visit Louisiana, he never received it, and he died in Paris in 1871, the same year as Mason.

Although the *Trent* affair marked a high point in the lives of some participants, and caused no more than a ripple in others, the six-week crisis held greater significance for relations between Great Britain and the United States. Some scholars, doubtlessly influenced by its comic features and peaceful settlement, have termed it "a popular but not necessarily a diplomatic crisis," an "isolated and overpublicized incident," and the "most farcical incident in the history of Anglo-American relations"; such scholars have cautioned against "exaggerating the likelihood of war resulting from it." In fact, historians have been captivated by the absurdity of war over such a minor matter. "It is hard," Peter Parish wrote, "to credit that Britain and the United States would ever actually have blundered into war over the unauthorized action of one self-important naval officer, and the fate of two diplomats representing a government which neither power recognized." While no one can say with certainty whether war would have developed if Mason and Slidell had not been surrendered, it is important to realize that for Britain the affair constituted a non-justiciable dispute. The Palmerston ministry adamantly opposed arbitration—the course favored by Lincoln, but normally confined to cases less important than the *Trent* affair—and embarked on preparations for war; their motivation did not necessarily stem from the principle involved, but from fear that the United States and its evil genius, Seward, had chosen that moment to provoke the hostilities so long predicted by Lyons.[35] More than one conflict has resulted from misperception by one or both of the involved parties, and the background of the *Trent* affair provided ample opportunity for poor judgment. Obviously, the incident should never have been allowed to go so far, but it did; minimizing the significance of the grievance in no way mitigates the seriousness of the crisis. If it contained all the ingredients of high melodrama, it also possessed the makings of tragedy.

The *Trent* affair turned out to be the gravest foreign crisis of the Civil War and marked the most perilous development in Anglo-American relations between the War of 1812 and the Venezuelan crisis of 1895. Although the two nations disagreed on many matters during the nineteenth century, they never reached a point where the question of war passed beyond the realm of speculation. It was fitting, perhaps, in view of their most lasting controversy, that in 1861 they nearly clashed a second time over the issues of neutral and belligerent rights; but it would have been bitterly ironic—a satiric commentary on the future of international peace—if war had resulted from violation of a principle accepted by both nations, a war that would have impaired, rather than improved, the rights of neutrals.

Abbreviations

AJIL   *American Journal of International Law.*

AMAE   Archives du Ministère des Affaires étrangères. Paris.

BM   British Museum. London.

DAB   Dictionary of American Biography.

DNB   Dictionary of National Biography.

FO   Foreign Office. London.

GPO   U.S. Government Printing Office. Washington, D.C.

HMC   Historical Manuscripts Commission. London.

LC   Library of Congress, Manuscripts Division.

MHS   Massachusetts Historical Society. Boston.

NA   National Archives. Washington, D.C.

NMM   National Maritime Museum. Greenwich, England.

NYPL   New York Public Library.

ORA   *The War of the Rebellion: A Compilation of the Official Records of the Union and Confederate Armies.* 130 vols. Washington, D.C.: GPO, 1880–1901.

ORN   *Official Records of the Union and Confederate Navies in the War of the Rebellion.* 30 vols. plus index. Washington, D.C.: GPO, 1894–1914.

PAC   Public Archives of Canada. Ottawa.

PRO   Public Record Office. London.

The following abbreviations are used for legal works cited in this volume.

Cranch   Cranch, William. *Reports of Cases Argued and Adjudged in the Supreme Court of the United States.* 9 vols. Philadelphia: Johnson, 1830–1854.

Dodson   Dodson, John. *Reports of Cases Argued and Determined in the High Court of Admiralty, Commencing with the Judgments of the Right Hon. Sir William Scott, Trinity Term, 1811.* 2 vols. London: A. Strahan, 1815–1828.

Edwards   Edwards, Thomas. *Reports of Cases Argued and Determined in the High Court of Admiralty, Commencing with the Judgments of the Right Hon. Sir William Scott, Easter Term, 1808–1812.* London: A. Strahan, 1812.

C. Rob.   Robinson, Christopher. *Reports of Cases Argued and Determined in the High Court of Admiralty, Commencing with the Judgments of the Right Hon. Sir William Scott, Michaelmas Term, 1798.* 6 vols. New York: Isaac Riley, 1801–1810.

U.S.   *United States Supreme Court Reports.* (The first 90 vols. are referred to by names of the reporters, as in Cranch above and Wallace and Wheaton below. Beginning with vol. 91, the reference is *U.S. Supreme Court Reports.*)

Wallace   Wallace, John W. *Cases Argued and Adjudged in the Supreme Court of the United States.* 21 vols. Washington, D.C.: Morrison, 1864–1875.

Wheaton   Wheaton, Henry. *Cases Argued and Decided in the Supreme Court of the United States.* 12 vols. Albany: Banks and Brothers, 1883.

Notes

1. The Capture of Mason and Slidell

1. Virginia Mason, *The Public Life and Diplomatic Correspondence of James M. Mason* (Roanoke: Stone Printing & Manufacturing, 1903), pp. 209–10; Wm. H. Trescott to R. M. T. Hunter, Oct. 12, 1861, ORN, 1st series, III: 281.

2. Jefferson Davis to Howell Cobb, Aug. 28, 1861; J. J. Hooper to Davis, Aug. 29, 1861; R. M. T. Hunter to Mason and Slidell, Sept. 23, 1861 (under separate covers), ORA, 2nd series, II: 1207–22.

3. M. B. Hammond, *The Cotton Industry* (New York: Macmillan, 1897; reprinted Johnson Reprint, 1966), pp. 252–54; Frank L. Owsley, *King Cotton Diplomacy* (Chicago: University of Chicago Press, 1959), pp. 3, 8; E. Merton Coulter, *The Confederate States of America, 1861–1865* (Baton Rouge: Louisiana State University Press, 1950), pp. 184–85.

4. Clement Eaton, *A History of the Southern Confederacy* (New York: Macmillan, 1954), p. 61; James A. B. Scherer, *Cotton as a World Power: A Study in the Economic Interpretation of History* (New York: Frederick A. Stokes, 1916), p. 239; William Howard Russell, *My Diary North and South*, 2 vols. (Boston: Burnham, 1863), I: 142, 178.

5. Robt. Toombs to Yancey, Rost, and Mann, Mar. 16, 1861, ORN, 2nd series, III: p. 195; R. M. T. Hunter to Mason, Sept. 23, 1861, ORA, 2nd series, II: 1209–10, 1213.

6. Allen Johnson and Dumas Malone, eds. *Dictionary of American Biography*, 11 vols. (New York: Scribner's, 1957), VI:365; Charles Francis Adams, Jr., *An Autobiography* (Boston and New York: Houghton Mifflin, 1916), p. 215; CFA, Jr., "The Trent Affair," *Proceedings of the Massachusetts Historical Society*, XLV (1911–12), p. 39; Howard C. Perkins, ed., *Northern Editorials on Secession*, 2 vols. (New York: D. Appleton-Century, 1942), II: 1028; Mary Boykin Chesnut, *A Diary from Dixie*, ed. Isabella D. Martin and Myrta L. Avary (New York: D. Appleton, 1905; reprinted Gloucester: Peter Smith, 1961), pp. 116–17; George M. Trevelyan, *The Life of John Bright* (London: Constable, 1913), p. 312.

7. [Joseph A. Scoville], *The Old Merchants of New York City*, 5 vols. (New York: Carleton, 1864–70; reprinted New York: Greenwood, 1968), II: 257–60; Marian Gouverneur, *As I Remember: Recollections of American Society During the Nineteenth Century* (New York: D. Appleton, 1911), pp. 94–5; Robert F. Lucid, ed., *The Journal of Richard Henry Dana*, 3 vols. (Cambridge, Mass.: Harvard University Press, 1968), I: 399; Burton J. Hendrick, *Statesmen of the Lost Cause: Jefferson Davis and His Cabinet* (Boston: Little, Brown, 1939), pp. 288–92; New York *Daily Tribune*, Nov. 18, 22, 25, 1861; DAB, IX: 210; W. H. Russell, *Diary*, p. 237; London *Times*, Dec. 10, 1861.

8. Adams, "*Trent* Affair," p. 41; Brian Jenkins, *Britain and the War for the Union* (Montreal: McGill-Queens, 1974), I: 215–16.

9. Virgil C. Jones, *The Civil War at Sea*, 3 vols. (New York: Holt, Rinehart & Winston, 1960–62), I: 294–95; Owsley, *King Cotton Diplomacy*, pp. 230–31, 261; Marcus W. Price, "Ships that Tested the Blockade of the Carolina Ports, 1861–1865," *American Neptune*, VIII (1948), p. 196; Slidell and Mason to Hunter, Oct. 3, 4, 1861, ORN, 2nd series, III: 275–76.

10. Mason to R. M. T. Hunter, Oct. 5, 9, 1861, ORN, 2nd series, III: 277, 1st series, I: 150; C.S.S. *Theodora*, ibid., 2nd series, III: 269; Price, "Ships that Tested the Blockade," p. 197; Mason, *Life*, pp. 199, 210.

Lately a few historians have argued that Confederate officials publicized the departure of Mason and Slidell in order to trap the Union navy into capturing the agents, thus precipitating an Anglo-American war crisis. The theory is over a hundred years old, as illustrated in W. G. Simms to James H. Hammond, Dec. 12, 1861; and Mary C. Simms Oliphant, Alfred T. Odell, and T. C. Duncan Eaves, eds., *Letters of William Gilmore Simms*, 5 vols. (Columbia: University of South Carolina Press, 1955), IV: 387–388. Lynn M. Case also looks suspiciously at the publicity, and asserts that Wilkes, Mason, and Slidell had planned the capture over lunch on board Wilkes's ship at Havana. This information comes from the diary of Attorney General Edward Bates. Bates had quoted statements of Secretary of War Simon Cameron, who got the information from an assistant who had received a letter from a consul in Scotland. The consul had learned the information from "respectable sources" in London, who attributed the information to the British mail agent on the *Trent*, Commander Williams. Williams, incidentally, did not mention it in his report to the Admiralty or to any public meeting. Thus, hearsay and circumstantial evidence constitute the base of Case's allegation. See Lynn M. Case and Warren F. Spencer, *The United States and France: Civil War Diplomacy* (Philadelphia: University of Pennsylvania Press, 1970), pp. 190–91. Daniel B. Carroll, *Henri Mercier and the American Civil War* (Princeton: Princeton University Press, 1971), p. 100, accepts the Case hypothesis. Simms, Case, and Carroll apparently believe that an ulterior motive, not carelessness, led the Confederate government and press to inform the North of the diplomats' plans. But the regularity with which Northern newspapers published details of Union military movements suggests that excessive candor was the hallmark of Civil War journalism.

11. Mason to R. M. T. Hunter, Oct. 18, 1861, ORN, 1st series, I: 151; Mason, *Life*, pp. 200, 209–11.

12. Mason, *Life*, pp. 200, 202, 211–13; Mason to R. M. T. Hunter, Oct. 18, 1861, ORN, 1st series, I: 151–52.

13. Crawford to Russell, Apr. 6, 1861 (no. 15), FO 72/1013, p. 109; Jenkins, *Britain*, p. 23; Helm to Benjamin, Jan. 23, 1864, ORN, 2nd series, III: 1007; Serrano to Helm, Oct. 23, 1861, ibid., p. 285; Mason, *Life*, pp. 201–3; Adams, "*Trent* Affair," p. 41; F. C. Drake, "The Cuban Background of the *Trent* Affair," *Civil War History*, XIX (1973), pp. 40–1.

After the commissioners left Havana and were captured at sea, Crawford found himself being roasted in the Northern press for his accommodation of the Confederates and, when questioned by the British Foreign Office, denied that he had conducted the men to Serrano's office. *See* Crawford to Russell, Dec. 3, 1861, FO 72/1013.

14. H. H. Bell to Gustavus V. Fox, Dec. 19, 1861, Robert M. Thompson and Richard Wainwright, eds., *Confidential Correspondence of Gustavus Vasa Fox, Assistant Secretary of the Navy, 1861–1865*, 2 vols. (New York: Naval Historical Society, 1918), I: 412–13; ORN, 2nd series, I: 200; Frank Moore, ed., *The Rebellion Record*, 11 vols. (New York: G. P. Putnam, 1861–65), III: 335; Michael S. Goldberg, "A History of United States Naval Operations During 1861," Ph.D. dissertation, University of New Mexico (1970), p. 31; John Sherman Long, "Glory-Hunting Off Havana: Wilkes and the *Trent* Affair," *Civil War History*, IX (1963), p. 133.

15. DAB, X: 217; Merle Curti, *The Growth of American Thought*, 2nd ed. (New York: Harper, 1951), p. 330; Geoffrey S. Smith, "Charles Wilkes and the Growth of American Naval Diplomacy," in *Makers of American Diplomacy*, ed. Frank Merli and Theodore Wilson (New York: Scribner's, 1974), pp. 136–38; William Stanton, *The Great United States Exploring Expedition of 1838–1842* (Berkeley and Los Angeles: University of California Press, 1975), pp. 312–13. *See also*: David B. Tyler, *The Wilkes Expedition: The First United States Exploring Expedition 1838–1842* (Philadelphia: American Philosophical Society, 1968); Vincent Ponko, Jr., *Ships, Seas, and Scientists: U.S. Naval Exploration and Discovery in the Nineteenth Century* (Annapolis: Naval Institute Press, 1974); and Charles Wilkes, *Narrative of the United States Exploring Expedition During the Years 1838, 1839, 1840, 1841, 1842*, 5 vols. (Philadelphia: C. Sherman, 1844).

16. James Fergusson, *Notes of a Tour in North America in 1861* (London: Wm. Blackwood & Son, 1861), p. 3; Daniel Henderson, *Hidden Coasts: A Biography of Admiral Charles Wilkes* (New York: Wm. Sloane, 1953), pp. 75, 210–11; Stanton, *Exploring Expedition*, pp. 220, 288; Clayton R. Barrow, ed., *America Spreads Her Sails: U.S. Seapower in the 19th Century* (Annapolis: Naval Institute Press, 1973), pp. 112–13.

17. Howard K. Beale, ed., *Diary of Gideon Welles, Secretary of the Navy under Lincoln and Johnson*, 3 vols. (New York: W. W. Norton, 1960), I: 73; John Sherman Long, "The Gosport Affair," *Journal of Southern History*, XXIII (1957), p. 169; William W. Jeffries, "The Civil War Career of Charles Wilkes," ibid., XI (1945), pp. 324–45, has an excellent character analysis. Wilkes was also a reformer who worked for abolition of the grog ration. *See* Harold D. Langley, *Social Reform in the United States Navy, 1789–1862* (Chicago: Illinois University Press, 1967), p. 250; Moore, *Rebellion Record*, III: 335; Long, "Glory-Hunting Off Havana," p. 134; Goldberg, "Naval Operations," pp. 375–79; James S. Palmer to Welles, Sept. 23, 1861, ORN, 1st series, I: 91; Henderson, *Hidden Coasts*, p. 236; John McIntosh Kell, *Recollections of a Naval Life; Including the Cruises of the Confederate States Steamers "Sumter" and "Alabama"* (Washington: Neale, 1900), p. 160, comments on French sympathy.

18. Palmer to Welles, Oct. 25, 1861, ORN, 1st series, I: 122; Raphael Semmes to Stephen R. Mallory, Nov. 9, 1861, ibid., p. 637, says he boarded the *Spartan* on Oct. 5; Kell, *Recollections*, pp. 158–59; D. D. Porter to William Mervine, Oct., 1861, ORN, p. 109; Wilkes to Palmer, Oct. 13, 1861, ibid., p. 120; Jones, *Civil War at Sea*, I: 298; Wilkes to Welles, Oct. 24, 1861, ORN, p. 119; Wilkes to Welles, Nov. 15, 19, 1861, ibid., p. 130. Maranham is the former name of São Luiz de Maranhão, now called São Luiz.

19. Louis R. Hamersly, comp., *The Records of Living Officers of the United States Navy and Marine Corps*, rev. ed. (Philadelphia: J. B. Lippincott, 1870), p. 121; Drake,

"Cuban Background," pp. 30, 38–9; R. W. Shufeldt to Seward, Nov. 4, 1861 (no. 76), NA, Letters Received by the Secretary of the Navy from the President and Executive Agencies, vols. 41–43; Shufeldt to Seward, Nov. 9, 1861 (no. 79), NA, Despatches from U.S. Consuls in Havana, vol. 41; Shufeldt to Wilkes, Dec. 20, 1861, LC, Charles Wilkes Papers, Special Correspondence, *Trent* Affair, Letters (Dec. 1861). Mason, *Life*, p. 215, claims that two of Wilkes's officers talked with him in the parlor of the Hotel Cubana, apparently trying to extract information, but other sources flatly contradict Mason. Norman Ferris, *The Trent Affair: A Diplomatic Crisis* (Knoxville: University of Tennessee Press, 1977), p. 19, accepts Mason's account.

20. Wilkes to Welles, Nov. 16, 1861, ORN, 1st series, I: 144; Charles Wilkes, "Journal," Nov. 6, 1861, Wilkes Papers.

21. Wilkes to Welles, Nov. 15, 1861, ORN, 1st series, I: 130; London *Times*, Dec. 5, 1861; H. P. Grace to Wilkes, Nov. 3, 1861, NA, Letters Received by the Secretary of the Navy, Captains' Letters, vol. 4.

In an official report of the accident, Wilkes claimed the *Jules et Marie* rammed him just as he was about to send over a boarding party. Boatswain H. P. Grace, the inspecting officer, also regarded the French captain as either negligent or incompetent and assessed damages to the foreign vessel at $30 to $40. However, a joint American and French naval commission, with an Italian naval officer as arbiter, thirteen months later absolved the French ship of responsibility, and concluded the *San Jacinto* caused the collision by failing to reverse her engine in time. Shufeldt and the French consul at Havana agreed on $9,500 compensation, slightly reduced from the original claim. House Exec. Doc. 4, 37 Cong., 3 Sess., 1862.

22. Charles Wilkes, Autobiography MS., X: 2283, Wilkes Papers; Wilkes to Welles, Nov. 15, 1861, ORN, 1st series, I: 130; A. Noel Blakeman, ed., *Personal Recollections of the War of the Rebellion*, 4 vols. (New York: G. P. Putnam, 1891–1912), II: 235–36; Cicero Price (comm., *Huntsville*) to Wm. W. McKean, Nov. 24, 1861, and James P. Couthouy (comm., *Kingfisher*) to Price, Nov. 8, 1861, NA, Naval Records Collection, Area 6, M-625, roll 56, 557, 749, verify the vessels' presence and negate testimony of *San Jacinto* officers; *see also*: Logs of the U.S.S. *Huntsville* and U.S.S. *Kingfisher*, NA, R.G. 24, Bureau of Naval Personnel; Robert H. Johnson and Clarence C. Buel, eds., *Battles and Leaders of the Civil War*, 4 vols. (New York: Thomas Yoseloff, 1956), II: 136; Drake, "Cuban Background," pp. 44–5, explains that the message meant that Wilkes would see the *Trent* on the afternoon of Nov. 8, the sixth day of his departure from Havana; Charles Wilkes, "Journal," Nov. 6, 1861, Wilkes Papers.

23. Protest of Mason and Slidell, Nov. 9, 1861, ORN, 1st series, I: 139; Secretary of the Admiralty to Edmund Hammond, enclosing Moir's protest, Dec. 27, 1861, Great Britain, *Command Papers*, LXII (1862), North America, no. 5 (Correspondence respecting the Seizure of Messrs. Mason, Slidell, McFarland, and Eustis from on board the Royal Mail-Packet "Trent" by the Commander of the United States Ship of War "San Jacinto"), p. 628; Mason, *Life*, p. 226; Royal Mail Lines, *125 Years of Maritime History, 1839–1964* (London: Royal Mail Lines, 1964), p. 8; John H. Kemble, "The Panama Route to California, 1848–1869," Ph.D. dissertation, University of California (1937), pp. 14–15; T. A. Bushell, *"Royal Mail": A Centenary History of the Royal Mail Line, 1830–1939* (London: Trade and Travel, 1940), pp. 10, 13, 17, 81–2, 100.

24. Charles Wilkes, "Journal," Nov. 7, 1861, Wilkes Papers; Logbook of *San Jacinto*, Nov. 8, 1861, ORN, 1st series, I: 132; Charles Wilkes, Autobiography MS., X: 2284–85; R. M. Hunter, "The Capture of Mason and Slidell," *The Annals of the*

War Written by Leading Participants North and South (Philadelphia: Times Publishing, 1879), pp. 795–96 (must be used carefully).

25. Mason, *Life*, pp. 215–16; Moir's protest, *Command Papers*, LXII: 628; Protest of Mason and Slidell, Nov. 9, 1861, ORN, 1st series, I: 140; Commander Williams to Capt. Patey, Nov. 9, 1861, *Command Papers*, LXII: 13; Statement of the *Trent's* purser, Nov. 8, 1861, in Moore, *Rebellion Record*, III: 330.

26. Protest of Mason and Slidell, Nov. 9, 1861, ORN, 1st series, I: 140; Logbook of *San Jacinto*, Nov. 8, 1861, ibid., p. 132; Statement of the *Trent's* purser, Nov. 8, 1861, in Moore, *Rebellion Record*, III: 330; Mason, *Life*, p. 216. John W. Dubose, *The Life and Times of William Lowndes Yancey* (Birmingham, Ala.: Roberts & Son, 1892), z. 625, states that the papers were given to Mr. Haskel of Charleston, who later delivered them to Yancey and company.

27. Report of Fairfax to Wilkes, Nov. 12, 1861, ORN, 1st series, I: 133; Wilkes's Instructions to Fairfax, Nov. 8, 1861, ibid., pp. 131–32.

28. Johnson and Buel, *Battles and Leaders*, II: 136–37; Fairfax's report, ORN, 1st series, I: 133; Moir's protest, *Command Papers*, LXII: 628.

29. Johnson and Buel, *Battles and Leaders*, II: 137–39; Fairfax's report, ORN, 1st series, I: 133; Report of James B. Houston to Wilkes, Nov. 13, 1861, ibid., p. 136; Report of H. P. Grace to Wilkes, Nov. 12, 1861, ibid., p. 139.

30. Johnson and Buel, *Battles and Leaders*, II: 138–39; Commander Williams's memorandum at the British Admiralty, Nov. 27, 1861, ORN, 1st series, I: 163; Houston's report, ibid., p. 136.

According to the company contract with the British government, the mail agent had no authority to act as Williams did. *See* Royal Mail Steam Packet Co., *A Link of Empire, or 70 years of British Shipping* (London: Royal Mail Steam Packet Co., 1909), p. 42.

31. Johnson and Buel, *Battles and Leaders*, II: 138–39; Slidell and Wilkes allegedly had been boyhood friends. Henderson, *Hidden Coasts*, p. 229.

32. Report of James A. Greer to Wilkes, Nov. 12, 1861, ORN, 1st series, I: 134; Report of George W. Hall to Wilkes, Nov. 13, 1861, ibid., p. 137.

33. Mason, *Life*, p. 219; Hunter, *Annals*, p. 799; Report of Robert G. Simpson to Wilkes, Nov. 13, 1861, ORN, 1st series, I: 138; Greer's report, ibid., p. 135; Hall's report, ibid., p. 137.

34. Fairfax's report, ORN, 1st series, I: 134; Greer's report, ibid., p. 135; Hunter, *Annals*, p. 799; Statement of the *Trent's* purser, in Moore, *Rebellion Record*, III: 331; Commander Williams's speech at the Royal Western Yacht Club of Milbay, Plymouth, Dec. 12, 1861, ibid., p. 333; Johnson and Buel, *Battles and Leaders*, II: 139–40; Jay Monaghan, *Diplomat in Carpet Slippers: Abraham Lincoln Deals with Foreign Affairs* (Indianapolis and New York: Bobbs-Merrill, 1945; Charter ed., 1962), p. 169, exemplifies how Miss Slidell's joust with Fairfax has been magnified.

35. Greer's report, ORN, 1st series, I: 135.

36. Ibid.; Williams's memorandum, ibid., p. 163; Williams's speech to Yacht Club, in Moore, *Rebellion Record*, III: 333; W. G. Romaine to Capt. Patey, Dec. 2, 1861, PRO, Adm. 13/14, Admiralty and Secretariat, Supplementary Correspondence.

37. Greer's report, ORN, 1st series, I: 135–36; Fairfax's report, ibid., p. 134; Hall's report, ibid., p. 137; Johnson and Buel, *Battles and Leaders*, II: 141–42; Houston's report, ORN, 1st series, I: 136–37.

38. Moir's protest, *Command Papers*, LXII: 628; Johnson and Buel, *Battles and Leaders*, II: 140.

39. Greer's report, ORN, 1st series, I: 135; Mason, *Life*, p. 222; Logbook of *San Jacinto*, Nov. 8, 1861, ORN, 1st series, I: 132; Commander Williams's memorandum, ibid., p. 163.

40. Johnson and Buel, *Battles and Leaders*, II: 140; Wilkes to Welles, Nov. 16, 1861, ORN, 1st series, I: 144; Wilkes, "Journal," Nov. 8, 1861, Wilkes Papers.

41. *House Ex. Doc.* 102, 38th Cong., 1st Sess., 1864, p. 157.

42. Wilkes to Welles, Nov. 15, 1861, ORN, 1st series, I: 131; Mason, *Life*, p. 222; Howard P. Nash, Jr., *A Naval History of the Civil War* (South Brunswick and New York: A. S. Barnes, 1972), p. 57; John D. Hayes, *Samuel Francis Dupont: A Selection from His Civil War Letters*, 3 vols. (Ithaca: Cornell University Press, 1969), I: lxxii, 252, 290.

43. L. M. Goldsborough to Welles, Nov. 15, 1861, ORN, 1st series, I: 142; Wilkes, Autobiography MS., X: 2278–80, Wilkes Papers; Wilkes to Welles, Nov. 15, 1861, ORN, 1st series, I: 142–43.

44. Mason, *Life*, pp. 223–24; Robert Murray to W. H. Seward, Nov. 25, 1861, ORA, 2nd series, II: 1100; Seward and Welles to Robt. Murray, Nov. 16, 1861, ibid., p. 1092.

45. Mason, *Life*, pp. 224–25; Wilkes to Welles, Nov. 20, 1861, ORN, 1st series, I: 145; telegram from Wilkes to Welles, enclosing prisoners' request, received Nov. 21, 1861, ibid., p. 146; telegram from Welles to Wilkes, Nov. 21, 1861, ibid.

46. Wilkes to Welles, Nov. 24, 1861, ORN, 1st series, I: 147; Mason, *Life*, p. 226.

47. Benson J. Lossing, *Pictorial History of the Civil War in the United States of America*, 3 vols. (Hartford: T. Belknap, 1868), II: 155; Francis J. Parker, *The Story of the Thirty-Second Regiment Massachusetts Infantry* (Boston: C. W. Calkins, 1880), pp. 5, 7, 14.

48. Mason, *Life*, p. 227; New York *Times*, Nov. 26, 1861; Slidell, Mason, McFarland, and Eustis to Wilkes, Nov. 15, 1861, ORA, 2nd series, II: 1092.

49. Mason, *Life*, pp. 227–28; Wilkes to Welles, Nov. 24, 1861, ORN, 1st series, I: 147; New York *Daily Tribune*, Nov. 16, 1861.

2. WELCOME TO WILKES!

1. Henry Sanford to Curtis, Nov. 29, 1861, General Sanford Memorial Library, Sanford, Florida, Henry Shelton Sanford Papers, reel 59 (box 100).

2. Boston *Daily Evening Transcript*, Nov. 22, 1861.

3. New York *Times*, Nov. 26, 1861; Wilkes, Autobiography MS., X: 2306–07, Wilkes Papers.

4. John Le Camp to Wilkes, Nov. 18, 1861, Wilkes Papers, General Correspondence (1861); W. H. S. Claridge to Wilkes, Nov. 27, 1871, ibid., Special Correspondence, *Trent* Affair, Letters (June–Nov. 1861); Mrs. Marion Wheeler to Wilkes, Nov. 23, 1861, ibid.; Eugene Batchelder to Wilkes, Nov. 26, 1861, ibid., General Correspondence (1861); D. N. Spooner to Wilkes, Nov. 25, 1861, ibid., Special Correspondence, *Trent* Affair, Letters (Dec. 1861); P. T. Barnam to Wilkes, Dec. 11,

1861, ibid., General Correspondence; P. T. Barnum, *Struggles and Triumphs: Or, Forty Years' Recollections* (Buffalo: Warren, Johnson, 1872), pp. 567–68.

5. Philo S. Shelton to R. W. Shufeldt, Nov. 25, 1861, LC, Robert W. Shufeldt Papers, Box 11; New York *Times*, Nov. 27, 29, 1861; Adams, "*Trent* Affair," p. 48.

6. Truman Smith to R. W. Shufeldt, Nov. 19, 1861, Shufeldt Papers, Box 18; Anthony Trollope, *North America*, 2 vols. (London: Chapman & Hall, 1862), I: 367–68.

7. Boston *Transcript*, Nov. 29, 1861; Adams, "*Trent* Affair," pp. 48, 82; Richard H. Dana, Jr., to CFA, Dec. 17, 1861, MHS, Adams Family Papers, Letters Received and Other Loose Papers; CFA, Jr., to CFA, Nov. 19, 1861, ibid.

8. Paul R. Frothingham, *Edward Everett, Orator and Statesman* (Boston and New York: Houghton Mifflin, 1925), p. 437; Everett to Seward, Nov. 18, 1861, MHS, Edward Everett Papers, vol. 115; Boston *Transcript*, Nov. 22, 1861; Everett to editor, Dec. 7, 1861, New York *Daily Tribune*, Dec. 24, 1861; Sir Robert J. Phillimore, *Commentaries upon International Law*, 4 vols. (London: Butterworth, 1871–74), II: 166–67.

9. The two precedents were the Laurens Case, previously discussed, and the incident involving Lucien Bonaparte. The latter had boarded an American vessel, the *Hercules*, in 1810, which was captured by a British warship and taken to Malta, while the prince was sent to London as a prisoner.

10. David Donald, *Charles Sumner and the Coming of the Civil War* (New York: Alfred A. Knopf, 1967), p. 129; Wilkes, Autobiography MS., X: 2309, Wilkes Papers; David Donald, *Charles Sumner and the Rights of Man* (New York: Alfred A. Knopf, 1970), pp. 31–2; Long, "Glory-Hunting Off Havana," p. 140; Victor H. Cohen, "Charles Sumner and the *Trent* Affair," *Journal of Southern History*, XXII (1956), pp. 208–09, believes that Sumner's initial reaction was to support Wilkes, but evidence is sketchy.

11. New York *Times*, Nov. 19, 1861; CFA, Jr., *Autobiography*, p. 128; Adams, "*Trent* Affair," pp. 59–60, 89–90, 94. The comment attributed to Mason by Winthrop may have been made by Robert Toombs.

12. Lawrence Sangston, *The Bastilles of the North* (Baltimore: Hedion, Kelley & Piet, 1863), pp. 94–5, 101; Mason, *Life*, pp. 205–09, 229–30, 234–35.

13. New York *Times*, Nov. 19, Dec. 4–5, 1861.

14. New York *Herald*, Dec. 5–6, 1861; New York *World*, Dec. 6, 1861; New York *Daily Tribune*, Dec. 6, 1861; New York *Herald Tribune*, Dec. 9, 1861.

15. New York *Herald Tribune*, Dec. 11, 1861.

16. Bray Hammond, *Sovereignty and an Empty Purse: Banks and Politics in the Civil War* (Princeton: Princeton University Press, 1970), pp. 123–25; New York *Daily Tribune*, Nov. 18, 20, 21, 30, Dec. 11, 1861; London *Economist*, Dec. 14, 1861; *Banker's Magazine*, Jan. 1862, p. 655; John Maginn to R. W. Shufeldt, Dec. 14, 1861, Shufeldt Papers General Correspondence, Box 11.

17. Fernando Wood to Caleb Cushing, Nov. 29, 1861, LC, Caleb Cushing Papers, General Correspondence, Box 90; George D. Morgan to Welles, Dec. 13, 1861, LC, Gideon Welles Papers, vol. 48; DAB, II: 623–27; Sister Mary Parent, "Caleb Cushing and the Foreign Policy of the United States, 1860–77," Ph.D. dissertation, Boston College (1958), pp. 5, 15, 43–4, 51; Sister M. M. Catherine Hodgson, *Caleb Cushing: Attorney General of the United States, 1853–1857* (Washington, D.C.: Catholic University of America Press, 1955), pp. 51, 77–8, 182; John Niven, *Gideon Welles: Lincoln's Secretary of the Navy* (New York: Oxford University Press, 1973), p. 248.

18. Cushing to Wood, Dec. 6, 1861, Cushing Papers, Box 90; New York *Times Supp.*, Dec. 18, 1861; Parent, "Cushing," pp. 54–6.

19. Parent, "Cushing," p. 61.

20. London *Times*, Dec. 3, 1861; Telegram from M. N. Falls to Thomas A. Scott, Nov. 16, 1861, LC, The Robert Todd Lincoln Collection of the Papers of Abraham Lincoln, roll 29, series I, p. 13020; New York *Times*, Nov. 27, 1861; Howard K. Beale, ed., *The Diary of Edward Bates, 1859–1866* (Washington, D.C.: American Historical Association, 1930), pp. 202, 205; Bates to E. M. Norton, Nov. 16, 1861, NA, Attorney General Letterbook B-4.

21. Gideon Welles, *Lincoln and Seward* (New York: Sheldon, 1874), p. 186; New York *Times*, Nov. 19, 1861.

22. DAB, X: 629–30; Charles O. Paullin, *Paullin's History of the Naval Administration, 1775–1911* (Annapolis: Naval Institute Press, 1968), pp. 250–51, 258; Niven, *Welles*, pp. 264, 268, 270; Charles O. Paullin, "President Lincoln and the Navy," *American Historical Review*, XIV (1908–09), p. 287.

23. Paullin, *History of Naval Administration*, p. 252; Charles A. Dana, *Recollections of the Civil War; with the Leaders at Washington and in the Field in the Sixties*, (New York: Appleton, 1902), p. 170; Edward Dicey, *Six Months in the Federal States*, 2 vols. (London: Macmillan, 1863), p. 235; Niven, *Welles*, pp. 448, 452; Noah Brooks, *Washington in Lincoln's Time* (New York: Century, 1895), pp. 33–4; W. Fletcher Thompson, Jr., *The Image of War: The Pictorial Reporting of the American Civil War*, (New York: Thomas Yoseloff, 1960), p. 103; Stuart L. Bernath, *Squall Across the Atlantic: American Civil War Prize Cases and Diplomacy* (Berkeley and Los Angeles: University of California Press, 1970), p. 13; Beale, *Diary of Welles*, I: 79.

24. Welles to Wilkes, Nov. 30, 1861, ORN, 1st series, I: 120–21; Gideon Welles, "The Capture and Release of Mason and Slidell," *Galaxy*, XV (1873), p. 648; Niven, *Welles*, pp. 446–47.

25. Thomas J. Peyton, Jr., "Charles Sumner and United States Foreign Relations During the American Civil War," Ph.D. dissertation, Georgetown University (1972), p. 101; London *Times*, Dec. 3, 1861; W. H. Russell, *Diary*, p. 575; LeRoy H. Fischer, *Lincoln's Gadfly: Adam Gurowski* (Norman, Okla.: University of Oklahoma Press, 1964), p. 84; Welles, *Lincoln and Seward*, pp. 185, 187; Lossing, *Pictorial History of Civil War*, II: 156–57.

Wilkes claimed that during an interview with Lincoln the president had remarked that Wilkes had "kicked up a buzz" but that he "intended to stand by me and rejoiced over the boldness . . . of my act." (Wilkes, Autobiography MS., X: 2308, Wilkes Papers.) Neither Lincoln nor any cabinet member mentioned such a meeting. Although Seward did not authorize the Wilkes operation, the assistant secretary of state, his son Frederick, later assured Consul Shufeldt in Havana that it was "entirely in accordance with the principles of international law laid down by the best and most authoritative writers on the subject." (F. W. Seward to R. W. Shufeldt, Nov. 22, 1861, NA, Instructions to U. S. Consuls in Havana, Record Group 84.)

26. Adam Gurowski, *Diary from March 4, 1861 to November 17, 1862*, 2 vols. (Boston: 1862; reprinted New York: Burt Franklin, 1968), II: 307; Dicey, *Six Months*, I: 30, 43; N. A. Woods, *The Prince of Wales in Canada and the United States* (London: Bradbury & Evans, 1861), p. 390; Thomas L. Nichols, *Forty Years of American Life*, 2 vols. (London: John Maxwell, 1864), I: 319, 322; Trollope, *North America*, II: 43.

27. Dicey, *Six Months*, I: 31, 41, 326; New York *Times*, Nov. 18, 19, 22, 1861; Nichols, *Forty Years*, I: 326–27, 330, 332; New York *Daily Tribune*, Nov. 18, 22, 23, 1861; Thurlow Weed to Seward, Nov. 30, 1861, Rush Rhees Library, University of

Rochester, William Henry Seward Papers; Bradford R. Wood to Chase, Dec. 24, 1861, LC, Salmon P. Chase Papers, General Correspondence, Series I, vol. 54; August Belmont to S. P. Chase, Aug. 15, 1861, LC, August Belmont Papers, Personal Papers, Miscellany; New York *Herald*, Nov. 17, 1861.

28. Philadelphia *Sunday Dispatch*, Nov. 17, 1861; Philadelphia *Inquirer*, Nov. 19, 29, 1861 (*See also*: The *Weekly Vincennes Western Sun*, Dec. 7, 1861); Harrisburg *Pennsylvania Daily Telegraph*, Nov. 19, 25, 1861; Washington *Evening Star*, Nov. 19, 1861; Boston *Daily Evening Transcript*, Nov. 18, 1861; Detroit *Daily Advertiser*, Nov. 19, 20, 1861; St. Louis *Daily Missouri Democrat*, Nov. 18, 20, 21, 1861; St. Paul *Pioneer and Democrat*, Nov. 24, 1861; Milwaukee *Morning Sentinel*, Nov. 19, 1861.

29. Cleveland *Morning Leader*, Nov. 18, 20, 1861; Cleveland *Daily Plain Dealer*, Nov. 19, 1861; Cincinnati *Daily Commercial*, Nov. 19, 1861; Cincinnati *Daily Enquirer*, Nov. 17, 1861.

30. Dubuque *Herald*, Nov. 22, 24, 1861; Atchison (Kansas) *Freedom's Champion*, Nov. 23, 1861; Sacramento *Daily Union*, Nov. 21, 25, 1861.

31. Portland *Eastern Argus*, Nov. 19, Dec. 24, 1861; Albany *Atlas and Argus*, Nov. 18, 21, 1861; London *Times*, Dec. 10, 1861.

32. Richmond *Enquirer*, Nov. 22, Dec. 18, 19, 1861; Richmond *Examiner*, Nov. 19, 1861; Atlanta *Southern Confederacy*, Nov. 19, 1861; Nashville *Patriot*, Nov. 20, 1861; New Orleans *Bee*, Nov. 18, 20, Dec. 5, 24, 1861; New Orleans *Picayune*, Nov. 23, 27, Dec. 20, 1861.

33. Kate E. Staton, comp., *Old Southern Songs of the Period of the Confederacy: The Dixie Trophy Collection* (New York: Samuel French, 1926), pp. 105–6.

34. John B. Jones, *A Rebel War Clerk's Diary at the Confederate States Capital*, ed. Howard Swiggett, 2 vols. (New York: Old Hickory Bookshop, 1935), I: 93; Jefferson Davis, "Message to the Congress of the Confederate States," Nov. 19, 1861, *Journal of the Congress of the Confederate States of America*, 7 vols. (Washington, D.C.: GPO, 1904–05), 58th Cong., 2nd Sess., Sen. Doc. 234, I: 471; R. M. T. Hunter to Yancey, Rost, and Mann, Nov. 20, 1861, ORN, 2nd series, III: 297; Hunter to Charles J. Helm, Nov. 30, 1861 (no. 1), LC, Records of Confederate States of America, Department of State, vol. 61 (Foreign Countries, 1861–64); Richmond *Enquirer*, Dec. 25, 1861; Jones, *Rebel Diary*, I: 101; Robert E. Lee, Jr., ed., *Recollections and Letters of General Robert E. Lee* (Garden City: Doubleday, Page, 1904), p. 59.

35. Gordon H. Warren, "The King Cotton Theory," in *Encyclopedia of American Foreign Policy: Studies of the Principal Movements and Ideas*, ed. Alexander DeConde, 3 vols. (New York: Scribner's, 1978), II: 517–18.

36. London *Economist*, Dec. 28, 1861; David D. Porter, *The Naval History of the Civil War* (New York: Sherman, 1886; reprinted Glendale, N.Y.: Benchmark, 1970), p. 71.

3. BRITAIN AND AMERICA IN THE SECESSION CRISIS

1. Kenneth Bourne, *The Foreign Policy of Victorian England, 1830–1902* (Oxford: Clarendon, 1970), pp. 87–88; Richard Van Alstyne, "Anglo-American Relations, 1853–1857," *American Historical Review*, XLII (1937), pp. 499–500.

2. Kenneth Bourne and D. C. Watt, eds., *Studies in International History: Essays Presented to W. Norton Medlicott* (London: Longmans, Green, 1967), pp. 149, 167,

169–70; Richard Van Alstyne, "British Diplomacy and the Clayton-Bulwer Treaty, 1850–1860," *Journal of Modern History*, XI (1939), pp. 181–82.

3. Robin W. Winks, *Canada and the United States: The Civil War Years* (Baltimore: Johns Hopkins Press, 1960), p. 6; Woods, *Prince of Wales*, pp. 286–383; George Templeton Strong, *Diary of the Civil War, 1860–1865*, ed. Allan Nevins (New York: Macmillan, 1962), pp. 34, 45; Barnum, *Struggles and Triumphs*, p. 544.

Fifty years later, American mourners placed on Edward VII's grave a wreath of leaves taken from the tree he had planted at Mount Vernon. Bradford Perkins, *The Great Rapprochement: England and the United States, 1895–1914* (New York: Atheneum, 1968), p. 266.

4. Newcastle to Palmerston, Oct. 14, 1860, University of Nottingham, Duke of Newcastle Papers, NeC 10889; Lyons to Russell, Oct. 22, 1860 (no. 272), PRO, FO 5/739; Theodore Martin, *The Life of the Prince Consort*, 5 vols. (London: Smith, Elder, 1880), V: 245.

5. Dicey, *Six Months*, I: 274; Edward A. Freeman, *Some Impressions of the United States* (London: Longmans, Green, 1883; reprinted Freeport, N.Y.: Books for Libraries Press, 1970), pp. 6–8, 264; Viscount Crichton, *A Tour in British North America and the United States, 1863* (Dublin: Hodges Smith, 1864), p. 59; Allan Nevins, ed., *American Social History as Recorded by British Travelers* (New York: Henry Holt, 1931), pp. 364–66, 294.

6. Nevins, *American Social History*, p. 365.

7. Nevins, *American Social History*, pp. 291–92, 350; Myron F. Brightfield, "America and the Americans, 1840–1860, as Depicted in the English Novels of the Period," *American Literature*, XXXI (1959), p. 311; Charles E. Shain, "English Novelists and the American Civil War," *American Quarterly*, XIV (1962), pp. 400–01, 405.

8. Nevins, *American Social History*, pp. 292, 322–23; Alexander J. B. Beresford-Hope, *England, the North, and the South* (London: James Ridgway, 1862), pp. 12–13; Charles Dickens, *American Notes* (London, 1840; reprinted London: Oxford University Press, 1970), p. 320.

9. Nevins, *American Social History*, p. 293; Freeman, *Some Impressions*, pp. 44–5; Shain, "English Novelists," p. 404; Frederic W. Maitland, *The Life and Letters of Leslie Stephen* (London: Duckworth, 1906), p. 120.

10. Palmerston to Hammond, April 21, 1861, PRO, Edmund Hammond Papers, FO 391/7; Van Alstyne, "Anglo-American Relations," pp. 494–95, 497–99; Wilbur D. Jones, *The American Problem in British Diplomacy, 1841–1861* (Athens: University of Georgia Press, 1974), p. 115.

11. Allen Johnson et al., eds., *Dictionary of National Biography*, 22 vols. and supps. (New York: Macmillan, 1922–74), XII: 358–59; Sir Edward Malet, *Shifting Scenes* (London: John Murray, 1901), pp. 25–6; Gurowski, *Diary*, I: 36; Bright to Cobden, Nov. 4, 1861, BM, John Bright MSS., Add. Mss. 43384; Cobden to Bright, Nov. 1, 1861, BM, Richard Cobden MSS., Add. Mss. 43651.

12. Lyons to Russell, Dec. 4, 1860 (no. 304), FO 5/740.

13. Lyons to Russell, Jan. 7, 1861, PRO, Lord John Russell Papers, PRO 30/22/35.

14. Lyons to Russell, Oct. 21, 1861 (no. 585), FO 5/772.

15. Glyndon G. Van Deusen, *William Henry Seward* (New York: Oxford University Press, 1967), pp. 7, 11, 185, 217; Hodgson, *Cushing*, p. 5; James M. Scovel, "Recollections of Lincoln and Seward," *Overland's Monthly*, XXXVIII (1901), p. 265; Gouverneur, *As I Remember*, p. 12; Dwight L. Dumond, ed., *Southern Editorials on Secession* (New York: Century, 1931), p. 404.

16. George E. Baker, ed., *The Works of William H. Seward*, 5 vols. (Boston: Houghton Mifflin, 1852–84), I: 184, 186, 192; IV: 124; Allan Nevins, ed., *The Diary of Philip Hone, 1828–1851* (New York: Dodd, Mead, 1927), p. 660.

17. Frank M. Anderson, *The Mystery of "A Public Man"* (Minneapolis: University of Minnesota Press, 1948), p. 202.

18. Henry Adams, *The Education of Henry Adams* (Boston: Houghton Mifflin, 1961), p. 104; Glyndon G. Van Deusen, *Thurlow Weed: Wizard of the Lobby* (Boston: Little, Brown, 1947), pp. 30, 269–70; Gordon H. Warren, "Imperial Dreamer: William Henry Seward and American Destiny," in *Makers of American Foreign Policy*, ed. Frank J. Merli and Theordor A. Wilson (New York: Scribner's, 1974), p. 197; Rollo Ogden, *Life and Letters of Edwin Lawrence Godkin*, 2 vols. (New York: Macmillan, 1907), I: 175; Strong, *Diary of Civil War*, p. 282; Theodore C. Pease and James G. Randall, eds., *The Diary of Orville Hickman Browning*, 2 vols. (Springfield: Illinois State Historical Collections, XX, 1925), I: 527; Gurowski, *Diary*, I: 31.

19. W. H. Russell, *Diary*, p. 34; J. C. Derby, *Fifty Years Among Authors, Books and Publishers* (New York: G. W. Carleton, 1884), p. 74; George A. H. Sala, *My Diary in America in the Midst of War*, 2 vols. (London: Tinsley Bros., 1865), I: 129–30; CFA, Jr., *Autobiography*, pp. 62, 79; Thomas McCormack, ed., *Memoirs of Gustave Koerner*, 2 vols. (Cedar Rapids, Ia.: Torch Press, 1909), II: 438; Lewis Einstein, *Napoleon III and American Diplomacy at the Outbreak of the Civil War* (London: [n.p.], 1905), p. 11; Donn Piatt, *Memories of the Men Who Saved the Union* (New York: Belford, Clark, 1887), pp. 151–52.

20. Newton Arvin, ed., *The Selected Letters of Henry Adams* (New York: Farrar, Strauss and Young, 1961), pp. 25–6; Ogden, *Godkin*, I: 258.

21. Newcastle to Edmund Head, June 5, 1861, Newcastle Papers, Private Letterbook, Series B, NeC 10885; Weed to Seward, Dec. 18, 1861, Jan. 28, 1862, Seward Papers.

22. CFA, "Reminiscences of his mission to Great Britain," Adams Papers, Miscellany; Edward W. Emerson and Waldo E. Forbes, eds., *Journals of Ralph Waldo Emerson*, 10 vols. (Boston: Houghton Mifflin, 1909–14), IX: 389–90; Newcastle to Head, June 5, 1861, Newcastle Papers, Private Letterbook, Series B, NeC 10885.

23. Weed letter, London *Times*, Dec. 14, 1861.

24. Ralph H. Lutz, " Rudolph Schleiden and the Visit to Richmond, April 25, 1861," American Historical Association *Annual Report* (1915), p. 210; Lyons to Russell, Feb. 4, 1861, PRO 30/22/35; Lyons to Russell, Feb., 12, 1861 (no. 59), FO 5/760.

25. Harry J. Carman and Reinhard H. Luthin, *Lincoln and the Patronage* (New York: Columbia University Press, 1943; reprinted Gloucester, Mass.: Peter Smith, 1964), p. 51; Henry W. Temple, "William H. Seward," in *The American Secretaries of State and Their Diplomacy*, ed. Samuel F. Bemis and Robert H. Ferrell, 18 vols. (New York: Pageant, 1958–70), IX: 22; Lyons to Russell, Feb. 4, 1861 (no. 40), FO 5/760;

Lutz, "Schleiden," p. 210; Nivens, *Welles*, pp. 329, 448; Beale, *Welles Diary*, I: 132; Alvan F. Sanborn, ed., *Reminiscences of Richard Lathers* (New York: Grafton, 1907), p. 229.

26. Lyons to Russell, Mar. 26, 1861, PRO 30/22/35; Carroll, *Mercier*, p. 52.

27. Allan Nevins, *The War for the Union*, 4 vols. (New York: Scribner's 1959–71), I: 22.

28. Roy P. Basler, ed., *The Collected Works of Abraham Lincoln*, 9 vols. (New Brunswick, N.J.: Rutgers University Press, 1953–55), IV: 317–18.

29. Lyons to Russell, Apr. 1, 15, 1861, PRO 30/22/35.

30. Donald, *Sumner and Rights of Man*, p. 22; Worthington C. Ford, ed., *Letters of Henry Adams, 1858–1891* (Boston and New York: Houghton Mifflin, 1930), p. 76.

31. Seward to Adams, Apr. 10, 1861 (no. 2); U.S. State Dept., comp., *Papers Relating to the Foreign Affairs of the United States, 1861–68*, 19 vols. (Washington, D.C.: GPO, 1862–69), *1861*: 76; Donald, *Sumner and Rights of Man*, p. 23; Warren, "Imperial Dreamer," p. 204.

32. Lord Stanmore, *Sidney Herbert: Lord Herbert of Lea; a memoir*, 2 vols. (London: John Murray, 1906), II: 430; Helen G. Macdonald, *Canadian Public Opinion on the American Civil War* (New York: Columbia University Press, 1926), p. 117; Fred M. Landon, "Canadian Opinion of Southern Secession, 1860–61," *Canadian Historical Review*, I (1920), p. 257.

33. George F. Milton, *Abraham Lincoln and the Fifth Column* (New York: Vanguard, 1942), p. 49; Jenkins, *Britain and the War*, I: 40; Alexander Somerville, *Canada, A Battle Ground; About a Kingdom in America* (Hamilton: Donnelley & Lawson, 1862), pp. 18–20; Lyons to Russell, May 11, 1861 (no. 194), FO 5/763; Lyons to Russell, Dec. 6, 1861 (no. 740), FO 5/766.

34. Lincoln Papers, series 1, roll 21, pp. 9303, 9465; Winks, *Canada*, p. 45; Jenkins, *Britain and the War*, I: 45; Lyons to Russell, May 2, 1861 (no. 171), FO 5/763; Lyons to Russell, Dec. 6, 1861 (no. 740), FO 5/766.

35. Lyons to Russell, May 6, 1861 (no. 185), 5/763; Lyons to Russell, May 6, 1861, PRO 30/22/35.

36. Lyons to Russell, May 20, 1861 (no. 206), FO 5/764.

37. Sister Mary M. O'Rourke, "The Diplomacy of William H. Seward During the Civil War: His Policies as Related to International Law," Ph.D. dissertation, Berkeley (1963), p. 26; William H. Seward, *An Autobiography from 1801 to 1834. With a Memoir of his Life, and Selections from his Letters* [title of vols. II and III is *Seward at Washington, as Senator and Secretary of State* by Frederick W. Seward], 3 vols. (New York: Derby & Miller, 1891), II: 575–76, 579; Case and Spencer, *U.S. and France*, p. 46.

38. Seward to CFA, May 21, 1861 (no. 10), State Dept., *Papers Relating to Foreign Affairs, 1861*: 87–90; Donald, *Sumner and Rights of Man*, p. 21.

39. Warren, "Imperial Dreamer," p. 205.

4. THE SUMMER OF DISCONTENT

1. Richard H. Dana, Jr., to CFA, June 4, 1861, Adams Papers, reel 554; George Bemis, *Hasty Recognition of Rebel Belligerency and Our Right to Complain of It* (Boston: A. Williams, 1865), p. 21; James Russell Lowell, *The Biglow Papers*, 2nd ser.

(Boston: Ticknor & Fields, 1867), p. 45; Sumner to Bright, Oct. 15, 1861, Bright MSS., Add. Mss. 43390, 124–25; Duchess of Argyll, ed., *Autobiography and Memoirs of the Duke of Argyll*, 2 vols. (London: John Murray, 1906), II: 173.

2. Martin B. Duberman, *Charles Francis Adams, 1807–1886* (Boston: Houghton Mifflin, 1961), pp. 260–61; Emmerich de Vattel, *The Law of Nations, or Principles of Natural Law Applied to the Conduct and Affairs of Nations and Sovereigns*, ed. Joseph Chitty and Edward D. Ingraham (Philadelphia: T. & J. W. Johnson, 1853), p. 291; Marjorie M. Whiteman, ed., *Digest of International Law*, 15 vols. (Washington, D.C.: GPO, 1963–73), II: 486–89, 501–3; Richard A. Falk, ed., *The International Law of Civil War* (Baltimore: Johns Hopkins University Press, 1971), pp. 46–7; James L. Brierly, *The Law of Nations*, 6th ed. (London: Oxford University Press, 1963), pp. 141–42.

3. CFA Diary, entry of Nov. 18, 1861, Adams Papers, reel 76; Richard Cobden to John Bright, May 23, 1861, Cobden MSS., Add. Mss. 43651; Lord Russell to Edward Everett, July 12, 1861, Everett Papers; Sheldon Van Auken, "English Sympathy for the Southern Confederacy: The Glittering Illusion," B. Litt. thesis, Oxford University (1957), p. 60; *Edinburgh Review*, CXIII: 586–87; London *Economist*, Jan. 19, 1861, p. 58.

4. Adams might have arrived in time to give the government second thoughts had he not postponed his departure from Boston to attend a son's wedding, but he almost never left at all. His rival for the post was Senator Sumner and, although the two men had once been close comrades in the antislavery trenches, they had battled over adoption of a new state constitution in the 1850s, the convening of the 1860 Peace Convention, and leadership of the Massachusetts Republicans. The appointment of Adams, whom Sumner described as unfit for the position, widened the breach. However, considering the senator's corrosive personality, the president had chosen well. Brooks Adams, "The Seizure of the Laird Rams, MHS *Proceedings*, XLV (1911–12), p. 249; Duberman, *Adams*, pp. 187–88, 250–51; Laura White, "Charles Sumner and the Crisis of 1860–61," in *Essays in Honor of William E. Dodd*, ed. Avery O. Craven (Chicago: University of Chicago Press, 1935), pp. 162–63, 165, 174, 178, 181; H. Adams, *Education*, pp. 27, 35; CFA, Jr., *Charles Francis Adams* (Boston: Houghton Mifflin, 1900), pp. 214–15.

5. Ephraim D. Adams, *Great Britain and the American Civil War*, 2 vols. (New York: Longmans, Green, 1925), I: 131; Irving Katz, *August Belmont: A Political Biography* (New York: Columbia University Press, 1968), p. 94; G. W. E. Russell, *Collections and Recollections by one who has kept a diary* (New York and London: Harper & Row, 1899), p. 12; CFA to Seward, Nov. 14, 1861 (no. 71), NA, Dept. of State, Despatches from United States Ministers to Great Britain, 1791–1906, M30, roll 74; CFA Diary, entry of May 18, 1861, Adams Papers, reel 76; CFA to Seward, May 21, 1861 (no. 2), M30, roll 73.

6. CFA to Seward, June 14, 1861 (no. 8), M30, roll 73.

7. CFA to Seward, May 21, 1861 (no. 2), May 31 (no. 4), June 7 (no. 5), June 21 (no. 9), July 12 (no. 14), M30, roll 73; CFA, "Reminiscences," Adams Papers, reel 296; CFA to R. H. Dana, Jr., June 14, 1861, to C. E. Douglas, June 15, 1861, to B. D. Silliman, July 12, 1861, Adams Papers, CFA Letterbook, reel 165; CFA to Edward Everett, July 12, 1861, Everett Papers; CFA to CFA, Jr., June 21, 1861, Adams Papers, reel 514.

8. CFA Diary, entry of June 10, 1861, Adams Papers, reel 76; H. Adams to CFA, Jr., June 10–11, 1861, ibid., reel 54.

9. Malet, *Shifting Scenes*, p. 12; Robert V. Bruce, *Lincoln and the Tools of War* (Indianapolis: Bobbs-Merrill, 1956; reprinted Westport, Conn.: Greenwood, 1973), p. 22; Margaret Leech, *Reveille in Washington, 1860–1865* (New York and London: Harper & Bros., 1941), pp. 8–9.

10. W. A. and P. W. Heaps, *The Singing Sixties: The Spirit of Civil War Days Drawn from the Music of the Times* (Norman: University of Oklahoma Press, 1960), p. 313; Lyons to Russell, May 23, 1861 (no. 209), May 30, 1861 (no. 231), FO 5/764; Lyons to Milne, May 25, 1861, ibid.

11. Lyons to Russell, May 23, 1861, PRO 30/22/35.

12. Archibald to Lyons, June 1, 1861, enclosed in Lyons to Russell, June 3, 1861 (no. 246), FO 5/765.

13. Lyons to Russell, June 3, 1861 (no. 246), FO 5/765; Head to Lyons, June 9, 1861 (extract), enclosed in Lyons to Russell, June 13, 1861 (no. 276), FO 5/766; Wodehouse to Rogers, July 1, 1861, PRO, CO 537/96.

14. Lyons to Russell, June 6, 1861 (no. 253), June 8, 1861 (no. 263), FO 5/765.

15. Lyons to Russell, June 10, 1861, PRO 30/22/34; Lyons to Russell, June 14, 1861 (no. 251), June 8, 1861 (no. 262), FO 5/765; Carroll, *Mercier*, p. 74.

16. Seward, *Autobiography*, III: 519, 587; Frederick W. Seward, *Reminiscences of a War-Time Statesman and Diplomat, 1830–1915* (New York and London: G. P. Putnam, 1916), pp. 179–80; Lyons to Russell, June 17, 1861 (no. 282), FO 5/766.

17. Seward to CFA, June 21, 1861, M77, roll 76; Seward to Dayton, June 22, 1861 (no. 22), State Dept., *Papers Relating to Foreign Affairs, 1861*: 229; Seward to CFA, July 21, 1861 (no. 42), ibid., p. 118; Seward to CFA, June 19, 1861, ibid., p. 108; Lyons to Russell, Aug. 1, 1861, PRO 30/22/35; Lyons to Russell, Aug. 12, 1861 (no. 422), FO 5/769.

18. Seward to CFA, June 21, 1861, M77, roll 76; Seward to CFA, Aug. 12, 1861 (no. 58), State Dept., *Papers Relating to Foreign Affairs, 1861*: 127; Seward to CFA, July 21, 1861 (no. 42), ibid., p. 118.

19. Lyons to Russell, July 20, Aug. 1 and 23, 1861, PRO 30/22/35; Lyons to Russell, Aug. 12, 1861 (no. 422), FO 5/769.

20. Hammond to Cowley, May 14, 17, 21, 1861, PRO, Lord Cowley Papers, FO 519/190; Peyton, "Sumner and U.S. Foreign Relations," pp. 68–9; Ellen T. Vaughn, ed., *Letters of the Hon. Mrs. Edward Twisleton written to her family 1852–1862* (London: John Murray, 1928), p. 310; Sir Gilbert F. Lewis, ed., *Letters of the Right Hon. Sir George Cornewall Lewis, bart., to various friends* (London: Longmans, Green, 1870), pp. 397–98.

21. Bernath, *Squall*, p. 162; James P. Baxter III, "The British Government and Neutral Rights, 1861–1865," *American Historical Review.*, XXXIV (1928), p. 10; Robert G. Albion and Jennie B. Pope, *Sea Lanes in Wartime: The American Experience, 1775–1942* (New York: W. W. Norton, 1942), p. 22; List of H.M.'s steam vessels on North American and West Indies Station, May 10, 1861, FO 27/1376.

The gunboat was the smallest of Britain's sea-going warships in the 1860s and carried two or three large-caliber guns. A gun-vessel was larger than a gunboat, and usually carreid five large-caliber guns. From the 1850s to the 1880s, the Royal Navy ordered 120 gun-vessels, and 262 gunboats. E. H. H. Archibald, *The Wooden Fighting Ship in the Royal Navy, AD 897–1860* (London: Blandford Press, 1968), pp. 90–91.

22. Bernath, *Squall*, p. 163; "Instructions for the guidance of cruizers employed on the Coasts of America for the protection of British Commerce," May 30, 1861, NMM, Admiral Sir Alexander Milne Papers, MLN/103/15(c).

23. Lyons to Milne, June 10, 1861, Milne Papers, MLN/107/1(a); Milne to Secretary of Admiralty, June 27, 1861 (no. 281), ibid., MLN/103/3(c); W. G. Romaine to Hammond, July 29, 1861, FO 5/799; Somerset to Palmerston, Aug. 19, 1861, HMC, Lord Palmerston Papers, GC/SO/58; Somerset to Palmerston, Sept. 26, 1861, ibid., GC/SO/60; Jenkins, *Britain and the War*, p. 87. An excellent discussion of British territorial defenses appears in Regis A. Courtemanche, *No Need of Glory: The British Navy in American Waters, 1860–1864* (Annapolis: Naval Institute Press, 1977), pp. 40–56.

24. Jasper Ridley, *Lord Palmerston* (New York: E. P. Dutton, 1971), p. 589; Colin F. Baxter, "Admiralty Problems during the Second Palmerston Administration, 1859–1865," Ph.D. dissertation, University of Georgia (1965), p. 30.

25. Bourne and Watt, *Studies*, p. 189; James P. Baxter III, *The Introduction of the Ironclad Warship* (Cambridge: Harvard University Press, 1933), pp. 133–34; F. A. Wellesley, *Secrets of the Second Empire: Private Letters from the Paris Embassy* (New York and London: Harper & Bros., 1929), p. 215.

26. Baxter, "Admiralty Problems," pp. 7, 9, 10, 37; Jones, *American Problem in British Diplomacy*, p. 194; Bourne and Watt, *Studies*, pp. 190–91; Baxter, *Ironclad Warship*, p. 140; Palmerston to Gladstone, July 19, 21, 1861, BM, William E. Gladstone MSS., Add. Mss. 44272; Stanmore, *Herbert*, II: 430.

Public demand for greater security led in 1859 to creation of the Volunteer Rifle Corps, which was celebrated by Alfred Tennyson in the recruitment poem:

> Be not deaf to the sound that warns!
>   Be not gull'd by a despot's plea!
> Are figs of thistles, or grapes of thorns?
>   How should a despot set men free?
>   Form! form! Riflemen form!
>   Ready, be ready to meet the storm!
>   Riflemen, riflemen, riflemen form!
>
> . . . .
> Form, be ready to do or die!
>   Form in Freedom's name and the Queen's!
> True that we have a faithful ally,
>   But only the Devil knows what he means.
>   Form! form! Riflemen form!
>   Ready, be ready to meet the storm!
>   Riflemen, riflemen, riflemen form!
>
>   (Baxter, *Ironclad Warship*, p. 138.)

Although 170,000 enrolled within two years, these Saturday soldiers offered little protection and served mainly as a costly morale booster. "Not a day passes," Adams observed from the American legation, "that we do not see regiments of mere boys busily engaged in military exercise." The dockyards were filled with "naval inventions to fortify ships and to increase the range of artillery fire." If it were not for European complications, Britain "might deal quite summarily with us." Palmerston to Gladstone, July

19, 1861, Gladstone MSS., Add. Mss. 44272; Jones, *American Problem in British Diplomacy*, pp. 57, 195; Baxter, "Admiralty Problems," pp. 9, 93–4; Baxter, *Ironclad Warship*, p. 141; Worthington C. Ford, ed., *A Cycle of Adams Letters, 1861–1865*, 2 vols. (Boston and New York: Houghton Mifflin, 1920), I: 39; CFA to R. H. Dana, Jr., Aug. 25, 1861, Adams Papers, CFA Letterbook, reel 165; Ridley, *Palmerston*, p. 534.

27. Woods, *Prince of Wales*, p. 420; Kenneth Bourne, *Britain and the Balance of Power in North America, 1815–1908* (Berkeley and Los Angeles: University of California Press, 1967), pp. 35, 44, 53, 223, 236; Milne to Sec. of Admiralty, Apr. 23, 1861 (no. 169), Milne Papers, MLN/103/2(B); By an Officer [Col. Sir Patrick L. Mac-Dougall], *Forts versus Ships: Also Defence of the Canadian Lakes and Its Influence on the General Defence of Canada* (London: James Ridgway, 1862), p. 46; George F. G. Stanley, *Canada's Soldiers: The Military History of an Unmilitary People*, rev. ed. (Toronto: Macmillan, 1960), p. 216; Andrew Robb, "The Toronto *Globe* and the Defence of Canada, 1861–1866," *Ontario History*, LXIV (1972), p. 66; David F. Krein, "Genesis of Isolation: Palmerston, Russell, and the Formation of British Foreign Policy, 1861–1864," Ph.D. dissertation, University of Iowa (1974), p. 14.

28. Palmerston memorandum, May 23, 1861, PRO 30/22/35; Russell memorandum, May 21, 1861, ibid.; Stanmore, *Herbert*, II: 429; Newcastle to Palmerston, May 25, 1861, Palmerston Papers, GC/NE/86; Newcastle to Head, June 5, 1861, Newcastle Papers, Private Letter Book, Series B, NeC 10885; Bourne, *Britain and Balance of Power*, p. 212.

29. Bourne, *Britain and Balance of Power*, pp. 212–13; John M. Brinnin, *The Sway of the Grand Saloon: A Social History of the North Atlantic* (New York: Delacorte, 1971), pp. 216–17; James Dugan, *The Great Iron Ship* (New York: Harper & Bros., 1953), pp. 97–9; Frank C. Bowen, *A Century of Atlantic Travel, 1830–1930* (London: Little, Brown, 1932), p. 109; Strong, *Diary of the Civil War*, p. 37.

30. Baxter, "Admiralty Problems," p. 109; CFA to Seward, June 14 (no. 8) and 28 (no. 10), 1861, M30, roll 73; Palmerston to Russell, July 9, 1861, PRO 30/22/21; Palmerston to Newcastle, Sept. 1, 1861, GC/NE/98.

31. Palmerston to Newcastle, Sept. 1, 1861, GC/NE/98.

32. Ridley, *Palmerston*, p. 551; London *Punch*, Dec. 21, 1861; Sir Adolphus W. Ward and George P. Gooch, *The Cambridge History of British Foreign Policy, 1783–1919*, 3 vols. (Cambridge, Eng.: University Press, 1922–23), II: 499; CFA to CFA, Jr., Sept. 7, 1861, Adams Papers, reel 555; Adams to Seward, Aug. 8, 1861 (no. 25), M30, roll 73; CFA to John M. Forbes, Aug. 30, 1861, Adams Papers, CFA Letterbook, reel 165; CFA to Edward Everett, Sept. 6, 1861, ibid.; Alexander J. B. Beresford-Hope, "A Popular View of the American Civil War," p. 37, in *The American Disruption* (London: Wm. Ridgway, 1863).

33. Russell to Palmerston, Aug. 26, 1861, Palmerston Papers, GC/RU/667; Russell to Palmerston, Aug. 21, 1861, ibid., GC/RU/666.

34. E. D. Adams, *Great Britain*, I: 184–86; Milledge L. Bonham, Jr., *The British Consuls in the Confederacy* (New York: Columbia University Press, 1911), p. 20.

35. E. D. Adams, *Great Britain*, I: 187–95; Russell to CFA, Sept. 9, 1861, 58 Cong., 1 Sess., Sen. Doc. 18 (*Neutrality of Great Britain in the Civil War*), p. 96; Case and Spencer, *U.S. and France*, pp. 114–17.

36. Lyons to Russell, Oct. 14, 1861, PRO 30/22/35; Russell to Palmerston, Oct. 29, 1861, ibid.; Hammond to Cowley, Sept. 4, 1861, Cowley Papers, FO 519/190; Russell to Palmerston, Nov. 12, 1861, Palmerston Papers, GC/RU/680; Russell to Cowley, Sept. 9, 1861, in *The Later Correspondence of Lord John Russell, 1840–1878*,

ed. George P. Gooch, 2 vols. (London: Longmans, Green, 1925), II: 320; Palmerston to Russell, Sept. 9, 1861, PRO 30/22/31; Palmerston to Newcastle, Sept. 1, 1861, Palmerston Papers, GC/NE/98; Russell to Palmerston, Sept. 11, 1861, ibid., GC/RU/670.

37. Argyll to Gladstone, Sept. 17, 1861, Gladstone MSS., Add. Mss. 44099; Newcastle to Palmerston, Aug. 30, Sept. 3, and Nov. 11, 1861, Palmerston Papers, GC/NE/87–89; Lewis to Head, Sept. 8, 1861, Lewis, *Letters*, p. 402; Gladstone to Lewis, Sept. 21, 1861, Gladstone MSS., Add. Mss. 44532; Argyll to Gladstone, Sept. 13, 1861, ibid., Add. Mss. 44099; Somerset to Palmerston, Aug. 30, 1861, Palmerston Papers, GC/SO/59; Jenkins, *Britain*, p. 179; London *Times*, Dec. 2, 1861.

38. H. Adams to CFA, Jr., Sept. 7, 1861, Adams Papers, Letters Received, reel 555; CFA to Seward, Oct. 11, 1861 (no. 58), M30, roll 73; CFA to Seward, Nov. 1, 1861 (*very confidential*), M30, roll 74; CFA to Seward, Nov. 15, 1861 (*confidential*), Adams Papers, Letterbook, reel 166.

39. New York *Times*, Oct. 17, 18, 1861; Philadelphia *Inquirer*, Oct. 21, 1861; *Leslie's Illustrated Newspaper*, Jan. 11, 1862; London *Times*, Nov. 7, 26, 1861.

40. Lyons to Russell, Oct. 18, 1861 (no. 569), FO 5/772; Lyons to Russell, Oct. 28, 1861 (no. 606), FO 5/773; Lyons to Russell, Oct. 28, 1861, PRO 30/22/35.

41. Palmerston to Russell, Oct. 18, 1861, Palmerston Papers, GC/RU/1139.

5. "OUTRAGE ON THE BRITISH FLAG"

1. Welles to DuPont, Oct. 15, 1861, ORN, 1st series, I: 113; DuPont to Welles, Oct. 16, 1861, ibid., p. 115; Breese to Comm. Woodhull, Oct. 16, 1861, ibid., p. 116; Marchand to Welles, Oct. 30, 1861, ibid., pp. 125–26; CFA to Seward, Nov. 8, 1861 (no. 69), Despatches, Great Britain, vol. 79; Goldberg, "Naval Operations During 1861," pp. 392–93.

2. Reuter's Telegrams, Oct. 15, 1861, FO 5/804, American, Domestic Various; Hammond to law officers, Nov. 9, 1861, FO 83/2212, Law Officers Reports, America, pp. 251–52.

3. Hammond to law officers, Nov. 9, 1861, FO 83/2212, pp. 253–54; Hammond to Palmerston, Nov. 9, 1861, Palmerston Papers, GC/HA/248.

4. Sir Roundell Palmer, *Memorials, Family and Personal, 1766–1865*, 2 vols. (London and New York: Macmillan, 1896), II: 378–81, 386–88; Norman Ferris, *Desperate Diplomacy: William H. Seward's Foreign Policy, 1861* (Knoxville: University of Tennessee Press, 1976), p. 203, erroneously contends that British leaders would not act before hearing from the law officers, and therefore adopted policy "invariably based on narrow (and often archaic) legalistic considerations rather than on those of either political realities or humanitarian concerns." Numerous, obvious examples of cabinet flexibility exist to contradict this statement.

5. Hammond to Cowley, Nov. 11, 1861, Cowley Papers, FO 519/190; Palmerston to John T. Delane, Nov. 11, 1861, Adams, "*Trent* Affair," pp. 54–5; Hammond memorandum, Nov. 11, 1861, PRO, Edmund Hammond Papers, FO 391/7; John P. MacKintosh, *The British Cabinet*, 2nd ed. (London: Steven & Sons, 1968), pp. 161, 166.

6. DNB, XII: 291–92; ibid., II: 428–29; Argyll, *Autobiography*, II: 66–9; F. L. Wiswall, Jr., ed., *The Development of Admiralty Jurisdiction and Practice since 1800* (Cambridge, Eng.: University Press, 1971), pp. 72–4.

7. Palmerston to Delane, Nov. 11, 1861, Adams, "*Trent* Affair," pp. 54–5.

8. Ibid.; Palmerston to Hammond, Nov. 11, 1861, Hammond Papers, FO 391/7; Argyll, *Autobiography*, II: 40.

9. Harding, Atherton, and Palmer to Russell, Nov. 12, 1861, FO 83/2212, pp. 263–65.

10. Baxter, "British Government and Neutral Rights," pp. 15–16. Among those historians who uncritically accept Baxter's hypothesis are D. P. Crook, *The North, the South, and the Powers, 1861–1865* (New York: John Wiley & Sons, 1974), p. 123; Jenkins, *Britain and the War*, I: 209; and Alice O'Rourke, "The Law Officers of the Crown and the *Trent* Affair," *Mid-America*, 54 (1972), p. 161, fn. 5.

11. Sarah A. Wallace and Frances E. Gillespie, eds., *The Journal of Benjamin Moran, 1857–1865*, 2 vols. (Chicago: University of Chicago Press, 1949), II: 904–5; Palmerston to CFA, Nov. 12, 1861, Adams, "*Trent* Affair," p. 54; Ridley, *Palmerston*, p. 302.

12. Evelyn Ashley, *Life and Correspondence of Lord Palmerston*, 2 vols. (London: Richard Bentley & Son, 1879), I: 309; G. M. Young, *Victorian England: Portrait of an Age*, 2nd ed. (London: Oxford University Press, 1964), p. 84; Henry J. T. Palmerston, *Opinions and Policy of the Right Honourable Viscount Palmerston* (London: Colburn, 1852; reprinted New York: Kraus, 1972), p. 472; Krein, "Genesis of Isolation," pp. 96–7.

13. Ridley, *Palmerston*, p. 153; Wallace and Gillespie, *Journal of Moran*, I: 51; Bourne and Watt, *Studies*, p. 145; CFA to Seward, Nov. 15, 1861, Despatches, Great Britain, vol. 78.

14. CFA to Seward, Nov. 15, 1861, Despatches, Great Britain, vol. 78; Palmerston to Victoria, Nov. 13, 1861, in *The Letters of Queen Victoria*, ed. Arthur C. Benson and Viscount Esher, 3 vols. (London: John Murray, 1908), III: 467.

15. CFA, "Reminiscences," Adams Papers.

16. Palmerston to Delane, Nov. 12, 1861, Adams, "*Trent* Affair," p. 55; Russell to Lyons, Nov. 16, 1861, Russell Papers, PRO 30/22/96, Correspondence (drafts) to legation in Washington.

17. George M. Dallas to Lewis Cass, Aug. 25, 1857, in George M. Dallas, *A Series of Letters from London*, 2 vols. (Philadelphia: J. B. Lippincott, 1869), I: 198.

18. CFA to Seward, Nov. 15, 1861, Adams Papers, Letterbook, reel 166; London *Times*, Nov. 11, 1861.

19. H. Adams, *Education*, p. 119; Wallace and Gillespie, *Journal of Moran*, II: 912–14.

20. James Pope-Hennessy, *Monckton Milnes: The Flight of Youth, 1851–85* (London: Constable, 1951), p. 168; CFA, "Reminiscences," Adams Papers, Miscellany; Moran to Adams, Nov. 27, 1861 (telegram), ibid., Letters Received; CFA Diary, entry of Nov. 27, 1861, ibid.; CFA, Jr., *Adams*, pp. 216–17; W. E. Forster to wife, Nov. 1861, in T. Wemyss Reid, *Life of W. E. Forster*, 2 vols. (London: Chapman & Hall, 1888), I: 343; CFA to H. Adams, Nov. 27, 1861, Adams Papers, Letters Received.

21. Wallace and Gillespie, *Journal of Moran*, II: 914–15; Gordon Waterfield, *Layard of Ninevah* (New York: F. A. Praeger, 1968), p. 294.

22. London *Times*, Nov. 28–30, 1861; William J. Stillman, *The Autobiography of a Journalist*, 2 vols. (Boston and New York: Houghton Mifflin, 1901), I: 337; Charles I. Glicksberg, "Henry Adams and the Civil War," *Americana*, 33 (1939), p. 458; New York *Daily Tribune*, Dec. 19, 1861.

23. London *Times*, Nov. 28, 1861.

24. Ibid.; A. J. Wilding to Seward, Nov. 29, 1861, NA, Despatches from U.S. Consuls in Liverpool, vol. 20.

25. Charles Mackay to Seward, Nov. 29, 1861, ORA, 2nd series, II: 1107; Stillman, *Autobiography*, I: 337; F. H. Morse to Seward, Nov. 29, 1861 (nos. 40, 41), NA, Despatches from U.S. Consuls in London, vol. 29.

26. London *Economist*, Nov. 30, 1861, pp. 1327, 1332; Anonymous to Russell, Nov. 29, 1861, FO 5/806; Fred Boucher to Russell, Nov. 28, 1861, ibid.; Vigil to Russell, Nov. 28, 1861, ibid.

27. Krein, "Genesis of Isolation," pp. 54, 56; Mackintosh, *British Cabinet*, pp. 101–7; Owsley, *King Cotton Diplomacy*, p. 195; Nevins, *American Social History*, p. 362; Graham Hutton, "Lincoln through British Eyes," *Abraham Lincoln Quarterly*, III (June, 1944), p. 70.

28. Albert to Newcastle, Nov. 1, 1861, Newcastle Papers, NeC 12778; London *Times*, Nov. 28, 1861.

29. London *Star*, London *Morning Post*, and Manchester *Guardian*, Nov. 28, 1861; London *Economist*, Nov. 30, 1861, pp. 1317–18.

30. London *Standard*; London *Times*; London *Examiner*; London *Star*; and *Saturday Review of Politics, Literature, Science and Art*; Nov. 30, 1861.

31. *The Irishman*, Dec. 7, 1861; Richard J. Purcell, "Ireland and the American Civil War," *The Catholic World*, CXV (1922), p. 81; Joseph M. Hernon, Jr., *Celts, Catholics, and Copperheads: Ireland Views the American Civil War* (Columbus: Ohio State University Press, 1967), pp. 46, 49–50; Henry Wisham to Russell, Dec. 28, 1861, FO 5/808.

32. London *Times*, Nov. 29, 1861; Layard to Palmerston, Palmerston to Layard, Nov. 27, 1861, BM, Austen Henry Layard MSS., Add. Mss. 38987; Bourne, *Britain and Balance of Power*, p. 220; Palmerston to Lewis, Nov. 27, 1861, Palmerston Papers, GC/LE/234.

33. Palmerston to Lewis, Nov. 27, 1861, Palmerston Papers, GC/LE/234; Lewis to Palmerston, Nov. 27, 1861, ibid., GC/LE/147; Wellesley, *Secrets*, pp. 223–25.

34. London *Times*, Nov. 29, 1861; Lord John Russell, *Recollections and Suggestions, 1813–1873* (Boston: Roberts Bros., 1875), p. 226; Sir Horace Rumbold, *Recollections of a Diplomatist*, 2 vols. (London: E. Arnold, 1902), II: 83.

35. Harding, Atherton, and Palmer to Russell, Nov. 28, 1861, FO 83/2212.

36. Russell to Lyons, Nov. 16, 1861 (copy), PRO 30/22/96; CFA to Seward, Nov. 29, 1861 (nos. 80, 81), Despatches, Great Britain, vol. 78; Algernon B. F. M. Redesdale, *Memories*, 2 vols. (New York: E. P. Dutton, [n.d.]), I: 128; J. L. Motley to wife, June 6, 1858, in *The Correspondence of John Lothrop Motley*, ed. George W. Curtis, 2 vols. (New York: Harper & Bros., 1889), I: 255; CFA Diary, entry of Nov. 29, 1861 (misdated Nov. 28), Adams Papers; Russell to Lyons, Nov. 30, 1861 (no. 445), FO 5/778; Wallace and Gillespie, *Journal of Moran*, II: 915.

37. Palmerston to Gladstone, Nov. 29, 1861, Gladstone MSS., Add. Mss. 44272; Hammond to Layard, Nov. 29, 1861, Layard MSS., Add. Mss. 38951; Palmerston to Victoria, Nov. 29, 1861, in Benson and Esher, *Letters of Victoria*, III: 469.

38. A. J. P. Taylor, *The Trouble Makers: Dissent over Foreign Policy, 1792–1939* (Bloomington: Indiana University Press, 1958), p. 64; Bright to Sumner, Nov. 30, 1861, in "Letters of John Bright, 1861–1862," ed. James Ford Rhodes, MHS *Proceedings*, XLV (1911–12), p. 149; John Morley, *The Life of William Ewart Gladstone*, 3 vols. (New York: Harper & Bros., 1903), II: 73.

39. London *Times*, Nov. 30, 1861; CFA, "Reminiscences," Adams Papers, Miscellany; CFA Diary, entry of Nov. 30, 1861, Adams Papers.

40. Harold B. Hancock and Norman B. Wilkinson, " 'The Devil to Pay!': Saltpeter and the *Trent* Affair," *Civil War History*, X (1964), pp. 21–2; Bruce, *Lincoln and Tools of War*, pp. 146–47; B. G. duPont, *E. I. duPont de Nemours and Co.: A History, 1802–1902* (Boston and New York: Houghton Mifflin, 1920), pp. 89–90.

41. Forbes Campbell to the Treasury, Nov. 27, 1861, FO 5/806; J. MacKenzie to Russell, Nov. 27, 1861, ibid.; Russell to Layard, memorandum of Nov. 27, 1861, Layard MSS., Add. Mss. 38987; F. H. Morse to Seward, Nov. 29, 1861, Despatches from London Consuls, vol. 29.

42. A. Howard Meneely, *The War Department, 1861: A Study in Mobilization and Administration* (New York: Columbia University Press, 1928), p. 293; Forbes Campbell, confidential memorandum, Nov. 28, 1861, FO 5/806. The vessel may have been the *Moses* (not *Cornelius*) *Grinnell*. London *Times*, Nov. 28, 1861; the *Times*'s suggestion of preventing Union agents from buying war material also appears in a Palmerston memorandum, Dec. 2, 1861, Palmerston Papers, Cabinet (1861).

43. J. D. Harding to Layard, Nov. 28, 1861, Layard MSS., Add. Mss. 39101.

44. Palmerston to Granville, Nov. 29, 1861, Granville Papers, PRO 30/29/18; Palmerston to Russell, Nov. 29, 1861 (2 letters), Russell Papers, PRO 30/22/21; Royal Proclamation, Nov. 29, 1861, *British and Foreign State Papers* (London: Foreign Office, 1868), LI (1860–61), p. 170; Palmerston memorandum, Nov. 30, 1861, Palmerston Papers, Cabinet (1861); Hancock and Wilkinson, "Devil to Pay," p. 24.

45. Sanford to Beckwith, undated letters in late Nov. and early Dec. 1861, Henry Sanford Memorial Library, Sanford, Florida, Henry Shelton Sanford Papers, box 100; Sanford to Simon Cameron, Dec. 3, 1861, ibid., box 99; Sanford to Beckwith, Dec. 7, 1861, ibid; Sanford to Foster, Dec. 20, 1861, ibid.; Sanford to Judge Goodrich, Dec. 20, 1861, ibid.; Sanford to Weed, Dec. 8, 1861, in Francis Balace, comp., *La guerre de sécession et la Belgique; documents d'archives américaines, 1861–1865* (Louvain: Nauwelaerts, 1969), p. 28; Joseph A. Fry, "An American Abroad: The Diplomatic Career of Henry Shelton Sanford," Ph.D. dissertation, University of Virginia (1974), p. 160; Leo T. Molloy, *Henry Shelton Sanford, 1823–1891: A Biography* (Derby, Conn.: Bacon, 1952), p. 20.

46. Russell to Lyons, Nov. 30, 1861 (no. 444), FO 5/758.

47. London *Times*, Dec. 2, 1861; Lord Edmund Fitzmaurice, *The Life of Granville George Leveson Gower, Second Earl Granville, K.G., 1815–1891*, 2 vols. (New York: Longmans, Green, 1905), I: 402; Gladstone to Argyll, Dec. 3, 1861, Gladstone MSS., Add. Mss. 44099; Lewis to Edward Twisleton, Nov. 30, 1861, Lewis, *Letters*, pp. 405–6; Russell to Palmerston, Dec. 1, 1861, Palmerston Papers, GC/RU/681.

48. Philip W. Wilson, ed., *The Greville Diary*, 2 vols. (Garden City: Doubleday, Page, 1927), II: 361–62, 582; Herbert C. Bell, *Lord Palmerston*, 2 vols. (London: Longmans, Green, 1936), II: 215; Cecil Woodham-Smith, *Queen Victoria: From her Birth to the Death of the Prince Consort* (New York: Alfred A. Knopf, 1972), pp. 416–17; Martin, *Prince Consort*, V: 416–17, 421–22; Victoria to Princess Royal, Nov. 30, 1861, in *Dearest Child: Letters Between Queen Victoria and the Princess Royal, 1858–1861*, ed. Roger Fulford (New York: Holt, Rinehart, 1964), p. 370.

49. Martin, *Prince Consort*, V: 421–22; Norman B. Ferris, "The Prince Consort, 'The Times,' and the 'Trent' Affair," *Civil War History*, VI (1960), pp. 154–55, and Ferris, *Trent Affair*, p. 51, claims on the basis of circumstantial evidence that *Times* editorials of Nov. 29 and 30, 1861, influenced the Prince's revisions. Ferris apparently is unaware of the Prince's low opinion of the paper.

50. Russell to Lyons, Nov. 30, 1861 (no. 446), FO 5/758; Russell to Lyons, Nov. 30, 1861 (no. 448), FO 96/13 (series I), Draft Dispatches; *Illustrated London News*, Dec. 14, 1861.

51. Yancey, Rost, and Mann to R. M. T. Hunter, Dec. 2, 1861 (no. 10), ORN, 2nd series, III: 305; Yancey, Rost, and Mann to Russell, Nov. 27, 1861, ibid., 1st series, I: 154; Yancey, Rost, and Mann to Russell, Nov. 29, 1861, ibid., 2nd series, III: 299.

52. Yancey, Rost, and Mann to Hunter, Dec. 2, 1861, ORN, 1st series, I: 156; Mann to Hunter, Dec. 2, 1861, ibid., 2nd series, III: 307; George H. Putnam, *Memories of My Youth, 1844–1865* (New York: G. P. Putnam, 1914), pp. 201–11; Mann to Judah P. Benjamin, ORN, 2nd series, III: 631; Russell to Yancey, Rost, and Mann, Dec. 7, 1861, FO 5/807.

53. H. Adams, *Education*, p. 119.

54. H. Adams to CFA, Jr., June 10–11, Nov. 30, 1861, Adams Papers, Letters Received.

55. Ibid.; H. Adams to CFA, Jr., Nov. 30, 1861, ibid.

56. CFA Diary, entry of Dec. 1, 1861, Adams Papers, reel 76; CFA to Seward, Dec. 6, 1861 (no. 84), M30, roll 74.

6. BRITAIN PREPARES FOR WAR

1. Confidential memorandum for the use of the cabinet, Dec. 4, 1861, FO 146/987.

2. Palmerston to Russell, Dec. 6, 1861, Russell Papers, PRO 30/22/21; Palmerston to Victoria, Dec. 5, 1861, in *Regina vs. Palmerston: The Correspondence Between Queen Victoria and Her Foreign and Prime Minister, 1837–1865*, ed. Brian Connell (Garden City: Doubleday, 1961), p. 347.

3. Gladstone to Russell, Dec. 12, 1861, Russell Papers, PRO 30/22/19; Gladstone to Cobden, Dec. 13, 1861, Gladstone MSS., Add. Mss. 44136; C. Collyer, "Gladstone and the American Civil War," 6 *Proc. Leeds Philosophical and Literary Society* (Pt. 8), p. 587.

4. Lewis to Clarendon, Dec. 9, 1861, Bodleian Library (Oxford), Papers of George William Frederick Villiers, 4th Earl of Clarendon, c. 531; Lewis to Twisleton, Dec. 11, 1861, Lewis, *Letters*, p. 407; Lewis to Clarendon, Dec. 10, 1861, in *The Life and Letters of George William Frederick, Fourth Earl of Clarendon*, ed. Herbert E. Maxwell, 2 vols. (London: E. Arnold, 1913), II: 250.

According to the Liverpool *Mercury* of Dec. 14, 1861, cited by New York *Times*, Dec. 24, 1861, and corroborated by Maxwell, *Clarendon*, II: 251, Lord Derby, leader of the opposition, already had approved of the government's actions.

5. Hammond to Cowley, Dec. 2, 4, 1861, Cowley Papers, FO 519/190; Hammond to Palmerston, Dec. 3, 1861, Palmerston Papers, GC/HA/250.

6. Palmerston memorandum, Dec. 2, 1861, Palmerston Papers, Cabinet (1861); Somerset to Palmerston, Dec. 6, 1861, ibid., GC/SO/69; Royal Proclamation of Dec. 4, 1861, *British and Foreign State Papers*, LI: 172.

7. Palmerston to Lewis, Dec. 6, 1861, Palmerston Papers, GC/LE/237; MacKintosh, *British Cabinet*, pp. 147–48; Bourne, *Britain and Balance of Power*, p. 220.

8. Capt. Noble's memorandum on Canada Lakes, Nov. 29, 1861, PAC, R. G. 8/c1671/Part III/9.

9. Sir John Burgoyne, "Thoughts on war with the United States, as regards operations by the land forces," Dec. 14, 1861, National Library of Wales, Harpton Court Collection (Sir George Lewis Papers), HC 2984.

10. Jay Luvaas, "General Sir Patrick MacDougall, the American Civil War, and the Defence of Canada," Canadian Historical Association *Annual Report*, 1962, pp. 4–5; Richard A. Preston, *Canada and "Imperial Defense": A Study of the Origins of the British Commonwealth's Defense Organization, 1867–1919* (Durham: Duke University Press, 1967), p. 46; Lieut. Col. Sir Patrick L. MacDougall, *The Theory of War*, 2nd ed. (London: Longmans, Brown, Green, Longmans, & Roberts, 1858), pp. 3, 73; Col. MacDougall, "On the Prospect of War with the U. States," Dec. 3, 1861, Lewis Papers, HC 2943.

11. Lewis to Palmerston, Dec. 2, 3, 1861, Palmerston Papers, GC/LE/148–49; Lewis memorandum, Dec. 4, 1861, Lewis Papers, HC 2951.

12. Lord Grey memorandum on America and defense of Canada, Dec. 1, 1861, Lewis Papers, HC 2941; Lord Grey, memorandum, Dec. 8, 1861, ibid., HC 2957.

13. Woods, *Prince of Wales*, p. 124; Sir E. W. Watkin, *Canada and the States: Recollections, 1851 to 1886* (London: Ward, Lock, 1887), pp. 65* [sic], 80–87; Jenkins, *Britain and the War*, pp. 216–18, 266; Cobden to Bright, Dec. 7, 1861, Cobden MSS., Add. Mss. 43651.

14. Memo from Canadian delegation on Halifax and Quebec R.R., Dec. 10, 1861, Lewis Papers, HC 2698; Edward Watkin to Newcastle, Dec. 3, 1861, Newcastle Papers, NeC 11275; Gladstone to Lewis, Dec. 22, 1861 (copy), Gladstone MSS., Add. Mss. 44532.

15. Confidential memorandum for cabinet use, Dec. 7, 1861, FO 5/806; confidential memoranda for cabinet use, Dec. 14, 26 (2), 1861, FO 115/250; W. S. Romaine to Hammond, Dec. 7, 1861, FO 5/807; Clarendon to Russell, Dec. 4, 1861, Russell Papers, PRO 30/22/29; Argyll to Gladstone, Dec. 7, 1861, Gladstone MSS., Add. Mss. 44099; Gladstone to Somerset, Dec. 13, 1861 (copy), ibid., Add. Mss. 44, 3–4; Gladstone to Sir John Sinclair, Dec. 16, 1861 (copy), ibid., Add. Mss. 44532.

16. Elizabeth Batt, *Monck: Governor General, 1861–1868* (Toronto: McClelland and Stewart, 1976), p. 20; Newcastle to Monck, Dec. 5, 1861, Newcastle Papers, NeC 10885; Newcastle to Monck, Dec. 11, 14, 1861, *ibid.,* NeC 10886; Newcastle to Arthur H. Gordon, Dec. 7, 1861, *ibid.,* NeC 10886/B3; Newcastle to Gordon, Dec. 21, 1861, NeC 10886; Newcastle to Monck, Dec. 28, 1861, Province of Canada, *Sessional Papers*, XX, no. 36 ("Return of Papers relative to Matapedia Road, June 2, 1862"); Newcastle to Alexander Bannerman, Dec. 14, 1861, Newcastle Papers, NeC 10886.

17. *Illustrated London News*, Dec. 14, 1861; London *Times*, Dec. 5, 1861; Bourne, *Britain and Balance of Power*, p. 230; Joseph H. Lehmann, *The Model Major-General: A Biography of Field-Marshal Lord Wolseley* (Boston: Houghton Mifflin, 1964), pp. 114–16; Wolseley to Biddulph, Dec. 10, 1861, Jan. 26, 1862, in "Canada and the American Civil War. More Wolseley letters," ed. H. Biddulph, *Society for Army Historical Research Journal* (London), XIX (1940), p. 115.

18. Thomas H. Dudley to Seward, Dec. 13, 1861, NA, M-141, roll T20; Edwin G. Rundle, *A Soldier's Life* (Toronto: William Briggs, 1909), p. 41; Somerset memorandum, Dec. 21, 1861, ADM. 1/5766; Bushell, *Royal Mail,* p. 101; *Illustrated London News*, Dec. 7, 28, 1861; Cecil Woodham-Smith, *Florence Nightingale, 1820–1910* (New York: McGraw-Hill, 1951), p. 257; London *Times,* Dec. 27, 1861; Somerset to Palmerston, Dec. 6, 1861, Palmerston Papers, GC/SO/69.

19. Weed to Seward, Dec. 20, 1861, Seward Papers; London *Spectator*, Dec. 21, 1861; *Illustrated London News*, Dec. 28, 1861, Jan. 4, 1862; *Hansard's Parliamentary Debates*, 3rd Series, V:165, 1455; Richard H. Dana, Jr., "The *Trent* Affair: An Aftermath," MHS *Proceedings*, XLV (1911-1912), p. 516; Somerset to Palmerston, Dec. 24, 1861, Palmerston Papers, GC/SO/75; War Office, 3rd Jan. 1862, CONFIDENTIAL LISTS, PAC, R.G. 8/c1671/Part II/12, 521-26; Bowen, *Century of Atlantic Travel*, p. 114; Batt, *Monck*, pp. 39-40; Edward Lugard to T. F. Elliott, Dec. 13, 1861, PRO, CO 6/33; Lewis memorandum, Dec. 26, 1861, Lewis Papers, HC 2988; Russell to Palmerston, Dec. 11, 1861, Palmerston Papers, GC/RU/684.

20. Sir John W. Fortescue, *A History of the British Army*, 13 vols. (London: Macmillan, 1902-30), XII:545-47; Dugan, *Great Iron Ship*, p. 104; Bourne, *Britain and Balance of Power*, p. 230; *Hansard's Parliamentary Debates*, 3rd Series, CLXV (1862), p. 292; Rundle, *Soldier's Life*, p. 43; J. Mackay Hitsman, "Winter Troop Movements to Canada, 1862," *Canadian Historical Review*, XLIII (1962), pp. 133-34; Somerset to Palmerston, Dec. 24, 1861, Palmerston Papers, GC/SO/75; F. Eardly to Chief of Staff in Montreal, March 10, 1862, PAC, R.G. 8/c 1671, Nova Scotia Command, *Trent* Affair, CR/Q/408, Part I/29, 223-33.

In his report, Paget claimed that 14, 436 officers and men were sent out; therefore, the accurate figure remains in doubt. Despite government defense of the expedition as a strategic and diplomatic necessity, critics viewed the logistical nightmare as no more than an expensive gesture for which the British public paid dearly and received little substance. Gladstone complained at the height of the crisis that there was "a vulgar idea in this country that when once war comes ever so remotely into view all thoughts of limiting expense ought to be cast aside." (Gladstone to Lewis, Dec. 15, 1861 (copy), Gladstone MSS., Add. Mss. 44532.) When the secretary of the Admiralty, Lord Clarence Paget, reported to the Commons in February 1862, he claimed somewhat disingenuously that the cost amounted to sixteen pounds per head or roughly 230,000 pounds, a figure that may have covered the direct outlay for transportation of officers, men, and dependents. Lewis reported on the same day that military expenses were approximately £607,194, but his and Paget's totals fell far short of actual expenses. The cost of troop movements approached a million and a half pounds, most of it going for arms and supplies, and London would have had to spend almost one million pounds annually to maintain the new level of strength in Canada. Most naval expenses resulted from consumption of coal by transports and the sending of 10,000 tons to Halifax, 9,000 to Bermuda, and 2,000 to the West Indies, a reasonable precaution in view of anticipated monthly wartime consumption of 10,000 tons at higher freight rates. *Hansard's Parliamentary Debates*, 3rd series, CXLV (1862), pp. 396, 165; Lewis to Palmerston, Feb. 8, 1862, Palmerston Papers, GC/LE/155; C. P. Stacey, *Canada and the British Army, 1846-1871* (London: Longmans, 1936), p. 122; Somerset to Palmerston, Dec. 24, 1861, Palmerston Papers, GC/SO/74-75.

21. Toronto *Globe*, Dec. 10, 1861; London *Times*, Jan. 8, 1862; Winks, *Canada*, pp. 87, 94; Quebec *Morning Chronicle*, Nov. 21, 1861; Montreal *Gazette*, Dec. 17-19, 1861; Ottawa *Tribune*, Dec. 20, 1861; Fred Landon, ed., "Extracts from the Diary of Mrs. Amelia Harris, 1857-77 of London, Ontario," London (Ontario) *Free Press*, Aug. 25, 1928; Charles Clarke, *Sixty Years in Upper Canada, with Autobiographical Recollections* (Toronto: W. Briggs, 1908), p. 119.

22. Toronto *Globe*, Nov. 18, 19, 22, Dec. 18, 21, 1861; Winks, *Canada*, p. 93; Toronto *Leader*, Nov. 18, 20, Dec. 26, 1861.

23. Ottawa *Citizen*, Nov. 19, Dec. 10, 24, 1861; Halifax *Morning Chronicle*, Dec. 17, 1861; Montreal *Gazette*, Dec. 14, 17, 1861.

24. C. F. Hamilton, "The Canadian Militia: from 1861 to Confederation," *Canadian Defence Quarterly*, VI (1929), pp. 200–1; Monck to Newcastle, Nov. 22, 1861, Newcastle Papers, NeC 11387; Preston, *Canada and "Imperial Defense,"* p. 38; Hansard's *Parliamentary Debates*, 3rd series, CLXV (1862), p. 388; F. W. Williams to Monck, Nov. 29 (copy), Dec. 1, 1861, PRO, Canada, Original Correspondence (Despatches), CO 42/628; Monck to Williams, Nov. 30, 1861, PAC, R.G. 7, G11, vol. 22 (4); MacDougall, *Theory of War*, p. 294; Stanley, *Canada's Soldiers*, p. 219; George H. Ham, *Reminiscences of A Raconteur between the '40s and the '20s* (Toronto: Musson, 1921), pp. 75–6; Toronto *Globe*, Dec. 25, 1861.

25. Toronto *Globe*, Dec. 17, 20, 1861; Stanley, *Canada's Soldiers*, pp. 218–19; Monck to Newcastle, Dec. 20, 1861, Newcastle Papers, NeC 11890; Bourne, *Britain and Balance of Power*, p. 225; J. P. Edwards, "The Militia of Nova Scotia, 1749–1867," Nova Scotia Historical Society *Collections*, XVII (1913), p. 99.

26. Monck to Newcastle, Dec. 20, 1861, Newcastle Papers, NeC 11890; Bourne, *Britain and Balance of Power*, p. 224; William H. Russell, *Canada and Its Defenses, Conditions and Resourcesn*(Boston: Burnham, 1865), pp. 35, 49–50, 55, 77; Milne to Newcastle, Nov. 30, 1861, Newcastle Papers, NeC 11389; Toronto *Globe*, Dec. 2, 1861; Monck to Newcastle, Nov. 24, 1861, Newcastle Papers, NeC 11388; entry of Dec. 19, 1861, PAC, R.G. 1, E 1 (Minute Books, United Canada), vol. 85; Monck to Newcastle, Dec. 19, 1861, R.G. 7, G2 (Despatches from CO to Monck), vol. 8; Toronto *Leader*, Dec. 3, 4, 1861; London *Times*, Dec. 23, 1861; Kenneth Bourne, "British Preparations for War with the North, 1861–1862," *English Historical Review*, LXXVI (1961), p. 619; Winks, *Canada*, p. 85.

27. Somerset to Palmerston, Dec. 6, 1861, Palmerston Papers, GC/SO/69–70.

28. London *Times*, Dec. 2, 1861; London *Spectator*, Jan. 4, 1862; *Illustrated London News*, Jan. 4, 1862.

29. Somerset to Russell, Dec. 6, 1861, Palmerston Papers, GC/SO/71; Milne to Sec. of Admiralty, Dec. 20, 1861 (no. 631), Milne Papers, MLN/103/3(c).

30. Somerset to Palmerston, Sept. 26, 1861, Palmerston Papers, GC/SO/60; Somerset to Russell, Dec. 6, 1861, ibid., GC/SO/71; F. H. Morse to Seward, Dec. 6, 1861 (no. 43), Despatches from U.S. Consuls in London, vol. 29; London *Times*, Dec. 3, 1861; *Illustrated London News*, Dec. 7, 1861; telegrams of Dec. 6, 7, 1861, PRO, Adm. 13/14; Somerset to Palmerston, Dec. 6, 1861, Palmerston Papers, GC/SO/69; Bourne, *Britain and Balance of Power*, p. 239. The *Conquerer* ripped open its bottom on a Bahama coral reef.

31. Somerset to Russell, Dec. 6, 1861, Palmerston Papers, GC/SO/71; Somerset to Milne, Dec. 16, 1861, Milne Papers, MLN/107/1(c); Somerset to Russell, Dec. 29, 1861, Russell Papers, PRO 30/22/24; Somerset to Palmerston, Dec. 6, 1861, Palmerston Papers, GC/SO/69.

32. Milne to Sec. of Admiralty, Dec. 20, 1861 (no. 631), Milne Papers, MLN/103/3(c); Russell to Lord Commissioners of Admiralty, Nov. 30, 1861 (5), *Command Papers*, LXII:616.

33. Moneiciff memorandum, Dec. 4, 1861, Lewis Papers, HC 2952; Somerset note, Dec. 3, 1861, PRO, Adm. 1/5766.

34. F. V. Longstaff, *Esquimalt Naval Base: A History of Its Works and Its Defences* (Victoria: Victoria Book & Stationery, 1941), p. 24; Richard C. Mayne, *Four Years in British Columbia and Vancouver Island* (London: John Murray, 1862), pp. 24–5; Benjamin F. Gilbert, "Rumours of Confederate Privateers Operating in Victoria, Vancouver Island," *British Colonial Historical Review*, XVIII (1954),

pp. 240–41; Thomas Maitland to Sec. of Admiralty, Jan. 13, 1862 (no. 22, copy), FO 5/856; Bourne, *Britain and Balance of Power,* p. 237; Barry M. Gough, *The Royal Navy and the Northwest Coast of North America, 1810–1914: A Study of British Maritime Ascendancy* (Vancouver: University of British Columbia Press, 1971), p. 201.

Milne's force also relied on American shipyards to make serious repairs. *See* Courtemanche, *No Need of Glory,* p. 42.

35. Somerset to Russell, Dec. 13, 1861, FO 5/807; Russell memorandum, Dec. 13, 1861, Russell to Somerset, Dec. 15, 1861, ibid.; Russell to T. Griffith, Dec. 16, 1861 (no. 75), FO 146/989; Russell to Lyons, Dec. 20, 1861 (no. 488), FO 5/758.

In addition to settling the Panama issue, London thought the two countries should reach agreement on the use of privateers in war. It would be improper, the government had decided, to issue letters of marque before ascertaining the American attitude. Somerset thought there was not the slightest chance of Lincoln being reasonable on the issue, but Russell still instructed Lyons to try. The British minister refused to speak to Seward about letters of marque or the Panama railroad because it would have interfered with a peaceful resolution of the crisis. *See* Somerset to Russell, Dec. 16, 1861, Russell Papers, PRO 30/22/24; Russell to Lyons, Dec. 20, 1861 (no. 489), FO 5/758; Lyons to Russell, Feb. 11, 1862 (no. 105), FO 115/298.

36. Lewis to Palmerston, Dec. 24, 1861, Palmerston Papers, GC/LE/159; Palmerston to Granville, Dec. 26, 1861, PRO, Second Earl Granville Papers, PRO 30/39/18; Palmerston to Russell, Dec. 27, 1861, Russell Papers, PRO 30/22/21; Bethell to Palmerston, Dec. 30, 1861, Palmerston Papers, GC/WE/132.

37. Palmerston to Victoria, Nov. 29, 1861, Benson and Esher, *Letters of Victoria,* III:469.

38. John T. Pickett to Jefferson Davis, Feb. 22, 1862, NA, Pickett Papers, I:9717; Percy Doyle to Lord Cowley, Dec. 3, 1861, FO 115/250; W. Reed West, *Contemporary French Opinion on the American Civil War* (Baltimore: Johns Hopkins, 1924), p. 53; Bigelow to Seward, Dec. 9, 1861, NA, M T-1, roll 12; Charles W. Elliott, *Winfield Scott, the Soldier and the Man* (New York: Macmillan, 1937), pp. 746, 748, 752; Harriet A. Weed, ed., *Autobiography of Thurlow Weed,* 2 vols. (Boston: Houghton Mifflin, 1884), I:654–55; John Bigelow, *Retrospections of an Active Life,* 5 vols. (New York: Baker & Taylor, 1909), I:387–90; *Illustrated London News,* Dec. 14, 1861.

39. Russell to Lyons, Dec. 1, 7, 1861, Russell Papers, PRO 30/22/96.

7. "WAITING FOR AN ANSWER"

1. James Lesley, Jr., to F. W. Seward, Dec. 4, 1861, Seward Papers; *La Patrie,* Dec. 2, 1861; New York *Times,* Dec. 25, 1861; London *Times,* Dec. 12, 1861; George E. Marindin, ed., *Letters of Frederic Lord Blachford, Under-Secretary of State for the Colonies, 1860–1871* (London: John Murray, 1896), p. 232; London *Times,* Dec. 4, 1861; Gordon N. Ray, *Thackeray: The Age of Wisdom, 1847–1863* (New York: McGraw-Hill, 1958), p. 316.

2. T. M. Mackay to Layard, Dec. 4, 1861, Layard MSS., Add. Mss. 39102; Manchester Chamber of Commerce to Russell, Dec. 9, 1861, FO 5/807; Wm. S. Lindsay to Layard, Dec. 10, 1861, Layard MSS., Add. Mss. 39102; Manchester *Guardian,* Dec. 7, 1861; Caleb D. Watson to Russell, Dec. 9, 1861, FO 5/807; A. Sleigh to Russell, Dec. 3, 1861, Lewis Papers, HC 2963.

3. *The Edinburgh Review,* CXV (Jan.–Apr. 1862), pp. 139–40; *McMillan's Magazine,* V (Nov. 1861–Apr. 1862), p. 263; London *Times,* Dec. 5, 1861.

4. *Illustrated London News,* London *Spectator, Saturday Review,* London *Examiner,* Dec. 7, 1861.

5. *Punch,* Dec. 7, 1861.

6. *Ibid.,* Dec. 14, 28, 1861.

7. London *Times,* Manchester *Guardian,* Dec. 17, 1861; London *Examiner,* Dec. 21, 1861.

8. London *Times,* Dec. 2, 4, 1861; London *Economist,* Dec. 7, 14, 28, 1861; London *Law Times,* Dec. 21, 1861; Peter Harnetty, "The Imperialism of Free Trade: Lancashire, India, and the Cotton Supply Question, 1861–1865," *Journal of British Studies,* VI (1966), p. 76.

9. Philip A. Smith, *The Seizure of the Southern Commissioners, considered with reference to International Law and to the Question of War or Peace* (London: James Ridgway, 1862), pp. 42–3; Trollope, *North America,* I:446–47; Rev. Newman Hall, *No War with America. A Lecture on the Affair of the Trent* (London: Eliot Stock, 1861), pp. 4, 6; Robert Botsford, "Scotland and the American Civil War," Ph.D. dissertation, University of Edinburgh (1955), pp. 468–72; London *Times,* Dec. 4, 26, 1861; Mary Ellison, *Support for Secession: Lancashire and the American Civil War* (Chicago: University of Chicago Press, 1972), pp. 134–35, 146; D. G. Wright, "Bradford and the American Civil War," *Journal of British Studies,* VIII (1969), pp. 78–9, 81; Karl Marx and Frederick Engels, *The Civil War in the United States* (New York: International, 1937), pp. 130–33; London *Observer,* Jan. 5, 1862.

10. Ridley, *Palmerston,* p. 526; Jenkins, *Britain and War,* p. 69.

11. Waterfield, *Layard,* p. 295; Herman Ausubel, *John Bright: Victorian Reformer* (New York: Wiley, 1966), pp. 48–9, 76, 105; Ridley, *Palmerston,* pp. 427–28; Royden Harrison, *Before the Socialists: Studies in Labour and Politics, 1861–1881* (London: Routledge & Kegan Paul, 1965), p. 55; New York *Daily Tribune,* Dec. 19, 1861.

12. John Bright, *Speeches on the American Question* (Boston: Little, Brown, 1865), pp. 53–66.

13. London *Examiner,* Dec. 7, 1861; Manchester *Guardian,* Dec. 9, 1861; London *Spectator,* Dec. 7, 1861; London *Times,* Dec. 6, 1861; *Punch,* Dec. 14, 1861.

14. Cobden to Bright, Dec. 3, 1861, Cobden MSS., Add. Mss. 43651; Cobden to Sumner, Dec. 6, 12, 1861, ibid., Add. Mss. 43676; Cobden to John Slagg, [n.d.] and Nov. 8, 1861, ibid. Cobden's grain theory cannot be substantiated.

15. London *Times,* Dec. 20, 1861; Cobden to Bright, Dec. 17, 1861, Cobden MSS., Add. Mss. 43651; Clarendon to Brougham, Jan. 4, 1862, University College Library (London), Baron Brougham Papers, BP 30,188; Cobden to Rev. Henry Richard, Dec. 18, 1861, Cobden MSS., Add. Mss. 43659; Cobden to Sumner, Dec. 5, 1861, ibid., Add. Mss. 43676. Cobden to Bright, Dec. 6, 1861, ibid., Add. Mss. 43651.

16. London *Times,* Dec. 3, 10, 1861; James Frazer to Russell, Nov. 29, 1861, FO 5/806; Donaldson Jordan and Edwin J. Pratt, *Europe and the American Civil War* (Boston: Houghton Mifflin, 1931), p. 39; Charles P. McIlvaine to Seward, Dec. 23, 1861, Seward Papers; Robert Ashson to Russell, Dec. 11, 1861, FO 5/807; Edward Richardson to Russell, Dec. 18, 1861, ibid.; J. H. Hinton to Russell, Dec. 20, 1861, FO 5/808; Committee of Congregational Union to Russell, Dec. 27, 1861, ibid.

17. David Large, "Friends and the American Civil War: The *Trent* Affair," Friends' Historical Society *Journal*, XLVIII (1957), pp. 164–66; petition from Society of Friends to Palmerston and Russell, Dec. 9, 1861, FO 5/807.

18. Large, "Friends," pp. 166–67; Ridley, *Palmerston*, pp. 503–4; London *Times*, Dec. 19, 1861.

19. Russell to Palmerston, Dec. 16, 1861, Palmerston Papers, GC/RU/685.

20. Lewis to Twisleton, Dec. 11, 1861, Lewis, *Letters*, p. 407; Lewis to Gladstone, Dec. 17, 1861, Gladstone MSS., Add. Mss. 44236; Cobden to Sumner, Jan. 23, 1862, Cobden MSS., Add. Mss. 43676.

21. Confidential memorandum, Dec. 7, 1861, FO 5/806; confidential memoranda for the cabinet, Dec. 14, 26, 28, 30, 1861, FO 115/289; Hammond to Lyons, Dec. 21, 1861, FO 5/758; Bethell to Russell, Dec. 21, 1861, FO 83/2212.

22. Hammond to law officers, Dec. 16, 1861, FO 83/2212; Harding, Atherton, and Palmer to Russell, Dec. 21, 1861, ibid.; Argyll to Gladstone, Dec. 10, 1861, Gladstone MSS., Add. Mss. 44099; Gladstone to Russell, Dec. 12, 1861, Russell Papers, PRO 30/22/19; Russell to Gladstone, Dec. 13, 1861, Gladstone MSS., Add. Mss. 44292; Russell to Bloomfield, Dec. 11, 1861, PRO, Lord Bloomfield Papers, FO 356/32.

23. Biglow to Seward, Dec. 9, 1861, NA, M T-1, roll 12; Robert M. Johnston, ed., *Memoirs of 'Malakoff'* [pseud.] *being extracts from the Correspondence and Papers of the late William Edward Johnston*, 2 vols. (London: Hutchinson, 1907), II:378, 380–82; West, *Contemporary French Opinion*, p. 46; Serge Gavronsky, *The French Liberal Opposition and the American Civil War* (New York: Humanities Press, 1968), p. 102.

24. Lynn M. Case, ed., *French Opinion on the United States and Mexico, 1860–1867* (New York: D. Appleton-Century, 1936), pp. xii–xiv, xviii, 29, 32, 37, 41, 244, 248–55; Case and Spencer, *U.S. and France*, p. 164.

25. Case and Spencer, *U.S. and France*, pp. 40–2, 191; West, *Contemporary French Opinion*, pp. 41–4, 49–50, 52–3; *La Patrie*, Dec. 1, 1861; *Journal des Débats*, Dec. 1, 22, 24, 1861; Gavronsky, *French Liberal Opposition*, pp. 102, 105–6; *Gazette des Tribunaux*, Dec. 5, 1861.

26. Laurent B. Hautefeuille, *Questions de droit maritime international* (Paris: Guillaumin, 1868 [1861], contains an essay entitled "Affaires du *Trent* et du *Nashville*," which was published in Paris by Charles Jouaust in 1861.

27. Cowley to Russell, Dec. 2, 1861, FO 519/229; Wm. L. Dayton to Seward, Nov. 30, 1861 (no. 87), NA, Despatches from U.A. Ministers to France, vol. 51; Cowley to Russell, Jan. 9, 1862, Russell Papers, PRO 30/22/57; Biglow to James Bowen, Dec. 6, 1861, Seward Papers; Hughes to Seward, Dec. 5, 1861, ibid.; Belmont to Chase, Dec. 8, 1861, Belmont Papers, Personal Papers Miscellany; Belmont to Dayton, Dec. 10, 1861, Princeton University Library, Wm. L. Dayton Papers, box 3.

28. Thouvenel to Mercier, Dec. 3, 1861, ORN, 1st series, I:164–65.

29. Dayton to Seward, Dec. 6, 1861 (no. 91), Despatches from U.S. Ministers to France, vol. 51; Hughes to Seward, Dec. 27, 1861, Seward Papers.

30. Benjamin P. Thomas, *Russo-American Relations, 1815–1867* (Baltimore: Johns Hopkins Press, 1930), p. 129; Clay to Seward, Dec. 10, 1861 (no. 13), NA, Despatches from U.S. Ministers to Russia, vol. 19.

31. Napier to Russell, Dec. 25 (no. 430), Dec. 27, 1861 (no. 438), Jan. 6, 1862 (no. 10), FO 115/284; Napier to Russell, Dec. 28, 1861, Russell Papers, PRO 30/22/83.

32. Russell to Napier, Jan. 10, 1862 (no. 3), FO 115/284; Hammond to Cowley, Jan. 11, 1862, Cowley Papers, FO 519/190.

33. Motley to Biglow, Dec. 19, 1861, Biglow, *Retrospections,* I:419; Motley to his mother, Dec. 1, 16, 1861, Curtis, *Correspondence of Motley,* II:43, 46, 49; Motley to Dayton, Dec. 17, 1861, Dayton Papers, box 3; Meneely, *War Department,* p. 291; M. Clair Lynch, *The Diplomatic Mission of John Lothrop Motley to Austria, 1861–1867* (Washington, D.C.: Catholic University of America Press, 1944), p. 81.

34. Bloomfield to Russell, Dec. 12, 1861 (no. 629), FO 115/250; Bloomfield to Russell, Dec. 12 (no. 630), Dec. 18, 1861 (no. 638), Bloomfield Papers, FO 356/17; Motley to Seward, Jan. 20, 1862, ORA, 3rd series, II:1183; Rechberg to Hülsemann, Dec. 18, 1861, ORN, 1st series, I:170.

35. Judd to Seward, Dec. 14, 1861 (no. 14), NA, Despatches from U. S. Ministers to the German States, vol. 12 (Prussia); Ralph Lutz, *Die Beziehungen zwischen Deutschland und den Vereinigten Staaten während des Sezessionskrieges* (Heidelberg: C. Winter, 1911), p. 11; Loftus to Russell, Dec. 28, 1861 (no. 502), FO 5/515; Case and Spencer, *U.S. and France,* p. 206.

36. Bernstorff to Gerolt, Dec. 25, 1861, ORN, 1st series, I:175; Seward to Gerolt, Jan. 14, 1862, ORA, 2nd series, II:1178; Gurowski, *Diary,* p. 141.

37. Marsh to Seward, Dec. 9 (no. 32), Dec. 23, 1861 (no. 34), NA, Despatches from U.S. Ministers to the Italian States, vol. 10; Seward to Marsh, Jan. 14, 1862 (no. 38), NA, Diplomatic Instructions, Italy, vol. 1.

38. Odo Russell to Russell, Dec. 17, 1861 (no. 10), FO 146/989; Wm. J. Stillman to Seward, Jan. 3, 1862, in *Consular Relations between the United States and the Papal States,* ed. Leo F. Stock (Washington, D.C.: American Catholic Historical Association, 1945), pp. 225–26.

39. Schurz to Seward, Dec. 7, 1861 (no. 44), NA, Despatches from U.S. Ministers to Spain, vol. 43; Horatio J. Perry to Seward, Dec. 28, 1861 (no. 17), ibid. Approving Britain's protest and viewing surrender of Mason and Slidell as the "only true course" open to the Lincoln administration, the Netherlands' Queen Sophie told the American minister that war would otherwise result between Britain and the United States. Sir Andrew Buchanan to Russell, Dec. 10, 1861 (no. 108), FO 115/250; James S. Pike to Seward, Jan. 9, 1862, ORA, 2nd series, II: 1165; Robert F. Durden, *James Shepherd Pike: Republicanism and the American Negro, 1850–1882* (Durham: Duke University Press, 1957), p. 103. The Swedish government likewise condemned the seizure as a violation of international law and a *casus belli* unless disavowed. The minister of foreign affairs, Count Manderstrom, informed Washington that he considered the act "utterly indefensible," and remarked to the British minister that since an Anglo-American conflict would come sooner or later, this would be an excellent time for England; it was prepared, was on good terms with France, and faced no civil disturbance in Canada. A permanent division of the United States, he said, would be "highly beneficial" to Europe. J. S. Haldeman to Seward, Dec. 10, 1861, ORA, 2nd series, II:1122; G. H. Jerningham to Russell, Dec. 23, 1861 (no. 159), FO 115/284.

40. Clarendon to Russell, Dec. 8, 1861, Russell Papers, PRO 30/22/29; Philip C. Jessup, *A Modern Law of Nations: An Introduction* (New York: Macmillan, 1948), pp. 37–9; Elihu Root, *Addresses on International Subjects,* ed. Robert Bacon and James B. Scott (1916; reprinted Freeport, N.Y.: Books for Libraries Press, 1969), pp. 421–24.

41. Bright to Cobden, Dec. 9, 1861, Bright MSS., Add. Mss. 44384; CFA to J. G. Palfrey, Dec. 13, 1861, Adams Papers, Letters Received, reel 556; CFA to CFA, Jr., Dec. 27, 1861, ibid.; CFA to R. H. Dana, Jr., Dec. 13, 1861, ibid., CFA Letterbook, reel 166; H. Adams to CFA, Jr., ibid., Letters Received, reel 556; CFA Diary, entry of Dec. 11, 1861, ibid., reel 76; CFA to Seward, Dec. 6, 1861 (no. 84), Despatches, Great Britain, vol. 78; CFA to CFA, Jr., Dec. 12, 1861, Ford, *Cycle of Letters,* p. 82; Francis J. Heppner, "Henry S. Sanford, United States Minister to Belgium, 1861–1869," M.A. thesis, Georgetown University (1955), pp. 109–14; Sanford to Seward, July 4, 1861, Lincoln Papers, series 1, roll 23; CFA to Seward, Dec. 11, 1861 (no. 85), Despatches, Great Britain, vol. 78.

42. Seward to CFA, Nov. 27, 1861 (*Confidential*), Instructions, Great Britain, vol. 18; Seward to CFA, Nov. 30, 1861 (no. 136), ibid.; Wallace and Gillespie, *Journal of Moran,* II:927; CFA to Russell, Dec. 18, 1861, FO 5/792.

43. CFA Diary, entry of Dec. 19, 1861, Adams Papers; CFA to Seward, Dec. 20, 1861 (no. 93), Despatches, Great Britain, vol. 78; Russell to Lyons, Dec. 19, 1861 (no. 483), FO 115/250.

44. Ibid.; Russell to Palmerston, Dec. 20, 1861, Palmerston Papers, GC/RU/686; Krein, "Genesis of Isolation," p. 150.

45. Wallace and Gillespie, *Journal of Moran,* II:928; Weed to Seward, Dec. 20, 1861, Seward Papers; CFA to Seward, Jan. 17, 1862 (no. 103), Despatches, Great Britain, vol. 78; Weed to Richard Blatchford, Jan. 10, 1862, Seward Papers; *see* Marx and Engels, *Civil War* for detailed discussion of the suppressed dispatch; CFA, "Reminiscences," Adams Papers.

46. Weed to Seward, Dec. 4, 7, 1861, Seward Papers; Weed to Archbishop Hughes, Dec. 7, 1861, Rush Rhees Memorial Library, University of Rochester, Thurlow Weed Papers; Weed to Lincoln, Dec. 11, 1861, Lincoln Papers, series I, roll 30, p. 13369; Van Deusen, *Weed,* pp. 278–79.

47. Weed to Seward, Dec. 13, 1861, Lincoln Papers, series I, roll 30, pp. 13405–6; Russell memorandum, Dec. 13, 1861, FO 5/807; *Illustrated London News,* Dec. 14, 1861; Weed, *Autobiography,* I:644, incorrectly gives Nov. 27 as the dinner date.

48. Martin, *Consort,* V:415–17; Wellesley, *Secrets of Second Empire,* p. 229; *Punch,* Dec. 21, 1861.

49. Wallace and Gillespie, *Journal of Moran,* II:926–30; Reginald Pound, *Albert: A Biography of the Prince Consort* (London: Michael Joseph, 1973), p. 351; London *Times,* Dec. 24, 1861; London *Spectator,* Dec. 28, 1861.

8. THE STORM PASSES

1. Albert G. Riddle, *Recollections of War Times: Reminiscences of Men and Events in Washington, 1860–1865* (New York: G. P. Putnam, 1895), pp. 75–6; Ben Perley Poore, *Reminiscences of Sixty Years in the National Metropolis,* 2 vols. (Philadelphia: Hubbard Bros., 1886), II:94; Trollope, *North America,* II:23, 27; Dicey, *Six Months,* pp. 43, 95; Sala, *Diary,* I:68–9; Stephen M. Weld, *War Diary and Letters of Stephen Minot Weld, 1861–1865* (Cambridge, Mass.: Riverside Press, 1912), p. 47; Milton, *Lincoln and Fifth Column,* pp. 59–60; Gurowski, *Diary,* I:97.

2. Woods, *Prince of Wales,* pp. 341–44; Max Berger, *The British Traveller in America, 1836–1860* (New York: Columbia University Press, 1943), p. 92; Fergusson, *Notes,* pp. 88–9.

3. *Congressional Globe,* 37 Cong., 2 Sess., pp. 5–6. Neither diplomat became the victim of congressional revenge, and British observers, expecting no less of men who represented the "ordinary rude and practical mass" that ruled the country, described the proceedings as "the mere echo of mob outcry, and the ebullition of hate against the Southern prisoners." London *Economist,* Dec. 21, 1861; Thomas C. Grattan, *England and the Disrupted States of America,* 3rd ed. (London: J. Ridgway, 1862), p. 5.

Among those who have mistakenly reported that Congress voted Wilkes a gold medal are: E. D. Adams, *Great Britain,* I:220; Benjamin P. Thomas, *Abraham Lincoln* (New York: Alfred A. Knopf, 1952), p. 281; Duberman, *Adams,* p. 279; Thornton K. Lothrop, *William H. Seward* (Boston and New York: Houghton Mifflin, 1896), p. 325; Nevins, *War for the Union,* I:338; and Donald, *Sumner and Rights of Man,* p. 31.

4. London *Times,* Dec. 17, 1861; ORN, 3rd series, I:703, 710–11.

5. Alexander Galt, memorandum of Dec. 5, 1861, PAC, Alexander Tilloch Galt Papers, MS Group 27, ID 8, vol. 7, 2652 A–E.

6. Lyons to Russell, Dec. 6, 28, 1861, Russell Papers, PRO 30/22/35.

7. F. G. Cartland, *Southern Heroes or The Friends in War Time* (Poughkeepsie: F. G. Cartland, 1897), p. 8; Bruce, *Lincoln and Tools of War,* p. 79.

8. George D. Morgan to Welles, Dec. 3, 1861, LC, Gideon Welles Papers, vol. 48, 28357; CFA, Jr., to H. Adams, Dec. 3, 1861, Adams Papers, Letters Received, reel 556; Nevins and Thomas, *Diary of Strong,* III:196–97.

9. Pease and Randall, *Diary of Browning,* I:513–14; George Meade, ed., *The Life and Letters of George Gordon Meade,* 2 vols. (New York: Scribner's, 1913), I:235.

10. Bruce, *Lincoln and Tools of War,* pp. 147–48; Silas W. Burt, *My Memoirs of the Military History of the State of New York during the War for the Union, 1861–1865* (Albany: J. B. Lyons, 1902), pp. 70–4; New York *Daily Tribune,* Dec. 17, 1861; Thomas Hillhouse to L. Thomas, Dec. 21, 1861, ORA, 3rd series, I:755.

11. Arnold S. Lott, *A Long Line of Ships: Mare Island's Century of Naval Activity in California* (Annapolis: U.S. Naval Institute, 1954), p. 76; Benjamin F. Gilbert, "Naval Operations in the Pacific, 1861–1866," Ph.D. dissertation, University of California (1951), pp. 7, 26–7; Aurora Hunt, "The Civil War on the Western Seaboard," *Civil War History,* IX (1963), pp. 178–79; Goldberg, "Naval Operations," pp. 69–71.

12. Fawn M. Brodie, *Thaddeus Stevens: Scourge of the South* (New York: W. W. Norton, 1959), p. 172; Abraham Hirsch, "Mitchell's Work on Civil War Inflation in His Development as an Economist," *History of Political Economy,* II (1970), p. 119; Ellis P. Oberholtzer, *Jay Cooke: Financier of the Civil War,* 2 vols. (Philadelphia: G. W. Jacobs, 1907), I:170; Peter J. Parish, *The American Civil War* (New York: Holmes-Meier, 1975), pp. 354–55; Fred. Perry Powers, "The Greenback in War," *Political Science Quarterly,* II (1887), pp. 86–7; Henrietta M. Larson, *Jay Cooke: Private Banker* (Cambridge, Mass.: Harvard University Press, 1936), p. 112; Hammond, *Sovereignty and Empty Purse,* pp. 109–22.

13. Wesley C. Mitchell, "The Suspension of Specie Payments, December 1861," *Journal of Political Economy,* VII (1889), pp. 320–23; *Banker's Magazine,* 16 (Jan. 1862), p. 559; New York *Daily Tribune,* Dec. 17, 1861.

14. New York *Herald Tribune*, Dec. 21, 1861; Hammond, *Sovereignty and Empty Purse*, pp. 151–53.

15. Pease and Randall, *Diary of Browning*, I:514–15; Mark A. DeWolfe Howe, *The Life and Letters of George Bancroft*, 2 vols. (New York: Scribner's, 1908), II:148; W. H. Russell, *Diary*, p. 587; Case and Spencer, *U.S. and France*, p. 215.

Interpreting Seward's outburst as a clumsy effort to frighten foreign powers into urging a peaceful settlement upon Britain, the French minister wrote Thouvenel, "You are going to say that the Americans are crazier than you thought, and you will be right." Privately, Seward told Mercier, "We will not have war; great nations like England and the United States do not make war out of passion." *See* Mercier to Thouvenel, Dec. 19, 1861 (no. 75), AMAE, Correspondance politique, États Unis, vol. 125: 290. In a blind defense that reveals that he does not understand Seward's complex personality, Ferris insists (*Trent Affair*, p. 243, fn. 25), that in my dissertation (Indiana University, 1969) I misinterpreted Russell's account of this incident and that Bancroft's testimony as to Seward's language cannot be trusted because of his political opposition to the secretary. Evidently, two witnesses count for nothing. The secretary's good humor the next day in no way casts doubt on the explosion of the previous evening. Seward often matched his mood to the occasion, acting in a contrived fashion. His naturally buoyant personality made a perpetually angry mood impossible.

16. *Congressional Globe*, 37 Cong., 2 Sess., p. 101.

17. Ibid., pp. 119–20.

18. Ibid., pp. 120–22; Richard N. Current, *Old Thad Stevens* (Madison: University of Wisconsin Press, 1942), p. 154.

19. Lyons to Russell, Nov. 22, 1861 (no. 690), FO 5/775; Lyons to Russell, Dec. 18, 1861 (no. 773), FO 5/777; New York *Daily Tribune*, Dec. 18, 20, 1861; Lyons to Russell, Dec. 19, 1861 (no. 777), FO 5/777; Case and Spencer, *U.S. and France*, p. 216.

20. Lyons to Russell, Dec. 19, 1861 (no. 777), FO 5/777; Lyons to Russell, Dec. 19, 1861, Russell Papers, PRO 30/22/35; W. H. Russell, *Diary*, p. 588; Edmund Monson to editor, London *Spectator*, Aug. 11, 1900; Lyons to Milne, Dec. 19, 1861, FO 115/277; Lyons to Milne, Dec. 19, 1861, Milne Papers, MLN/107/1(a).

21. Lyons to Russell, Dec. 23, 1861 (no. 790), FO 5/777.

22. Carroll, *Mercier*, pp. 8, 69, 110; Lyons to Russell, Dec. 23, 1861, T. W. L. Newton, *Lord Lyons: A Record of British Diplomacy*, 2 vols. (New York: Longmans, Green, 1913), I:68, 70; Mercier to Thouvenel, Dec. 23, 1861 (no. 76), AMAE, Correspondance politique, États Unis, vol. 125.

23. James R. Doolittle to Lincoln, Dec. 19, 1861, Lincoln Papers, series I, roll 30, p. 13478.

24. Francis Lieber to Sumner, Dec. 27, 1861, Root, *Addresses*, p. 99; Edward L. Pierce, *Memoir and Letters of Charles Sumner*, 4 vols. (Boston: Roberts Bros., 1878–94), IV:58; Peyton, "Sumner," p. 129; Cobden to Sumner, Nov. 29, 1861, Cobden MSS., Add. Mss. 43676; Sumner to Bright, Dec. 23, 30, 1861, Bright MSS., Add. Mss. 43390.

25. Pease and Randall, *Diary of Browning*, I:517; memorandum for Seward's reply to Lyons, Dec. 1861, Lincoln Papers, series I, roll 30, pp. 13623–25.

Lynn Case in "La France et l'affaire du 'Trent'," *Revue Historique*, CCXXVI (1961), pp. 75–6, claims that Lincoln received his arbitration idea from a Weed letter to Seward, Dec. 4, 1861, and a Bright letter to Sumner, Dec. 5, 1861. Case's evidence does not justify his conclusion. Arrival of the two letters indicates nothing except that Weed and Bright were thinking of arbitration, along with many Americans and Britons, including newspaper editors in both countries.

26. Lyons to Russell, Dec. 23, 1861 (nos. 790, 791), FO 5/777.

27. Lyons to Russell, Dec. 23, 1861 (no. 791), FO 5/777; Lyons to Russell, Dec. 23, 1861, Russell Papers, PRO 30/22/14c.

28. Lyons to Russell, Dec. 23, 1861 (no. 791), FO 5/777; Lyons to Russell, Dec. 23, 1861, Russell Papers, PRO 30/22/14c; Lyons to Gov. of Jamaica, Dec. 22, 1861, FO 5/777.

29. Milne to G. Hancock, Dec. 25, 1861, FO 5/854; New York *Daily Tribune,* Dec. 24, 1861.

30. Biglow, *Retrospections,* I:439.

Adams in "*Trent* Affair," p. 65, doubts Lincoln's alleged remark. However, even if the conversation is not accurately quoted, there is no reason to question its authenticity, since it fits the president's reluctance to surrender the men.

31. Seward, *Autobiography,* III:25.

32. Howard K. Beale, ed., *The Diary of Edward Bates, 1859–1866* (Washington, D.C.: American Historical Association, 1930), pp. 213–14; Sumner to Bright, Dec. 23, 30, 1861, Bright MSS., Add. Mss. 43390.

It is not clear whether the cabinet discussed the *Trent* on Dec. 24–25 (as some documents state), or on Dec. 25–26. However, the latter dates have been accepted because they agree with Seward's testimony. *See* Seward to Weed, Jan. 22, 1862, Seward, *Autobiography,* II:42–3. Ferris asserts (*Trent Affair,* p. 174) without proof that Bright's letters influenced Lincoln's draft note.

33. Thouvenel to Mercier, Dec. 3, 1861, ORN, 1st series, I:164–65. Lynn M. Case ("France et l'affaire du 'Trent'," pp. 72–3), Jordan and Pratt (*Europe and American Civil War,* p. 206), and Carroll (*Mercier,* p. 116) all claim that Thouvenel's note clinched the argument for surrender and brought Lincoln over to Seward's side. The French note may have reinforced the cabinet's inclination toward surrender, but it is more likely that the reasons cited by Bates, and believed by others, were more compelling arguments. There are indications that some cabinet members had made their decisions prior to the meeting.

34. Remarks of Secretary Chase at the cabinet meeting, Dec. 25, 1861, Chase Papers, Series V, Diaries, box 123. Indeed, General Benjamin Butler had received a telegram canceling his expedition against New Orleans until the government disposed of the *Trent* affair. *See* Benjamin F. Butler, *Autobiography and Personal Reminiscences* (Boston: A. M. Thayer, 1892), p. 324; Beale, *Bates Diary,* pp. 213–17; Niven, *Welles,* p. 445.

35. Seward, *Autobiography,* III:26.

36. Ibid., I:52; Seward to Lyons, Dec. 26, 1861, ORN, 1st series, I:177–87; Warren, "Imperial Dreamer," p. 209.

Steadfastly believing that high government officials cannot think for themselves, Ferris (*Trent Affair,* p. 184) gives Adams credit for furnishing Seward with "the crucial ingredient in his argument." He also takes issue with criticism, in my dissertation, of the note's content, alleging that amendments "apparently added by others" tend to "invalidate much of the criticism." The fact remains that Seward signed the note, automatically approving its language and accepting full responsibility. The essential arguments, nevertheless, were Seward's.

37. Winks, *Canada,* p. 105; Warren, "Imperial Dreamer," p. 209.

9. THE BLACK ABYSS

1. Gurowski, *Diary*, II:313; Henry James, *William Wetmore Story and His Friends*, 2 vols. (Boston: Houghton Mifflin, 1903), II:109; London *Times*, Dec. 10, 1861; Thomas Milner-Gibson to Cobden, Dec. 2, 1861, Cobden MSS., Add. Mss. 43662.

2. Colby M. Chester, "Diplomacy of the Quarter Deck," AJIL, 8 (1914), pp. 444–45.

3. Wilkes, Autobiography MS., X:2315, Wilkes Papers; William J. Morgan, David B. Tyler, Joye L. Leonhart, Mary F. Loughlin, eds., *Autobiography of Rear Admiral Charles Wilkes, U.S. Navy, 1798–1877* (Washington, D.C.: Naval History Division, Dept. of Navy, 1978), p 846. Ferris (*Trent Affair*, p. 131) accepts Wilkes's unsubstantiated contention that Lincoln had assured Wilkes that he would stand by him.

4. Thirty Hogsheads of Sugar, 9 Cranch 198 (1815).

5. Vattel, *Law of Nations*, pp. 452, 455.

6. *The Caroline*, 6 C. Rob. 467–68 (1808).

7. Phillimore, *Commentaries*, II: 163–64, III:459.

8. James Kent, *Commentaries on American Law*, 10th ed., 4 vols. (Boston: Little, Brown, 1860), I:47.

9. Lucid, *Dana Journal*, II:367; Joel Parker, "International Law," *North American Review*, 95 (July 1862), p. 18.

10. "Contraband of War," *American Law Review*, V (1870–71), p. 268.

11. Henry Wheaton, *Elements of International Law*, 6th ed., ed. William Beach Lawrence (Boston: Little, Brown, 1855), pp. 275–76; Phillimore, *Commentaries*, II:158.
The American government consistently denied that the rebellion was a civil war. Even the United States Naval War Code of 1900 insists on a distinction. Article 150 reads: "Civil War is war between two or more portions of a country or state, each contending for the mastery of the whole, and each claiming to be the legitimate government. The term is also sometimes applied to war of rebellion, when the rebellious provinces or portions of the state are contiguous to those containing the seat of government." And article 151: "The term rebellion is applied to an insurrection of large extent, and is usually a war between the legitimate government of a country and portions of provinces of the same who seek to throw off their allegiance to it and set up a government of their own." See Naval War College, "United States Naval War Code of 1900," *International Law Discussions*, 1903, p. 138.

12. Vattel, *Law of Nations*, p. 457; *The Caroline*, 6 C. Rob. 466–67 (1808).

13. Kent, *Commentaries*, I:159; *The Nereide*, 9 Cranch 426–27 (1815); *The Maria*, 1 C. Rob. 359 (1799).

14. "Belligerents and Neutrals," *The Edinburgh Review*, CXV:274–75; Charles I. Bevans, comp., *Treaties and Other International Agreements of the United States of America, 1776–1949*; 12 vols. (Washington, D.C.: GPO 1968–74), XII:104.

15. Parker, "International Law," p. 49; *The Lord Hobart*, 2 Dodson 100–05 (1815); *The Maria*, 1 C. Rob. 359 (1799).

16. Georg[sic] Schwarzenberger, *International Law*, 2 vols. (London: Stevens, 1968), p. 595; C. John Colombos, *The International Law of the Sea*, 6th ed. (New York: David McKay, 1967), p. 766; Lassa F. L. Oppenheim, *International Law: A Treatise*, ed. Hersh Lauterpacht, 8th ed., 2 vols. (New York: Longmans, Green, 1955–57), II:852; Robert Tucker, *The Law of War and Neutrality at Sea*, U.S. Naval

War College, *International Law Studies, 1955*, p. 336; Theodore D. Woolsey, *Introduction to the Study of International Law*, 5th ed. (New York: Scribner's, 1879), p. 368.

17. *The Dos Hermanos*, 2 Wheaton 78 (1817); Kent, *Commentaries*, I:167; Philip C. Jessup and Francis Déak, *Neutrality: Its History, Economics and Law*, 4 vols. (New York: Columbia University Press, 1935–36), I:228; *The Maria*, 1 C. Rob. 360 (1799). Fairfax also did not enter notification of his visit in the ship's log, a normal procedure for the visiting officer. It became impossible when Moir refused to produce the papers. Colombos, *International Law of Sea*, p. 766.

18. *The Alexander*, 8 Cranch 180 (1814); *The Grotius*, 9 Cranch 369–70 (1815).

19. *The Friendship*, 6 C. Rob. 420 (1807); Norman L. Hill, "The Origin of the Law of Unneutral Service," AJIL, 23 (1929), pp. 56, 61, 65–7; Naval War College, "Unneutral Service," pp. 79–80; Julius Stone, *Legal Controls of International Conflict: A Treatise on the Dynamics of Disputes- and War-Law* (New York: Rinehart, 1954), pp. 512–13; Oppenheim, *International Law*, II:832; T. J. Lawrence, *The Principles of International Law*, 4th ed. (Boston: D. C. Heath, 1910), pp. 724–25; ibid., 3rd ed. (1906), p. 633.

20. Thomas Jefferson to Robert Livingston, Sept. 9, 1801, Carlton Savage, *Policy of the United States Toward Maritime Commerce in War*, 2 vols. (Washington, D.C.: GPO, 1934–36), I:235.

21. Oppenheim, *International Law*, II:799–802.

The *Digest of International Law*, ed. John Bassett Moore, 8 vols. (Washington, D.C.: GPO, 1906), VII:667, contains the text of a Russian decree (1877) specifying contraband of war. Herbert A. Smith, *The Law and Custom of the Sea*, 3rd ed. (London: Stevens and Sons, 1959), p. 136, fn. 12. Although Seward referred to Cornelis van Bynkershoek, *Quaestionum Juris Publici Libri Duo* (1737), the work contains no information helpful to the American case. *See* the version edited by James B. Scott (Oxford: Clarendon Press, 1930).

22. Tucker, *Law of War*, p. 271; *The Imina*, 3 C. Rob. 167–68 (1800); *see also The Commercen*, 1 Wheaton 382 (1816).

23. Herbert W. Briggs, "Removal of Enemy Persons from Neutral Vesselsnon the High Seas," AJIL, 34 (1940), pp. 253–54; Tucker, *Law of War*, p. 325; Norman L. Hill, "Recent Development in the Law of Unneutral Service," AJIL, 21 (1927), p. 495; *The Friendship*, 6 C. Rob. 429 (1807); *The Orozembo*, 6 C. Rob. 434 (1807).

24. John Westlake, *International Law*, 2 vols. (Cambridge, Eng.: University Press, 1904–07), II:262.

25. *The Caroline*, 6 C. Rob. 465 (1808); *The Atalanta*, 6 C. Rob. 446, 460 (1808); Hill, "Origins of Law of Unneutral Service," pp. 57, 66; *The Rapid*, Edwards 228 (1810); T. Baty and J. H. Morgan, *War: Its Conduct and Legal Results* (New York: E. P. Dutton, 1915), pp. 389–90; C. John Colombos, *A Treatise on the Law of Prize* (London: Sweet and Maxwell, 1926), p. 208; William E. Hall, *A Treatise on International Law*, 8th ed., ed. A. Pearce Higgins (Oxford: Clarendon Press, 1924), p. 818; *The Madison*, Edwards 224 (1810).

26. *The Atalanta*, 6 C. Rob. 444, 460 (1808).

27. Henry Wheaton, *International Law*, 8th ed., ed. Richard H. Dana, Jr. (Boston: Little, Brown, 1866), pp. 651–52.

28. Phillimore, *International Law*, II:167; Wheaton-Dana, *Elements*, p. 506; Sir William G. V. V. Harcourt, *Letters by Historicus on Some Questions of International*

Law (London and Cambridge: Macmillan, 1863), p. 197; Francis Wharton, ed., *Digest of the International Law of the United States,* 3 vols. (Washington, D.C.: GPO, 1886), III:453.

29. Lawrence, *Principles* (3rd ed., 1906), p. 635.

30. *The Peterhoff,* 5 Wallace 61 (1866); Moore, *Digest,* VII:481–82; Bernath, *Squall,* pp. 63–84.

31. Thomas E. Holland, *A Manual of Naval Prize Law, Founded upon the Manual Prepared in 1866 by Godfrey Lushington* (London: H. M. Stationery Office, 1888), p. 27.

32. Amos S. Hershey, "The so-called Inviolability of the Mails," AJIL, 10 (1916), pp. 581–82. McKinley's proclamation naturally did not apply to Spanish mail ships destined for use as warships. *The Panama,* 176 U.S. 535 (1900); U.S. Naval War College, "Unneutral Service," *International Law Topics and Discussions, 1905* (Washington, D.C.: GPO, 1908), p. 182; H. Reason Pyke, *The Law and Contraband of War* (Oxford: Clarendon Press, 1915), p. 202; Lord Arnold D. McNair, ed., *International Law Opinions,* 3 vols. (Cambridge, Eng.: University Press, 1956), III:269–70; U.S. Naval War College, "Mail and Passengers in Time of War," *International Law Topics, 1906* (Washington, D.C.: GPO, 1907), pp. 92–3.

33. William M. Malloy, et al., eds., *Treaties, Conventions, International Acts, Protocols, and Agreements Between the United States and Other Powers. 1776–1937,* 4 vols. (Washington, D.C.: GPO, 1910–38), II:2348; Hersey, "Inviolability of Mails," p. 580.

34. Tucker, *Law of War,* p. 327; Stone, *Legal Controls,* pp. 518–19; Briggs, "Removal," p. 257; U.S. Naval War College, "Enemy Persons on Neutral Vessels," *International Law Situations, 1928* (Washington, D.C.: GPO, 1929), pp. 83–4.

35. Tucker, *Law of War,* p. 328, fn. 16. After World War I the United States, along with France, Germany, Italy, and other nations, accepted the principle embodied in Article 47.

36. AJIL, Supplement, 9 (July 1915), "Diplomatic Correspondence between the United States and Belligerent Governments Relating to Neutral Rights and Commerce," 3 vols., I:353–59; Green H. Hackworth, ed., *Digest of International Law,* 8 vols. (Washington, D.C.: GPO, 1940–44), VI:625–26.

37. AJIL, Supplement, 10 (Oct. 1916), "Diplomatic Correspondence," II:427–37.

38. Hackworth, *Digest,* VI:628. Briggs, "Removal," p. 255.

39. Ibid., p. 629.

40. Ellery C. Stowell and Henry F. Munro, *International Cases,* 2 vols. (Boston and New York: Houghton Mifflin, 1916), II:466; Hackworth, *Digest,* VI:629–32; Briggs, "Removal," p. 255.

41. Whiteman, *Digest,* X:780–83.

42. Ibid., 778–79.

10. THE ACCOUNTING

1. Lyons to Russell, Dec. 27, 1861 (no. 801), FO 5/777; Lyons to Russell, Dec. 27, 1861, Russell Papers, PRO 30/22/35.

2. Madeline V. Dahlgren, ed., *Memoir of Admiral John A. Dahlgren* (Boston: James R. Osgood, 1882), p. 351; Seward, *Autobiography,* II:586; Charles K. Tucker-

man, *Personal Recollections of Notable People at Home and Abroad*, 2 vols. (London: Richard Bentley & Son, 1895), p. 117; (New York *Times*, Dec. 28, 1861; Pease and Randall, *Diary of Browning*, I:519.

3. Henry S. Foote, *Casket of Reminiscences* (Washington, D.C.: Chronicle, 1874), p. 76; *Congressional Globe*, 37 Cong., 2 sess., Part I, pp. 177–78, 181, 208, 210–13, 240, 235, 333.

4. Donald, *Sumner and Coming of War*, pp. 213–17, 247; George W. Smalley, *Anglo-American Memories* (London: Duckworth, 1910), p. 108; Gouverneur, *As I Remember*, p. 241; Ogden, *Godkin*, I:304–05.

5. Donald, *Sumner and Rights of Man*, pp. 41–2; Smalley, *Anglo-American Memories*, p. 109; *Congressional Globe*, 37 Cong., 2 sess., Part I, pp. 241–45.

6. Peyton, "Sumner and U.S. Foreign Relations," p. 133.
The senator's remarks, two weeks in preparation, appeared erudite only because the secretary of state had composed such a dismal note and because Sumner had confidential copies of the Crown law officers' opinions of November 12 and 24, from which he drew material. Lyons to Russell, Feb. 3, 1862 (no. 76), FO 5/824.

7. John P. Kennedy to Seward, Dec. 28, 1861, Seward Papers; Robert B. Minturn to Seward, Dec. 28, 1861, ibid.; Robert C. Winthrop to Seward, Dec. 31, 1861, ibid.; Charles Norton to George W. Curtis, Dec. 31, 1861, in *Letters of Charles Eliot Norton*, 2 vols., ed. Sara Norton and Mark A. DeWolfe Howe (Boston: Houghton Mifflin, 1913), I:250; Philadelphia *Sunday Dispatch*, Philadelphia *Public Ledger*, Dec. 29, 1861; Cleveland *Plain Dealer*, Washington *Evening Star*, Dec. 30, 1861; New York *Herald Tribune*, Dec. 27, 1861; New York *Faily Tribune*, Dec. 31, 1861; Robert Murray to Weed, Jan. 8, 1862, Weed Papers; W. H. Russell, *Canada*, p. 30.

8. Edward Everett to CFA, Jan. 5, 1862, Adams Papers, Letters Received, reel 557.

9. Lowell, *Bigelow Papers*, 71.

10. *The Liberator*, Jan. 17, 1862; Dubuque *Herald*, Dec. 29, 1861; Harrisburg *Daily Telegraph*, Dec. 30, 1861; Vincennes *Western Sun*, Jan. 4, 1862; Detroit *Daily Advertiser*, Dec. 30, 1861; Harrisburg *Daily Telegraph*, Jan. 1, 1862; Atchison *Freedom's Champion*, Jan. 4, 1862; S. F. DuPont to wife, Jan. 6, 1862, Hayes, *DuPont Letters*, I:311; James R. Hawley to Welles, Dec. 30, 1861, Welles Papers, vol. 48, 28415; Lyons to Russell, Dec. 31, 1861, Russell Papers, PRO 30/22/35.

11. *Harper's Weekly*, Jan. 11, 1862; Philadelphia *Inquirer*, Jan. 1, 1862; Albany *Atlas and Argus*, Dec. 30, 1861.

12. Pierce, *Sumner*, VI:60–1; Horace Porter, *Campaigning with Grant* (New York, 1897; reprinted Bloomington, Ind.: Indiana University Press, 1961), pp. 408–9.

13. Seward, *Autobiography*, III:36; Lyons to Russell, Dec. 31, 1861 (no. 806), FO 5/777.

14. Edward W. Emerson, *The Early Years of the Saturday Club, 1855–1870* (Boston: Houghton Mifflin, 1918; reprinted Freeport, N.Y.: Books for Libraries Press, 1967), p. 257; Sangston, *Bastilles of the North*, p. 124; Parker, *32nd Massachusetts Regiment*, p. 16–17; Seward, *Autobiography*, III:36; Dimmick to Seward, Jan. 1, 1862, ORA, 2nd series, II:1162.

15. Lyons to Russell, Dec. 31, 1861 (no. 805), FO 5/777; Lyons to Hewett, Dec. 30, 1861 (enclosed in no. 805), ibid.; Hewett to Lyons, Jan. 1, 1862, FO 115/330; Mason, *Life*, pp. 236–41; London *Spectator*, Feb. 1, 1862.

16. New Orleans *Picayune,* Jan. 12, 1862; Savannah *Morning News,* Dec. 25, 1861, Jan. 1, 6, 1862.

17. Note, Jan. 8, 1862, FO 5/853.

18. Wallace and Gillespie, *Journal of Moran,* II:940, 950; London *Economist,* Jan. 1, 1862; London *Times,* Jan. 6, 8, 9, 1862; *Punch,* Jan. 18, 1862; resolutions of Jan. 27, 1862, meeting of working men, enclosed in CFA to Seward, Jan. 31, 1862 (no. 110), M-30, roll 74; *Hansard's Parliamentary Debates,* 3rd series, CXLV (1862), p. 1639; Paul Edmund de Strzelecki to Gladstone, Jan. 9, 1862, Gladstone MSS., Add. Mss. 44398; James H. North to S. R. Mallory, Mar. 16, 1862, ORN, 2nd series, II:167; Bright to Sumner, Feb. 27, 1862, Sumner Papers, bms Am 1, 19; Nancy Mitford, ed., *The Stanleys of Alderley* (London: Hamish Hamilton, 1968), p. 280; Edward Law to Brougham, Jan. 13, 1862, Brougham Papers, 28,797; Stewart M. Ellis, ed., *A Mid-Victorian Pepys: The Letters and Memoirs of Sir William Hardman, M.S., F.R.G.S.* (London: George H. Doran, 1923), p. 83.

19. Wallace and Gillespie, *Journal of Moran,* II:935; CFA to Seward, Feb. 27, 1862 (no. 95), M-30, roll 74; CFA to CFA, Jr., Jan. 3, 1862, Adams Papers, Letters Received, reel 557.

20. Seward to CFA, Dec. 27, 1861 (no. 150), Instructions, Great Britain, M-77, roll 77; Seward to CFA, Dec. 30, 1861, ORA, 2nd series, II:1159; Seward to Weed, Dec. 30, 1861, Seward Papers; Seward to CFA, Jan. 31, 1862, ORA, 2nd series, II:1193.

21. CFA to CFA, Jr., Jan. 10, 1862, Adams Papers, Letters Received, reel 557; CFA to Seward, Jan. 10, 1862 (no. 99), M-30, roll 74; CFA Diary, entries of Jan. 8, 15, 1862, Adams Papers; CFA to Seward, Feb. 13, 1862 (no. 114), Despatches, Great Britain, vol. 78; CFA to R. H. Dana, Jr., Feb. 6, 1862, Adams Papers, Letterbook.

22. George E. Buckle, ed., *The Letters of Queen Victoria,* 2nd series, 3 vols. (London: John Murray, 1926–28), I:7–8; Russell to Lyons, Jan. 10, 1862 (no. 11), FO 5/817; Argyll to Sumner, Jan. 10, 1862, Sumner Papers, bms Am 1.4; Somerset to Milne, Jan. 18, 1862, Milne Papers, MLN/107/1(c); Russell to Lyons, Jan. 11, 1862 (no. 13), FO 5/818; E. M. Archibald to Lyons, Dec. 27, 1861 (no. 187), FO 5/799.

23. Harding, Atherton, and Palmer to Russell, Jan. 15, 1862, FO 83/2213.

24. Memorandum on law officers' answer to Seward, Jan. 16, 1862, Russell Papers, PRO 30/22/27; Clarendon to Lewis, Jan. 19, 1862, Clarendon Papers, c. 533; Lewis to Clarendon, Jan. 20, 1862, ibid., c. 531; Russell to Lyons, Jan. 23, 1862 (no. 39), FO 5/817.

25. Evelyn Ashley to editor, Aug. 18, 1900, London *Spectator,* LXXXV (1900); Cowley to Russell, Jan. 24, 1862, Cowley Papers, FO 519/229; Palmerston note (incorrectly dated "? Nov., 1861"), Russell Papers, PRO 30/22/21.

26. *Illustrated London News,* Feb. 8, 1862; John Bright, *The Diaries of John Bright* (London: Cassell, 1930), p. 259; *Hansard's Parliamentary Debates,* 3rd series, CLXV (1862), pp. 381–85.

27. *Hansard's Parliamentary Debates,* 3rd series, CLXV (1862), pp. 389–92.

28. Ibid., p. 393.

29. Lyons to Russell, Jan. 31, 1862, Russell Papers, PRO 30/22/36; Seward to Lyons, Feb. 21, 1862, ORA, 2nd series, II:1200; Henry Murray to Russell, Jan. 10, 1862 (no. 3), FO 5/846; Edmondstone, Allan and Company to R. Rollo, Jan. 13, 1862, ibid.; Lyons to Russell, Jan. 17, 1862 (nos. 39–40), FO 5/823; Lyons to Russell,

Jan. 20, 1862, Russell Papers, PRO 30/22/36; Lyons to Russell, Feb. 7, 1862 (no. 96), FO 115/298; Archbishop Hughes to Seward, Jan. 24, 1862, Seward Papers.

30. Adams, "*Trent* Affair," p. 48; Henry S. Commager, *The Blue and the Gray: The Story of the Civil War as Told by Participants,* 2 vols. (Indianapolis: Bobbs-Merrill, 1950), p. 269.

31. Russell to Gladstone, Jan. 26, 1862, Gladstone MSS., Add. Mss. 44292; E. D. Adams, *Great Britain,* II:72.

32. Among those who professed this belief are Thomas A. Bailey, *A Diplomatic History of the American People,* 10th ed. (Englewood Cliffs, New Jersey: Prentice-Hall, 1980), p. 330; Robert B. Mowat, *The Diplomatic Relations of Great Britain and the United States* (New York: Longmans, 1925), pp. 174, 179; Adams, "*Trent* Affair," p. 43; and James G. Randall, *Lincoln the President,* 4 vols. (New York: Dodd, Mead, 1945–55).

33. Lewis to Gladstone, Dec. 24, 1861, Gladstone MSS., Add. Mss. 44236; London *Economist,* Jan. 11, 1862.

34. Ridley, *Palmerston,* p. 583; DNB, XVII:463.

35. Winks, *Canada,* p. 103; Martin P. Claussen, "The United States and Great Britain, 1861–1865: Peace Factors in International Relations," Ph.D. dissertation, University of Illinois (1938), p. 13; Parrish, *American Civil War,* pp. 412–13; Brougham Villiers [*pseud.*] and W. H. Chesson, *Anglo-American Relations, 1861–1865* (London: T. F. Unwin, 1919), p. 51; H. B. Jacobini, *International Law; a text,* rev. ed. (Homewood, Ill.: Dorsey, 1968), p. 235.

Ferris (*Desperate Diplomacy,* pp. 196–97) also plays down the incident, asserting that war might just as easily have erupted over the Bunch affair or the *Nashville*'s sinking of the *Harvey Birch.* Although in 1969 I first advanced the thesis that British sensitivity resulted from Lyons's reports about Seward, and am pleased that Ferris's duplicate research supports mine, I regret that he still does not understand the seriousness of the *Trent* affair and the important principles at stake. As hasty as the British overreaction may have been, it was based on long-term, as well as temporary, concerns.

Bibliography

1. MANUSCRIPT SOURCES

The following list of manuscript collections refers, with some exceptions, only to those cited in the previous pages and does not include other, numerous collections that were searched.

Boston. Massachusetts Historical Society. Adams Family MSS. Diaries and papers of Francis Adams and his family.

Washington, D.C. Library of Congress. August Belmont MSS.

London. Public Record Office, FO 356. John Bloomfield, 2nd Baron MSS.

London. British Museum. John Bright MSS.

London. University College Library. Lord Henry Brougham MSS.

Washington, D.C. Library of Congress. Salmon P. Chase MSS.

Nottingham. University of Nottingham Library, by permission of the trustees of the Newcastle estate. Henry Pelham Fiennes Pelham Clinton, 5th Duke of Newcastle MSS.

London. British Museum. Richard Cobden MSS.

Washington, D.C. Library of Congress. Confederate State Papers.

London. Public Record Office. FO 519. Henry Wellesley Cowley, 1st Earl MSS.

Washington, D.C. Library of Congress. Caleb Cushing MSS.

Princeton, New Jersey. Princeton University Library. William L. Dayton MSS.

Boston. Massachusetts Historical Society. Edward Everett MSS.

Ottawa, Canada. Public Archives of Canada. Alexander Tilloch Galt MSS.

London. British Museum. William Ewart Gladstone MSS.

London. Public Record Office. PRO 30/29. George Leveson-Gower Granville, 2nd Earl MSS.

London. Public Record Office. FO 391. Edmund Hammond MSS.

London. British Museum. Sir Austen Henry Layard MSS.

Aberystwyth, Wales. Harpton Court Collection, National Library of Wales. George Cornewell Lewis MSS.

Washington, D.C. Library of Congress. Abraham Lincoln MSS.

Greenwich, England. National Maritime Museum. Sir Alexander Milne MSS.

Washington, D.C. Library of Congress. John T. Pickett MSS.

London. Public Record Office. PRO 30/22. John Russell, 1st Earl MSS.

Sanford, Florida. General Sanford Memorial Library. Henry Shelton Sanford MSS.

Rochester, New York. Rush Rhees Library, University of Rochester. Robert W. Shufeldt MSS.

Cambridge, Massachusetts. Houghton Library, Harvard University. Charles Sumner MSS.

London. Historical Manuscripts Commission, by permission of the trustees of Broadlands Archives. Henry John Temple, 3rd Viscount Palmerston MSS.

Paris. Archives du Ministère des Affaires étrangères. Memoires et Documents. Antoine Edouard Thouvenel. Papiers de Thouvenel.

Oxford. Bodleian Library. George William Frederick Villers, 4th Earl of Clarendon, Deposit.

Rochester, New York. Rush Rhees Library, University of Rochester. Thurlow Weed MSS.

Washington, D.C. Library of Congress. Gideon Welles MSS.

Washington, D.C. Library of Congress. Charles Wilkes MSS.

Paris. Archives du Ministère des Affaires étrangères. Correspondance politique, des États Unis, des Consuls (New York, Philadelphia, Baltimore, Charleston, New Orleans, St. Louis, Richmond, Boston, San Francisco, Los Angeles.)

Washington, D.C. National Archives. Naval Records Collection, Department of the Navy. Area 6, M-625; Admirals', Commodores', and Captains' Letters (entry 37); Captains' Letters (M-125); Confidential Letters (entries 14, 15); Letters to Officers Commanding Squadrons or Vessels (entry 16); Letters to the President and Federal Executive Agents (M-472); Letters received by the Secretary of the Navy from the President and

Executive Agencies, vols. 41–43; Letters sent to Officers of Ships of War (M-149); Miscellaneous Letters received from Congress (entry 27); Miscellaneous Letters received from the President and Federal Executive Agents (M-517); Miscellaneous Letters Sent (M-209); Record Group 24, Bureau of Naval Personnel (logs of U.S.S. *Kingfisher* and U.S.S. *Huntsville*); Record Group 45; Squadron Letters (M-89); Supplemental Letters Received (entry 36).

Washington, D.C. Records of the Department of State. Diplomatic Instructions and Diplomatic Despatches, 1861–62, for Austria, Belgium, France, Great Britain, Italy, Papal States, Prussia, Russia, Spain; Special Mission (1859–1871); Consular Instructions and Despatches for Havana, London, Liverpool, Naples, Paris, Quebec, St. Johns, Southampton, Vienna.

Washington, D.C. Records of the Office of Attorney General. Letter Book B-4.

London. Public Record Office. FO 5, series II (America, United States); FO 7 (Austria, General Correspondence); FO 27 (France, General Correspondence); FO 45 (Italy, General Correspondence); FO 64 (Prussia and Germany, General Correspondence); FO 83 (Great Britain and General); FO 96, series II (Draft Despatches, Minutes, Memoranda, etc.); FO 115 (Embassy and Consular Archives, America, United States); FO 146 (Embassy and Consular Archives, France); ADM. 1 (Admiralty and Secretariat Papers); ADM. 3 (Admiralty and Secretariat Minutes); ADM. 13 (Admiralty and Secretariat, Supplementary Correspondence); CO 6 (British North America, Original Correspondence); CO 42 (Canada, Original Correspondence); CO 537 (Supplementary Correspondence).

Ottawa, Canada. Public Archives. Record Group I (Executive Council, United Canada), known as "E" Series; Record Group VII (Military Papers), known as "G" Series.

2. NEWSPAPERS AND MAGAZINES

Albany *Atlas and Argus*
Atchison *Freedom's Champion*
Atlanta *Southern Confederacy*
Banker's Magazine
Boston *Daily Evening Transcript*
Boston *Liberator*
Cincinnati *Commercial*
Cincinnati *Enquirer*
Cleveland *Leader Daily*
Cleveland *Plain Dealer*
Dublin *Irishman*
Dubuque *Herald*
Edinburgh Review
Gazette des Tribunaux
Halifax *Morning Chronicle*
Harper's Weekly

Harrisburg *Daily Telegraph*
Illustrated London News
Journal des Débats
La Patrie
Leslie's Illustrated Newspaper
London *Economist*
London *Examiner*
London (Ontario) *Free Press*
London *Law Times*
London *Morning Post*
London *Punch*
London *Spectator*
London *Standard*
London *Star*
London *Times*
McMillan's Magazine
Manchester *Guardian*
Montreal *Gazette*
Nashville *Patriot*
New Orleans *Bee*
New Orleans *Times-Picayune*
New York *Daily Herald*
New York *Daily Tribune*
New York *Times*
New York *World*
Ottawa *Citizen*
Ottawa *Tribune*
Philadelphia *Inquirer*
Philadelphia *Public Ledger*
Philadelphia *Sunday Dispatch*
Portland *Daily Eastern Argus*
Quebec *Morning Chronicle*
Richmond *Enquirer*
Richmond *Examiner*
Sacramento *Daily Union*
St. Louis *Daily Missouri Democrat*
St. Paul *Pioneer and Democrat*
St. Paul *Pioneer-Press*
Saturday Review of Politics, Literature, Science and Art
Savannah *Morning News*
Toronto Globe
Toronto *Leader*
Vincennes *Western Sun*
Washington *Evening Star*

3. PUBLISHED SOURCES

Adams, Charles F., Jr. *An Autobiography.* Boston and New York: Houghton Mifflin, 1916.
Adams, Henry. *The Education of Henry Adams.* Boston: Houghton Mifflin, 1961.
Argyll, Duchess of, ed. *Autobiography and Memoirs of the Duke of Argyll.* 2 vols. London: John Murray, 1906.
Arvin, Newton, ed. *The Selected Letters of Henry Adams.* New York: Farrar, Straus and Young, 1951.
Baker, George E., ed. *The Works of William H. Seward.* 5 vols. Boston: Houghton Mifflin, 1852–84.
Balace, Francis, comp. *La guerre de sécession et la Belgique; documents d'archives américaines, 1861–1865.* Louvain: Nauwelaerts, 1969.
Barnum, Phineas T. *Struggles and Triumphs: Or, Forty Years' Recollections.* Buffalo: Warren, Johnson, 1872.
Basler, Roy P., ed. *The Collected Works of Abraham Lincoln.* 9 vols. New Brunswick: Rutgers University Press, 1953–55.
Beale, Howard K., ed. *The Diary of Edward Bates, 1859–1866.* Washington, D.C.: American Historical Association, 1930.

———. *Diary of Gideon Welles.* 3 vols. New York: W. W. Norton, 1960.

Belmont, Perry. *An American Democrat: The Recollections of Perry Belmont.* 2nd ed. New York: AMS Press, 1967.

Bemis, George. *Hasty Recognition of Rebel Belligerency and Our Right to Complain of It.* Boston: A. Williams, 1865.

Benson, Arthur C., and Esher, Viscount, eds. *The Letters of Queen Victoria, 1837–1861.* 3 vols. London: John Murray, 1908.

Beresford-Hope, A. J. B. *The American Disruption.* London: William Ridgway, 1863.

———. *England, the North, and the South.* London: James Ridgway, 1862.

Bevans, Charles I., comp. *Treaties and Other International Agreements of the United States of America, 1776–1949.* 12 vols. Washington, D.C.: GPO, 1968–74.

Biddulph, H., ed. "Canada and the American Civil War. More Wolseley letters." *Society for Army Historical Research Journal* (London), XIX (1940), 112–17.

Bigelow, John. *Retrospections of an Active Life.* 5 vols. New York: Baker & Taylor, 1909.

Blakeman, A. Noel, ed. *Personal Recollections of the War of the Rebellion: Addresses Delivered Before the Commandery of the State of New York, Military Order of the Loyal Legion of the United States.* 4 vols. New York: G. P. Putnam's Sons, 1891–1912.

Bright, John. *The Diaries of John Bright.* London: Cassell, 1930.

———. *Speeches on the American Question.* Boston: Little, Brown, 1865.

Brooks, Noah. *Washington in Lincoln's Time.* New York: Century, 1895.

Buckle, George E., ed. *The Letters of Queen Victoria.* 2nd series. 3 vols. London: John Murray, 1926–28.

Burt, Silas W. *My Memoirs of the Military History of the State of New York During the War for the Union, 1861–1865.* Albany: J. B. Lyon, 1902.

Butler, Benjamin, F. *Autobiography and Personal Reminiscences.* Boston: A. M. Thayer, 1892.

Bynkershoek, Cornelis van. *Quaestionum Juris Publici Libri Duo.* Edited by James B. Scott. Oxford: Clarendon, 1930.

Cartland, F. G. *Southern Heroes or The Friends in War Time.* Poughkeepsie: F. G. Cartland, 1897.

Case, Lynn M., ed. *French Opinion on the United States and Mexico, 1860–1867.* New York: D. Appleton-Century, 1936.

Chesnut, Mary Boykin. *A Diary from Dixie.* Gloucester, Mass.: Peter Smith, 1961.

Clarke, Charles. *Sixty Years in Upper Canada, with Autobiographical Recollections.* Toronto: W. Briggs, 1908.

Congressional Globe, 37th Congress.

Connell, Brian, ed. *Regina vs. Palmerston: The Correspondence Between Queen Victoria and Her Foreign and Prime Minister, 1837–1865.* Garden City: Doubleday, 1961.

Cranch, William. *Reports of Cases Argued and Adjudged in the Supreme Court of the United States.* 9 vols. Philadelphia: Johnson, 1830–1854.

Curtis, George W., ed. *The Correspondence of John Lothrop Motley.* 2 vols. New York: Harper & Bros., 1889.

Dahlgren, Madeline V., ed. *Memoir of Admiral John A. Dahlgren.* Boston: James R. Osgood, 1882.

Dallas, George M. *A Series of Letters from London.* 2 vols. Philadelphia: J. B. Lippincott, 1869.

Dana, Charles A. *Recollections of the Civil War; with the Leaders at Washington and in the Field in the Sixties.* New York: Appleton, 1902.

Derby, J. C. *Fifty Years Among Authors, Books and Publishers.* New York: G. W. Carleton, 1884.

Dicey, Edward. *Six Months in the Federal States.* 2 vols. London: Macmillan, 1863.

Dickens, Charles. *American Notes and Pictures from Italy.* London: Oxford University Press, 1970.

"Diplomatic Correspondence between the United States and Belligerent Governments Relating to Neutral Rights and Commerce." 3 vols. *American Journal of International Law*, *Supp.*, 9–11 (July 1915–October 1917).

Dodson, John. *Reports of Cases Argued and Determined in the High Court of Admiralty, Commencing with the Judgments of the Right Hon. Sir William Scott, Trinity Term, 1811.* 2 vols. London: A. Strahan, 1815–28.

Dumond, Dwight L., ed. *Southern Editorials on Secession.* New York: Century, 1931.

Edwards, Thomas. *Reports of Cases Argued and Determined in the High Court of Admiralty, Commencing with the Judgments of the Right Hon. Sir William Scott, Easter Term, 1808–1812.* London: A. Strahan, 1812.

Ellis, Stewart M., ed. *A Mid-Victorian Pepys: The Letters and Memoirs of Sir William Hardman, M.A., F.R.G.S.* London: George H. Doran, 1923.

Emerson, Edward Waldo. *The Early Years of the Saturday Club, 1855–1870.* Boston: Houghton Mifflin, 1918; reprinted Freeport, N.Y.: Books for Libraries Press, 1967.

Emerson, Edward W., and Forbes, Waldo E., eds. *Journals of Ralph Waldo Emerson.* 10 vols. Boston: Houghton Mifflin, 1909–14.

Erne, John Henry Crichton, 4th earl of. *A Tour in British North America and the United States, 1863. . . .* Dublin: Hodges, Smith, 1864.

Fergusson, James. *Notes of a Tour in North America in 1861*. London: William Blackwood & Son, 1861.

Foote, Henry S. *Casket of Reminiscences*. Washington, D.C.: Chronicle, 1874.

Ford, Worthington C., ed. *A Cycle of Adams Letters, 1861–1865*. 2 vols. Boston and New York: Houghton Mifflin, 1920.

———. *Letters of Henry Adams, 1858–1891*. Boston and New York: Houghton Mifflin, 1930.

Foreign Office, *British and Foreign State Papers*, LI (1860–61). London: Foreign Office, 1868.

Freeman, Edward A. *Some Impressions of the United States*. London: Longmans, Green, 1883; reprinted Freeport, N.Y.: Books for Libraries Press, 1970.

Fulford, Roger, ed. *Dearest Child: Letters Between Queen Victoria and the Princess Royal, 1858–1861*. New York: Holt, Rinehart, 1964.

Gooch, George P., ed. *The Later Correspondence of Lord John Russell, 1840–1878*. 2 vols. London: Longmans, Green, 1925.

Gouverneur, Marian. *As I Remember: Recollections of American Society During the Nineteenth Century*. New York: D. Appleton, 1911.

Grattan, Thomas C. *England and the Disrupted States of America*. 3rd ed. London: James Ridgway, 1862.

Gurowski, Adam. *Diary from March 4, 1861 to November 17, 1862*. 2 vols. Boston, 1862; reprinted New York: Burt Franklin, 1968.

Hall, Newman. *No War with America. A Lecture on the Affair of the Trent*. London: Eliot Stock, 1861.

Ham, George H. *Reminiscences of A Raconteur between the '40s and the '20s*. Toronto: Musson, 1921.

Hamersly, Louis R., comp. *The Records of Living Officers of the United States Navy and Marine Corps*. Rev. ed. Philadelphia: J. B. Lippincott, 1870.

Harcourt, William G. V. V. *Letters by Historicus on Some Questions of International Law*. London and Cambridge: Macmillan, 1863.

Hautefeuille, Laurent B. *Questions de droit maritime international*. Paris: Guillaumin, 1868 [1861]. "Affaires du Trent et du Nash-ville." Paris: Charles Jouaust, 1861.

Hayes, John D., ed. *Samuel Francis DuPont: A Selection from His Civil War Letters*. 3 vols. Ithaca: Cornell University Press, 1969.

Holland, Thomas Erskine. *A Manual of Naval Prize Law, founded upon the manual prepared in 1866 by Godfrey Lushington*. London: H. M. Stationery Office, 1888.

Hunter, R. M., ed. *The Annals of the War Written by Leading Participants North and South*. Philadelphia: Times, 1879.

Johnson, Robert U., and Buel, Clarence C., eds. *Battles and Leaders of the Civil War.* 4 vols. New York: Century, 1887–88; reprinted Thomas Yoseloff, 1956.

Johnston, Robert M., ed. *Memoirs of 'Malakoff' [pseud.] being extracts from the Correspondence and Papers of the late William Edward Johnston.* 2 vols. London: Hutchinson, 1907.

Jones, John B. *A Rebel War Clerk's Diary at the Confederate States Capital.* Edited by Howard Swiggett. 2 vols. New York: Old Hickory Bookshop, 1935.

Journal of the Congress of the Confederate States of America. 7 vols. Washington, D.C.: GPO, 1904–05.

Kell, John McIntosh. *Recollections of a Naval Life; Including the Cruises of the Confederate States Steamers "Sumter" and "Alabama."* Washington, D.C.: Neale, 1900.

Kent, James. *Commentaries on American Law.* 10th ed. 4 vols. Boston: Little, Brown, 1860.

Koerner, Gustave. *Memoirs of Gustave Koerner.* Edited by Thomas McCormack. 2 vols. Cedar Rapids, Ia.: Torch, 1909.

Landon, Fred, ed. "Extracts from the Diary of Mrs. Amelia Harris, 1857–77 of London, Ontario." London (Ontario) *Free Press,* July 14–Nov. 17, 1928, art. 4.

Lee, Robert E., Jr., ed. *Recollections and Letters of General Robert E. Lee.* Garden City: Doubleday, Page, 1904.

Lewis, Gilbert F., ed. *Letters of the Right Hon. Sir George Cornewall Lewis, bart., to various friends.* London: Longmans, Green, 1870.

Lowell, James Russell. *The Biglow Papers.* 2nd ser. Boston: Ticknor & Fields, 1867.

Lucid, Robert F., ed. *The Journal of Richard Henry Dana.* 3 vols. Cambridge, Mass.: Belknap Press (Harvard University Press), 1968.

MacCarthy, Desmond, and Russell, Agatha, eds. *Lady John Russell: A Memoir with Selections from her Diaries and Correspondence.* London: Methuen, 1910.

[MacDougall, Patrick L.] *Forts versus Ships: Also Defence of the Canadian Lakes and Its Influence on the General Defence of Canada.* London: James Ridgway, 1862.

MacDougall, Patrick L. *The Theory of War.* 2nd ed. London: Longmans, Brown, Green, Longmans, & Roberts, 1858.

Malet, Edward. *Shifting Scenes.* London: John Murray, 1901.

Malloy, William M.; Redmond, C. F.; and Treworth, E. J.; eds. *Treaties, Conventions, International Acts, Protocols, and Agreements between the United States and Other Powers, 1776–1937.* 4 vols. Washington, D.C.: GPO, 1910–38.

Marindin, George E., ed. *Letters of Frederic Lord Blachford, Under-*

Secretary of State for the Colonies, 1860–1871. London: John Murray, 1896.

Marx, Karl, and Engels, Frederick. *The Civil War in the United States.* New York: International, 1937.

Mayne, Richard C. *Four Years in British Columbia and Vancouver Island.* London: John Murray, 1862.

Meade, George, ed. *The Life and Letters of George Gordon Meade.* 2 vols. New York: Scribner's, 1913.

Moore, Frank, ed. *The Rebellion Record.* 11 vols. New York: G. P. Putnam, 1861–65.

Morgan, William J.; Tyler, David B.; Leonhart, Joye L.; and Loughlin, Mary F.; eds. *Autobiography of Rear Admiral Charles Wilkes, U. S. Navy, 1798–1877.* Washington, D.C.: Naval History Division, Dept. of Navy, 1978.

Nevins, Allan, ed. *American Social History as Recorded by British Travellers.* New York: Henry Holt, 1931.

———. *The Diary of Philip Hone, 1828–1851.* New York: Dodd, Mead, 1927.

Nichols, Thomas L. *Forty Years of American Life.* 2 vols. London: John Maxwell, 1864.

Norton, Sara, and Howe, Mark A. DeWolfe, eds. *Letters of Charles Eliot Norton.* 2 vols. Boston: Houghton Mifflin, 1913.

Official Records of the Union and Confederate Navies in the War of the Rebellion. 30 vols. Washington, D.C.: GPO, 1894–1914.

Oliphant, Mary C. Simms; Odell, Alfred T.; and Eaves, T. C. Duncan; eds. *Letters of William Gilmore Simms.* 5 vols. Columbia: University of South Carolina Press, 1955.

Palmer, Roundell. *Memorials, Family and Personal, 1766–1865.* 2 vols. London and New York: Macmillan, 1896.

Palmerston, Henry J. T. *Opinions and Policy of the Right Honourable Viscount Palmerston.* London: Colburn, 1852; reprinted New York: Kraus, 1972.

Parker, Francis J. *The Story of the Thirty-Second Regiment Massachusetts Infantry.* Boston: C. W. Calkins, 1880.

Parker, Joel. "International Law." *North American Review,* 95 (July 1862), 1–54.

Pease, Theodore C., and Randall, James G., eds. *The Diary of Orville Hickman Browning.* 2 vols. Springfield: Illinois State Historical Collections, XX, 1925.

Perkins, Howard C., ed. *Northern Editorials on Secession.* 2 vols. New York: D. Appleton-Century, 1942.

Piatt, Donn. *Memories of the Men Who Saved the Union.* New York: Belford, Clark, 1887.

Poore, Ben Perley. *Reminiscences of Sixty Years in the National Metropolis.* 2 vols. Philadelphia: Hubbard Bros., 1886.

Porter, Horace. *Campaigning with Grant*. Bloomington: Indiana University Press, 1961.

Putnam, George H. *Memories of My Youth, 1844-1865*. New York: G. P. Putnam's Sons, 1914.

Redesdale, Algernon B. F. M., *Memories*. 2 vols. New York: E. P. Dutton, [n.d.].

Rhodes, James Ford, ed. "Letters of John Bright, 1861-1862." Massachusetts Historical Society *Proceedings*, XLV(1911-12), 148-59.

Riddle, Albert G. *Recollections of War Times: Reminiscences of Men and Events in Washington, 1860-1865*. New York: G. P. Putnam's Sons, 1895.

Robinson, Christopher. *Reports of Cases Argued and Determined in the High Court of Admiralty, Commencing with the Judgments of the Right Hon. Sir William Scott, Michaelmas Term, 1798*. 6 vols. New York: Issac Riley, 1801-10.

Root, Elihu. *Addresses on International Subjects*. Edited by Robert Bacon and James B. Scott. Freeport, N.Y.: Books for Libraries Press, 1916; reprinted 1969.

Rumbold, Horace. *Recollections of a Diplomatist*. 2 vols. London: E. Arnold, 1902.

Rundle, Edwin, G. *A Soldier's Life*. Toronto: William Briggs, 1909.

Russell, G. W. E. *Collections and Recollections by one who has kept a diary*. New York and London: Harper & Row, 1899.

Russell, John. *Recollections and Suggestions, 1813-1873*. Boston: Roberts Bros., 1875.

Russell, William H. *Canada and Its Defenses, Conditions and Resources*. Boston: Burnham, 1865.

———. *My Diary North and South*. 2 vols. Boston: Burnham, 1863.

Sala, George A. H. *My Diary in America in the Midst of War*. 2 vols. London: Tinsley Bros., 1865.

Sanborn, Alvan F., ed. *Reminiscences of Richard Lathers*. New York: Grafton Press, 1907.

Sangston, Lawrence. *The Bastilles of the North*. Baltimore: Hedion, Kelley & Piet, 1863.

Scott, James B., director. *Prize Cases Decided in the United States Supreme Courts, 1798-1918*. 3 vols. Oxford: Clarendon Press, 1923.

Scovel, James M. "Recollections of Lincoln and Seward," *Overland's Monthly*, XXXVIII (Oct. 1901), 265-71.

Seward, Frederick W. *Reminiscences of a War-Time Statesman and Diplomat, 1830-1915*. New York and London: Putnam, 1916.

Seward, William H. *An Autobiography from 1801-1834. With a Memoir of his Life, and Selections from his Letters*. 3 vols. New York: Derby & Miller, 1891. (Title of vols. II and III is

Seward at Washington, as Senator and Secretary of State by Frederick W. Seward.)

Smalley, George W. *Anglo-American Memories.* London: Duckworth, 1910.

Smith, Philip A. *The Seizure of the Southern Commissioners, considered with reference to International Law and to the Question of War or Peace.* London: James Ridgway, 1862.

Somerville, Alexander. *Canada, A Battle Ground; About a Kingdom in America.* Hamilton: Donnelley & Lawson, 1862.

Staton, Kate E., comp. *Old Southern Songs of the Period of the Confederacy: The Dixie Trophy Collection.* New York: Samuel French, 1926.

Stillman, William J. *The Autobiography of a Journalist.* 2 vols. Boston and New York: Houghton Mifflin, 1901.

Stockmar, E. von. *Memories of Baron Stockmar.* Edited by F. Max Muller. 2 vols. London: Longmans, Green, 1872.

Strong, George Templeton. *The Diary of the Civil War, 1860–1865.* Edited by Allan Nevins. New York: Macmillan, 1962.

Thompson, Robert M., and Wainwright, Richard, eds. *Confidential Correspondence of Gustavus Vasa Fox, Assistant Secretary of the Navy, 1861–1865.* 2 vols. New York: Naval Historical Society, 1918.

Trollope, Anthony. *North America.* 2 vols. London: Chapman & Hall, 1862.

Tuckerman, Charles K. *Personal Recollections of Notable People at Home and Abroad.* 2 vols. London: Richard Bentley & Son, 1895.

United States Congress, House of Representatives. *Letter from the Secretary of the Navy Transmitting the Proceedings of the Court-Martial Which Tried Commodore Charles Wilkes.* House Ex. Doc. 102–3, 38th Cong., 1st Sess., 1864.

———. *Message from the President of the United States in Relation to the Collision Between the U. S. War Steamer* San Jacinto *and the French Brig* Jules et Marie. House Ex. Doc. 4, 37th Cong., 3rd Sess., 1862.

United States Department of State. *Neutrality of Great Britain in the Civil War.* Sen. Doc. 18, 58th Cong., 1st Sess., 1903.

United States Supreme Court Reports.

Vattel, Emmerich de. *The Law of Nations, or Principles of Natural Law Applied to the Conduct and Affairs of Nations and Sovereigns.* Edited by Joseph Chitty and Edward D. Ingraham. Philadelphia: P. & J. W. Johnson, 1853.

Vaughn, Ellen T., ed. *Letters of the Hon. Mrs. Edward Twisleton written to her family, 1852–1862.* London: John Murray, 1928.

Wallace, John W. *Cases Argued and Adjudged in the Supreme Court of the United States.* 21 vols. Washington, D.C.: Morrison, 1864–75.

Wallace, Sarah A., and Gillespie, Frances E., eds. *The Journal of Benjamin Moran, 1857–1865.* 2 vols. Chicago: University of Chicago Press, 1949.

The War of the Rebellion: A Compilation of the Official Records of the Union and Confederate Armies. 130 vols. Washington, D.C.: GPO, 1880–1901.

Watkin, E. W. *Canada and the States: Recollections, 1851 to 1886.* London: Ward, Lock, 1887.

Weed, Harriet A., ed. *Autobiography of Thurlow Weed.* 2 vols. Boston: Houghton Mifflin, 1884.

Weld, Stephen M. *War Diary and Letters of Stephen Minot Weld, 1861–1865.* Cambridge, Mass.: Riverside Press, 1912.

Welles, Gideon. "The Capture and Release of Mason and Slidell." *Galaxy,* XV (1873), 640–51.

———. *Lincoln and Seward.* New York: Sheldon, 1874.

Wellesley, F. A. *Secrets of the Second Empire: Private Letters from the Paris Embassy. Selections from the Papers of Henry Richard Charles Wellesley, 1st Earl Cowley, Ambassador at Paris, 1852–1867.* New York and London: Harper & Bros., 1929.

Wheaton, Henry. *Cases Argued and Decided in the Supreme Court of the United States.* 12 vols. Albany: Banks and Bros., 1883.

———. *Elements of International Law.* 6th ed. Edited by William Beach Lawrence. Boston: Little, Brown, 1855; 8th ed. Edited by Richard H. Dana, Jr. Boston: Little, Brown, 1866.

Wilkes, Charles. *Narrative of the United States Exploring Expedition During the Years 1838, 1839, 1840, 1841, 1842.* 5 vols. Philadelphia: C. Sherman, 1844.

Wilson, Philip W., ed. *The Greville Diary.* 2 vols. Garden City: Doubleday, Page, 1927.

Woods, N. A. *The Prince of Wales in Canada and the United States.* London: Bradbury & Evans, 1861.

4. SECONDARY WORKS

Adams, Brooks. "The Seizure of the Laird Rams." Massachusetts Historical Society *Proceedings,* XLV (1911–12), 243–333.

Adams, Charles F., Jr. *Charles Francis Adams.* Boston: Houghton Mifflin, 1900.

———. "The *Trent* Affair." Massachusetts Historical Society *Proceedings,* XLV (1911–12), 35–148.

Adams, Ephraim D. *Great Britain and the American Civil War.* 2 vols. New York: Longmans, Green, 1925.

Albion, Robert G., and Pope, Jennie B. *Sea Lanes in Wartime: The*

American Experience, 1775–1942. New York: W. W. Norton, 1942.

Andersen, Arlow W. *The Immigrant Takes His Stand: The Norwegian-American Press and Public Affairs, 1847–1872*. Northfield, Minn.: Norwegian-American Historical Associations, 1953.

Anderson, Frank M. *The Mystery of "A Public Man"*. Minneapolis: University of Minnesota Press, 1948.

Archibald, E. H. H. *The Wooden Fighting Ship in the Royal Navy, AD 897–1860*. London: Blandford Press, 1968.

Ashley, Evelyn. *Life and Correspondence of Lord Palmerston*. 2 vols. London: Richard Bentley & Son, 1879.

Ausubel, Herman. *John Bright: Victorian Reformer*. New York: John Wiley, 1966.

Bailey, Thomas A. *A Diplomatic History of the American People*. 10th ed. Englewood Cliffs, N. J.: Prentice-Hall, 1980.

Barrow, Clayton R., ed. *America Spreads Her Sails: U. S. Seapower in the 19th Century*. Annapolis: Naval Institute Press, 1973.

Batt, Elizabeth. *Monck: Governor General, 1861–1868*. Toronto: McClelland and Stewart, 1976.

Baty, T., and Morgan, J. H. *War: Its Conduct and Legal Results*. New York: E. P. Dutton, 1915.

Baxter, James P. III. "The British Government and Neutral Rights, 1861–1865." *American Historical Review*, XXIV (1928), 9–29.

———. *The Introduction of the Ironclad Warship*. Cambridge: Harvard University Press, 1933.

Bell, Herbert C. *Lord Palmerston*. 2 vols. London and New York: Longmans, Green, 1936.

Berger, Max. *The British Traveller in America, 1836–1860*. New York: Columbia University Press, 1943.

Bernath, Stuart L. *Squall Across the Atlantic: America Civil War Prize Cases and Diplomacy*. Berkeley and Los Angeles: University of California Press, 1970.

Bonham, Milledge L., Jr. *The British Consuls in the Confederacy*. New York: Columbia University Press, 1911.

Bourne, Kenneth. *Britain and the Balance of Power in North America, 1815–1908*. Berkeley and Los Angeles: University of California Press, 1967.

———. "British Preparations for War with the North, 1861–1862." *English Historical Review*, LXXVI (1961).

———. *The Foreign Policy of Victorian England, 1830–1902*. Oxford: Clarendon Press, 1970.

Bourne, Kenneth, and Watt, D. C., eds. *Studies in International History: Essays Presented to W. Norton Medlicott*. London: Longmans, Green, 1967.

Bowen, Frank C. *A Century of Atlantic Travel, 1830–1930.* London: Little, Brown, 1932.

Brierly, James L. *The Law of Nations.* Edited by Sir Humphrey Waldock. 6th ed. London: Oxford University Press, 1963.

Briggs, Herbert W. "Removal of Enemy Persons from Neutral Vessels on the High Seas." *American Journal of International Law,* 34 (1940), 249–59.

Brightfield, Myron F. "America and the Americans, 1840–1860, as Depicted in English Novels of the Period." *American Literature,* XXXI (1959), 309–24.

Brinnin, John M. *The Sway of the Grand Saloon: A Social History of the North Atlantic.* New York: Delacorte, 1971.

Brodie, Fawn M. *Thaddeus Stevens: Scourge of the South.* New York: W. W. Norton, 1959.

Bruce, Robert V. *Lincoln and the Tools of War.* Indianapolis: Bobbs-Merrill, 1956; reprinted Westport, Conn.: Greenwood, 1973.

Bushell, T. A. *"Royal Mail": A Centenary History of the Royal Mail Line, 1830–1939.* London: Trade & Travel, 1940.

Carman, Harry J., and Luthin, Reinhard H. *Lincoln and the Patronage.* New York: Columbia University Press, 1943; reprinted Gloucester, Mass.: Peter Smith, 1964.

Carroll, Daniel B. *Henri Mercier and the American Civil War.* Princeton: Princeton University Press, 1971.

Case, Lynn. "La France et l'affaire du 'Trent.' " *Revue Historique,* CCXXVI (1961), pp. 57–86.

Case, Lynn M., and Spencer, Warren F. *The United States and France: Civil War Diplomacy.* Philadelphia: University of Pennsylvania Press, 1970.

Chester, Colby M. "Diplomacy of the Quarter Deck." *American Journal of International Law,* 8 (1914), 443–76.

Claussen, Martin P. "Peace Factors in Anglo-American Relations, 1861–1865." *Journal of American History,* XXVI (1940), 511–22.

Cohen, Victor H. "Charles Sumner and the *Trent* Affair." *Journal of Southern History,* XXII (1956), 205–19.

Collyer, C. "Gladstone and the American Civil War." *6 Proc. Leeds Philosophical and Literary Society* (Pt. 8), 583–94.

Colombos, C. John. *The International Law of the Sea.* 6th ed. New York: David McKay, 1967.

———. *A Treatise on the Law of Prize.* London: Sweet & Maxwell, 1926.

Commager, Henry S. *The Blue and the Gray: The Story of the Civil War as Told by Participants.* 2 vols. Indianapolis: Bobbs-Merrill, 1950.

"Contraband of War." *American Law Review* V (1870–71), 247–71.

Coulter, E. Merton. *The Confederate States of America, 1861–1865.* Baton Rouge: Louisiana State University Press, 1950.

Courtemanche, Regis A. *No Need of Glory: The British Navy in American Waters, 1860–1864.* Annapolis: Naval Institute Press, 1977.

Crook, D. P. *The North, the South, and the Powers, 1861–1865.* New York: John Wiley & Sons, 1974.

Current, Richard N. *Old Thad Stevens.* Madison: University of Wisconsin Press, 1942.

Curti, Merle. *The Growth of American Thought.* New York: Harper, 1951.

Dana, Richard H., Jr. "The *Trent* Affair: An Aftermath." Massachusetts Historical Society *Proceedings,* XLV (1911–1912), 508–30.

Donald, David. *Charles Sumner and the Coming of the Civil War.* New York: Alfred A. Knopf, 1967.

———. *Charles Sumner and the Rights of Man.* New York: Alfred A. Knopf, 1970.

Drake, F. C. "The Cuban Background of the *Trent* Affair." *Civil War History,* XIX (1973), 29–49.

Duberman, Martin B. *Charles Francis Adams, 1807–1886.* Boston: Houghton Mifflin, 1961.

Dubose, John W. *The Life and Times of William Lowndes Yancey.* Birmingham, Ala.: Roberts & Son, 1892.

Dugan, James. *The Great Iron Ship.* New York: Harper & Bros., 1953.

du Pont, Bessie G. *E. I. du Pont de Nemours and Company: A History, 1802–1902.* Boston and New York: Houghton Mifflin, 1920.

Durden, Robert F. *James Shepherd Pike: Republicanism and the American Negro, 1850–1882.* Durham: Duke University Press, 1957.

Eaton, Clement. *A History of the Southern Confederacy.* New York: Macmillan, 1954.

Edwards, J. P. "The Militia of Nova Scotia, 1749–1867." Nova Scotia Historical Society *Collections,* XVII (1913), 98–105.

Einstein, Lewis. *Napoleon III and American Diplomacy at the Outbreak of the Civil War.* London: [n.p.], 1905.

Elliott, Charles W. *Winfield Scott, the Soldier and the Man.* New York: Macmillan, 1937.

Ellison, Mary. *Support for Secession: Lancashire and the American Civil War.* Chicago: University of Chicago Press, 1972.

Falk, Richard A., ed. *The International Law of Civil War.* Baltimore: Johns Hopkins Press, 1971.

Ferris, Norman. *Desperate Diplomacy: William H. Seward's Foreign Policy, 1861.* Knoxville: University of Tennessee Press, 1976.

———. "The Prince Consort, 'The Times,' and the 'Trent' Affair." *Civil War History,* VI (1960), 152–56.

———. *The Trent Affair: A Diplomatic Crisis.* Knoxville: University of Tennessee Press, 1977.

Fischer, LeRoy H. *Lincoln's Gadfly: Adam Gurowski.* Norman: University of Oklahoma Press, 1964.

Fitzmaurice, Edmund. *The Life of Granville George Leveson Gower, Second Earl Granville, K.G., 1815–1891.* 2 vols. New York: Longmans, Green, 1905.

Fortescue, John W. *A History of the British Army.* 13 vols. London: Macmillan, 1902–30.

Frothingham, Paul R. *Edward Everett, Orator and Statesman.* Boston and New York: Houghton Mifflin, 1925.

Gavronsky, Serge. *The French Liberal Opposition and the American Civil War.* New York: Humanities, 1968.

Gilbert, Benjamin F. "Rumours of Confederate Privateers Operating in Victoria, Vancouver Island." *British Columbia Historical Quarterly,* XVIII (1954), 239–55.

Glicksberg, Charles I. "Henry Adams and the Civil War." *Americana,* 33 (1939), 443–62.

Gough, Barry M. *The Royal Navy and the Northwest Coast of North America, 1810–1914: A Study of British Maritime Ascendancy.* Vancouver: University of British Columbia Press, 1971.

Hackworth, Green H., ed. *Digest of International Law.* 8 vols. Washington, D.C.: GPO, 1940–44.

Hall, William E. *A Treatise on International Law.* Edited by A. Pearce Higgins. 8th ed. Oxford: Clarendon Press, 1924.

Hamilton, C. F. "The Canadian Militia: from 1861 to Confederation." *Canadian Defence Quarterly,* VI (1929), 199–211.

Hammond, Bray. *Sovereignty and an Empty Purse: Banks and Politics in the Civil War.* Princeton: Princeton University Press, 1970.

Hammond, M. B. *The Cotton Industry.* New York: Macmillan, 1897; reprinted New York: Johnson Reprint, 1966.

Hancock, Harold B., and Wilkinson, Norman B. " 'The Devil to Pay!': Saltpeter and the *Trent* Affair." *Civil War History,* X (1964), 20–32.

Harnetty, Peter. "The Imperialism of Free Trade: Lancashire, India, and the Cotton Supply Question, 1861–1865." *Journal of British Studies,* VI (1966), 70–96.

Harris, Thomas L. *The Trent Affair, including a Review of English and American Relations at the Beginning of the Civil War.* Indianapolis and Kansas City: Bowen-Merrill, 1896.

Harrison, Royden. *Before the Socialists: Studies in Labour and Politics, 1861–1881.* London: Routledge & Kegan Paul, 1965.

Heaps, W. A., and Heaps, P. W. *The Singing Sixties: The Spirit of Civil War Days Drawn from the Music of the Times.* Norman: University of Oklahoma Press, 1960.

Henderson, Daniel. *Hidden Coasts: A Biography of Admiral Charles Wilkes.* New York: William Sloan, 1953.

Hendrick, Burton J. *Statesmen of the Lost Cause: Jefferson Davis and His Cabinet.* Boston: Little, Brown, 1939.

Hernon, Joseph M., Jr. *Celts, Catholics, and Copperheads: Ireland Views the American Civil War.* Columbus: Ohio State University Press, 1967.

Hersey, Amos S. "The so-called Inviolability of the Mails." *American Journal of International Law*, 10 (1916), 580–84.

Hill, Norman L. "The Origin of the Law of Unneutral Service." *American Journal of International Law,* 23 (1929), 56–67.

———. "Recent Development in the Law of Unneutral Service." *American Journal of International Law,* 21 (1927), 490–98.

Hirsch, Abraham. "Mitchell's Work on Civil War Inflation in His Development as an Economist." *History of Political Economy,* 2 (1970), 118–32.

Hitsman, J. MacKay. "Winter Troop Movement to Canada, 1862." *Canadian Historical Review,* XLIII (1962), 127–35.

Hodgson, Sister M. Michael Catherine, O. P. *Caleb Cushing: Attorney General of the United States, 1853–1857.* Washington, D.C.: Catholic University of America Press, 1955; reprinted Ann Arbor: University Microfilms, 1973.

Howe, Mark A. DeWolfe. *The Life and Letters of George Bancroft.* 2 vols. New York: Scribner's, 1908.

Hudson, Manley O., ed. *Cases and Other Materials on International Law.* 3rd ed. St. Paul: West, 1951.

Hunt, Aurora. "The Civil War on the Western Seaboard." *Civil War History,* IX (1963), 178–86.

Hutton, Graham. "Lincoln through British Eyes." *Abraham Lincoln Quarterly,* III (1944), 63–92.

Jacobini, H. B. *International Law; a text.* Rev. ed. Homewood, Ill.: Dorsey, 1968.

James, Henry. *William Wetmore Story and His Friends.* 2 vols. Boston: Houghton Mifflin, 1903.

Jeffries, William W. "The Civil War Career of Charles Wilkes." *Journal of Southern History,* XI (1945), 324–48.

Jenkins, Brian. *Britain and the War for the Union.* Vol. 1. Montreal: McGill-Queens, 1974.

Jessup, Philip C. *A Modern Law of Nations: An Introduction.* New York: Macmillan. 1948.

Jessup, Philip C., and Déak, Francis. *Neutrality: Its History,*

Economics and Law. 4 vols. New York: Columbia University Press, 1935–36.

Johnson, Allen, and Malone, Dumas, eds. *Dictionary of American Biography.* 11 vols. New York: Scribner's, 1957.

Johnson, Allen, et al., eds. *Dictionary of National Biography.* 22 vols., supps. New York: Macmillan, 1922–74.

Jones, Virgil C. *The Civil War at Sea.* 3 vols. New York: Holt, Rinehart & Winston, 1960–62.

Jones, Wilbur D. *The American Problem in British Diplomacy, 1841–1861.* Athens: University of Georgia Press, 1974.

Jordan, Donaldson, and Pratt, Edwin J. *Europe and the American Civil War.* Boston: Houghton Mifflin, 1931.

Katz, Irving. *August Belmont: A Political Biography.* New York: Columbia University Press, 1968.

Landon, Fred M. "Canadian Opinion of Southern Secession, 1860–61." *Canadian Historical Review,* I (1920), 255–66.

Langley, Harold D. *Social Reform in the United States Navy, 1789–1862.* Chicago: Illinois University Press, 1967.

Large, David. "Friends and the American Civil War: The *Trent* Affair." *Friends' Historical Society Journal,* XLVIII (1957), 163–67.

Larson, Henrietta M. *Jay Cooke: Private Banker.* Cambridge: Harvard University Press, 1936.

Lawrence, T. J. *The Principles of International Law.* 3rd and 4th eds. Boston and New York: D. C. Heath, 1906, 1910.

―――. *War and Neutrality in the Far East.* London: Macmillan, 1904.

Leech, Margaret. *Reveille in Washington, 1860–1865.* New York and London: Harper & Bros., 1941.

Lehmann, Joseph H. *The Model Major-General: A Biography of Field-Marshall Lord Wolseley.* Boston: Houghton Mifflin, 1964.

Long, John Sherman. "Glory-Hunting Off Havana: Wilkes and the *Trent* Affair." *Civil War History,* IX (1963), 133–44.

―――. "The Gosport Affair, 1861." *Journal of Southern History,* XXIII (1957), 155–72.

Longstaff, F. V. *Esquimalt Naval Base: A History of Its Works and Its Defences.* Victoria: Victoria Book & Stationery, 1941.

Lossing, Benson J. *Pictorial History of the Civil War in the United States of America.* 3 vols. Hartford: T. Belknap, 1868.

Lothrop, Thornton K. *William H. Seward.* Boston and New York: Houghton Mifflin, 1896.

Lott, Arnold S. *A Long Line of Ships: Mare Island's Century of Naval Activity in California.* Annapolis: Naval Institute Press, 1954.

Lutz, Ralph. *Die Beziehungen zwischen Deutschland und den Vereinigten Staaten während des Sezessionskrieges.* Heidelberg: C. Winter, 1911.

Lutz, Ralph H. "Rudolph Schleiden and the Visit to Richmond, April 25, 1861," American Historical Association *Annual Report, 1915*, 209–16.

Luvaas, Jay. "General Sir Patrick MacDougall, the American Civil War, and the Defence of Canada." Canadian Historical Association *Annual Report, 1962*, 44–54.

Lynch, M. Clair. *The Diplomatic Mission of John Lothrop Motley to Austria, 1861–1867*. Washington, D.C.: Catholic University of America Press, 1944.

Macdonald, Helen G. *Canadian Public Opinion on the American Civil War*. New York: Columbia University Press, 1926.

MacKintosh, John P. *The British Cabinet*. 2nd ed. London: Stevens & Sons, 1968.

McNair, Arnold D. *International Law Opinions*. 3 vols. Cambridge, Eng.: University Press, 1956.

Maitland, Frederic W. *The Life and Letters of Leslie Stephen*. London: Duckworth, 1906.

Martin, Theodore. *The Life of the Prince Consort*. 5 vols. London: Smith, Elder, 1880.

Mason, Virginia. *The Public Life and Diplomatic Correspondence of James M. Mason*. Roanoke: Stone, 1903.

Maxwell, Herbert E. *The Life and Letters of George William Frederick, Fourth Earl of Clarendon*. 2 vols. London: E. Arnold, 1913.

Meneeley, A. Howard. *The War Department, 1861: A Study in Mobilization and Administration*. New York: Columbia University Press, 1928.

Milton, George F. *Abraham Lincoln and the Fifth Column*. New York: Vanguard, 1942.

Mitchell, Wesley C. "The Suspension of Specie Payments, December 1861." *Journal of Political Economy*, VII (1889), 289–326.

Mitford, Nancy, ed. *The Stanleys of Alderley*. London: Chapman & Hall, 1939; reprinted London: Hamish Hamilton, 1968.

Molloy, Leo T. *Henry Shelton Sanford, 1823–1891: A Biography*. Derby, Conn.: Bacon, 1952.

Monaghan, Jay. *Diplomat in Carpet Slippers: Abraham Lincoln Deals with Foreign Affairs*. Indianapolis and New York: Bobbs-Merrill, 1945; Charter ed., 1962.

Moore, John Bassett, ed. *Digest of International Law*. 8 vols. Washington, D.C.: GPO, 1906.

Morley, John. *The Life of William Ewart Gladstone*. 3 vols. New York: Harper & Bros., 1903.

Mowat, Robert B. *The Diplomatic Relations of Great Britain and the United States*. New York: Longmans, Green, 1925.

Nash, Howard P., Jr. *A Naval History of the Civil War*. South Brunswick and New York: A. S. Barnes, 1972.

Nevins, Allan. *The War for the Union.* 4 vols. New York: Scribner's, 1959–71.

Newton, T. W. L. *Lord Lyons: A Record of British Diplomacy.* 2 vols. New York: Longmans, Green, 1913.

Nicolay, Helen. *Lincoln's Secretary: A Biography of John G. Nicolay.* New York: Longmans, Green, 1949.

Niven, John. *Gideon Welles: Lincoln's Secretary of the Navy.* New York: Oxford University Press, 1973.

Oberholtzer, Ellis P. *Jay Cooke: Financier of the Civil War.* 2 vols. Philadelphia: G. W. Jacobs, 1907.

Ogden, Rollo. *Life and Letters of Edwin Lawrence Godkin.* 2 vols. New York: Macmillan, 1907.

Oppenheim, Lassa F. L. *International Law: A Treatise.* Edited by Hersh Lauterpacht. 8th ed. 2 vols. New York: Longmans, Green, 1955–57.

O'Rourke, Alice. "The Law Officers of the Crown and the *Trent* Affair." *Mid-America,* 54 (1972), 157–71.

Owsley, Frank L. *King Cotton Diplomacy: Foreign Relations of the Confederate States of America.* Chicago: University of Chicago Press, 1959.

Parish, Peter J. *The American Civil War.* New York: Holmes-Meier, 1975.

Paullin, Charles O. *Paullin's History of the Naval Administration, 1775–1911.* Annapolis: Naval Institute Press, 1968.

———. "President Lincoln and the Navy," *American Historical Review,* XIV (1908–09), 284–303.

Perkins, Bradford. *The Great Rapprochement: England and the United States, 1895–1914.* New York: Atheneum, 1968.

Phillimore, Robert J. *Commentaries upon International Law.* 4 vols. London: Butterworth, 1871–74.

Pickard, Samuel T. *Life and Letters of John Greenleaf Whittier.* 2 vols. Boston: Houghton Mifflin, 1894.

Pierce, Edward L. *Memoir and Letters of Charles Sumner.* 4 vols. Boston: Roberts Brothers, 1878–94.

Ponko, Vincent, Jr. *Ships, Seas, and Scientists: U. S. Naval Exploration and Discovery in the Nineteenth Century.* Annapolis: Naval Institute Press, 1974.

Pope-Hennessy, James. *Monckton Milnes: The Flight of Youth, 1851–85.* London: Constable, 1951.

Porter, David D. *The Naval History of the Civil War.* New York: Sherman, 1886; reprinted Glendale, N.Y.: Benchmark, 1970.

Pound, Reginald. *Albert: A Biography of the Prince Consort.* London: Michael Joseph, 1973.

Powers, Fred. Perry. "The Greenback in War." *Political Science Quarterly,* 2 (1887), 79–90.

Preston, Richard A. *Canada and "Imperial Defense": A Study of the*

Origins of the British Commonwealth's Defense Organization, 1867–1919. Durham: Duke University Press, 1967.

Price, Marcus W. "Ships that Tested the Blockade of the Carolina Ports, 1861–1865." *American Neptune,* VIII (1948), 196–241.

Purcell, Richard J. "Ireland and the American Civil War." *Catholic World,* 115 (1922), 72–84.

Pyke, H. Reason. *The Law of Contraband of War.* Oxford: Clarendon Press, 1915.

Ray, Gordon N. *Thackeray: The Age of Wisdom, 1847–1863.* New York: McGraw-Hill, 1958.

Reid, T. Wemyss. *Life of W. E. Forster.* 2 vols. London: Chapman & Hall, 1888.

Ridley, Jasper. *Lord Palmerston.* New York: E. P. Dutton, 1971.

Robb, Andrew. "The Toronto *Globe* and the Defence of Canada, 1861–1866." *Ontario History,* LXIV (1972), 65–77.

Royal Mail Lines. *125 Years of Maritime History, 1839–1964.* London: Royal Mail Lines, 1964.

Royal Mail Steam Packet Co. *A Link of Empire, or 70 Years of British Shipping; Souvenir of the 70th Year of Incorporation of the Royal Mail Steam Packet Company.* London: Royal Mail Steam Packet Co., 1909.

Savage, Carlton. *Policy of the United States Toward Maritime Commerce in War.* 2 vols. Washington, D.C.: GPO, 1934–36.

Scherer, James A. B. *Cotton as a World Power: A Study in the Economic Interpretation of History.* New York: Frederick A. Stokes, 1916.

Schwarzenberger, Georg [*sic*]. *International Law.* 2 vols. London: Stevens, 1968.

[Scoville, Joseph A.]. *The Old Merchants of New York City by Walter Barrett, Clerk.* 5 vols. New York: Carleton, 1864–70; reprinted New York: Greenwood, 1968.

Shain, Charles E. "English Novelists and the American Civil War." *American Quarterly,* XIV (1962), 399–421.

Smith, Geoffrey S. "Charles Wilkes and the Growth of American Naval Diplomacy." In *Makers of American Diplomacy,* edited by Frank J. Merli and Theodore A. Wilson, pp. 135–64. New York: Scribner's, 1974.

Smith, Herbert A. *The Law and Custom of the Sea.* 3rd ed. London: Stevens & Sons, 1959.

Stacey, C. P. *Canada and the British Army, 1846–1871.* London: Longmans, 1936.

Stanley, George F. G. *Canada's Soldiers: The Military History of an Unmilitary People.* Rev. ed. Toronto: Macmillan, 1960.

Stanmore, Lord [A. H. Gordon]. *Sidney Herbert: Lord Herbert of Lea; a memoir.* 2 vols. London: John Murray, 1906.

Stanton, William. *The Great United States Exploring Expedition of*

1838–1842. Berkeley and Los Angeles: University of California Press, 1975.
Stock, Leo F. *Consular Relations Between the United States and the Papal States*. Washington, D.C.: American Catholic Historical Association, 1945.
Stone, Julius. *Legal Controls of International Conflict: A Treatise on the Dynamics of Disputes- and War-Law*. New York: Rinehart, 1954.
Stowell, Ellery C., and Munro, Henry F. *International Cases*. 2 vols. Boston and New York: Houghton Mifflin, 1916.
Taylor, A. J. P. *The Trouble-Makers: Dissent over Foreign Policy, 1792–1939*. Bloomington: Indiana University Press, 1958.
Temple, Henry W. "William H. Seward." Vol. IX in *The American Secretaries of State and Their Diplomacy*, edited by Samuel F. Bemis and Robert H. Ferrell. 18 vols. New York: Pageant, 1958–70.
Thomas, Benjamin P. *Abraham Lincoln*. New York: Alfred A. Knopf, 1952.
———. *Russo-American Relations, 1815–1867*. Baltimore: Johns Hopkins Press, 1930.
Thompson, W. Fletcher, Jr. *The Image of War: The Pictorial Reporting of the American Civil War*. New York: Thomas Yoseloff, 1960.
Trevelyan, George M. *The Life of John Bright*. London: Constable, 1913.
Tucker, Robert. *The Law of War and Neutrality at Sea*, U. S. Naval War College, *International Law Studies, 1955*. Washington, D.C.: GPO, 1957.
Tyler, David B. *The Wilkes Expedition: The First United States Exploring Expedition 1838–1842*. Philadelphia: American Philosophical Society, 1968.
Upton, Francis H. *The Law of Nations Affecting Commerce During War: With a Review of the Jurisdiction, Practice and Proceedings of Prize Courts*. 3rd ed. New York: John S. Voorhies, 1863.
U. S. Naval War College. "Enemy Persons on Neutral Vessels." In *International Law Situations, 1928*, pp. 73–108. Washington, D.C.: GPO 1929.
———. "Mail and Passengers in Time of War." In *International Topics and Discussions, 1906*, pp. 88–104. Washington, D.C.: GPO, 1907.
———. "Unneutral Service." *International Law Topics and Discussions, 1905*, pp. 171–88. Washington, D.C.: GPO, 1908.
Van Alstyne, Richard. "Anglo-American Relations, *1853–1857.*" *American Historical Review*, XLII (1937), 491–505.
———. "British Diplomacy and the Clayton-Bulwer Treaty, 1850–1860." *Journal of Modern History*, XI (1939), 149–83.

Van Deusen, Glyndon G. *Thurlow Weed: Wizard of the Lobby.* Boston: Little, Brown, 1947.

——. *William Henry Seward.* New York: Oxford University Press, 1967.

Villiers, Brougham [*pseud.*], and Chesson, W. H. *Anglo-American Relations, 1861–1865.* London: T. F. Unwin, 1919.

Ward, Adolphus W., and Gooch, George P. *The Cambridge History of British Foreign Policy, 1783–1919.* 3 vols. Cambridge, Eng.: University Press, 1922–23.

Warren, Gordon H. "Imperial Dreamer: William Henry Seward and American Destiny." In *Makers of American Diplomacy,* edited by Frank J. Merli and Theodore A. Wilson, pp. 195–222. New York: Scribner's, 1974.

——. "The King Cotton Theory." In *Encyclopedia of American Foreign Policy: Studies of the Principal Movements and Ideas,* 3 vols., edited by Alexander DeConde, II:515–20. New York: Scribner's, 1978.

Waterfield, Gordon. *Layard of Ninevah.* New York: F. A. Praeger, 1968.

West, W. Reed. *Contemporary French Opinion on the American Civil War.* Baltimore: Johns Hopkins Press, 1924.

Westlake, John. *International Law.* 2 vols. Cambridge, Eng.: University Press, 1904–07.

Wharton, Francis, ed. *Digest of the International Law of the United States.* 3 vols. Washington, D.C.: GPO, 1886.

White, Laura. "Charles Sumner and the Crisis of 1860–61." In *Essays in Honor of William E. Dodd,* edited by Avery O. Craven. Chicago: University of Chicago Press, 1935.

Whiteman, Marjorie M., ed. *Digest of International Law.* 15 vols. Washington, D.C.: GPO, 1963–73.

Winks, Robin W. *Canada and the United States: The Civil War Years.* Baltimore: Johns Hopkins Press, 1960.

Wiswall, F. L., Jr., ed. *The Development of Admiralty Jurisdiction and Practice since 1800.* Cambridge, Eng.: University Press, 1971.

Woodham-Smith, Cecil. *Florence Nightingale, 1820–1910.* New York: McGraw-Hill, 1951.

——. *Queen Victoria: From her Birth to the Death of the Prince Consort.* New York: Alfred A. Knopf, 1972.

Woolsey, Theodore D. *Introduction to the Study of International Law.* 5th ed. New York: Scribner's, 1879.

Wright, D. G. "Bradford and the American Civil War." *Journal of British Studies,* VIII (1969), 69–85.

Young, G. M. *Victorian England: Portrait of an Age.* 2nd ed. London: Oxford University Press, 1964.

5. UNPUBLISHED WORKS

Anderson, Mary A. "Edmund Hammond, Permanent Under-Secretary of State for Foreign Affairs, 1854–1873." Ph.D. dissertation, London University, 1956.

Baxter, Colin F. "Admiralty Problems during the Second Palmerston Administration, 1859–1865." Ph.D. dissertation, University of Georgia, 1965.

Botsford, Robert. "Scotland and the American Civil War." Ph.D. dissertation, University of Edinburgh, 1955.

Claussen, Martin P. "The United States and Great Britain, 1861–1865: Peace Factors in International Relations." Ph.D. dissertation, University of Illinois, 1938.

Fry, Joseph A. "An American Abroad: The Diplomatic Career of Henry Shelton Sanford." Ph.D. dissertation, University of Virginia, 1974.

Gilbert, Benjamin F. "Naval Operations in the Pacific, 1861–1866." Ph.D. dissertation, University of California, 1951.

Goldberg, Michael S. "A History of United States Naval Operations During 1861." Ph.D. dissertation, University of New Mexico, 1970.

Heppner, Francis J. "Henry S. Sanford, United States Minister to Belgium, 1861–1869." M.A. thesis, Georgetown University, 1955.

Kemble, John H. "The Panama Route to California, 1848–1869." Ph.D. dissertation, University of California, 1937.

Krein, David F. "Genesis of Isolation: Palmerston, Russell, and the Formation of British Foreign Policy, 1861–1864." Ph.D. dissertation, University of Iowa, 1974.

O'Rourke, Sister Mary Martinice. "The Diplomacy of William H. Seward during the Civil War: His Policies as Related to International Law." Ph.D. dissertation, University of California, 1963.

Parent, Sister Mary of St. Celine. "Caleb Cushing and the Foreign Policy of the United States, 1860–1877." Ph.D. dissertation, Boston College, 1958.

Peyton, Thomas J., Jr. "Charles Sumner and United States Foreign Relations During the American Civil War." Ph.D. dissertation, Georgetown University, 1972.

Van Auken, Sheldon. "English Sympathy for the Southern Confederacy: The Glittering Illusion." B. Litt. thesis, Oxford University, 1957.

Warren, Gordon Harris. "The *Trent* Affair, 1861–1862." Ph.D. dissertation, Indiana University, 1969.

Index

Page references in italics indicate illustrations

DATE DUE
